AFRICAN AMERICA
AND HAITI

The Right Reverend James T. Holly. Courtesy of The Archives of the Episcopal Church, USA.

AFRICAN AMERICA AND HAITI

Emigration and Black Nationalism in the Nineteenth Century

Chris Dixon

Contributions in American History, Number 186
Jon L. Wakelyn, Series Editor

GREENWOOD PRESS
Westport, Connecticut • London

Library of Congress Cataloging-in-Publication Data

Dixon, Chris, 1960–
   African America and Haiti : emigration and Black nationalism in the nineteenth
century / Chris Dixon.
      p.   cm.—(Contributions in American history, ISSN 0084–9219 ; no. 186)
   Includes bibliographical references (p.) and index.
   ISBN 0–313–31063–7 (alk. paper)
   1. Free Afro-Americans—History—19th century. 2. Black nationalism—United
States—History—19th century. 3. Black nationalism—Haiti—History—19th century. 4.
Haiti—Emigration and immigration—History—19th century. 5. United States—Emigration
and immigration—History—19th century. I. Title. II. Series.
E185.18.D59   2000
   304.8′7294073   21—dc21   99–043506

British Library Cataloguing in Publication Data is available.

Library of Congress Catalog Card Number: 99–043506
ISBN: 0–313–31063–7
ISSN: 0084–9219

First published in 2000

Greenwood Press, 88 Post Road West, Westport, CT 06881
An imprint of Greenwood Publishing Group, Inc.
www.greenwood.com

Printed in the United States of America

The paper used in this book complies with the
Permanent Paper Standard issued by the National
Information Standards Organization (Z39.48–1984).

10 9 8 7 6 5 4 3 2

FOR SAM

Contents

Preface

For those of us accustomed to dramatic images of people desperately fleeing the Caribbean nation of Haiti, seeking sanctuary in the United States, the notion that several thousand African Americans would voluntarily migrate in the opposite direction seems puzzling, implausible even. Twice during the nineteenth century, however, in the face of continuing oppression in the free as well as slave states, black Americans contemplated emigrating to Haiti, a nation that they hoped could provide civic freedom, material well-being, and political equality. The interest in Haitian emigrationism was both a logical reaction to the racial injustices faced by blacks in the United States, and a reflection of the positive light in which many African Americans viewed Haiti. Having thrown off the brutal yoke of French colonialism at the end of the eighteenth century, the Haitians had established a black nationality that had survived as a potent symbol of black independence. For African Americans, because the Haitian Revolution was irrevocably antagonistic to the political and racial imperatives that underpinned American racism, the survival of the Haitian nationality was doubly significant. Because a clear majority of white Americans regarded Haiti as the archetype of racial disorder and violence, it was not surprising that the United States refused to acknowledge Haitian independence.

Antebellum black emigrationism produced several prominent African American leaders. Martin Delany's interest in Africa, and his contribution to nineteenth-century black nationalism, are widely acknowledged. Delany, however, was not the only proponent of black emigration; significant, too, was James Theodore Holly, who not only advocated emigration to Haiti for a decade preceding the Civil War, but who in 1861 relocated—permanently—to the black republic. As this book makes clear, Holly's emigrationism was more than an exercise in material advancement—it was also a spiritual mission. Carrying his version of Christian civilization to Haiti, and formulating an early form of black nationalism, Holly's black Manifest Destiny reflected the paradoxes of African America: while he was determined to promote black emigration from the United States, and although he was appalled by the racism that so pervasively tainted American social relations and political life, he was equally certain that American blacks were uniquely equipped to elevate Haitians from their material and spiritual wilderness. Consequently, even as the black nationalism that was very much a part of antebellum emigrationism renounced American racism, it reflected a deep-seated belief that American blacks were more advanced than African peoples elsewhere.

African American emigrationism has often been associated—erroneously, in most cases—with white-sponsored schemes to remove blacks from the United States, the most notorious of which was sponsored by the American Colonization Society. The departure of six thousand African Americans for Haiti during the 1820s suggests that while black Americans had decisively repudiated the Colonization Society's attempt to "repatriate" them "back" to Africa, they remained receptive to the idea of emigration to alternative destinations. And although the Haitian emigration movement of the 1820s ended in failure, black Americans remained conscious of Haiti's significance as the world's first independent black republic. That awareness was one imperative behind the dramatic revival of interest in Haitian emigrationism during the 1850s. The antebellum period was one of rapid change and uncertainty, but for black Americans each moment in the increasingly bitter sectional conflict suggested that emancipation for the Southern slaves was becoming more distant, and that Northern blacks' already marginal freedom was becoming ever more precarious.

Much of the emigrationist sentiment of the early 1850s focused on Canada, and—during the middle of the decade—on the possibility of a movement to Africa. By the late 1850s, however, although a tiny minority clung to their African dream, Haiti had become the most viable option for those blacks who had despaired of ever achieving meaningful freedom in the United States. Indeed, during the 1850s, African Americans' interest in Haiti stood at the center of their deliberations concerning freedom and equality. On the eve of the Civil War, with the Haitian government providing tangible support to emigrationism, the scene was set for a movement to the island republic. Under the auspices of the Haitian Bureau of Emigration—whose white leader, James Redpath, played a significant, albeit contentious part in the movement—two thousand blacks left the United States to settle in Haiti. Examining that movement allows not only an analysis of the black nationalism of the movement's leaders, but also the contemplation of what emigrationism meant to the African American populace. As is seen here, ambitious dreams of black nationalism counted for little when emigrants encountered hardship and disappointment in their new home. Accordingly, in detailing an important, but little understood aspect of the black diaspora, this study also investigates the development of black nationalism, the relationship between racial and national identity, the divisions within the African American leadership, and the often divergent aspirations of that leadership and the black masses. Haitian emigrationism thus provides clues to a range of issues that have been central to the black experience in the United States.

ACKNOWLEDGMENTS

My initial interest in black America was sparked during my undergraduate studies at the University of Western Australia, where Tony Barker and Frank Broeze brought a witty, but appropriately critical approach to the study of American history. During the latter stages of this project Tony read the entire manuscript: although he was at that stage basking in the well-earned glory—and, hopefully, the royalties—of having written the definitive study of the Western Australian Cricket Association, the manuscript has benefited from his keen eye and deep knowledge of black history and antebellum reformism. It is now many years since I took Frank's course on Maritime History, and although I have long since forgotten the intricacies of the Battle of Midway, Frank's boundless enthusiasm and energy continue to inspire.

Anyone who has delved into black history will appreciate that the assistance of archivists and librarians is crucial in locating and accessing primary source materials. This study is no exception. To the staff at the following libraries and institutions, I offer my thanks: the Library of Congress, the Massachusetts Historical Society, the Rare Book and Manuscript Room at the Boston Public Library, the Schomburg Center for Research in Black Culture, the National Archives, the Rare Book, Manuscript, and Special Collections Library at Duke University, the New Orleans Public Library, and the Sterling Memorial Library at Yale University. For their speedy and efficient help, I especially thank Jennifer Peters and her colleagues at the Archives of the Episcopal Church at Austin, Texas.

Researching American history from Australia presents substantial logistical difficulties and expenses. I am grateful to the Inter-Library Loan Staff in the Auchmuty Library at the University of Newcastle, who not only procured material from other libraries in Australia, but who also obtained a number of obscure yet nonetheless invaluable items from overseas. In addition, I take this opportunity to acknowledge the support provided by the University of Newcastle's Research Management Committee and Outside Studies Program Committee. Their generous assistance enabled me to gain access to the aforementioned overseas libraries and archives, without which this study could not have been completed. While the tyranny of distance can also complicate the process of liaison between author and publisher, Heather Staines, Emma

Moore, and the rest of the crew at Greenwood Press did a splendid job of turning this manuscript into a book.

The support of family, friends, and colleagues has been crucial in enabling me to see this project through to completion. To my mother, and to Louise, David, and Michael, I extend my heartfelt thanks. For their camaraderie and good cheer, thanks go to my colleagues in the History Department at the University of Newcastle. Michael Fellman, Roger Bell, and Steven Piott have provided encouragement, good counsel, and valued support for my academic career. In the United States, Mark C. Boissy offered hospitality and good company. Despite the demands of their own teaching and research, a number of people have taken the time to read and comment upon all or some of this manuscript: I'm obliged to Shane White, Allan Johnson, and Sean Brawley for their helpful comments and critiques. I owe a particular debt to Ian Tyrrell, who not only suggested that the subject of Haitian emigration was worthy of investigation, but who read and offered a characteristically incisive critique of an early draft of this manuscript.

Lorna Davin has lived with this project for many years; I remain grateful for her unwavering love, support, and patience. Finally, although Sam Dixon arrived just in time to delay completion of the manuscript, his enthusiastic annotations on a number of pages—the most incisive of which were written with a thumbnail dipped in Vegemite—were more valuable than he realizes.

Introduction

From the early decades of the nineteenth century, emigrationism has been an integral aspect of the black experience in the United States. By raising vital questions about African American aspirations, as well as the origins of black nationalism, emigrationists broached issues that have long been central to the preoccupations of students of black America.[1] Writing at the beginning of the twentieth century, the black activist and scholar W.E.B. Du Bois described the contradictory feeling of "two-ness," of being both "an American" and "a Negro." In articulating the "two unreconciled strivings" of black Americans, Du Bois identified a long-standing tension in African American thought and culture.[2] Yet although many blacks responded to that tension by focusing their energies on the quintessentially American notion of individual self-advancement, and by standing firm in their demands for the rights of citizenship within the United States, the questions of racial and national self-identity raised by Du Bois transcended the aspirations and experiences of individual African Americans. For some blacks, emigrationism—coupled with the establishment of an assertive black nationality—was not only a means of achieving individual self-advancement, but was also a political expression of their racial identity. Through their efforts to reconcile individual and collective action, African Americans both reflected, and confronted, the tension between individualism and collectivity that has long been evident in American culture.

Since the era of the American Revolution, emigrationist sentiment among black Americans has often been directed toward Africa. It is not surprising, then, that in discussing emigrationism, and the associated question of black nationalism, historians have tended to focus their attentions on the connections between black Americans and Africa.[3] Without slighting black Americans' connections with their ancestral origins, it is suggested here that historians have understated African Americans' relationship with the island republic of Haiti, a nation that excited the imagination of those interested in the elevation of black people, which for many Americans also illustrated blacks' apparent inability to achieve political, social, or economic advancement independent of whites. Similarly, while not denying the nineteenth-century interest in African emigrationism, this study contends that the Haitian emigration movement of the Civil War era represented a more significant climax to the history of black aspirations in the era of slavery than the more romantically appealing, but far less realistic, back-to-Africa schemes of the 1850s. Besides casting light on various aspects of the black experience in America, and highlighting the dilemmas of racial and national identification to which Du Bois so eloquently referred, the story of nineteenth-century African American emigration to Haiti is a dramatic element of the black diaspora, that locates the history of black Americans in a broader, international context. Accordingly, African American emigration to Haiti provides a window into the complex interplay of "race" and "nationality" in nineteenth-century history.

Haiti has long occupied a prominent—albeit contentious—place in America's racial consciousness.[4] Often maligned, and much misunderstood, Haiti has, in the words of Melville J. Herskovits, "fared badly at the hands of its literary interpreters."[5] For some Americans, the Haitians' success in ousting the brutal French colonial regime that had inflicted so much hardship on its black subjects suggested the Haitian revolutionaries were heirs to the Americans' quest for independence. At the same time, however, for many Americans, Haiti conjured the most dreadful fears of all: black revolution and race war. In part, Haiti was so contentious because it exposed the gaping contradiction in American life. From the early nineteenth century, Haiti highlighted the tension between Americans' stated principles of freedom and liberty on the one hand, and the realities of slavery and racism on the other. As David Brion Davis has said, the black revolution in Haiti "put the American ideology to its most critical test: if slaves could demonstrate their capacity for freedom by fighting for it, then how could white Americans retain their double standard and still remain loyal to their Revolutionary ideals?"[6] Indeed, the black revolution in Haiti and the continuing survival of the island republic in the face of considerable adversity were recurring themes in nineteenth-century American discourses about race and slavery.

Black Americans were active participants in those discourses. Eugene Genovese has argued that the "Haitian manifestation" of the "international bourgeois-democratic revolution of the last quarter of the eighteenth century" had "an impact on Afro-America that transcended the political and ideological shaping of the black struggle for justice." Similarly, Ira Berlin has noted that following "the slaves' success in creating the Haitian republic, neither master nor slave could doubt the possibility of a world turned upside down."[7]

Haiti's influence was profound, but it was also ambiguous. This study reveals that the black nationalists of the mid-nineteenth century regarded the Haitian Revolution as fundamentally incomplete. Convinced that black Americans were best placed to provide the commercial, agricultural, and industrial acumen that was required to bring the Haitian Revolution to a successful conclusion, and certain that African Americans could transplant Christian civilization to the benighted Haitians, proponents of Haitian emigrationism identified a common destiny between black America and the island republic. Haitian emigrationism was thus an essential element of nineteenth-century black nationalism.

Although that nationalism was the subject of widespread debate during the 1850s, black emigrationism can be traced to an earlier period of American history, one that saw the formation of free black communities in a number of northern cities. Emerging in the era of the American Revolution, these black communities were positive expressions of African American consciousness, born partly from the adversities of American racism. During the 1820s, that racism was one factor impelling free blacks to consider the relative merits of colonization to Africa, and emigration to Haiti. Analyzing the black response to colonization during the decade following the establishment of the American Colonization Society (ACS) in 1817 helps to explain the failure of African emigrationism and colonization in the longer antebellum period, as well as the appeal of Haitian emigration during the 1820s, and again during the 1850s and 1860s.[8]

In the long term, only a handful of blacks left the United States, and the dream of black nationalism was in many respects unrealized. But emigration schemes had a significance far beyond the scant numbers of black Americans who actually settled in Haiti, Africa, or elsewhere. Not only does the adage that the extraordinary can help us understand the ordinary suggest something about the significance of antebellum emigrationism, but the *ideas* behind black emigrationism—and the white-sponsored schemes for black colonization that were also very much a part of nineteenth-century America's racial debate—demand attention. Consequently, while this study considers (in so far as it is possible to do so) the experiences of those African Americans who emigrated to Haiti, a major theme is an analysis of the ideology of Haitian emigrationism and of the obstacles that stood in the way of a successful movement of black Americans to the island republic. Not only does the evolution of the emigrationist and colonizationist ideologies reveal much about black and white attitudes in antebellum America, but the efforts that were made to translate those ideas into tangible actions warrant fresh investigation. As William W. Freehling has observed, proposals for black colonization have too frequently been disparaged by historians as "preposterous" panaceas to the enormous difficulties facing the United States during the nineteenth century—and beyond. The important point, as Freehling emphasized, is that historians must analyze antebellum colonization on its own terms. The "key to crediting proposals to deport blacks," he wrote, "is to realize that controversial new migrations into and out of a multicultural social world everywhere conditioned antebellum Americans' angles of vision." Whether it be in terms of westward expansion, the influx of European immigrants, the beginnings of women's move from the private sphere to the public realm, or discussions of Southern secession from the Union, nineteenth-century America—like much of the European world—appeared to be a society on the move.[9] It is well to remember, too, that nineteenth-century black society and culture were no less the products of migration, albeit involuntary. Consequently, although it is easy to disparage African American emigrationism and colonization as unrealistic and fanciful solutions to the bitterly divisive issues of race and slavery that beset the United States during the pre-Civil War period, it is essential to remember that black emigration and colonization were not unrealistic to many antebellum Americans.

As with almost all aspects of the black experience, the historiography of African American emigrationism is inextricably connected to the post–World War II shifts in studies of slavery. It is only since the 1950s, when black demands for equality have become more militant, that historical studies have come to emphasize the active response of slaves to their predicament, rather than portray them merely as passive victims of the South's "peculiar institution." If the first response of historians to the civil rights activism of the post–World War II era was to stress the cruelties of slavery, this in turn quickly led to insistence that African Americans had not been crushed by its rigors. It was only in the same recent decades that the existence of 450,000 free blacks in the antebellum period was even properly recognized. But once Leon Litwack "rescued" them from obscurity, largely by describing the extent of legal and racial discrimination they endured, the focus of interpretation soon paralleled the slave studies.[10]

Free blacks had more opportunity to express collective concern for separatist or other goals, most notably through participation in the black convention movement. But, despite the fact that all blacks endured racism, and notwithstanding an emerging sense of African American racial consciousness during the nineteenth century, the free black community was not a homogenous group. At the same time as black leaders quarreled over the best means for African Americans to achieve self-elevation and racial advancement, a majority of blacks were preoccupied with surviving amid a racist environment that relegated them to the margins of white society. The distinctions within African America had direct implications for the black nationalism of the 1850s, raising questions regarding the significance of Haiti, and particularly the Haitian Revolution, for those blacks who were not part of the educated minority. Although there is no doubt that the African American leadership understood the implications of the Haitian Revolution, and although there is compelling evidence that the free black populace and slaves were also conscious of Haiti's significance, the history of Haiti since the overthrow of French rule exposed significant differences among black Americans.[11]

These differences were perhaps predictable given the difficulties facing the black republic. Nineteenth-century Haiti had not suffered the environmental degradation that is now a characteristic of the island, but its tropical climate and physical geography were at the very least unfamiliar—indeed, probably unappealing—to many free blacks, especially those residing in the northern states. Similarly, post-revolutionary Haiti was cursed by recurrent political instability and social upheaval that would be familiar to any modern observer of what remains a contentious example of black rule. Persistent depictions of the island republic as the epitome of political and social disorder, coupled with the widespread knowledge of the grinding poverty endured by its citizens, stood in tension alongside Haiti's reputation as a nemesis of slaveholders everywhere. Black Americans' various responses to Haiti's woes were exposed most clearly by their reactions to proposals for emigration to the Caribbean island. These reactions, in turn, were at the center of ongoing debates regarding the wider question of black freedom and equality in the United States. At the same time, however, as African American leaders—emigrationists and anti-emigrationists alike—debated the best means by which black Americans could achieve meaningful freedom, their disputes frequently betrayed more personal rivalries. Accordingly, although this study begins from the premise that emigrationism must be viewed *within* the tradition of antebellum black activism, rather than as an aberrant distraction, the fact that the Haitian movement of the Civil War era reached an operational level that led to a formally organized movement of black Americans meant the debates it aroused were particularly vitriolic.

Black proposals for emigration have often been confused with white-sponsored schemes to remove African Americans from the United States. The idea of black colonization—often understood to mean the forced expatriation of blacks from America—attracted support from such distinguished statesmen as Thomas Jefferson and Abraham Lincoln. In contemplating the "Negro problem," a majority of white Americans would have concurred with Walt Whitman's 1858 statement: "Who believes that Whites and Blacks can ever amalgamate in America? Or who wishes it to happen? Nature has set an impassable seal against it. Besides, is not America for the Whites? And is it not better so?"[12] Whitman opposed the extension of slavery into the western regions of the United States, but his opposition to the expansion of slavery was a reflection of fears that the South's peculiar institution could undermine economic and social development throughout the nation, rather than an expression of support for the principles of racial equality. For Whitman, as for many other whites, America's destiny was a racially distinct one that offered little scope for black advancement. Given the depth of those assumptions among white Americans, it was not surprising that many blacks expressed uncompromising opposition to white-organized schemes to remove them from the United States. The best known of these schemes was that of the ACS, which established the west African colony of Liberia in 1818. Although the ACS survived into the early twentieth century, it achieved only marginal success in expatriating black Americans "back" to Africa.[13]

The long prevalent assumption that African Americans were little more than dependants of whites inevitably meant that until the 1960s scholarly interest in black colonization and emigration focused largely on the ACS.[14] However, the desire to argue for a degree of black autonomy in all facets of nineteenth-century life has equally inevitably focused attention on African Americans' own plans for emigration from the United States, independent of the ACS. A pioneering student of black aspirations was Howard H. Bell, whose 1953 doctoral dissertation on the African American convention movement preceded the controversies and reinterpretations stimulated by Stanley Elkins' controversial depiction of the slaves as "psychic casualties" of the South's peculiar institution. It was to be sixteen years before Bell's dissertation was published in a period now much more sensitive to black activism.[15] In the meantime, however, the increasing focus on African Americans' nineteenth-century efforts to determine their own future was reflected in the publication of a number of articles by Bell, drawn from the findings he had made in his 1953 study. Ever attentive to evidence of black nationalist sentiment or action among African Americans, Bell asserted at the end of the 1950s that the antebellum "emphasis on emigration and Negro sovereignty can best be described as a kind of Negro nationalism." In Bell's view, this black nationalism was "one of the dominant forces affecting the free Negro in the decade before the Civil War."[16]

Not surprisingly, the decade of black militancy in the 1960s saw others echo and elaborate on those ideas. With much of this attention directed toward schemes for black emigration to Africa, Martin Delany was belatedly recognized as a significant figure in African American history. Following Frederick Douglass' 1862 depiction of Delany as the most intense "embodiment of black nationalism" to be encountered "outside of the valley of the Niger," twentieth-century scholars have characterized Delany as a telling influence on an embryonic black nationalism that did much to alert black Americans to their African heritage. As Harold Cruse noted in 1967, not only was Delany "the real prototype of Afro-American Nationalism," but "every Pan-Africanist trend of the twentieth century, including Garvey's, had its roots in nineteenth-century American Negro trends."[17]

Implicit within some of these analyses was the assumption that Delany's brand of emigrationism was more valuable than the assimilationism of other black leaders, particularly Frederick Douglass. In part, these issues have been contentious because the language, strategies, and goals of black leaders have often been amorphous. Black separatism, for example, did not necessarily entail physical removal from the United States—it could mean an endorsement of black economic independence from white capital, or a sense of pride in black culture. But given that a number of nineteenth-century black leaders themselves emphasized their differences with each other, it is perhaps not surprising that some historians have represented the antebellum black leadership in dichotomic terms. As Cruse pointed out in 1967, this proclivity to focus on often exaggerated opposites has often rested in "historical arguments between personalities" such as Douglass and Delany.[18]

Yet, although African American activism has often been conceptualized in terms of binary opposites, the black leadership, and the ideologies and strategies they formulated, cannot be so easily categorized. Sterling Stuckey has offered useful advice for those contemplating African American efforts to achieve freedom and equality. On the one hand, Stuckey identified the competing principles that have long characterized black activism in the United States. In an important study published in 1987, Stuckey observed that the "period from 1830 to 1860, in which the forces of integrationism and nationalism first seriously contended for ascendancy, prefigured similar struggles among black Americans in the twentieth century." Judging the "integrationist contribution to liberation theory in the slave era" as "almost non-existent," Stuckey credited the "nationalists" with marking "out the material and to some extent the spiritual lines along which genuine liberation might be attained." Stuckey thus signaled his own views regarding the efficacy of activist methods, styles, and goals. At the same time, however, although he contrasted black nationalism with integrationism, Stuckey also stressed that Frederick Douglass' declaration that "we are Americans," was "no integrationist argument, nothing so simple as that."[19] Fifteen years earlier, moreover, when contemporary debates over Black Power had loomed large in the historical as well as popular consciousness, Stuckey had emphasized that the terms "integrationist" and "black nationalist" do not adequately signify the complexities and contradictions within black thought in antebellum America, and beyond. As he noted, thinking solely in terms of "integrationism" and "black nationalism" prevents "us from understanding major movements and ideologies."[20] And, as James Oliver Horton and Lois E. Horton have pointed out, any "dichotomy" that posits "integration versus black nationalism, where the implication is that integration means replacing an African identity with an American identity" disregards "the African heritage carried by all Americans."[21]

Put bluntly, integrationism and black nationalism are not necessarily mutually exclusive, and the terms should be applied with caution. Accordingly, although antebellum black nationalism was certainly not a "fantasy," due attention must be paid to the nuances of nineteenth-century black thought and activism.[22] Analyzing Haitian emigrationism provides an opportunity to investigate these nuances, by exposing the two, frequently contradictory principles—separatism, or integration—that have often shaped the historiography and politics of black America.

As well as analyzing differences within black America, this book considers emigrationists' attitudes toward black people elsewhere. In his recent study of African Americans' attitudes toward their ancestral homeland, Tunde Adeleke spoke of "Un-African Americans," whose romantic rhetoric of black nationalism masked a condescension toward—or even distaste for—the "real" Africa. Ironically, however, in forcefully deconstructing the notion of a black community—which has not only been an ideal for which black leaders have frequently aspired, but which has also served as an organizing principle among scholars of slavery and other aspects of the black experience—Adeleke curiously ignored Haiti's role in African Americans' nineteenth-century constructions of black nationalism.[23] Not only was Haiti crucial to those constructions, but the antebellum interest in the black republic offers a unique prism through which African American attitudes toward non-American blacks can be assessed.

Analyzing black American attitudes toward Haiti serves also to connect African American history to the notion of American exceptionalism. Implicit within that notion, and encapsulated within the African American experience, were deep-seated assumptions regarding "civilization"—which, in turn shaped constructions of "the nation." Consequently, black emigrationists' discussions of race and nationality should be placed within the context of the wider antebellum discourses of nationalism, many of which explicitly defined American civilization in terms of Anglo-Saxon hegemony. Bearing in mind that "civilization" and "culture" were frequently used interchangeably during the nineteenth century, and acknowledging that antebellum black nationalism was as much a cultural construction as it was a political and economic imperative, this study considers the relationship between the nationalist vision articulated by black emigrationists, and the wider values of antebellum America.

The attention lavished on Martin Delany's proposals for African emigration helps explain why there has been considerably less interest in African American emigration to Haiti.[24] A corrective to this historiographical neglect is long overdue, given that during the 1820s, and again on the eve of the Civil War, Haitian emigrationism reached an organizational state of development far beyond that of any black proposals for African emigration. In the process of sending two thousand emigrants out of the United States, the Haitian movement of the Civil War era clearly engaged the interest of at least some of the black populace; this, in turn, exposed the leaders of the Haitian scheme to the accusation that they favored an en-masse exodus of African Americans—a charge that had long been leveled against the despised ACS. Haitian emigrationism thus offers insights into the mind-set of the black masses, as well as the black leadership, during the antebellum period.

During the 1850s, the best known proponent of Haitian emigrationism was James Theodore Holly, a free-born black. In raising black Americans' consciousness about the significance of the Haitian Revolution, and paving the way for the emigration of African Americans during the early 1860s, Holly played a key role in laying the groundwork for what was arguably the closest approximation of a "political" mass movement among black Americans in the antebellum period. Determined to carry his particular brand of Christian-based black nationality to Haiti, Holly was a tireless advocate of emigration to the island republic. For Holly, his commitment to what might be labeled

"Christian-emigrationism" proved to be the first stage in his life-long devotion to the spiritual elevation of Haiti. But despite his long-standing commitment to Haiti, when the Haitian government committed money to the project in 1860, and established a Bureau of Emigration in the United States, Holly was overlooked in favor of James Redpath, a Scottish-born abolitionist. For some black Americans at the time, and perhaps for subsequent generations of scholars, the appointment of Redpath undermined the black nationalist credentials of Haitian emigrationism. Indeed, the appointment of Redpath as chief administrator of the Haitian scheme probably helps account for the relative historiographical neglect of Haitian emigration vis-à-vis African emigrationism. As this study reveals, however, the appointment of Redpath was just one of many apparent inconsistencies in the formulation of black nationality; the implication that the movement would have enjoyed more success if it had been led by a black person requires careful analysis.

Just as the political climate of the 1960s has shaped the historiography of emigrationism and black nationalism, Haiti's turbulent history is another factor behind the general neglect of African American emigration to Haiti. Noting Melville Herskovits' warning that "condescension and caricature have" often been used in explaining Haiti's people and its institutions, Haitian emigrationism can only be properly understood within the context of the island republic's agonizing quest for economic advancement, and social and political stability—and of black Americans' perceptions of Haiti and its population.[25] One twentieth-century observer described his time in Haiti as the "best nightmare on earth"; the phrase also connotes much about the hopes, along with the disappointments and hardships, of those African Americans who sought a new life in Haiti during the early 1860s. It is, moreover, an equally apposite summary of nineteenth-century attitudes, including black attitudes, toward the former French colony.[26]

Another visitor to Haiti, writing at the end of the nineteenth century, summed up the underlying ambivalence and mystique that surrounded the black republic: "Hayti the Mysterious! Her appeal to the imagination is inevitable."[27] This reference to "imagination" not only suggests a new way of approaching African American perceptions of Haiti, but also returns one to the vexed question of black nationality. The historical constructions of nationality have occupied the attentions of many scholars. One of the most perceptive of those scholars, Benedict Anderson, has noted that "nationality, or, as one might prefer to put it in view of that word's multiple significations, nation-ness, as well as nationalism are cultural artefacts of a particular kind." As Anderson explained, all nationalisms are *imagined*. Yet the allure of the nation is among the most compelling historical forces; at the heart of those sentiments rests a sense of *community*. In Anderson's view, "regardless of the actual inequality and exploitation that may prevail in each" nation, it "is always conceived as a deep, horizontal comradeship."[28] These imperatives are helpful in understanding antebellum black nationalism, in all its guises.

The middle decades of the nineteenth century constituted an important moment in the history of "race" in the United States. As the nation stumbled toward Civil War, politicians, scientists, and theologians spoke with increasing assertiveness on the question of racial difference. In articulating an ideology of black nationalism, emigrationists were confronting racial values and beliefs that were deeply embedded in the nation's culture. And even as they grappled with racial views that held wide currency in nineteenth-century white America, black emigrationists' linkage of race with nationality reflected a process that was already well established in the United States, and elsewhere.[29]

From the early nineteenth century Haiti stood as a tangible expression of those links between race and nationality. Ironically, although American merchants established a lively trade with Haiti, white Americans pointed frequently to the island republic's economic difficulties as evidence of blacks' inability to act independently of whites. Equally significant, because Haiti cast terror into the minds of many white Americans, and provoked such deep concerns about slave rebellion, the United States refused to grant formal diplomatic recognition to the Haitian government. Because the Haitian government gave James Redpath the responsibility for securing diplomatic recognition for Haiti from the United States—and hence legitimation for the notion of a black nationality—emigration to the island republic took place within the wider context of white America's self-proclaimed Manifest Destiny in the Caribbean. Again, the question arises of how Haiti was represented and perceived in the United States during the nineteenth century. Accordingly, the various depictions of the black republic that were offered from the late eighteenth century from black and white Americans form an important part of this analysis.

Proponents of Haitian emigration hoped a successful movement of African Americans would play a part in addressing each of these issues. The study of international relations has advanced well beyond the examination of relation between governments: Patterns of migration, along with cultural assumptions and values (including racial and ethnic stereotypes), are all intrinsic aspects of a more complete appreciation of the way in which nations and their citizens interact. Nineteenth-century African American emigrationism demonstrates these links, and foreshadows the twentieth-century emigrationism and black nationalism of Marcus Garvey, and others.[30] But before tracing the rise and fall of Haitian emigrationism in the Civil War era, it is necessary to consider an earlier period, when the first schemes for black colonization and emigration were formulated, and when the young black republic of Haiti attracted the attention of the emerging African American communities in the United States.

NOTES

1. Defining "black nationalism"—and indeed, "nationalism"—is a complex task. Discussing the difficulties involved in reaching a "precise definition of nation" (not an

identical task, of course, to defining "nationalism"), Craig Calhoun has noted that perhaps the best one can do is identify "a common pattern." Identifying "three dimensions" to nationalism—"nationalism as discourse," "nationalism as project," and "nationalism as evaluation"—Calhoun suggested that nationalism "is a rhetoric for speaking about too many different things for a single theory to explain it." Calhoun is right to argue that no single theory can explain nationalism, but the phrase is used widely, and demands some form of definition. The task is to define—and use—"black nationalism" in an inclusive way, without making it so general as to rob the phrase of meaning. In broad terms, I have defined black nationalism as a racial consciousness and pride based around common—if not identical—experiences, leading to an emphasis on black self-reliance, and possibly, the establishment of a black nation-state. See Calhoun, *Nationalism* (Buckingham: Open University Press, 1997), 5–6, 8. See also E. U. Essien-Udom, *Black Nationalism: A Search for an Identity in America* (New York: Dell, 1964), 6; Wilson Jeremiah Moses, "Introduction" to *Classical Black Nationalism: From the American Revolution to Marcus Garvey*, ed. Wilson J. Moses (New York: New York University Press, 1996), 2–5.

2. Du Bois, *The Souls of Black Folk* (1903; reprint, New York: Dover Publications, 1994), 2.

3. A typical example of this imbalance is Philip Foner's *History of Black Americans*. In the second volume of that series, *From the Emergence of the Cotton Kingdom to the Compromise of 1850*, Foner devoted the better part of a chapter to the 1820s controversy surrounding the American Colonization Society. But Haitian emigration, which attracted the interest of a significant number of free blacks, including the six thousand who emigrated to the island republic during that decade, is dealt with in just one paragraph—and with the cursory and misleading comment that "few free blacks actually did emigrate to Haiti." See Foner, *History of Black Americans: From the Emergence of the Cotton Kingdom to the Compromise of 1850* (Westport, Conn.: Greenwood Press, 1983), Chapter 13 (quote on 303).

4. The most comprehensive assessment of Haiti's influence on the United States during the nineteenth century is Alfred N. Hunt, *Haiti's Influence on Antebellum America: Slumbering Volcano in the Caribbean* (Baton Rouge: Louisiana State University Press, 1988).

5. Herskovits, *Life in a Haitian Valley* (1937; reprint, New York: Octagon Books, 1964), vii.

6. Davis, *The Problem of Slavery in the Age of Revolution, 1770–1823* (Ithaca, N.Y.: Cornell University Press, 1975), 327.

7. Genovese, *From Rebellion to Revolution: Afro-American Slave Revolts in the Making of the Modern World* (New York: Vintage Books, 1979), 92; Berlin, *Many Thousands Gone: The First Two Centuries of Slavery in North America* (Cambridge, Mass.: Harvard University Press, 1999), 222.

8. "Emigrationism" is used herein to refer to black-led proposals for African American emigration; "colonization" refers to white initiatives to expatriate, or otherwise remove, African Americans from the United States.

9. Freehling, " 'Absurd' Issues and the Causes of the Civil War: Colonization as a Test Case," in *The Reintegration of American History: Slavery and the Civil War*, ed. Freehling (New York: Oxford University Press, 1994), 138–57 (quotes on 138).

10. Litwack, *North of Slavery: The Negro in the Free States, 1790–1860* (Chicago: University of Chicago Press, 1961). Other studies of free blacks include Ira Berlin,

Slaves Without Masters: The Free Negro in the Antebellum South (New York: Oxford University Press, 1974); Leonard P. Curry, *The Free Black in Urban America, 1800–1850: The Shadow of the Dream* (Chicago: University of Chicago Press, 1981); Julie Winch, *Philadelphia's Black Elite: Activism, Accommodation, and the Struggle for Autonomy, 1787–1848* (Philadelphia: Temple University Press, 1988); James Oliver Horton and Lois E. Horton, *In Hope of Liberty: Culture, Community, and Protest Among Northern Free Blacks, 1700–1860* (New York: Oxford University Press, 1997).

11. In claiming that the Haitians "were revered by blacks throughout the Americas," and in arguing that African Americans were highly conscious of the Haitian Revolution, James O. Jackson has asserted, rather than demonstrated, that the black populace shared their leaders' attitudes toward Haiti's past. See Jackson, "The Origins of Pan-African Nationalism: Afro-American and Haytian Relations, 1800–1863" (Ph.D. diss., Northwestern University, 1976), 118–47 (quotes on 119–20).

12. Whitman, "Prohibition of Colored Persons," in the *Brooklyn Daily Times*, 6 May 1858, in *Race and the American Romantics*, ed. Vincent Friemarck and Bernard Rosenthal (New York: Schocken Books, 1971), 47.

13. Between 1820 and 1861, the ACS despatched 10,517 African Americans to Liberia. See Philip J. Staudenraus, *The African Colonization Movement, 1816–1865* (New York: Columbia University Press, 1961), 251.

14. The major studies of the ACS are Early Lee Fox, *The American Colonization Society, 1817–1840* (Baltimore: Johns Hopkins University Press, 1919); Staudenraus, *African Colonization Movement.*

15. See Elkins, *Slavery: A Problem in American Institutional and Political Life* (Chicago: University of Chicago Press, 1959); Bell, *A Survey of the Negro Convention Movement, 1830–1861* (New York: Arno Press, 1969).

16. Bell, "The Negro Emigration Movement, 1849–1854: A Phase of Negro Nationalism," *Phylon*, 20 (1959): 132. See also Bell, "Negro Nationalism: A Factor in Emigration Projects, 1858–1861," *Journal of Negro History*, 47 (1962): 42–53; Bell, "Negro Nationalism in the 1850s," *Journal of Negro Education*, 35 (1966): 100–104. Adelaide Hill and Martin Kilson have argued that a "conscious search among Negro Americans for an understanding of, and identity with, their African heritage began during the mid 1800s." See Hill and Kilson, eds., *Apropos of Africa: Sentiments of Negro American Leaders on Africa from the 1800s to the 1950s* (London: Frank Cass, 1969), xiii.

17. *Douglass' Monthly*, August 1862; Cruse, *The Crisis of the Negro Intellectual* (New York: William Morrow, 1967), 558. See also Lerone Bennett, Jr., *Before the Mayflower: A History of the Negro in America, 1619–1964*, Rev. Ed. (Harmondsworth: Penguin, 1966), 137.

18. Cruse, *Crisis of the Negro Intellectual*, 6.

19. Stuckey, *Slave Culture: Nationalist Theory and the Foundations of Black America* (New York: Oxford University Press, 1987), 224, 231.

20. Stuckey, *The Ideological Origins of Black Nationalism* (Boston: Beacon Press, 1972), 26. Utilizing a literary, rather than historical analysis, Robert S. Levine's work on Martin Delany and Frederick Douglass offers a sophisticated and nuanced discussion of the two men and their ideologies. Careful to emphasize the "instabilities and overlappings" in African American thought and activism, Levine also pointed out that "by the 1850s," Delany and Douglass "regarded themselves as in conflict with each other over issues of absolutely crucial importance." See Levine, *Martin Delany, Fre-*

derick Douglass, and the Politics of Representative Identity (Chapel Hill: University of North Carolina Press, 1997), 5–6. See also Wilson Jeremiah Moses, *The Golden Age of Black Nationalism, 1850–1920* (Hamden, Conn.: Archon Books, 1978), 45; Bernard R. Boxhill, "Douglass Against the Emigrationists," in *Frederick Douglass: A Critical Reader*, ed. Bill E. Lawson and Frank M. Kirkland (Malden, Mass.: Blackwell, 1999), 21–49.

21. Horton and Horton, *In Hope of Liberty*, xii.

22. Theodore Draper, "The Fantasy of Black Nationalism," *Commentary*, 48 (1969): 27–54.

23. Adeleke, *UnAfrican Americans: Nineteenth-Century Black Nationalists and the Civilizing Mission* (Lexington: University Press of Kentucky, 1998), 127, 143, passim.

24. Haitian emigrationism has not been entirely neglected. See Willis D. Boyd, "James Redpath and American Negro Colonization in Haiti, 1860–1862," *The Americas*, 12 (1955): 169–82; William Seraile, "Afro-American Emigration to Haiti During the American Civil War," *The Americas*, 35 (1978): 185–200; David McEwen Dean, *Defender of the Race: James Theodore Holly, Black Nationalist Bishop* (Boston: Lambeth Press, 1979); John McKivigan, "James Redpath and Black Reaction to the Haitian Emigration Bureau," *Mid-America*, 69 (1987): 139–53; Jackson, "Origins of Pan-African Nationalism." The most comprehensive account of antebellum emigrationism is Floyd J. Miller, *The Search for a Black Nationality: Black Emigration and Colonization, 1787–1863* (Urbana: University of Illinois Press, 1975). Although Miller's study devotes some attention to Haitian emigrationism, it glosses over the longer term relationship between black Americans and Haiti, and says little about the place of Haiti in African Americans' conception of black nationality.

25. Herskovits, *Life in a Haitian Valley*, vii.

26. Herbert Gold, *The Best Nightmare on Earth: A Life in Haiti* (New York: Touchstone, 1991).

27. Hesketh Prichard, *Where Black Rules White: A Journey Across and About Hayti* (1900; reprint, Freeport, N.Y.: Books for Libraries Press, 1971), 4.

28. Anderson, *Imagined Communities: Reflections on the Origins and Spread of Nationalism* (London: Verso, 1983), 13–16.

29. On the relationship between racial thought and the emergence of American nationalism, see Reginald Horsman, *Race and Manifest Destiny: The Origins of American Racial Anglo-Saxonism* (Cambridge, Mass.: Harvard University Press, 1981).

30. For a critical analysis of Garvey's black nationalism, see Clarence Walker, *Deromanticizing Black History: Critical Essays and Reappraisals* (Knoxville: University of Tennessee Press, 1991), 34–55.

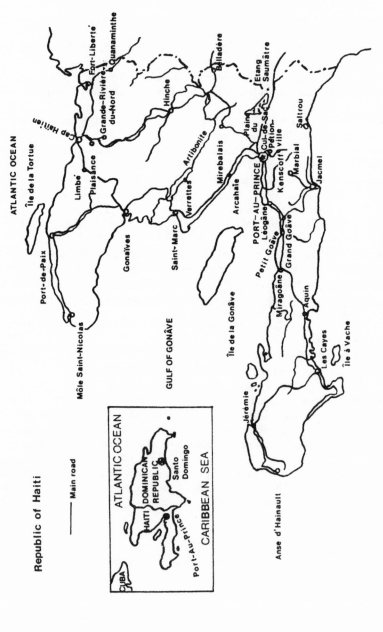

Republic of Haiti

—— Main road

1

Revolution and Emigration: Black America and Haiti, 1773–1830

The antecedents of African American emigrationism during the Civil War era, and the black nationalism with which it was frequently associated, can be traced to the late eighteenth century. While the period following the War of Independence witnessed an end to slavery throughout the North, and the beginning of well-organized communities of free blacks in a number of northern cities, African Americans soon realized that the lofty rhetoric of the Revolutionary era did not translate into racial equality. Not for the last time in American history, racism proved more resilient than slavery. Confronting social, political, and economic discrimination at every turn, black Americans contemplated whether they should leave the young republic that was so vigorously denying them the rights of citizenship. The early decades of the nineteenth century were also significant in establishing black Americans' impressions of Haiti, whose bloody revolution at the end of the eighteenth century not only influenced white Americans' attitudes toward race relations, but also affected the ideologies and tactics of African Americans seeking the abolition of slavery.

The 1820s emerges as a key period in the history of black America, providing insights into the long-term appeal of Haitian emigrationism vis-à-vis African colonization, and casting light on the long-term relationship between black Americans and the island republic of Haiti. Paradoxically, although that relationship was probably never as close as some black leaders hoped, or many white Americans feared, the persistent fear of slave conspiracy highlighted for many Americans the threat of trans-national racial violence, based on the Haitian experience. Of course, for most African Americans it was not the Haitian Revolution that was of concern, but the individual and institutionalized violence associated with American racism. Those concerns played a part in shaping the black response to the fiercely debated issues of emigration and colonization. Indeed, speaking in 1827, one African American remarked that of all the "temporal subjects that agitate the public mind," there was "none in which the free population of our brethren" was "so deeply interested," as emigration and colonization.[1] Much of that interest, however, comprised opposition to the expatriation of black Americans to Africa. Largely as a consequence of that black opposition, the white-led American Colonization Society (ACS) failed to dispatch more than a handful of African Americans to its African colony of Liberia. More significant, however, was a scheme that sent six-thousand black Americans to Haiti during the mid-1820s. Although that movement ended in failure, it offers clues to the later interest in Haitian emigration, as well as telling insights into African American aspirations in the period preceding the growth of radical abolitionism. This chapter examines black American emigrationism from the pre-Revolutionary period through to the early 1830s, paying particular attention to the 1820s, when Haitian emigrationism was a direct—and for a time apparently successful—rival to African colonization.

The earliest schemes for African American colonization were enunciated during the Revolutionary period, when northerners, as well as southerners expressed interest in the idea. An early white proponent of black colonization was the Reverend Samuel Hopkins, a well-known Rhode Island Congregationalist clergyman. Opposed to slavery and to the slave trade, Hopkins believed both practices could be abolished by the establishment of Christian settlements in Africa, led by black ministers trained in America. In 1773, Hopkins outlined a plan for sending blacks to Africa. But the members of the Rhode Island legislature, unwilling to finance any scheme for foreign colonization, refused to support Hopkins' plan. William Thornton, a West Indian, was another early advocate of black colonization. But when the Massachusetts Assembly refused to support his plans, Thornton's proposals lapsed. In 1790, Ferdinando Fairfax, a wealthy Virginian, elaborated the first detailed plan for African American expatriation. Envisaging a national scheme of colonization, Fairfax proposed that a colony of free blacks should travel to Africa, to pave the way for groups of manumitted slaves.[2]

The best known advocate of colonization during this early period was Thomas Jefferson. Favoring the ultimate emancipation of the slaves, Jefferson headed a 1777 committee of the Virginian legislature that detailed a plan for the gradual emancipation and expatriation of the blacks in that state. In principle, Jefferson was an opponent of slavery; in practice he reflected the common racialist assumptions of his time. Certain that the most urgent question raised by the prospect of emancipation was the removal of the freed blacks, he asserted that both races would benefit if they were separated.[3] Yet, not even an individual of Jefferson's political and social stature could translate these early endorsements of black colonization into tangible action.

As the eighteenth century drew to a close, interest in black deportation declined among white Americans. During this period, slavery became more firmly entrenched in the South, eventually becoming the basis for an economic and political order—indeed, a whole way of life—that was vastly different from that which developed in the North. A major factor in that process was the development in 1793 of the cotton gin by Eli Whitney. In the wake of Whitney's invention—which expedited the removal of the seeds from raw cotton—the production of cotton expanded dramatically, reinvigorating slavery as a labor system. Convinced that their economic and social well-being was dependent on slavery, white southerners' increasing reluctance to contemplate emancipation also reflected deep-seated fears concerning the possibility of social turmoil in the wake of emancipation. On this issue, white Americans were influenced by events in the United States, and by events abroad. During the 1790s, the black slaves in the French colony of Saint Domingue overthrew their white masters. Amid the ensuing bloodshed, it "did not take long for slaveholders to envision an American Saint Domingue."[4] More is said later regarding the significance of the revolution in Saint Domingue, and its impact on black consciousness in America. But the point should be made early that one of the enduring themes in antebellum white southern culture and politics was a fear of slave rebellion. Notwithstanding their repeated declarations that the slaves were content with their lot, southern slaveholders worried constantly about the prospect of black insurrection. Although the uprisings that did take place in the United States failed to overthrow the South's peculiar institution, they caused unremitting distress to whites. From the late eighteenth century, southern interest in black colonization was based less on the perception that it should be a corollary to emancipation, than it was on the belief that black deportation was a possible solution to the problems caused by the presence of free blacks—widely regarded as a dangerous and subversive element—in the United States.

At the same time as slavery was becoming more firmly entrenched in the South, emancipation was taking place in the North. Yet, although emancipation brought significant changes for African Americans in the North, the freedom they achieved was always tempered by the often brutal realities of American racism. Disadvantaged in terms of their education levels, economic position, and social status, free blacks lived on the margins of white society. Partly as a consequence of the rejection they faced from white America, northern blacks expressed interest in colonization during the post-Revolutionary period. Some blacks had expressed interest in leaving America even before the War of Independence. In a 1773 petition to their local "Representative," four Boston slaves determined to "leave the province" as "soon as" their "joynt [*sic*] labours" enabled them to "procure money to transport" themselves "to some part of the coast of Africa," where they hoped to establish a "settlement."[5]

18

Nothing came of that 1773 proposal, but following the turmoil of the Revolutionary years, there were renewed expressions of interest among some black Americans in African emigration. In 1787 a committee of the African Lodge, representing Boston's black Masons, petitioned the Massachusetts legislature regarding a "return to Africa." Arguing they could "live among" their "equals and be more comfortable and happy" in their "native country," these Boston blacks hoped the Massachusetts legislators would provide tangible assistance in their quest to emigrate to Africa. As was the case on other occasions, however, although there was considerable sympathy among whites for the idea of black colonization, no funds were forthcoming to facilitate an emigration movement.[6] Even at this early stage, proposals for black emigration to Africa, from black and white Americans alike, were thwarted by the logistical difficulties of transporting significant numbers of people across the Atlantic. A movement in the opposite direction had proved profitable for slave traders, but in the absence of a significant means of profiting from a movement back to Africa, the costs of transporting blacks from the United States to Africa were a significant impediment to an effective emigration movement.

The post-Revolutionary interest in colonization and emigration among blacks was connected to the growing social and political consciousness among sections of the African American population. During the latter decades of the eighteenth century, when northern blacks "constructed the social, religious, and emotional ligaments of their communities," an impressive array of separate black organizations was established in the cities of the North. Groups such as the African Union Society of Newport, Rhode Island, and the Free African Society of Philadelphia, were interested in a diverse range of issues, ranging from the abolition of the slave trade, to temperance.[7] Most significantly, free blacks established and joined their own churches. Responding to racial discrimination within the white denominations, and reflecting "the gradual rise of a community of interest" among those blacks being drawn to the cities in the post-emancipation period, the first "African" churches emerged in the late eighteenth century. As Leonard P. Curry has remarked, these churches were "dynamic instruments" for developing black community consciousness. But it is equally true that these institutions were "rooted in white culture."[8] This tension—reflecting an allegiance to race on one hand, and the influence of white America on the other—was to resonate through antebellum black emigrationism.

Colonization to Africa was conceivably more appealing to black Americans during this early period than was the case in later decades. For some blacks at least, dissatisfaction with life in America might well have been reinforced by links with Africa that were stronger than they were for subsequent generations. The language used by African Americans offers insights into this issue. As Gary Nash, and others, pointed out, the self-conscious use of the term "African" was more than a mere token; it was also a potentially effective means of encouraging racial solidarity. Moreover, the frequency with which black

Americans invoked the phrase "African" to name their institutions might also have reflected a desire to preserve their links with their ancestral past. As Ira Berlin has noted of the pre-Revolutionary period, an increase in the number of slaves transported directly to the United States possibly "reawakened Afro-Americans to their African past," and enabled northern blacks to incorporate "African culture into their own Afro-American culture." Of course, as Julie Winch remarked, "a renewed sense of cultural identity" among African Americans was not necessarily tantamount to a "desire to emigrate to Africa."[9] Conceivably, too, blacks' apparent willingness to consider—and their occasional expressions of support for—the notion of African colonization perhaps reflected the fact that the idea was simply that: an idea. When firm arrangements were in place to transport blacks to Africa, the appeal of an abstract notion faded in the face of the prospect of actual emigration. Early black emigrationists gave several reasons for favoring a "return" to Africa. Complementing their desire to escape the prejudice they suffered in the United States, they hoped to help emancipate those in bondage. Emigrationists also referred to the importance of carrying civilization—especially Christianity—to Africa. Regardless of their motives, however, early black supporters of emigration lacked the material resources to implement their plans.[10]

One African American in a better position to finance black colonization was a prosperous Quaker, Paul Cuffe, who had made his fortune out of merchant shipping. Following a trip to the west African colony of Sierra Leone in 1810, Cuffe proposed the establishment of a settlement of black Americans in Africa. Sierra Leone was already regarded as a bulwark in the fight against slavery. A group of freed black slaves from England had first settled in Sierra Leone in 1787, under the sponsorship of the British abolitionist, Granville Sharp. In 1808, the year after the British Parliament legislated against the slave trade, the British government took over the settlement in Sierra Leone, developing it as a naval base against the international trade in slaves.[11] Cuffe's plan to sail to Sierra Leone with a group of black emigrants from the United States was interrupted by the War of 1812. At the cessation of hostilities, however, he resumed his efforts with renewed enthusiasm. In late 1815 Cuffe sailed from Boston with thirty-eight emigrants willing to try their luck in the British colony. Although Cuffe's colonists were eventually granted land, the British governor in Sierra Leone, Charles McCarthy, was disappointed that the emigrants lacked sufficient experience and skill in tropical agriculture.[12] By implying that the "wrong" type of African American had emigrated to Sierra Leone, McCarthy foreshadowed a persistent explanation for the failure of subsequent schemes for black colonization and emigration.

Historians have disagreed over Cuffe's motives for supporting colonization. But whether he was motivated by a desire for financial profit, by a wish to contribute to the well-being of his black compatriots in the United States, or by a determination to abolish the slave trade, it is clear that Cuffe betrayed the cultural and hierarchical assumptions that were characteristic of African

American emigrationism.[13] Believing that the benighted Africans needed moral and spiritual guidance, he assumed black Americans could carry the blessings of civilization and Christianity with them to Africa. Although Cuffe's plans received wide publicity in the United States, his scheme aroused little support within the free black community, and ended with his death in September 1817.[14]

Cuffe's efforts to transport just a single group of colonists to Africa demonstrated that the expenses involved were so high that the scheme could never succeed without government support. That lesson was not lost on a group of whites (with whom Cuffe had been in contact prior to his death) who convened in Washington during December 1816 to establish the American Society for Colonizing the Free People of Colour in the United States.[15] This organization, more commonly known as the American Colonization Society, attracted the routine endorsement of, if not tangible support from, many prominent white Americans during the antebellum period. Traditionally, historians have played down, or ignored altogether, black interest in the ACS. However, that is somewhat misleading, and it is ultimately more revealing of black aspirations to confront directly the fact that more than five thousand African Americans did emigrate to Liberia before 1850. Analysis of this phenomenon serves only to emphasize the extent and spontaneity of opposition to the ACS among the embattled black communities of the North. That opposition was partly the result of a growing awareness of the realities of ACS motives and of conditions in the Society's west African colony of Liberia. It would be too strong to say that blacks became disillusioned with the venture for few had ever expressed enthusiasm. But for some at least an initial curiosity was being answered in a negative way by that increasing knowledge. It is impossible to accurately quantify Mary Frances Berry and John Blassingame's contention that "about 20% of the free blacks supported emigration between 1817 and 1861." Yet there can be no denying that the "thousands of letters" from African Americans—both free and slave—in the ACS files do reflect some interest even in that white-organized scheme.[16] Evidently, many free blacks were as yet far from convinced that their best hopes for the future lay in the United States.

Established in 1818, by late 1824 the ACS colony of Liberia encompassed 150 square miles, with six communities of expatriate African Americans. Although more than one thousand American blacks emigrated to Liberia during the 1820s, difficult conditions prevailed in the ACS colony, where settlers faced great physical hardship, ranging from hostile natives to often fatal bouts of fever.[17] The mortality rate—particularly during the colony's early years—was high, with between one fifth and one quarter of all settlers succumbing to malaria or other diseases within a year of their arrival.[18] Predictably, opponents of African colonization focused on the problems encountered by emigrants to the west African colony. Given those adversities, it was not surprising that most African Americans who emigrated were ex-slaves, many of whom had secured their emancipation on the specific condition that they leave the United States under the aegis of the ACS program.[19] Betraying assumptions regarding social and cultural hierarchies among black people that mirrored those of the African American elite, the emigrant community from the United States soon developed into an elite class amid the native African population.[20]

The difficulties endured by the settlers in Liberia contributed significantly to the opposition to the ACS that emerged among free blacks in the United States. Yet, even before the establishment of Liberia, the mass of African Americans had made clear their opinion of the ACS. That hostility, far more than the ACS' financial woes, organizational difficulties, or personnel problems, explained the failure of black colonization. Although some letters from African Americans may signify curiosity about colonization, more striking is the early evidence of mass hostility. Within a month of the formation of the ACS, blacks began expressing their opposition to the scheme. In late January 1817, three thousand blacks gathered at the Bethel Church in Philadelphia, where they registered their unanimous opposition to the ACS. That expression of feeling testifies to an underlying community spirit among African Americans during the early nineteenth century that doubtlessly existed in a number of cities, but which was particularly pronounced in Philadelphia. Gary Nash has noted that by the 1820s, African Americans in that city "had created an institutional life that was richer than that of the lower income whites."[21] Although that assertion places emphasis on formal black institutions, there is convincing evidence that anti-colonization sentiment was broadly based and spontaneous. Indeed, the most prominent of all black Philadelphians, James Forten, revealed a private (and sometimes unacknowledged) sympathy with colonization that he dared not express publicly in the face of mass hostility. Forten's statement—an early indication of the disjunction between the aspirations of the African American leadership on the one hand, and the views of the black populace on the other—hinted at an incipient black nationalism among sections of the African American leadership. Black Americans, Forten confided to Paul Cuffe soon after the gathering at Bethel Church, "will never become a people until they com [*sic*] out from among the white people, but as the majority is decidedly against me I am determined to remain silent."[22]

The majority's hostility to African colonization was manifest not only on that particular occasion in Philadelphia, but throughout the following decades in the conspicuous reluctance of northern blacks to emigrate to Liberia, notwithstanding their letters of enquiry to the ACS. The most revealing and succinct summary of their attitudes lies in the statistics of the ACS itself, which reveal that in the period from 1820 to 1833 a mere 169 northern blacks actually emigrated to Liberia.[23] In the longer run, even emigration schemes organized by blacks themselves would be jeopardized by similar reluctance. It may be that on those later occasions black leaders, separated from the masses by virtue of greater income and more advanced education, were proposing schemes that seemed unrealistic to a majority preoccupied with individual survival and indifferent to questions of collective racial advancement. But if similar divisions were already potentially present at that early stage, Forten's reticence kept them hidden. General black opposition to Liberia was clearly motivated by suspicions of ACS motives strong enough to prompt mass protest in 1817 and steadily reinforced by transparently false ACS propaganda during ensuing decades. Accordingly, although the notion of black colonization continued to beguile many white Americans, a majority of the antebellum free black population was convinced that white proponents of black colonization sought to reinforce the racial barriers that stood in the way of African American advancement.

White colonizationists' failure to win over black Americans lay partly in the growing Americanization of the black community. There are vigorous debates concerning the extent to which African customs and attitudes survived among the black communities in the United States. While there can be no disputing the survival of certain African beliefs and practices, it is equally evident that the "African American" culture, or cultures, that emerged in North America was an amalgam of African and American values and beliefs.[24] Nevertheless, as the decades passed, and American blacks' links with Africa became more tenuous, free blacks' aspirations focused increasingly on their entitlement to meaningful freedom within the United States. In the face of those aspirations, the growing knowledge of the difficulties encountered in Liberia compounded a negative image of Africa. Although life was hard for American blacks, their problems were trivial compared to those faced by Liberian colonists.

Whereas recruitment for Liberian colonization was increasingly undermined by those realities, African Americans continued to denounce the motives of white colonizationists. The ACS defies easy categorization. Unquestionably, some white supporters of the ACS were genuinely concerned with the well-being of African Americans, and some were interested in the abolition of the slave trade.[25] However, although certain colonizationists did espouse humanitarian objectives, they were never able to convince a majority of blacks of their altruism. African Americans understood that many whites viewed colonization as a convenient means of removing the "black problem" from the United States. For the duration of the antebellum period, the ACS struggled unsuccessfully to reconcile the contradictions inherent in its propaganda. At the same time as colonizationists sought to persuade white Americans that they were encouraging the removal of a dangerous element from within the United States, ACS propaganda directed toward African Americans stressed that these very same blacks were the chosen people to set about the tasks of Christianizing and "civilizing" Africa. Henry Clay, a prominent politician and long-time supporter of the ACS, summarized the views of many white colonizationists: "Of all the classes of our population, the most vicious is that of the free coloured. Contaminated themselves they extend their vices all around them, to the slaves, to the whites." But for Clay, and other white colonizationists, these same degraded blacks were destined to perform a higher service. "Every emigrant to Africa," he wrote, "is a missionary carrying the credentials in the holy cause of civilization, religion, and free institutions."[26]

African Americans found it galling that white colonizationists could attest that blacks were fellow human beings, but could then deny them the right to participate fully in American society. The common black attitude toward the ACS was succinctly stated by Peter Williams, a prominent black New Yorker, in 1830: "How inconsistent are those who say that Africa will be benefitted by the removal of the free people of colour of the United States there, while they say they are the *most vile and degraded* people in the world. If we are as vile and degraded as they represent us, and they wish Africans to be rendered a virtuous, enlightened and happy people, they should not *think* of sending *us* among them, lest we make them worse instead of better." Williams thus identified the underlying contradiction in white-sponsored schemes for black colonization: How could Africa be redeemed via the immigration of degraded and undesirable blacks from the United States? Insisting that the ACS was determined to render slavery more secure by removing all free blacks from the United States, African Americans such as Williams repudiated the colonizationists' assumption that whites and blacks could never coexist peacefully, on equal terms.[27] Black leaders maintained that colonizationists intended to remove "every incentive to virtue, to industry, to improvement, and to enterprise" from the African American community. Judging the ACS to be a tool of the slaveholders, black Americans were convinced that colonizing "the free people of colour in Africa," was "never going to facilitate emancipation, but rather retard its progress."[28]

African American opposition to the ACS was thus based on a range of factors. Alongside their skeptical response to white colonizationists' declarations of their humanitarian objectives, African Americans expressed little enthusiasm for emigrating to Liberia. Above all, blacks asserted that they were entitled to all the rights and benefits of citizenship in the United States. The Reverend Richard Allen raised these issues in an address to the first national convention of black Americans, held in Philadelphia in 1830. A co-founder of the Free African Society of Philadelphia, and bishop of the African Methodist Episcopal Church, Allen had been pastor of the Bethel Church in Philadelphia where African Americans had passionately condemned the ACS in 1817. Although Allen conceded "the debt which these United States may owe to injured Africa," and acknowledged that the "sons" and "daughters" of Africa had been dreadfully wronged, he was certain that "we who have been born and nurtured on this soil, we, whose habits, manners, and customs are the same in common with other Americans, can never consent to take our lives in our hands, and be the bearers of the redress offered by that Society to that much afflicted country."[29] In Allen's view, blacks had contributed too much to the United States to be exiled to Africa. Moreover, in noting "this land which we have watered with our *tears* and *our blood*, is now our *mother country*," Allen appeared to reject the notion that black Americans' loyalties to Africa were in some respects more significant, if more elusive, than their obligations to the United States.[30] Allen's remarks might have reflected a need to repudiate unequivocally the suggestion—expressed by some white colonizationists in their more unguarded moments—that black Americans were "African," and therefore not entitled to the benefits of American citizenship. But his comments did imply that African Americans' loyalties to the United States transcended their African origins. This view stood in contrast to the arguments of Martin Delany, and others, who during the 1850s would argue that black Americans could only establish their true identity, or nationality, once they acknowledged the primacy of their African heritage.

The overall failure of the ACS is important in several ways. In the long term its controversial activities would provide a stumbling block for those promoting very different emigration schemes. During the 1820s, however, that was not yet the case. In the short term, the widespread opposition to the ACS helps delineate with some precision black aspirations because the same period saw considerable enthusiasm among blacks for an alternative emigration scheme. This alternative, focusing on emigration to the black republic of Haiti, attracted wide interest within the African American community during the 1820s.

African American emigration to Haiti is best seen in conjunction with Haiti's turbulent history. That history shaped American blacks' perceptions of the island republic, and provided the context in which they would debate the question of emigration during the 1820s, and again during the 1850s and early 1860s. Following the arrival of Christopher Columbus in 1492, the island of Espanola that now includes Haiti and the Dominican Republic was a Spanish colony until 1697. In that year Spain ceded the western third of the colony to France; Saint Domingue, as the French colony became known, was among the most prosperous of the European colonies in the New World.[31] The spectacular economic growth in Saint Domingue was based on the labor of hundreds of thousands of African slaves. On the eve of the French Revolution the thirty thousand whites on the island—themselves divided between those who were born in France, and those born in Saint Domingue—were outnumbered by half a million black slaves. Complicating this volatile racial mix was the presence of nearly thirty thousand free mulattoes and blacks, most of whom regarded themselves as closer in status to the whites than to the slaves. Indeed, mulattoes, enjoying many more privileges than blacks, considered themselves as an entirely different class.[32] Differences between these groups were to affect political and social life in the island republic for decades to come.

The onset of the French Revolution in 1789 precipitated corresponding tensions in Saint Domingue. The "great revolution" that followed, leading ultimately to the establishment of the black republic of Haiti, was "the turning point in the history of slave revolts in the New World," and an important influence on race relations in the United States.[33] It is helpful to recount, briefly, the history of the Haitian Revolution—and to make the point that several of the major leaders of the Haitian revolt had "received their military education in the American Revolution." In particular, the Fontages Légion, a contingent of free blacks from Saint Domingue, fought on behalf of the Americans in their quest for independence, making a vigorous contribution to the siege of Savannah in 1779.[34]

In August 1791, the brutally mistreated black slaves in Saint Domingue revolted; the ensuing carnage brought terror on all sides. With the French endeavoring to retain power, and with black and mulatto Haitians maneuvering for control, the situation was further confused by the presence of British and Spanish military contingents sent to harass the French. From this muddled situation, two powerful figures emerged: the mulatto General André Riguad, who enjoyed the allegiance of the free blacks and mulattoes; and the black Pierre Dominique Toussaint L'Ouverture, who became a hero to the slaves. Shortly after Toussaint's forces gained the ascendancy over Riguad, Napoleon Bonaparte decided that France should not yield its prized colony without further struggle. By April 1802, the army sent by Napoleon had gained the upper hand, and by an act of "shameless treachery" the French General Charles Leclerc succeeded in persuading Toussaint to place himself in French hands. Toussaint died in a French prison within a year—an incongruous end for a man who was destined to become a martyr, and symbol of black revolution well beyond the Caribbean, during the decades that followed.[35]

The demise of Toussaint did not render the French position any more secure. With his armies in Saint Domingue devastated by yellow fever, aware of the high price France would have to pay seeking to maintain control in Haiti, and concluding that affairs in Europe demanded no New World distractions, Napoleon decided against sending more troops to the island. The chiefs of the revolutionary army in Saint Domingue recognized Jean-Jacques Dessalines as leader; on January 1, 1804, he proclaimed independence for the new nation, adopting the name used by the island's original Indian inhabitants.[36] Thus was born the world's first independent black republic.

Independence, however, did not bring stability to Haiti. Following the assassination of Dessalines in 1806, two rival governments were established. Alexandre Sabès Pétion, a mulatto, assumed control in the south, whereas Henry Christophe, a black, ruled in the North. It was not until the 1820s, when Jean-Pierre Boyer, a mulatto, was able to secure control of both the northern and southern parts of Haiti, that a semblance of political unity was established. Haiti's ongoing racial and political tensions were underpinned by economic chaos—during the early decades of the nineteenth century agricultural production was a tiny proportion of what it had been in the years preceding the slaves' uprising. These ongoing economic woes were a key imperative for successive Haitian leaders hoping to lure black immigrants from the United States.

Haiti's economic plight was one aspect of the wider picture drawn by Americans of the black republic and its revolutionary heritage. Americans, of course, were not alone in taking a keen interest in events in the black republic; Caryn Cossé Bell is right to argue that "[i]mages of Saint Domingue, the Haitian Revolution, and the establishment of the black republic inspired a generation of Romantic writers." But for Americans, the survival of slavery and the depth of racism meant issues of race were inevitably controversial. It was only predictable, then, that Haiti loomed large in Americans' racial and political consciousness, evoking a range of images and responses within the United States.[37] African Americans, of course, regarded the founding and survival of the island republic as tangible proof that blacks were not inferior to whites, and were capable of shaping their own destiny. Some white Americans, too, praised the establishment of Haitian independence as evidence that the United States' overthrow of colonial rule was a model for liberty-loving people everywhere. Yet many white Americans—including those who professed to be acting in the best interests of the island republic—regarded Haiti in condescending terms. Most contentious was the explicitly racial aspect to Haitian independence, offering both optimism and apprehension on the question of race relations in the United States. Indeed, the Haitian Revolution haunted many white Americans, including those who neither owned slaves, nor had little sympathy with the South's peculiar institution. The ongoing political strife and violence associated with Haiti during the late eighteenth and early nineteenth centuries—widely reported in the American press—served as a warning of what might happen should African American slaves revolt against the Southern slaveocracy.[38] Prizing their own republican experiment, many whites' views of the overthrow of French rule in Saint Domingue, and the subsequent establishment of the independent Haitian state, were formed not by dispassionate analysis, but by their reading of sensational and dramatically titled tracts such as *Secret History, or, the Horrors of St. Domingo*, published in 1808.[39]

Conscious that their achievement of black independence had international, as well as domestic implications, there were occasions when the Haitian leadership proved willing to play a part in the international politics of race. Not only had Toussaint L'Ouverture intended to "sail an armed force to West Africa to end the slave trade," but he had also invaded "the Spanish colony that shared Hispaniola with Haiti and freed the slaves there." The Haitians, moreover, were instrumental in the abolition of slavery on the entire island in 1801. No less provocative was the Haitians' support for "The Liberator," Simon Bolivar, in his struggles against the Spanish colonial authorities. Many Americans would not have been displeased to see challenges to Spain's colonial authority in the Americas, but the Haitians' support for Bolivar, along with the anti-slavery dimension to his rebellions, was an affront to white Americans' racial values.[40]

A further challenge to white Americans' racial sensibilities occurred during the rule of Henry Christophe, when Haitian naval vessels were "used against slave traders" who were flouting the "various bi-lateral treaties" that had been "devised in the aftermath of the Congress of Vienna."[41] The United States had legislated to prohibit the importation of African slaves after 1808, but the Haitians' apparent willingness to assert the rights of black people everywhere meant the island republic figured prominently in white Americans' fears of slave rebellion. Defenders of slavery, concerned that knowledge of the events in Haiti would embolden American slaves to attempt a similar revolt, sought to keep the slaves ignorant of their Haitian counterparts' success in ousting their French masters and establishing a black republic. Ironically, by exerting so much energy denouncing Haiti, white Americans perhaps increased the slaves' awareness of events in Haiti. Moreover, an influx of more than twelve thousand refugee planters and their slaves from the former French colony in the late eighteenth and early nineteenth centuries compounded white Americans' fears of black uprising. A number of Haitian blacks ended up in Northern cities, where their religion and poverty made them subjects of deep suspicion; many other refugees and their slaves found their way to South Carolina and Louisiana. Having "seen and heard much" during the turmoil in Haiti, the slaves who accompanied their masters to their new homes "became carriers of new doctrines."[42]

African Americans understood the significance of Haitian independence. As Robert L. Paquette has noted: "Existence proves possibility."[43] It is, of course, impossible to ascertain with precision the extent to which American slaves were aware of Haiti during the 1820s—or at any other time. There is, however, considerable evidence to suggest they were aware of Haiti's history. In some cases, such as in South Carolina during 1840, when slaves were "interpreting news" from the island republic "as a harbinger of their own liberation," and in Louisiana during the mid-nineteenth century, when slaves sang "revolutionary songs" originating from the early period of the Haitian Revolution, Haiti's influence did not lead directly to large-scale uprisings. Nonetheless, whites and blacks alike understood that Haiti's importance was more than symbolic.[44] Indeed, Sylvia R. Frey has argued the revolt in Saint Domingue "provided the inspiration" for "organized resistance" among African Americans during the 1790s. White Americans discovered to their chagrin that they could not isolate African Americans from events in Haiti. Black awareness of events in the former French colony was manifest on several levels. The lively trade with revolutionary Saint Domingue and then with the young republic of Haiti proved profitable for many white American merchants and mariners, but black seamen from the United States and elsewhere took advantage of the Haitian authorities' willingness to "challenge the authority of white ship masters and American commercial officials." Within the United States, information on happenings in Haiti, much of it originating from black sailors working on ships trading in the Caribbean, was spread via word of mouth, as well as through refugees and newspapers. As Frey explained, knowledge among African Americans of events in Haiti, compounded by the presence of the refugees from the island republic, was one imperative behind several instances of black rebelliousness in the United States during the 1790s.[45]

A 1795 uprising in Louisiana—at that time still in Spanish hands—revealed the extent to which whites in North America were alarmed by the Haitian Revolution. Numbers of refugees from Saint Domingue, including slaves, free blacks, and whites, had made their way to the Spanish colony. The potential danger posed by the influx of these people was recognized by the Spanish colonial authorities in Louisiana, who during the early 1790s demanded vigilance from the slaveholders. Despite such warnings, trouble broke out in the Pointe Coupée Parish, north of New Orleans, in 1795. The uprising was quickly quelled, and the ringleaders executed or deported. But it was widely believed—and not without some justification, since the conspirators had "worked alongside slaves" from Saint Domingue—that the violence in Pointe Coupée could be attributed to the influence of the French Caribbean colony on Louisiana blacks.[46] Further north, in 1798, the fears exposed by rumors that between two hundred and three hundred slaves owned by French refugees from Saint Domingue were planning to march on Philadelphia further highlighted Americans' anxieties regarding the influence of the slave rebellion in the troubled Caribbean island.[47]

Notwithstanding the fears raised during the 1790s, it was "General" Gabriel Prosser's rebellion at the turn of the century that most vividly highlighted white Americans' concerns. Prosser, a Virginian slave, launched an abortive uprising in August 1800 that confirmed the worst fears of many white Americans, and sapped any lingering emancipationist sentiments in the slave states. It is impossible to determine precisely Haiti's influence on Gabriel. But as Eugene Genovese has noted, Prosser "consciously looked to Haiti for inspiration and support," a process rendered easier by the presence in Virginia of significant numbers of slaves from Saint Domingue whose owners had found sanctuary in the United States.[48]

Although Prosser's rebellion was thwarted, the rebellious spirit among black Americans did not dissipate. An 1811 uprising in southern Louisiana, described by Genovese as "the biggest in American history," compounded whites' fears. While the 1811 rebellion remains "obscure," it is significant that one of its leaders, Charles Deslonde, hailed from Saint Domingue. With white Louisianans fearful that the rebellion could precipitate an outbreak of violence to match that which had occurred in Saint Domingue, the authorities moved quickly to quell the uprising "of over three hundred defiant, though poorly armed, slave rebels."[49] Although white Americans overstated the likelihood of a Haitian-type rebellion within the United States, the survival of the Haitian experiment not only constituted a challenge to American slavery, but was a tangible beacon of freedom for blacks seeking sanctuary from American racism. In 1818, for example, when the black crew on the American brig *Holkar* mutinied off Curacao, killing their captain, mate, and a passenger, "they bore away for St. Domingue."[50]

White Americans were further unsettled by the discovery in 1822 that Denmark Vesey, a free black resident of Charleston, South Carolina, was plotting
an uprising against slavery. A former slave, Vesey was well aware of the Haitian
Revolution. After spending several years in the Danish Caribbean colony of St.
Thomas, Denmark had been taken to Saint Domingue in 1781, where he was
sold by his owner, Captain Joseph Vesey. Finding Denmark to be "unsound
and subject to epileptic fits," his new owner returned him to Captain Vesey.
The young slave then spent two years sailing throughout the Caribbean, with
at least one trip to Africa, on his master's slave trading vessel.[51] As a consequence of the time he had spent in Saint Domingue, and of his contacts with
Haitian emigrés who had settled in South Carolina, Haiti loomed large in
Vesey's consciousness: Indeed, as Genovese has remarked, Vesey "brooded
over the meaning of Haiti." Even more troubling for white Americans, Vesey
not only "looked to Haiti as a model and for inspiration," but also for "material support." These concerns regarding Vesey's conspiracy were compounded
by the belief that the conspirators had planned to flee to Haiti.[52] Vesey, moreover, wrote two letters to the island republic, seeking the Haitians' assistance in
overthrowing American slavery. While those letters were intercepted, Vesey's
plans for black rebellion had an unmistakably trans-national dimension, that
looked explicitly to Haiti as a model and as a source of material assistance.[53]

The Vesey conspiracy was foiled before white blood was spilled. No less dis-
quieting for whites were the events that took place in Southampton County,
Virginia, in August 1831, when Nat Turner led the most notorious antebellum uprising among African American slaves. Whilst Turner left no record that
he sought to emulate the feats of the Haitian revolutionaries, it is implausible
that he was not at least generally aware of the Haitian Revolution. Although it
might have been coincidence that Turner planned his uprising to begin on 22
August—forty years to the day after "the famous secret meeting" that had
"launched the Haitian Revolution"—white southerners almost instinctively
linked his failed rebellion to the overthrow of slavery in the former French colony.[54] White fears at this time were intensified by the belief that a letter to Governor Floyd of Virginia spoke of a well-organized black underground movement
among American slaves, with clear links to Haiti. Having escaped from slavery,
the alleged leader of this movement had made his way to the black republic,
where a well-funded revolutionary army was already training "several dozen
members." With agents already in place in several southern states, the alleged
conspiracy was especially troubling because the author of the letter to Governor Floyd "invoked" the name Toussaint L'Ouverture: Mention of the famous
Haitian revolutionary never failed to send shivers up the spines of white Southerners. Although the letter was almost certainly a hoax, and quite possibly the
work of a white man, it fed white concerns that American slaves were not only
inspired by, but were also in collusion with, their Haitian brethren.[55] Ironically,
in presupposing cooperation and common intent between blacks in different
regions, white Americans were imagining a type of Pan-Africanism—or even

black nationalism—that black emigrationists subsequently felt was sorely lacking in the African American populace.

In the wake of Turner's uprising, white attitudes in the South continued to be premised on fears of Haitian-type violence. One immediate consequence of Turner's rebellion was to put the final nail in the coffin of emancipationist sentiment in the South, as the results of the 1832 debate on emancipation in the Virginian legislature demonstrated.[56] In 1832 Thomas R. Dew, a prominent Southern scholar and political commentator, alluded to white Southerners' enduring fears of slave rebellion—and to African Americans' connections to Haiti's revolutionary past. Denying the possibility that rebellious slaves were in any way comparable to genuine revolutionary heroes, and implying that the Haitians' quest for independence should not be confused with an authentic revolution, such as the American Revolution, Dew referred to "the hellish plots of Dessalines, Gabriel, and Turner." For Dew, as for many other white Americans, it was but a short step from Haiti to the southern plantation.[57] As in other slave societies, vigilance, if not paranoia, was an ever-present aspect of American slavery, right down to the Civil War. In these circumstances it was hardly surprising that white Americans expressed concern about Haiti, and refused to extend diplomatic recognition to the black republic.

As evidenced by the practice of gathering to celebrate Haitian independence, free blacks, even in the southern states, have also left evidence that they attached great meaning to the Haitian Revolution.[58] Both as a symbol, and as an unparalleled example of black will, Haiti represented many of the aspirations of free blacks in the United States. Some African Americans interpreted the bloodshed in Haiti as evidence of the necessity for peaceful, voluntary emancipation throughout the southern states of America. David Walker, a black resident of Boston whose 1829 *Appeal* to the "Coloured Citizens of the World" was perhaps the most notorious antebellum treatise enjoining African Americans to militant action, included specific references to events in Haiti. Although Walker lamented that Haiti was "plagued with that scourge of nations, the Catholic religion," and hoped the nation would "adopt in its stead the Protestant faith," he was unequivocal in acknowledging Haiti's political and racial significance, describing the island republic as "the glory of the blacks and the terror of tyrants." Emphasizing *manhood* as a measure of black self-worth, Walker noted that if "tyrants" did seek to injure the black republic, Haitians would "be cut off to man, before they would yield to the combined forces of the whole world." Indeed, Walker expressed deep confidence in the Haitians' resolve, asserting that "if the whole world was combined against them, it could not do any thing with them, unless the Lord delivers them up." Walker regarded—and depicted—events in Haiti as a "warning" to all Americans. In admonishing African Americans to support a "Hannibal" when one emerged from within the ranks of the black community, he asserted that "the history" of Haiti provided a telling "warning." When blacks in the French colony had been disunited and uncertain of their objectives, they had been "butchered by the whites." By calling for unity among black Americans, and in his apparently messianic belief in the notion of a black leader who could lead African Americans to freedom and equality, Walker was articulating views that held wide currency within the black leadership, and within the black community, for much of the nineteenth century—and beyond. With reference to black leaders, no individual had a greater international reputation during the nineteenth century than Toussaint L'Ouverture. Although Walker did not refer specifically to Toussaint, and while the violence frequently associated with Toussaint's revolutionary leadership was at odds with many African Americans' hopes for the peaceful elevation of their race within the United States, there was widespread admiration among black Americans for the way in which the Haitian hero had resisted French attempts to re-colonize Haiti. Finally, although Walker's *Appeal* was ostensibly directed toward a black audience, in noting that "some of them [whites] will curse the day they ever saw us," there can be no doubt that he expected white Americans to heed his exhortation: emancipate the slaves, or expect bloodshed similar to that which Haiti had experienced during the late eighteenth century.[59]

Free African Americans of rather less notoriety than Walker also betrayed the ongoing significance of the Haitian Revolution. In 1825, addressing a meeting of Baltimore blacks who had gathered to celebrate France's recent recognition of Haitian independence, the black abolitionist William Watkins articulated these issues in political terms. "Of all that has hitherto been done in favor of the descendants of Africa," he wrote, "I recollect nothing so fraught with momentous importance—so pregnant with interest to millions yet unborn—as the recent acknowledgment of Haytien Independence, by one of the European Powers, under whom the African population of that island had long groaned in the most abject bondage." As Watkins said, "our feelings upon this occasion, are unutterable. The joy which swells our bosoms is incommunicable." Speaking at the same time as an organized scheme for African American emigration to the black republic was underway, it is telling that Watkins, an opponent of African colonization, declared that Haiti stood as "an irrefutable argument to prove . . . that the descendants of Africa never were designed by their Creator to sustain an inferiority, or even a mediocrity, in the chain of being." Instead, they were "as capable of intellectual improvement as Europeans, or any other nation upon the face of the earth." At the same time as Watkins argued that African Americans' position within the United States was improving, his emphasis on Haiti's significance as both agent and symbol of black elevation implied that Haiti's fortunes affected the status of African Americans.[60] This prototypical black nationalism that was enunciated by Watkins was much less detailed, and certainly less contentious than that associated with the Haitian emigration scheme of the 1850s and 1860s. Nevertheless, as Watkins' statement revealed, from the early nineteenth century the significance of the Haitian Revolution was not lost on black America.

At the same time, however, as free blacks supported the principles of black liberation, and acknowledged the significance of the Haitian Revolution, their attitudes toward Haiti were complicated by conflicting imperatives. Following the emergence of Garrisonian abolitionism during the early 1830s, with its emphasis on moral suasionism and a peaceful end to slavery, some blacks were caught in a difficult situation: They could not allow their determination to abolish slavery in the United States to be confused with any apparent endorsement of the bloodshed in Haiti.[61] As was the case for many abolitionists, the question became one of means and ends. In this instance, although there were reservations regarding the way in which the Haitians had achieved their liberty, there was no denying the value of their final accomplishment. Consequently, despite concerns regarding the propriety of a violent end to slavery, a number of African American leaders had significant contacts with Haiti. As a subsequent chapter explains, these contacts were one factor impelling some blacks toward an endorsement of Haitian emigrationism during the pre–Civil War period.

It was from this historical and ideological context that interest in Haitian emigrationism emerged during the early decades of the nineteenth century. This interest was first manifested at the turn of the century. During the protracted struggles for control of Haiti, some Americans—including Thomas Jefferson, who regarded the "tropic zone" as "the proper residence of the negro"—had favored African American colonization in the former French colony.[62] Haitian leaders, too, had expressed interest in attracting black Americans to their young nation. In 1804, during the reign of Jean-Jacques Dessalines, monetary rewards were offered to American ship captains if they would transport African Americans to the island. Fearful that France was not yet ready to relinquish its prized former colony, Dessalines hoped an immigration of American blacks, along with a return of refugees who had fled to the United States during the Revolution, would increase the black republic's population. Not surprisingly, given the troubled situation in Haiti, and given that Dessalines hoped immigrants would serve in the army, there is no evidence that any more than a handful of blacks decided to emigrate, or return, to the island republic at that early stage.[63]

The next proposal for African American emigration to Haiti grew largely from the efforts of a young black New Englander, Prince Saunders. A teacher at the African School in Boston, Saunders had not only expressed support for Paul Cuffe (and married his daughter), but had also contemplated emigrating to Sierra Leone. Between the end of the War of 1812, and the early 1820s, Saunders was the most persistent advocate of Haitian emigrationism. Identifying the connections between African American emigration to the black republic on the one hand, and the importance of ensuring that Haiti remained prominent in America's racial consciousness on the other, he strived to maintain an awareness and interest in Haiti among black Americans. Saunders' involvement in emigrationism evolved out of his contacts with the British abolitionists William Wilberforce and Thomas Clarkson, who had encouraged him to visit Britain, and Haiti, where he conferred with government officials. Meanwhile, the Haitian leadership continued to express interest in attracting black migrants from the United States. Pursuing the policy initiated by Dessalines of encouraging immigration, Henry Christophe offered prospective black immigrants from the United States all the privileges of Haitian citizenship. At this early stage, the Haitians expressed particular interest in recruiting teachers from abroad, whom they hoped would play a part in improving the republic's education system.[64]

In 1816, in an effort to "excite a more lively concern for the promotion of the best interests, the improvement, the definite independence, and happiness of the Haytian people," Saunders published the *Haytian Papers*. However, despite his praise for Christophe's regime, and notwithstanding his endorsement of the island republic, Saunders' depiction of Haiti unwittingly raised doubts about its suitability as a destination for black emigrants from the United States. His reference to the need to establish "definite independence" in Haiti implied the republic was still beholden to the colonial system. This, of course, was an accurate assessment because Haiti remained in what would later be described as a state of neo-colonialism. But Saunders' judgment would hardly have reassured prospective emigrants. Moreover, in supporting African American emigration to the island republic, he envisioned that black Americans could play a part in reconciling the warring factions in Haiti.[65] The implication was that Haiti was hardly a bastion of political and social stability, and hence an unlikely destination for those blacks contemplating a departure from the United States. This contradiction would plague subsequent schemes for Haitian emigration down to the Civil War.

Despite such difficulties, Saunders and his British allies continued to advocate emigration to Haiti. As would be the case on subsequent occasions, the likelihood of a successful emigration in large measure depended on the support of the Haitian government. During 1818–1819, doubts emerged regarding the Haitian authorities' commitment to the project. In part, these concerns stemmed from Christophe's reservations concerning Saunders, whose prominence among Philadelphian blacks was potentially significant in building support for emigration. When Saunders temporarily fell out of favor with Christophe, the prospects for a successful movement dimmed. Soon back in favor with the Haitian leader, Saunders traveled to Haiti, where Christophe suggested that a ship, and a sum of money, be provided to Saunders to facilitate African American emigration to the island republic. A few African Americans took advantage of Christophe's offer to grant immigrants the privileges of Haitian citizenship, as did some Haitian refugees who had fled the island during the years of turmoil. Meanwhile, the British abolitionists who had done much to awaken Saunders' interest in Haiti in the first instance continued to work toward an emigration of black Americans. In 1820, Thomas Clarkson, in collaboration with Saunders, outlined a plan by which emancipated slaves from the United States would be transported to Haiti. Certain that a movement of African Americans to Haiti would benefit the island republic, Clarkson also hoped the American government could be enticed into participating in the project. He wondered whether the United States government could be persuaded to purchase the Spanish part of the island and cede it to Haiti. This suggests that even before 1823, when President James Monroe declared American opposition to any new attempts by the European powers to colonize the Americas, some observers believed the United States was interested in securing the Caribbean from European intrigues. But Clarkson's proposal that the United States should acquire territory only to hand it over to a government widely regarded as antithetical to the interests of the southern slaveocracy was fanciful. In any case, an uprising in Haiti, and Christophe's suicide, brought discussions of African American emigration to Haiti to a temporary standstill.[66]

Undeterred by these setbacks, Saunders continued to hold out hopes for a large-scale migration to Haiti. In 1823, he remained certain that thousands of African Americans were keen to migrate to Haiti.[67] Saunders' endeavors contributed to black Americans' awareness of Haiti, and helped lay the groundwork for subsequent emigration schemes to the black republic. By early 1824, however, Saunders's role as the major advocate of Haitian emigrationism within the United States had been taken by a white man, the Reverend Loring Dewey. A disenchanted agent of the ACS who had found it extremely difficult to persuade black Americans of the virtues of Liberia, Dewey sensed an interest in Haitian emigrationism among blacks in New York, where he was based. In March 1824, he wrote to President Boyer, inquiring what degree of assistance the Haitian government would provide to prospective settlers from the United States. Asking Boyer a range of specific questions pertaining to the conditions under which African Americans could emigrate to Haiti, Dewey raised concerns regarding prospective emigrants' spiritual, as well as material, well-being. Evincing the impecunious condition of the African American populace, Dewey sought the Haitians' assistance in defraying the costs of passage to the island. Land ownership, too, was a critical issue, and Dewey solicited Boyer's assurance that emigrants would be given land. The black church was the most important institution in black society in the United States, and African Americans, fearful of the treatment they would receive in Haiti, sought guarantees that their religious practices and institutions would be tolerated. Perhaps most contentiously, Dewey inquired whether the Haitians would permit a colony to be planted in their country that had its own laws, courts, and legislature—"in *all* respects like one of the States of the United States, and *connected with* and *subject to* the government of Hayti."[68] Dewey's letter was significant in several respects. In the first instance, it attested to the concerns expressed by potential emigrants. But in articulating these concerns, Dewey also suggested the extent to which prospective emigrants sought to recreate the institutions and lifestyle to which they were accustomed—further evidence both of the "Americanization" of the black population, and of the existence of a distinctly "African American" culture in the United States. Perhaps most significant, in seeking the replication in Haiti of American institutions and customs, emigrationists were implicitly endorsing the superiority of those institutions and customs. This expression of American exceptionalism—a curious phenomenon given the racism to which African Americans were subjected in the United States—was a recurrent characteristic of antebellum emigrationism.

Boyer was receptive to the prospect of black immigration from the United States. Motivated largely by a determination to improve Haiti's economic position, which by the 1820s had not recovered from the devastation wreaked by the struggle for independence, Boyer set out to restore the republic's agricultural base. Like Christophe and Dessalines before him, Boyer considered an agricultural revival to be the essential base on which future prosperity would depend. Haitian leaders were wary about antagonizing the politically and economically powerful large landowners, but one means of facilitating an agricultural revival was to increase the number of Haitians who owned the land on which they worked. Boyer's immediate predecessor, Christophe, had made some efforts toward the end of his reign to redistribute land among the Haitian people. Similarly, during the early part of Boyer's presidency, a "growing number of peasants acquired smallholdings of land." A consequence of this measured redistribution of land was that large landowners found it increasingly difficult to procure agricultural laborers. One response during Boyer's regime was to contemplate the importation of "indentured labor from India or China."[69]

Seen in this light, Haitian attempts during the 1820s to induce African Americans to settle in the black republic reflected little more than a desire to alleviate the shortage of agricultural laborers. As becomes clear here, many immigrants from the United States had rather more grandiose expectations. On occasion, their aspirations grew logically from the propaganda used to entice them to the black republic. For his part, Boyer hoped free black immigrants from the United States would carry with them the agricultural expertise required to rejuvenate the Haitian economy. With that in mind, Boyer reacted promptly to Dewey's inquiries. Assuring Dewey that financial assistance would be forthcoming to transport emigrants from the United States, the Haitian president also asserted that fertile land would be provided for African American settlers in Haiti, and promised that the emigrants' religious values and practices would be respected. But Dewey's questions concerning the legal status of a colony in Haiti elicited a predictably negative response from Boyer. Noting that the "laws of the republic are general—and no particular laws can exist," he sought to assure Dewey that emigrants would "enjoy happiness, security, tranquility, such as we ourselves possess, however our defamers declare the contrary." Predicating these assurances on Haiti's role in a nascent Pan-Africanism, and assuming that "African-ness" was based on racial affiliations and consciousness as well as on the legalities of citizenship, Boyer declared that those "who come, being children of Africa, shall be Haytians as soon as they put their feet on the soil of Hayti."[70]

To facilitate an emigration, Boyer announced he would send an agent to New York City, where Dewey was establishing a "Society for Promoting the Emigration of Free Persons of Colour to Hayti." New York City blacks, cautious of links between Haitian emigration and the ACS, initially regarded whites' involvement in the new scheme with suspicion. They were, nevertheless, curious about the overtures of the Haitian government. Shortly afterward, they established a black auxiliary to the emigration society, and the movement was further stimulated by the arrival of Boyer's agent, Jonathan Granville, in New York City. Granville immediately set about allaying African Americans' concerns regarding conditions in Haiti.[71] Foremost among those concerns was the issue of religion. In the pre–Civil War decade, when James T. Holly promoted emigration to Haiti, he did so with the self-conscious intention of carrying black American Christian values to the island republic. During the 1820s, however, perhaps because African American religious institutions and values were less well developed than they would be three decades later, Haitian emigrationism was not characterized by such an explicit proselytizing spirit.[72]

Regardless of the extent to which they were motivated by a missionary spirit, African American emigrants to Haiti confronted a set of unfamiliar religious values and practices. This was not surprising, given the different directions that Christianity and African religious beliefs had taken in the various regions of the New World. There were, to be sure, connections between the black religious cultures of New World societies. But equally telling were the differences, which were particularly profound when the United States was contrasted with Haiti. Prior to the overthrow of French colonial authority in Saint Domingue, there was a continued large-scale importation of African laborers, who were used to replenish the slave population that was constantly depleted by the harsh conditions of the French slave system. Consequently, Africa continued to loom large in Haiti, particularly in respect to religion, where the African influence was most profoundly felt in the widespread faith in voodoo.[73] This was a very different situation to that which prevailed in North America. Although "an underground stream of magical shamanism," did survive in the United States, this stream was never large; as Charles Joyner has observed, this aspect "of African cosmology maintained a subterranean existence outside of and inimical to African American Christianity." As Joyner noted, that African American Christianity comprised a "unique and creative synthesis" of Christianity and African religious values and practices.[74]

With that cultural context it mind, it was only predictable that proponents of Haitian emigration acknowledged that a majority of potential emigrants would find the Haitian amalgam of Catholicism and voodoo doubly alien. Recognizing these differences, Granville declared that religious differences would not be a source of division between emigrants and Haitians. "We all worship the same God," he assured black New Yorkers. Anticipating that emigrants would be drawn primarily from the youthful elements of American society, Granville insisted they would easily habituate themselves to the Haitian community. An effective and energetic advocate of emigration, Granville's assurances had the desired effect, not only in New York, but in other northern cities as well. In New York, the Haitian Emigration Society was chaired by Peter Williams; Philadelphia's society was led by the Reverend Richard Allen.[75] The involvement of Williams and Allen, both of whom were staunch opponents of the ACS during the 1820s, demonstrates that some African Americans at least regarded Haitian emigrationism in a different light to the African colonization scheme.

Further evidence of this distinction was the reaction of the ACS to Haitian emigrationism. At one point advocates of the Haitian scheme hoped the ACS might cooperate with the movement. But mindful that both schemes were essentially competing for the same constituencies, members of the ACS regarded Haitian emigrationism as a "dangerous rival," and collaboration proved impossible.[76] Perhaps demonstrating their real motive for favoring the departure of African Americans, many white colonizationists undoubtedly worried that encouraging the Haitians would be tantamount to endorsing an end to slavery.

Compounding this fear among white colonizationists was the support given to Haitian emigrationism by abolitionists. Benjamin Lundy, founder and editor of the *Genius of Universal Emancipation*, and the best known opponent of slavery in the period preceding the emergence of radical abolitionism during the early 1830s, corresponded with members of the Haitian government. In 1824, Lundy expressed support for Haitian emigration, and asserted that emigration to the island republic was a better option for black Americans than the ACS colony of Liberia.[77] From the outset, Lundy made it clear that he believed emigration to the island republic could assist the anti-slavery cause. He was adamant, moreover, that his endorsement of Haitian emigration was not a sign that he had joined those who rejected the possibility of free blacks living permanently in the United States as American citizens. Lundy's objective was to emancipate the slaves, not rid the United States of its free black population.[78] Later, when he set about cataloguing his *Life, Travels, and Opinions*, Lundy would present his interest in Haitian emigrationism as very much an aspect of his wider anti-slavery endeavors. During the 1820s, however, not all blacks accepted that reasoning. It was partly with such criticisms in mind that Lundy "repaired" to Haiti in 1825, seeking to assess for himself the prospects for African American emigrants, and "make arrangements with the government of that country for the settlement of any emancipated slaves who might be sent thither."[79] Satisfied with conditions in Haiti, and persuaded that President Boyer's interest in emigration was genuine, Lundy was an important figure in Haitian emigrationism during the 1820s.

Lundy's *Genius of Universal Emancipation* devoted considerable attention to the issue of Haitian emigration, providing information for prospective emigrants, and publishing letters from African Americans who had settled in the island republic. But Lundy's paper was more than a mouthpiece for proponents of Haitian emigration: opponents, as well as advocates of the scheme were able to use the paper to explain their arguments and persuade African Americans of the merits, or otherwise, of the island republic. In late 1824, Lundy had used the *Genius of Universal Emancipation* to spell out his personal views on Haitian emigration. Alongside his assertions that he viewed emigrationism as an anti-slavery device, Lundy discussed the advantages of emigration for free blacks. Beginning with the premise "that the country in which a man is born, is his rightful home, if he makes it his choice," he nonetheless outlined the potential advantages of emigration. Given "the degraded condition" of the free black population, their position "might be greatly meliorated by their removal to Hayti, where all would be placed strictly upon an equality; where they would no longer be tantalized with the idea of mental inferiority; and where, of course, they would feel themselves removed from the fancied chains of moral debasement." In Haiti, Lundy continued, the "road would be open to honour and preferment, they would feel an inducement to cultivate their minds and exercise their talents in the various departments of science and literature." Perhaps most significantly, Lundy raised the issue of nationality. In Haiti, he argued, African American emigrants "would enjoy the proud satisfaction of possessing a share in the sovereignty of a free, independent and enlightened nation."[80]

Mindful of the continuing enslavement of African Americans in the southern states, Lundy explained how emigration to Haiti could contribute to the emancipation of those in bondage. As he noted, Haiti was capable of receiving large numbers of freed slaves from the United States. Indeed, he referred to the possibility of an annual movement of fifty to sixty thousand people, at an estimated cost of twelve dollars per migrant. The island republic, Lundy asserted optimistically, could sustain a population of eight to ten million people. And although he rejected the argument that all blacks should be compelled to leave the United States, he did claim that if American legislators provided tangible support to the Haitian scheme, an en-masse movement was possible.[81]

Lundy was not the only white person to embrace black emigration to Haiti. The motives of these Americans varied from an unashamed desire to expel free blacks from the United States, to those who professed more charitable goals. A group of New Jersey legislators and white citizens, resolving in late 1824 to support efforts to establish churches and religious societies in Haiti, argued it was vital to supply "competent teachers among the emigrants to Hayti," and "thus prevent them from becoming a disorganized and vicious community."[82] The implication, of course, was that having set themselves adrift from the civilizing influence of white America, African Americans in Haiti could easily lapse back into the condition of "savagery" from which many white Americans believed blacks had come.

Benjamin Lundy's expressions of support for emigration helped persuade some African Americans of the scheme's merits. Equally significant, however, were the tangible inducements offered by the Haitian authorities. These inducements reflected the Haitian leadership's aforementioned desire to improve Haiti's agricultural output, by increasing the number of "agriculturalists" in the country. African American emigrants were explicitly encouraged to settle in rural regions. Seeking particularly to exploit the country's uncultivated regions, the Haitian authorities offered the greatest incentives to those emigrants willing to settle on undeveloped lands. Accordingly, emigrants were categorized into three distinct classes, with different terms of passage applying to each. Those willing to settle on "uncultivated or neglected lands" (First Class Emigrants) were not required to repay the cost of their passage to Haiti. Second Class migrants, who elected to work on lands already planted, had to repay their passages within six months of their arrival in the black republic, as did those of the Third Class, who comprised mechanics, traders, clerks, and school teachers. First Class emigrants, moreover, were to be given an initial land grant of fifteen acres, to be augmented later by a similar allocation. In an implicit admission that emigrants would encounter difficulties assimilating into Haitian society, those who elected to live on uncultivated lands were encouraged to settle in groups in the same neighborhood. Such a settlement pattern, it was anticipated, would help protect emigrants from being adversely affected by "their ignorance of the language of the country."[83]

The concern shown by proponents of Haitian emigration for the potential difficulties confronting emigrants to the island republic was a reflection of one of the major obstacles standing in the way of the movement: Despite their grandiose claims concerning the ability of African Americans to adapt to the material and spiritual conditions in Haiti, it was well-recognized by all those involved in the Haitian emigration scheme that for most black Americans, the island republic was a remote and obscure place, that conjured up ambivalent sentiments regarding the future of the black race. These contradictory views reflected, and contributed to, the wider American ambivalence regarding Haiti.

For black Americans, that ambivalence was reinforced by the experiences of African American emigrants to Haiti. During 1823, even before Loring Dewey contacted the Haitian government, small numbers of African Americans had departed for Haiti. The first formally organized group of emigrants sailed from Philadelphia in August 1824, with more groups following soon after. Within the United States, at least in the short term, there was considerable enthusiasm for the scheme. Indeed, as late as December 1827, two years after the movement had effectively faltered, the black editors of *Freedom's Journal* were prepared to reprint an article from Lundy's *Genius of Universal Emancipation*, describing the advantages of Haitian emigration, and emphasizing the virtues of the black nationality established by the Haitians. Besides lauding the physical advantages of Haiti, and the associated prospect of material well-being, the political virtues of Haiti remained self-evident. From "the moment" African Americans "touch the soil of Hayti," they would "be emphatically free," and "under the protection of a republican government, composed of their brethren."[84]

Initially, the Haitian scheme appeared to be a success, with African American emigrants speaking enthusiastically of conditions in Haiti. In Haiti, the semi-official *Société Philanthropique d'Haiti* assisted African Americans to settle in the island republic.[85] Writing in late 1823, one emigrant reported that as well as visiting President Boyer, and being "received by him in a most friendly manner," the Haitian president was "so kind as to furnish" him with "all the means necessary for farming." If that was not sufficient inducement, the same emigrant noted that Boyer had "promised" that "he would give me provisions for ten families until they can support themselves." Encouraging other African Americans to settle in Haiti, he assured prospective emigrants that they could do well for themselves in the island republic.[86] Serena M. Baldwin, another, younger emigrant, also spoke favorably about Haiti. Having been warmly received by the Haitian leadership, she pointed out that one of the first places to which her group of emigrants was taken was the local chapel, which she suggested was a grand building.[87] The Haitian authorities were evidently keen to impress on the immigrants that the nation's religious culture was essentially a Christian one, even if Catholicism was the dominant denomination in the republic.

According to a report in the January 1825 edition of the *Genius of Universal Emancipation*, the emigrants "were generally well pleased with their new situation, and the government has completely fulfilled the reasonable expectations of all who have gone" to the island republic. Although some emigrants did express discontent, it was claimed that those individuals had gone to Haiti with the "wildest notions of immediate wealth and grandeur."[88] Throughout 1825 some emigrants at least continued to send positive reports to the United States, declaring their "highest satisfaction" with conditions in the island republic. Dr. Belfast Burton, writing from the Samaná Peninsula in mid-1825, extolled the physical and spiritual conditions in Haiti. Not only had the Haitian government fulfilled its obligations to the emigrants, but Burton also reported that the "natives are hospitable in the extreme, and appear to be much pleased in seeing them [the emigrants] here rendering every assistance in their power, for the comfort of the emigrants."[89] Burton thus raised an important issue, concerning the reception offered to African American emigrants from the Haitian populace. Indeed, the support of the Haitian masses was a prerequisite for a successful emigration to Haiti. Another emigrant, Daniel Copelain, enthusiastic about conditions in his new home, described his success in producing coffee and emphasized that emigrants to Haiti were "received with love, and its attendant civilities.[90] Notwithstanding such assertions, however, we know little about the extent to which the Haitian masses welcomed the influx of African Americans. James O. Jackson's assertion that "in the spirit of brotherhood and mutual benefit," Haitians "actively supported the emigration of Afro-Americans to their country" says more about his determination to present this early emigration movement as an early expression of Pan-Africanism than it does about the reception accorded to the majority of American emigrants. Jackson's subsequent remark that "the Haytian people" must have "been somewhat uneasy" when large numbers of African Americans arrived in their country was a more accurate comment on the relationship between African American immigrants and native Haitians.[91]

Despite African American emigrants' early enthusiasm for Haiti, problems soon arose in their new homes. Contrary to assurances given before they left the United States, emigrants discovered that they could not easily surmount the linguistic, religious, and social differences between themselves and the Haitians. Both the ACS and anti-emigrationists emphasized these problems. While Benjamin Lundy initially dismissed the objections to the Haitian scheme, claiming that opposition was coming mainly from "those who wish to hold their fellow men in bondage, and to live at ease on the production of their labor," doubts were growing about the Haitian movement.[92] As early as 1824, disaffected emigrants were expressing serious concerns with the administration of the movement; in particular, a number of emigrants found the government's system of granting land both inefficient and burdensome.[93] Many emigrants realized that in the short term at least their destiny in Haiti was as agricultural laborers, rather than as independent farmers. By late 1824, increasing numbers of emigrants were choosing to return to the United States.

Reports of emigrants' dissatisfactions in Haiti did much to undermine the Haitian movement. Significant, too, were Benjamin Lundy's growing reservations about the scheme. Although he used the columns of the *Genius of Universal Emancipation* to detail specific cases in which slaveholders had emancipated their slaves and helped them to settle in Haiti, Lundy's personal enthusiasm for Haitian emigration was less persuasive to black Americans when it became clear that only a handful of slaves had been freed and sent to the island republic.[94] While the Haitian scheme promised to assist in the expatriation of the free blacks, a group regarded with extreme suspicion by many whites, there was no widespread sentiment among slaveholders in favor of emancipation. Indeed, only a tiny minority of slaveholders were prepared to emancipate their slaves and despatch them to Haiti. As was the case for free blacks, it was relatively straightforward for many slaveholders to express support for the principles of emancipation and colonization while the discussion remained a theoretical one. But when the abstract idea became a tangible alternative, the economic, social, and political imperatives that underpinned slavery took precedence over the marginal sentiment in favor of emancipation.

Lacking support from slaveholders, and viewed with increasing suspicion by free blacks, the Haitian movement suffered a further setback in May 1825, when the Haitian secretary-general, Joseph Balthazar Inginac, announced that all payments to aid the transportation of emigrants would be terminated. Inginac accused the captains of some of the ships that had carried African Americans to Haiti of greed and misappropriation, but he was especially critical of the emigrants. Expressing surprise at the efforts that were being made to undermine the scheme, he asserted that some emigrants were themselves "in connivance" with those who sought to discredit emigrationism. Explaining that a number of emigrants had quickly become discontented, he said that many had refused to stay in Haiti, and had demanded permits to leave the island soon after their arrival. Alarmingly, Inginac asserted that some wished to leave Haiti "even before the expiration of the four months of rations granted by the state." However, the emigrants' unwillingness to persist in Haiti was not the only factor behind the Haitian authorities' decision to withdraw support for the movement. Another, rather more direct imperative was also significant. The decision to terminate the subsidies was also a response to the embezzlement, by one of Boyer's agents, of some of the funds allocated to attract emigrants. Finally, reflecting the turbulent nature of political life in Haiti, Boyer became wary of enticing too many emigrants, lest they establish themselves as a significant political force in the island republic.[95]

These comments hinted at a common view among those seeking to explain the difficulties facing the Haitian scheme: African American emigrants who were dissatisfied with conditions in the island republic had unrealistic expectations, and lacked the skills and initiative required to succeed as emigrants. There was a certain irony to this judgment, because fears had been expressed in the United States that the emigration movement was robbing the African American community of its brightest talents. Indeed, the editors of the *Genius of Universal Emancipation* argued in November 1824 that this was as it should be. In a reference to the British penal colonies that had been established in what would become Australia, they reasoned it "would be very ungenerous" to "attempt to make a 'Botany Bay' of that Island."[96] Nevertheless, it was widely believed that the failure of the Haitian movement was attributable, at least in part, to the shortcomings of the emigrants. Supporters of the scheme sought to play down the emigrants' discontent, suggesting on occasions that those who emigrated were of poor character, and unaccustomed to hard work. Charles W. Fisher, who had left Baltimore to settle in Haiti, remarked on this issue in early 1825. Although he conceded that "many of the emigrants" were dissatisfied with conditions (particularly the quality of the foodstuffs available in Haiti), he left no doubt that such criticisms reflected poorly on the emigrants, rather than the opportunities available in Haiti. "They are impatient, and indulge in complaints," he wrote, "like the children of Israel, when in the wilderness, not knowing the good prospects that await them." Those who "will bear a little privation at first," he continued, "can live here, and do well."[97] Two months later, detailing the success of his farming venture, Fisher stated "the production of my land is in good order, yielding coffee, corn, sweet potatoes, yams, banannas [*sic*], oranges, pine-apples, cotton trees in abundance, and oil trees."[98]

Fisher's success proved to be rare among African American emigrants. For the editors of the *Genius of Universal Emancipation*, the issue was clear, at least during the early stages of the movement; those emigrants who found themselves in "distressed circumstances" did so for one reason—*because they will not cultivate the land.*[99] Arguing that only enterprising African Americans should emigrate, one report disparaged many of the emigrants in gendered terms, that not only reflected the concerns of the wider black community, but which also suggested the significance that was attached to masculine self-reliance, as it was commonly defined in early nineteenth-century America: "Hundreds of effeminate, lazy wretches, taught by their *worthless tutors* to despise honest labour, and having learned to ape their manners, by 'playing high life below the stairs,' have palmed themselves upon the generosity of the Haytiens." The Reverend Dewey's argument that in Haiti "manliness" was one of the character traits that was in abundant supply was a further expression of the significance of masculinity in the United States during the 1820s.[100] As the argument went, the island republic was attracting dependent and often unskilled blacks, rather than agriculturalists imbued with the requisite spirit of self-reliance.

Holding individual emigrants responsible for their disillusionment in Haiti was a persuasive argument so long as the consensus of opinion among the settlers remained positive. (It was, moreover, a tactic that was repeated by defenders of Haitian emigrationism during the 1850s and 1860s.) But during the mid-1820s, as the tide of opinion turned ever more decisively against emigration to the island republic, and when increasing numbers of African Americans returned with firsthand details of the difficulties they had encountered in Haiti, it became immeasurably more difficult to blame individual emigrants for the problems they were encountering. Clearly, criticizing the character, motives, and skills of the emigrants was an inadequate and ultimately unpersuasive explanation for the movement's woes.

As would be the case during the Civil War era, critics as well as proponents of emigration expressed concern for the moral well-being of the Haitians—and of those American blacks who elected to settle in the island republic. Responding to suggestions that the Haitians' gender and marital relations were less advanced than those of Americans, black and white, and signifying his own views of the moral status of the African American populace, Loring Dewey defended the Haitians. "As bad as are their practices, in relation to marriage," he declared, "there is, I am satisfied, as much real marriage among them as there is among the great mass of our coloured people, and far less promiscuous debauchery; and they have laws in reference to marriage, which is not the case, as relates to the coloured people, in most of our slave states."[101] These references to the significance of what were regarded as proper marriage relations, like the references to gender-specific character traits, said something about the ascendancy of middle-class domestic values in the United States as early as the 1820s. In part, as Dewey's reference to "our coloured people" implied, his remarks reflected an attempt to impose those values on black Americans. At the same time, however, as their long-term interest in moral reform and self-help movements reveals, there is ample evidence that many African Americans were already persuaded of the merits of those values.

The perceived immorality of Haitian society was one factor behind the criticism of the emigration movement. In part, this criticism reflected a deep-seated skepticism of the Haitian government, and of the alleged failure of the experiment in black government. These issues were linked to the contentious issue of U.S. diplomatic recognition of Haitian independence. White Americans did occasionally express support for Haitian independence. One such argument appeared in the New York *Observer* in mid-1825. Referring to French recognition of Haiti's independence, this author reiterated the significance of the Haitian Revolution, and asserted that Haitian advancement "settles the question of liberty for a continent." No longer, he asserted, could it be argued that Africans were unfit to be ranked "with civilized nations."[102]

Another commentator, writing in 1826, also suggested there would be positive consequences from an American recognition of Haiti; but his motives were firmly grounded in racialist assumptions, and a determination to preserve what he regarded as America's racial integrity. For this individual, the question of American recognition of Haitian independence had to be seen in light of commercial considerations, which were far from insignificant. If those concerns were taken into account, he argued, there could be no equivocation: "We must either have the Haytiens as friends or as enemies—there is no middle ground."[103] This writer identified the profound contradiction between refusing to accept black diplomats in Washington, while carrying on what was an increasingly significant "commercial intercourse" with the island republic. Typically, this issue was connected to the question of emigration, and it was here that this writer's deeper feelings about black Americans became evident. While some observers were arguing that "the reception of an ambassador from Hayti would be the signal for" African Americans "to revolt," this author argued there was another, more likely, consequence. The presence of a Haitian ambassador in Washington, he submitted, "would be the signal for all our sable [black] and free population who could find the means of embarkation for Hayti to adopt that measure, and to live among a community of their species, where they could enjoy" various "envied advantages." Clearly, in this instance, support for American recognition of Haiti was premised firmly on pragmatic considerations of commercial advantage and the removal of a potentially troublesome free black population from the United States.[104]

Although there were some proponents of American recognition of Haitian independence during the 1820s, more telling was the sustained critique of the Haitian experiment, with all its implications for race relations. These critiques, or concerns, could come from unlikely sources. In late 1824, Amos Phelps—who during the 1830s would become a prominent radical abolitionist—discussed the alternative destinations available to African Americans contemplating emigration. Phelps conceded that Haiti offered certain logistical advantages over Africa, but he was swayed more by other, more self-serving imperatives. Having concluded that most of the black Americans who would go to Haiti were "extremely ignorant," he worried that if a war was to break out in the region, a Haiti "allied to our enemies," and strengthened by the presence of immigrants from the United States, would "become a dangerous and powerful foe." Like other commentators, however, Phelps' argument appeared to rest on a contradiction regarding the status and role of black Americans: In this case the ignorant and degraded blacks would nevertheless become capable of offering significant support to Haiti. Blacks who traveled to Haiti, Phelps suggested, would become more educated and civilized while in the island republic; but rather than expressing gratitude, they would become resentful of their former "unjust confinement." One of Phelps's particular concerns was that when blacks had "learned the art of navigation," there would be "many" who—"activated by a spirit of revenge"—would "play the part of pirates with cruelty and success."[105] Phelps was writing as a twenty-year old student, and he was no friend of slavery. His thoughts, moreover, were undoubtedly still in the process of being formed. Nonetheless, in expressing anxiety over the perceived consequences of emigration, he had raised concerns that were common among white Americans.

Another, more emphatic critique of Haiti was evident in an 1825 report in the *National Intelligencer*, which noted that there "is not, in the christian world at least, from what we can learn, a more despotic government than that of Hayti." Although this remark implied that the Haitians' Christianity at least elevated them from absolute savagery, the emphasis on Haitian despotism was a typical assessment of the black republic among white Americans. Black Americans, therefore, were advised to think carefully before embarking for Haiti. Emigrants to the island republic, the contributor to the *National Intelligencer* claimed, "have suffered themselves to be seduced from a land of freedom to place themselves under the sway of a political and religious tyranny, of which they had no conception until the prison bolts were drawn. Those persons who were born, and have been educated under this free and tolerant government, cannot be otherwise than miserable under a government politically and religiously despotic, in comparison with ours."[106] Black Americans, of course, rejected such self-congratulatory assertions regarding American freedoms.

Another critic of the Haitian scheme, publishing his views in the Virginian *Petersburg Intelligencer*, attested back-handedly to the dangers posed by a successful black nationality. "We confess," he wrote, "there is something in the *geographical position* of Hayti which we do not like: we should not wish to see a powerful nation of blacks rise up so near us."[107] In the context of the Monroe Doctrine, announced just two years previously, these remarks were an early hint that the United States' avowed determination to prevent the extension of European colonialism in the Western hemisphere was paralleled by a similar resolve to ensure that the political structures and institutions that developed in the region were not antithetical to white American interests. As the contributor to the *Petersburg Intelligencer* revealed, these concerns were expressed in explicitly racial terms from the early decades of the nineteenth century.

Given the depth of these concerns, it was only predictable that the United States refused to grant formal diplomatic recognition to Haiti, even as European powers grudgingly accepted the reality of the Haitian Revolution. Here was America's great contradiction writ large. Although white Americans judged independence from European colonization a laudable achievement, and while they commonly regarded their republican form of government as a model for the rest of the world to emulate, the domestic imperatives of slavery and race relations figured prominently in U.S. foreign policy. Consequently, even after the Monroe Doctrine had repudiated European colonization in the Americas, and at the same time as the United States was in the process of recognizing a number of the Latin America republics that had recently secured their independence from Spain, American policymakers continued to spurn Haiti. If American policymakers had their way, the black republic would remain a pariah state.

Ironically, it is conceivable that American recognition of Haiti would have encouraged more black Americans to emigrate to the island republic. Estimates vary as to the number of African Americans who emigrated to Haiti during the 1820s. The Haitian government subsidized the passage of six thousand, although the total number of emigrants might have been higher.[108] Little is known of the fate of most of those black Americans who emigrated to the island republic during the 1820s. Of those who remained in Haiti, few succeeded as farmers, and from all accounts many of the emigrants returned to the United States. Joseph Balthazar Inginac estimated that by April 1826 "one-third" of the six thousand African Americans who had emigrated under the auspices of the Haitian Government's scheme had returned to the United States.[109] Later, one visitor to the island republic noted that after 1836 none of the emigrants were living on the land assigned to them by the government.[110] Some prominent African Americans did remain in Haiti. Prince Saunders, for example, stayed in the island republic until his death in 1839, having served as attorney general under President Boyer.[111]

Aside from their individual contributions to Haiti, there is evidence that African American immigrants' presence was felt in another, perhaps more significant way. Without providing specific details on individual settlers, M. B. Bird, who was "Nearly Thirty Years a Resident Missionary in the Haytian Republic," remarked in 1869 that although "many" emigrants returned to the United States, "many" others did remain in the island republic, becoming "respectable and useful in various branches of industry." In discussing the emigrants' religious contributions to Haiti, Bird provided insights into the emigrants' experiences, as well as the political and religious culture of the island republic. "Some" of the emigrants, he wrote, "who persevered in remaining" in Haiti "became ministers of the Gospel, and proved to be of sound character, both of the Methodist and Baptist denominations." "Small churches soon sprung up," Bird explained, "both in the French and Spanish" sections of the island. In Port-au-Prince, he continued, "a neat little edifice was raised by" the American immigrants, that could "accommodate some two hundred hearers." The immigrants' faith, however, was a challenge to the prevailing religious order in Haiti. The fact that most of the immigrants were "African Episcopal Methodists," Bird explained, "tested in a salutary manner the reigning thoughts of Roman Catholic Hayti on the general question of religious liberty." Despite early signs that the black republic would pass the test of religious freedom—"in fact Hayti really did receive the Gospel, notwithstanding difficulties"—the Haitian leadership ultimately baulked at the prospect of alternative religious values and hierarchies. Religion and politics proved inseparable. President Jean Pierre Boyer, fearful of the potential influence of African Americans over the Haitian masses, vowed that the republic's authorities would not meddle with the emigrants' "religious belief," as long as they did "not seek to make proselytes." As Bird noted, the "camp meetings, which were at first allowed," were "an interesting test to the reigning thoughts of the day." But because the meetings were a challenge to the prevailing religious order (and because they were generally conducted "in the English language") the Haitian authorities "feared" they would be "likely to be abused by revolutionists, or other ill-disposed persons." Consequently, further meetings were "disallowed." Apparently, then, the Haitian authorities did not directly fear that African American immigrants would themselves foment political strife. Rather, the concern was that the values and institutions they carried to Haiti might provide opportunities for Haitian malcontents to challenge the nation's social and political structures. Although Bird did not directly connect the perceived dangers of African American religion in Haiti to his earlier remarks regarding the "entirely military character and habits of Hayti," the two themes were linked. As he noted, the military nature of the island republic was "unsuitable to the American immigrants."[112]

The demise of the Haitian movement of the mid-1820s did not mean African American interest in the island republic had faded completely. Following graduation from Bowdoin College in 1826, the Jamaican-born John Browne Russwurm chose Haiti as the subject of his commencement address. Russwurm, who would soon become co-founder and co-editor of *Freedom's Journal*, subsequently became an advocate of African colonization. But in his 1826 address, his attentions were focused on Haiti. Beginning from the premise that it "is in the irresistible course of events that all men who have been deprived of their liberty shall recover this precious portion of their indefeasible inheritance," he argued "the Revolution in Haiti holds a conspicuous place" among the "many interesting events of the present day." Foremost among the Haitians' accomplishments was their success in establishing and maintaining a "republican form of government." As Russwurm noted, not only were the Haitians' political values and institutions recognizable to black Americans, but "the independence of Haiti" had "laid the foundations of an empire that" he

anticipated would "take a rank with the nations of the earth." Praising the Haitians' valor and commitment to liberty, Russwurm did not resile from the
bloodshed that had characterized the overthrow of French rule in Haiti. "If
cruelties were inflicted during the revolutionary war," he insisted, "it was ow-
ing to the policy pursued by the French commanders, that compelled them to
use retaliatory measures." Barbarism was not a characteristic of the black race,
as Haiti's detractors were fond of claiming. Instead, it was an inevitable response from men who had been "hunted with bloodhounds, who have been
threatened with auto-da-fé, whose relations and friends have been hanged on
gibbets before their eyes," and "sunk by hundreds in the sea." The implication, of course, was that if American slaveholders continued to brutalize their
slaves, the United States would be beset by similar turmoil to that which had
tormented Haiti.[113]

Although Russwurm did not act on his plan to emigrate to Haiti, and although the organized emigration movement to the black republic collapsed,
Haiti remained prominent in the black press.[114] During the 1820s, and beyond, newspaper editorialists, and others, left no doubt about the significance
they attached to the island republic. In early 1827, Russwurm and Samuel
Cornish, his co-editor of *Freedom's Journal*, cautioned "the dissatisfied and
envious" in the United States "to desist from their unmanly attacks upon a
brave and hospitable people." Aware that much of the so-called "News from
Hayti" was nothing more than malicious rumor, they emphasized that having
forged an independent "standard of liberty," the Haitians "fear none."[115] Besides offering hope for the slaves' emancipation, the Haitian Revolution provided evidence that the brutalities of slavery had not completely obliterated
the "finer sensibilities" of those who had been enslaved: "though trodden
down in the dust by the foot of the oppressor," Haitians "still possessed the
proper spirit and feelings of a man."[116] Implicit here was a conviction that
American slaves had not lost their essential humanity, nor the capacity to contribute to civilized society. No longer could it be argued, for example, that "the
descendants of Africa" were incapable "of self-government."[117] As Cornish
and Russwurm remarked in May 1827, the history of Haiti "presented the
most incontestable proofs, that the negro is not, in general, wanting in the
higher qualifications of the mind; and that, with the same advantages of liberty,
independence and education, as their white brethren in Europe and America,
the race would not be found deficient in hearts pregnant with heroic energies,
and hands capable of wielding the sword of war, or swaying the rod of empire."[118]

Through the late 1820s, as black leaders rejected the "wretched doctrine"
of the ACS, there were measured expressions of support for African American
migration to what Samuel Cornish described in 1829 as the "beautiful island
of Hayti." While he assured his readers that he had no "wish for them to emigrate," Cornish was convinced that if individual African Americans did decide
in favor of emigration, they would be much better off in Haiti than they would

be in Africa. Suggesting that "emigrants of industrious and economical habits" stood "every chance for obtaining wealth and influence" in Haiti, Cornish also believed that "the people" of Haiti were "civilized," and the "laws good and well administered."[119] David Walker, too, preferred Haitian emigration over African colonization. In the fourth "Article" of his *Appeal*—entitled "Our Wretchedness in Consequence of the Colonizing Plan"—Walker's first choice for those who elected to leave the United States was to settle among "those who have been for many years, and are now our greatest earthly friends and benefactors—the English." If that alternative did not appeal, or was not feasible, Walker counseled African Americans to "go to" their "brethren, the Haytians, who according to their word, are bound to protect and comfort us."[120] Despite Walker's lukewarm endorsement of black emigration to the island republic, there can be no doubt that like many black leaders he preferred Haitian emigration over the ACS's Liberian scheme.

The white abolitionist Benjamin Lundy also remained interested in emigrationism through the late 1820s and into the 1830s. In 1829, visiting the island for a second time, Lundy took with him "twelve more emancipated slaves, which a man in Maryland had given up to me for that purpose." Lundy's continuing enthusiasm for Haiti was evident from his report on conditions there. Having found "affairs" in Haiti "much better" than on his earlier visit, he outlined what he regarded as the generous conditions under which emigrants would be received in the black republic. Although emigrants would no longer enjoy the assistance of the Haitian government in making their way to Haiti, Lundy did declare that he was "ready to make arrangements" to transport emancipated slaves who wanted to emigrate. Once in Haiti, he asserted, ex-slaves "could obtain leases of plantations, with dwellings on them, for seven years, the first two years to be *gratis*, and the remaining five at a moderate rent." The emancipated slaves who had left the United States to settle in Haiti, Lundy claimed, had obtained nine-year leases of "the richest kind of land." With regard to the vexed issue of religion, Lundy asserted that "no country on earth was more free."[121]

Notwithstanding Lundy's continued interest in Haitian emigration, by the early 1830s the anti-emigrationist position of the black leadership had firmed to the point where the delegates to the 1832 national convention resolved "to discountenance, by all just means in their power, any emigration to Liberia or Hayti." For those present at the 1832 meeting, discussion of emigration to Haiti was as damaging to black aspirations as white colonizationists' proposals for black deportation to Liberia. Both schemes, the black leadership concluded, were "only calculated to distract and divide the whole colored family."[122] Yet, although the black leadership railed against emigration, the fact they went to such lengths to denounce such proposals implied there was at least some interest from within the black populace in emigration.[123]

During the early 1830s, Haiti and Liberia were not the only alternatives for African Americans contemplating a future beyond the United States. The prospect of finding a refuge from slavery in the British provinces to the north of the United States had long proved a powerful allure to black Americans. Slavery remained legal in Canada until its abolition by the British parliament in 1833, but most observers agreed that white racism was less virulent in Canada than it was in the United States. Growing partly out of the specific problems facing the free black community in Cincinnati, the first national convention of African Americans, held in Philadelphia in 1830, discussed the prospect of black emigration to Canada.[124] As Richard Allen told the convention, under the British administration in Upper Canada "no invidious distinction of colour is recognised, but there we shall be entitled to all the rights, privileges, and immunities of other citizens." Allen pointed to Canada's other advantages over Africa, including the fact that "the language, climate, soil, and productions" were similar to those of the United States: again, African Americans were being encouraged to take advantage of what was familiar to them. Finally, Allen noted that with affordable land, and a ready market for the produce that could be raised in Canada, the British provinces offered a degree of economic independence that was denied to all but a few blacks in the United States.[125]

The 1830 convention led to the establishment of the "American Society of Free Persons of Colour, for Improving their Condition in the United States; for Purchasing Lands; and for the Establishment of a Settlement in Upper Canada." Land was acquired for those Cincinnati blacks who chose to emigrate, and the Wilberforce settlement was formed to provide them with support when they arrived in Canada. Despite grandiose pronouncements, however, the Wilberforce project attracted fewer emigrants than had been anticipated. Ultimately, the scheme ended in failure. A subsequent African American emigration program to Canada, known as the Dawn Settlement, was established during the early 1840s. Although this project lingered on until 1868, its failure had been apparent many years earlier.[126]

Ultimately, Canada proved an imperfect refuge for black Americans. But for most blacks during the 1830s and 1840s, it was unquestionably a better alternative than the ACS colony of Liberia. In the United States, the black leadership continued to offer support for those blacks who were threatened with expulsion to Africa. For many years, the ACS sought financial support from the federal and state governments. In response to that possibility, the delegates at the 1833 national convention of African Americans resolved that if individual state legislatures sought to expatriate their black citizens, they would "give" such blacks "all the aid" in their "power to enable them to remove and settle in upper Canada, or elsewhere," so they would not be "compelled to sacrifice their lives in the insalubrious climate of Liberia."[127] The fact that the delegates remarked it would be better for besieged African Americans to settle in upper Canada, or elsewhere, suggested they had shifted ground from their resolution of the preceding year: Presumably Haiti was again being regarded as a more preferable site for emigration than Africa. In practice, the support offered by the black conventions to assist the African American populace was inevitably meager. But the delegates' resolution did signal the ongoing distinction they drew between African colonization and emigration to other destinations.

Despite occasional expressions of support for black emigration, however, during the 1830s there was a widespread determination among African Americans to remain in the United States. From the early years of that decade, the prospect of finding a refuge from slavery in the British provinces to the north of the United States was not the only imperative shaping the African American response to colonization and emigration. This period witnessed the rise of radical abolitionism, whose advocates spurned black colonization. During the 1820s, Benjamin Lundy, and other white opponents of slavery had been willing to consider the virtues of colonization, but the abolitionists of the 1830s were uncompromisingly opposed to the principles of the ACS. Demanding an immediate and unconditional end to slavery, radical abolitionists' caustic opposition to the ACS reflected African Americans' continued denunciations of the "evil purposes" of the colonizationists.[128] Although several thousand African Americans fled to Canada during the early 1830s, most blacks remained in the United States, where they sought equality and an end to slavery.

In choosing to stay and fight for freedom and equality in the United States, African Americans embraced many of the tenets of the individualism characteristic of antebellum America. By 1830, there were nearly 125,000 free blacks in the North, most of them comprising an unskilled or semi-skilled labor force, concentrated in and about certain urban areas in Massachusetts, New York, Pennsylvania, and Ohio. Meeting in regular local, state, and national conventions, and hoping to instill within the black populace the skills required to elevate themselves in white society, black leaders pronounced the virtues of thrift, temperance, piety, and moral reform. As a report to the 1831 Annual Convention of the Free People of Colour stated, *"Education, Temperance,* and *Economy,* are best calculated to promote the elevation of mankind to a proper rank and standing among men."* Ironically, as we will see, these were the very same virtues black emigrationists hoped African American settlers would carry to Haiti, Africa, and other destinations during the 1850s and early 1860s. In the process of encouraging self-elevation among blacks, African American leaders aimed to prove to whites that blacks were worthy of the full benefits of American citizenship.[129] It was in this context that a clear majority of African Americans spurned emigrationism during the 1830s and into the 1840s.

By the end of the 1820s, complex and often contradictory images of Africa and Haiti were well entrenched in the consciousness of black Americans. African Americans agreed that the redemption and elevation of Africa were worthwhile objectives. But physically far removed from their ancestral homeland, and increasingly separated from Africa with each generation, most free blacks looked askance at white-led schemes to expatriate them to Africa. While the colonization and emigration movements of the 1820s ended in failure, they were significant portents of later debates concerning emigrationism and black nationalism. If nothing else, the black response to white colonizationists' efforts to coerce them "back" to Africa contributed to the growing sense of community among urban blacks in the North. Although the failure of the ACS permanently tainted all back-to-Africa schemes—as evidenced by the anti-ACS resolutions that were passed almost as a matter of course at African American conventions down to the Civil War—the subsequent black interest in emigration to Haiti showed that black Americans were able to distinguish African colonization from Haitian emigrationism. Haiti itself presented contradictory images. At the same time as the island republic evoked images of bloodshed and terror, the Haitians' success in overthrowing their colonial oppressors, and establishing and defending the world's first independent black republic, was a source of pride for black Americans. That pride contributed to the African American interest in Haiti during the early nineteenth century.

The Haitian movement of the 1820s was a significant episode in African American history. Although the scheme failed, it attested to the level of discontent within the black community in the United States during the early decades of the nineteenth century. And while the movement of the 1820s was less clearly associated with sentiments of black nationality than was the case with Haitian emigrationism during the Civil War era, there were signs during the 1820s that some black Americans, at least, shared the Haitians' concern for trans-national racial unity. Perhaps most significant, although the demise of the scheme lingered long in the collective memory of black Americans, this early movement hinted at an awareness among African Americans of the possibilities presented by Haiti. This was evidenced by the efforts taken by proponents of Haitian emigration during the 1850s and 1860s, who—as subsequent chapters explain—went to considerable lengths to distinguish their proposals from the movement of the 1820s. After the failure of the Haitian scheme during the 1820s, it was not until the late 1840s that black Americans again gave serious attention to the virtues of emigrationism. The period preceding the Civil War witnessed divisive and bitter debates surrounding African Americans' future in the United States. Again, although many blacks found refuge in Canada during the 1850s, and although Africa attracted the interest of a number of black leaders, thousands of African Americans looked to Haiti as the most realistic and appealing destination beyond the United States.

NOTES

1. *Freedom's Journal*, 31 August 1827.

2 Winthrop Jordan, *White Over Black: American Attitudes Toward the Negro, 1550–1812* (1968; reprint, New York: Norton, 1977), 546–55.

3. John Chester Miller, *The Wolf by the Ears: Thomas Jefferson and Slavery* (New York: Free Press, 1977), 264, passim.

4. Ira Berlin, *Slaves Without Masters: The Free Negro in the Antebellum South* (New York: Vintage Books, 1974), 82.

5. "Petition of Peter Bestes, Sambo Freeman, Felix Holbrook, and Chester Joie," Boston, April 20, 1773, in *Early Negro Writings, 1760–1837*, ed. Dorothy Porter (Boston: Beacon Press, 1971), 255.

6. Cited in Foner, *History of Black Americans: From Africa to the Emergence of the Cotton Kingdom* (Westport, Conn.: Greenwood Press, 1975), 579.

7. Gary B. Nash, "Forging Freedom: The Emancipation Experience in the Northern Seaport Cities, 1775–1820," in *Slavery and Freedom in the Age of the American Revolution*, ed. Ira Berlin and Ronald Hoffman (Charlottesville: University Press of Virginia, 1983), 42.

8. William Douglass, *Annals of the First African Church in the United States of America* . . . (Philadelphia, 1862), quoted in Nash, "Forging Freedom," 44; Leonard P. Curry, *The Free Black in Urban America, 1800–1850: The Shadow of the Dream* (Chicago: University of Chicago Press, 1981), 174, 194.

9. Nash, "Forging Freedom," 45–46; Berlin, "Time, Space, and the Evolution of Afro-American Society," *American Historical Review*, 85 (1980): 53; Winch, *Philadelphia's Black Elite: Activism, Accommodation, and the Struggle for Autonomy, 1787–1848* (Philadelphia: Temple University Press, 1988), 27.

10. Floyd Miller, *The Search for a Black Nationality: Black Emigration and Colonization, 1787–1863* (Urbana: University of Illinois Press, 1975), 4–20; George E. Brooks, Jr., "The Providence African Society's Sierra Leone Scheme, 1794–1795: Prologue to the African Colonization Movement," *International Journal of African Historical Studies*, 7 (1974): 183–202.

11. On Sierra Leone, see Christopher Fyfe, *A History of Sierra Leone* (London: Oxford University Press, 1962); Richard West, *Back to Africa: A History of Sierra Leone and Liberia* (London: Jonathan Cape, 1970).

12. Miller, *Search for a Black Nationality*, 40–42.

13. On Cuffe, see Lamont D. Thomas, *Rise to Be a People: A Biography of Paul Cuffe* (Chicago: University of Illinois Press, 1986); Sheldon Harris, *Paul Cuffe: Black America and the African Return* (New York: Simon & Schuster, 1972); Henry N. Sherwood, "Paul Cuffee," *Journal of Negro History*, 8 (1923): 153–229.

14. Miller, *Search for a Black Nationality*, 51–53.

15. Henry N. Sherwood, "The Formation of the American Colonization Society," *Journal of Negro History*, 2 (1917): 209–28.

16. Berry and Blassingame, *Long Memory: The Black Experience in America* (New York: Oxford University Press, 1982), 400. Even more doubtful is Elizabeth Rauh Bethel's recent assertion that "between 1820 and 1860, 20 percent of the free African-American population quit the United States to establish new lives in Liberia, Haiti, the British West Indies, and Canada." See Bethel, *The Roots of African-American Identity: Memory and History in Free Antebellum Communities* (New York: St. Martin's Press, 1997), 76.

17. Philip J. Staudenraus, *The African Colonization Movement, 1816–1865* (New York: Columbia University Press, 1961), 251.

18. Phil Samuel Sigler has estimated that one quarter of all black emigrants to Liberia died within a year of their arrival, and Tom W. Shick's detailed analysis revealed that in the period preceding 1844, 21 percent of all emigrants to Liberia died within a year of their arrival of the colony. See Sigler, "The Attitudes of Free Blacks Towards Emigration to Liberia" (Ph.D. diss., Boston University, 1969), 20; Shick, "A Quanti-

tative Analysis of Liberian Colonization from 1820 to 1843 with Special Reference to Mortality," *Journal of African History*, 12 (1971): 45–59.

19. Early Lee Fox, *The American Colonization Society, 1817–1840* (Baltimore: Johns Hopkins University Press, 1919), 89.

20. See Philip S. Foner, *History of Black Americans: From the Emergence of the Cotton Kingdom to the Eve of the Compromise of 1850* (Westport, Conn.: Greenwood Press, 1983), 304; Imanuel Geiss, *The Pan African Movement,* trans. Ann Keep (London: Methuen, 1974), 82; Yekutiel Gershoni, *Black Colonialism: The Americo-Liberian Scramble for the Hinterland* (Boulder, Colo.: Westview Press, 1985).

21. Nash, "Forging Freedom," 47. See also Winch, *Philadelphia's Black Elite*, 4–15; Gary B. Nash, *Forging Freedom: The Formation of Philadelphia's Black Community, 1720–1840* (Cambridge, Mass.: Harvard University Press, 1988), 237–38.

22. Forten to Cuffe, January 25, 1817, in *Eyewitness: The Negro in American History*, ed. William Loren Katz (New York: Pitman, 1967), 146–47. See also Winch, *Philadelphia's Black Elite*, 35–37. For examples of the way in which Forten has been depicted as a devout opponent of the ACS, see William C. Nell, *The Colored Patriots of the American Revolution* (1855; reprint, New York: Arno Press, 1968), 177–78; Ray Allen Billington, "James Forten: Forgotten Abolitionist," in *Blacks in the Abolitionist Movement*, ed. John H. Bracey, August Meier, and Elliot Rudwick (Belmont, Calif.: Wadsworth, 1971), 8–10.

23. *African Repository*, 10 (1834): 292.

24. Early protagonists in this debate were E. Franklin Frazier, who argued that the process of enslavement effectively robbed African slaves of much of their "culture," and Melville J. Herskovits, who contended there were significant continuities between African culture and the African American culture that evolved in North America. See Frazier, *The Negro in the United States*, rev. ed. (New York: Macmillan, 1957); Herskovits, *The Myth of the Negro Past* (1958, reprint, Boston: Beacon Press, 1970).

25. Fox, *Colonization Society*, 11, 218. See also Douglas R. Egerton, " 'Its Origin Is Not a Little Curious': A New Look at the American Colonization Society," *Journal of the Early Republic*, 5 (1985): 463–80.

26. Clay, in the Tenth Annual Report of the ACS (1826), as quoted in Amos J. Beyan, *The American Colonization Society and the Creation of the Liberian State: A Historical Perspective, 1822–1900* (Lanham, Md.: University Press of America, 1991), 4.

27. Williams' speech at St. Philips Church, New York City, 4 July 1830, in *Negro Orators and Their Orations*, ed. Carter G. Woodson (1925; reprint, New York: Russell & Russell, 1969), 79.

28. *Rights of All*, 18 September 1829; *Freedom's Journal*, 31 August 1827.

29. *Constitution of the American Society of Free Persons of Colour, for Improving Their Condition in the United States; for Purchasing Lands; and for the Establishment of a Settlement in Upper Canada, also the Proceedings of the Convention, with Their Address to the Free Persons of Colour in the United States* (Philadelphia: J. W. Allen, 1831), 10.

30. *Freedom's Journal*, 2 November 1827.

31. Robert I. Rotberg, *Haiti: The Politics of Squalor* (Boston: Houghton Mifflin, 1971), 25.

32. Alfred N. Hunt, *Haiti's Influence on Antebellum America: Slumbering Volcano in the Caribbean* (Baton Rouge: Louisiana State University Press, 1988), 11–12.

33. Eugene Genovese, *From Rebellion to Revolution: Afro-American Slave Revolts in the Making of the Modern World* (New York: Vintage Books, 1979), 87.

34. Sylvia R. Frey, *Water from the Rock: Black Resistance in a Revolutionary Age* (Princeton, N.J.: Princeton University Press, 1991), 191; Hunt, *Haiti's Influence*, 19.

35. David Brion Davis, *The Problem of Slavery in the Age of Revolution, 1770–1823* (Ithaca, N.Y.: Cornell University Press, 1975), 557. See also Ronald Segal, *The Black Diaspora* (London: Faber and Faber, 1995), 105–25.

36. James G. Leyburn, *The Haitian People* (1941; reprint, New Haven: Yale University Press, 1966), 23–24; Rotberg, *Politics of Squalor*, 52.

37. Caryn Cossé Bell, *Revolution, Romanticism, and the Afro-Creole Protest Tradition in Louisiana, 1718–1868* (Baton Rouge: Louisiana State University Press, 1997), 98. On the early reactions within the United States to the revolution in Haiti, see Donald R. Hickey, "America's Response to the Slave Revolt in Haiti, 1791–1806," *Journal of the Early Republic*, 2 (1982): 361–79; Jordan, *White Over Black*.

38. On the American press and Haiti, see Shane White, *Somewhat More Independent: The End of Slavery in New York City, 1700–1810* (Athens: University of Georgia Press, 1991), 65, 67–68.

39. See Mary Hassal, *Secret History, or, The Horrors of St. Domingo in a Series of Letters: Written by a Lady at Cape Francois to Colonel Burr, Late Vice-President of the United States, Principally During the Command of General Rochambeau* (Philadelphia: Bradford & Innskeep, 1808).

40. James O. Horton and Lois E. Horton, *In Hope of Liberty: Culture, Community, and Protest Among Northern Free Blacks, 1700–1860* (New York: Oxford University Press, 1997), 192; Bell, *Revolution, Romanticism, and the Afro-Creole Protest Tradition*, 61.

41. See Robin Blackburn, *The Overthrow of Colonial Slavery, 1776–1848* (London: Verso, 1988), 256.

42. Genovese, *From Rebellion to Revolution*, 94. See also Berlin, *Slaves Without Masters*, 89, 114–16; Davis, *The Problem of Slavery in the Age of Revolution*, 329; Paul F. Lachance, "The Foreign French," in *Creole New Orleans: Race and Americanization*, ed. Arnold R. Hirsch and Joseph Logsdon (Baton Rouge: Louisiana State University Press, 1992), 103–11.

43. Paquette, "Revolutionary Saint Domingue in the Making of Territorial Louisiana," in *A Turbulent Time: The French Revolution and the Greater Caribbean*, ed. David Barry Gaspar and David Patrick Geggus (Bloomington: Indiana University Press, 1997), 205.

44. Genovese, *From Rebellion to Revolution*, 95–97. See also John M. Murrin et al., *Liberty, Equality, Power: A History of the American People* (Fort Worth, Tex.: Harcourt Brace, 1996), 278; Bethel, *Roots of African-American Identity*, 93–94.

45. Frey, *Water From the Rock*, 226–32; W. Jeffrey Bolster, *Black Jacks: African American Seamen in the Age of Sail* (Cambridge, Mass.: Harvard University Press, 1997), 145. On the assistance rendered to black seamen by the authorities in "revolutionary St. Domingue or republican Haiti," see also Ira Berlin, *Many Thousands Gone:*

The First Two Centuries of Slavery in North America (Cambridge, Mass.: Belknap Press of Harvard University Press, 1999), 305–6.

46. Berlin, *Many Thousands Gone*, 354. See also Hunt, *Haiti's Influence*, 24–26.

47. Nash, *Forging Freedom*, 175–76.

48. Genovese, *From Rebellion to Revolution*, 95; Douglas R. Egerton, *Gabriel's Rebellion: The Virginia Slave Conspiracies of 1800 and 1802* (Chapel Hill: University of North Carolina Press, 1993), 46–47.

49. Genovese, *From Rebellion to Revolution*, 43; Bell, *Revolution, Romanticism, and the Afro-Creole Protest Tradition*, 46.

50. Bolster, *Black Jacks*, 146.

51. Donald R. Wright, *African Americans in the Early Republic, 1789–1831* (Arlington Heights, Ill.: Harlan Davidson, 1993), 100–101.

52. Genovese, *From Rebellion to Revolution*, 130, 49. See also Murrin, *Liberty, Equality, Power*, 363; Sterling Stuckey, ed., *The Ideological Origins of Black Nationalism* (Boston: Beacon Press, 1972), 5; Jackson, "Origins of Pan-African Nationalism," 126.

53. Foner, *History of Black Americans: From the Emergence of the Cotton Kingdom to the Eve of the Compromise of 1850*, 145; Robert S. Starobin, "Denmark Vesey's Slave Rebellion of 1822: A Study in Rebellion and Repression," in *American Slavery: The Question of Resistance*, ed. John H. Bracey, Jr., August Meier, and Elliot Rudwick (Belmont, Calif.: Wadsworth, 1971), 143. Richard Wade has suggested that Vesey's Conspiracy existed only in the minds of fearful whites. See Wade, "The Vesey Plot: A Reconsideration," *Journal of Southern History*, 30 (1964): 143–61.

54. Peter H. Wood, "Nat Turner: The Unknown Slave as Visionary Leader," in *Black Leaders of the Nineteenth Century*, ed. Leon Litwack and August Meier (Urbana: University of Illinois Press, 1988), 27.

55. Wood, "Nat Turner," 35–36.

56. See James Brewer Stewart, *Holy Warriors: The Abolitionists and American Slavery* (New York: Hill and Wang, 1976), 61.

57. Dew, cited in Louis Filler, *The Crusade Against Slavery, 1830–1860* (New York: Harper Torchbooks, 1960), 55.

58. On African Americans' celebrations of Haitian independence, see Berlin, *Slaves Without Masters*, 314–15; Christopher Phillips, *Freedom's Port: The African American Community of Baltimore, 1790–1860* (Urbana: University of Illinois Press, 1997), 221.

59. Walker, *Appeal, in Four Articles, Together with a Preamble, to the Coloured Citizens of the World, But in Particular, and Very Expressly to those of the United States of America*, 3rd ed., 1830, reprinted in *"One Continual Cry": David Walker's Appeal to the Colored Citizens of the World (1829–1830)*, ed. Herbert Aptheker (New York: Humanities Press, 1965), 83–84.

60. *Genius of Universal Emancipation*, August, 1825. See also Berlin, *Slaves Without Masters*, 314.

61. William Lloyd Garrison, for example, refused to accept any responsibility for Nat Turner's uprising. Immediatist abolitionists, he insisted, were committed to the *peaceful* emancipation of the slaves. As Garrison saw it, if the South exploded in bloodshed, responsibility would rest with the slaveholders, who refused to countenance the possibility of emancipation. See Russel B. Nye, *William Lloyd Garrison and the Humanitarian Reformers* (Boston: Little, Brown, and Co., 1955), 53–54.

62. Jefferson, cited in Hunt, *Haiti's Influence*, 6. See also Miller, *Wolf by the Ears*, 270; John Edward Baur, "Mulatto Machiavelli: Jean Pierre Boyer, and the Haiti of His Day," *Journal of Negro History*, 32 (1947): 325.

63. See Miller, *Search for a Black Nationality*, 74–75. See also W. W. Harvey, *Sketches of Haiti From the Expulsion of the French to the Death of Christophe* (1827; reprint, London: Frank Cass, 1971), 236.

64. Horton and Horton, *In Hope of Liberty*, 192–93; Miller, *Search for a Black Nationality*, 75; Arthur O. White, "Prince Saunders: An Instance of Social Mobility Among Antebellum New England Blacks," *Journal of Negro History*, 60 (1975): 527–28.

65. Saunders, *Haytian Papers. A Collection of the Very Interesting Proclamations and Other Official Documents, Together with Some Account of the Rise, Progress, and Present State of the Kingdom of Hayti* (1816; reprint, Boston: Caleb Bingham & Co., 1818), v; Saunders, *A Memoir Presented to the American Convention for the Abolition of Slavery, and Improving the Condition of the African Race, December 11th, 1818* . . . (Philadelphia: n.p., 1818), 12–15. See also Winch, *Philadelphia's Black Elite*, 50–51.

66. Clarkson to Henry Christophe, 20 February 1819, in *Henry Christophe and Thomas Clarkson: A Correspondence*, ed. Earl Leslie Griggs and Clifford H. Prator (1952; reprint, New York: Greenwood, 1968), 124–25; White, "Prince Saunders," 530–33; Harvey, *Sketches of Haiti*, 237–40; Winch, *Philadelphia's Black Elite*, 51–52; Hubert Cole, *Christophe: King of Haiti* (London: Eyre & Spottiswoode, 1967), 246.

67. Miller, *Search for a Black Nationality*, 75–76.

68. Dewey to Boyer, 30 April 1824, in *Correspondence Relative to the Emigration to Haiti of the Free People of Colour in the United States, together with Instructions to the Agent Sent by President Boyer*, comp. Loring Dewey (New York: Mahlon Day, 1824), 3–6.

69. David Nicholls, *From Dessalines to Duvalier: Race, Colour and National Independence in Haiti*, 3rd ed. (London: Macmillan, 1996), 68.

70. Boyer to Dewey, 30 April 1824, in Dewey, *Correspondence*, 6–11.

71. Miller, *Search for a Black Nationality*, 77–78.

72. Gary Nash has pointed out that some of the emigrants from Philadelphia were "probably inspired" by Richard Allen's "dreams of stretching the arms of the Methodist Episcopal Church to the Caribbean." See Nash, *Forging Freedom*, 244.

73. Hunt, *Haiti's Influence*, 15–16.

74. Joyner, " 'Believer I Know': The Emergence of African-American Christianity," in *African-American Christianity: Essays in History*, ed. Paul E. Johnson (Berkeley: University of California Press, 1994), 34, 37.

75. Dewey, *Correspondence*, p. 31; Baur, "Mulatto Machiavelli," 325; Miller, *Search for a Black Nationality*, 78; John W. Blassingame, ed., *The Frederick Douglass Papers. Series One: Speeches, Debates, and Interviews. Volume 2: 1847–54* (New Haven: Yale University Press, 1982), 316n. On Williams' attitude toward Haitian emigrationism, see James O'Dell Jackson III, "The Origins of Pan-African Nationalism: Afro-American and Haytian Relations, 1800–1863" (Ph.D. diss., Northwestern University, 1976), 64–65.

76. Staudenraus, *Colonization Movement*, 84.

77. *Genius of Universal Emancipation*, June 1824.

78. Merton L. Dillon, *Benjamin Lundy and the Struggle for Negro Freedom* (Urbana: University of Illinois Press, 1966), 87–90.

79. Benjamin Lundy, *The Life, Travels, and Opinions of Benjamin Lundy, Including His Journeys to Texas and Mexico; With a Sketch of Contemporary Events, and a Notice of the Revolution in Hayti.* Compiled Under the Direction and on Behalf of His Children (1847; reprint, New York: Negro Universities Press, 1969), 23–24.

80. *Genius of Universal Emancipation*, October 1824.

81. *Genius of Universal Emancipation*, November 1824.

82. *Genius of Universal Emancipation*, April 1825.

83. Boyer's "Circular" in Dewey, *Correspondence*, 12; Haytien Emigration Society, *Information for the Free People of Colour Who Are Inclined to Emigrate to Hayti* (Philadelphia: H. Cunningham, 1825), 3, 7–11.

84. *Freedom's Journal*, 21 December 1827.

85. Miller, *Search for a Black Nationality*, 79–80.

86. *Genius of Universal Emancipation*, June 1824.

87. Baldwin to Abigail Field Mott, September 29, 1824 [incorrectly dated as 1834] in *Biographical Sketches and Interesting Anecdotes of Persons of Color. To Which is Added, a Selection of Pieces of Poetry*, 2nd ed. comp. Abigail Field Mott (New York: Mahlon Day, 1837), 215.

88. *Genius of Universal Emancipation*, January 1825.

89. *Genius of Universal Emancipation*, June 1825.

90. *Genius of Universal Emancipation*, August 1825.

91. Jackson, "Origins of Pan-African Nationalism," 57, 80.

92. *Genius of Universal Emancipation*, January 1825.

93. Baur, "Mulatto Machiavelli," 327; Miller, *Search for a Black Nationality*, 81.

94. *Genius of Universal Emancipation*, February 1825; June 1825; 3 December 1827. See also Lundy, *Life, Travels, and Opinions*, 23, 29.

95. *Genius of Universal Emancipation*, May, 1825. See also Baur, "Mulatto Machiavelli," 326–27; Miller, *Search for a Black Nationality*, 81; Dillon, *Benjamin Lundy*, 95; Geiss, *Pan-African Movement*, 86.

96. *Genius of Universal Emancipation*, November 1824.

97. *Genius of Universal Emancipation*, July 1825. One nineteenth-century commentator remarked that although "many respectable people" emigrated to Haiti during the 1820s, "many" of those who went there "were a perfect misfortune to themselves and the community which they had come to join." See M. B. Bird, *The Black Man; or, Haytian Independence. Deduced from Historical Notes, and Dedicated to the Government and People of Hayti* (1869; reprint, New York: Books for Libraries Press, 1971), 152.

98. Fisher, as reprinted in Mott, *Biographical Sketches*, 217.

99. *Genius of Universal Emancipation*, July 1825.

100. *Genius of Universal Emancipation*, April 1825.

101. *Genius of Universal Emancipation*, June 1825.

102. *New York Observer*, cited in *Genius of Universal Emancipation*, August 1825.

103. *Genius of Universal Emancipation*, 18 February 1826. On American commercial relations with Haiti during this period, see Michel-Rolph Trouillot, *Haiti: State Against Nation. The Origins and Legacy of Duvalierism* (New York: Monthly Review Press, 1990), 53.

104. *Genius of Universal Emancipation*, 25 February 1826. See also Lester D. Langley, *The Americas in the Age of Revolution, 1750–1850* (New Haven, Conn.: Yale University Press, 1996), 85.

105. Phelps, "Is the Transportation of Slaves to Hayti or to Africa Preferable?" Phelps Papers, Anti-Slavery Collection, Rare Book and Manuscript Room, Boston Public Library.

106. *National Intelligencer*, cited in *Genius of Universal Emancipation*, June 1825.

107. *Petersburg Intelligencer*, cited in *Genius of Universal Emancipation*, June 1825.

108. Writing after a visit to Haiti, Benjamin Lundy claimed that eight thousand African Americans had emigrated during the 1820s. Historian John Edward Baur claimed thirteen thousand African Americans emigrated to Haiti. See the *African Repository*, 5 (1829): 185; Baur, "Mulatto Machiavelli," 326. A handful of English-speaking descendants of those emigrants still reside on the Samaná Peninsular in the Dominican Republic. (Haiti occupied the Spanish part of the island from 1822 to 1824.) See James Cerutti, "The Dominican Republic: A Caribbean Comeback," *National Geographic*, 152 (1977): 538, 544–45; Harry Hoetink, " 'Americans' in Samaná," *Caribbean Studies*, 2 (1962): 3–22; E. Valerie Smith, "Early Afro-American Presence on the Island of Hispaniola: A Case Study of the 'Immigrants' of Samaná," *Journal of Negro History*, 72 (1987): 33–41.

109. Miller, *Search for a Black Nationality*, 81.

110. Benjamin S. Hunt, *Remarks on Hayti as a Place of Settlement for Afric-Americans and on the Mulatto as a Race for the Tropics* (Philadelphia: n.p., 1860), 11–12.

111. White, "Prince Saunders," 535.

112. Bird, *The Black Man*, 152–53; Boyer, cited in Baur, "Mulatto Machiavelli," 326.

113. Russwurm, "The Condition and Prospects of Haiti," in *The Voice of Black America: Major Speeches by Negroes in the United States, 1797–1973*, ed. Philip S. Foner, 2 vols. (New York: Capricorn Books, 1975), 1:43–45. See also William M. Brewar, "John B. Russwurm," *Journal of Negro History*, 13 (1928): 413–22; Bella Gross, "Freedom's Journal and the Rights of All," *Journal of Negro History*, 17 (1932): 241–86.

114. On Russwurm's plans to emigrate to Haiti, see Foner, *History of Black Americans: From the Emergence of the Cotton Kingdom to the Eve of the Compromise of 1850*, 227.

115. *Freedom's Journal*, 16 March 1827.

116. *Freedom's Journal*, 6 April 1827.

117. *Freedom's Journal*, 12 October 1827.

118. *Freedom's Journal*, 4 May 1827.

119. *The Rights of All*, 18 September 1829; 16 October 1829; 9 October 1829.

120. Walker, *Appeal*, 121.

121. Lundy, *Life, Travels, and Opinions*, 29, 232. See also Dillon, *Benjamin Lundy*, 100–101; *Genius of Universal Emancipation*, 2 September 1829.

122. *Minutes and Proceedings of the Second Annual Convention, for the Improvement of the Free People of Color, in these United States, Held by Adjournments in the*

City of Philadelphia, from the 4th to the 13th of June Inclusive, 1832 (Philadelphia: Martin and Boden, 1832), 8.

123. Howard H. Bell, *A Survey of the Negro Convention Movement, 1830–1861* (New York: Arno Press, 1969), 32.

124. Bell, *Survey of the Negro Convention Movement,* 12–13.

125. *Constitution of the American Society . . . 1830,* 10–11.

126. Robin Winks, *The Blacks in Canada: A History* (London: Yale University Press, 1971), 195–204; Jane H. Pease, and William H. Pease, *Black Utopia: Negro Communal Experiments in America* (Madison: State Historical Society of Wisconsin, 1963), 63–83.

127. *Minutes of the Proceedings of the Third Annual Convention, for the Improvement of the Free People of Colour in these United States, held by Adjournments in the City of Philadelphia, From the 3d to the 13th of June Inclusive, 1833* (New York: Published by Order of the Convention, 1833), 23.

128. William Hamilton, *Address to the Fourth Annual Convention of the Free People of Color of the United States. Delivered at the Opening of Their Session in the City of New York, June 2, 1834* (New York: S. W. Benedict, 1834), 5.

129. *Minutes and Proceedings of the First Annual Convention of the Free People of Colour, Held by Adjournments in the City of Philadelphia, From the Sixth to the Eleventh of June, Inclusive, 1831* (Philadelphia: Published by Order of the Committee of Arrangements, 1831), 5. See also Jane H. Pease and William H. Pease, *They Who Would Be Free: Blacks' Search for Freedom, 1830–1861* (New York: Atheneum, 1974), 27.

2

Rejecting America: Emigrationism Resurgent and the Beginnings of Black Nationalism, 1843–1854

In August 1843, after an eight-year hiatus, the African American leadership assembled in Buffalo, New York to consider their "moral and political conditions as American citizens." Passionately demanding emancipation and the rights of citizenship for black Americans, the ex-slave Henry Highland Garnet expressed support for radical political action. All too aware, however, that the political culture and institutions of the United States left little scope for black freedom and elevation, Garnet was not prepared to pin his hopes solely on political abolitionism. Instead, in rhetoric reminiscent of the Haitian revolutionaries, and referring specifically to Toussaint L'Ouverture, the best-known black hero of the Haitian rebellion, he demanded the slaves' right to overthrow the slaveocracy. It would be better, he insisted, for those in bondage to "*die freemen, than live to be slaves.*" Garnet's speech provoked a spirited debate, exposing the range of opinions within the black leadership. But although the delegates praised Garnet's "masterly effort," a slender majority, led by Frederick Douglass, concluded that Garnet's position was too militant, and decided against publication of his "Address."[1] In effect, where Douglass continued to rest his hopes in *evolutionary* change, as represented by the ideology of the American Revolution, Garnet had moved to an advocacy of *revolutionary* change, as exemplified by the Haitians' successful quest for independence and nationality.

Despite the defeat of Garnet's resolution, the events in Buffalo in 1843 portended a dramatic shift in sensibilities among the black leadership. During the next two decades, as increasing numbers of blacks rejected the notion that the United States was, as Frederick Douglass put it in 1849, "the abode of civiliza-

tion and religion," the activist stance articulated by Garnet would be manifested in a myriad of ways by many within the African American leadership.[2]
Frustrated by white abolitionists' failure to secure freedom for the slaves,
aware that racism was an American, rather than a southern problem, and
acutely concerned about the deepening sectional crisis that beset the United
States from the late 1840s, black Americans discussed how they could achieve
meaningful freedom. Although some blacks contemplated a violent revolution
against slavery, emigrationism proved the most contentious issue among African Americans.

The pre–Civil War decade witnessed the emergence of Martin Delany,
whose interest in emigration to Africa has been celebrated in the historiography of nineteenth-century black America. Yet, while Delany's interest in Africa
was of considerable significance, due attention must be given to the emerging
black interest in Caribbean—and particularly Haitian—emigrationism. This
entails an analysis of James Theodore Holly, whose devotion to Haiti was both
more consistent, and arguably more practicable, than Delany's advocacy of African emigrationism. In tracing Holly's emergence as a key figure in antebellum black activism during the early 1850s, this chapter identifies a number of
themes that he, and others, would apply to Haitian emigrationism at the end of
the decade. Accordingly, although Holly's emigrationist odyssey traversed a
number of potential sites during the 1850s, the underlying theme of a black
nationality—albeit one that reflected blacks' experiences in America—was
evident throughout. African American leaders did not concur on what black
nationality meant as an ideology, and they argued vigorously about what it implied in practical terms. But there was a sense of black nationality, and the halt-
ing—indeed, often hesitant—articulation of that ideology from the
mid-1840s through to the 1854 National Emigration Convention is a major
theme of this chapter. Moreover, as becomes clear here, although antebellum
black nationalism has most frequently been associated with emigrationists,
from the early 1850s proponents of the stay-and-fight doctrine were also influenced by the nationalist rhetoric that was very much a part of nineteenth-
century culture.

The growing black interest in emigration during the 1850s grew logically
from the events of the preceding decade. During the 1830s African Americans
had placed considerable faith in William Lloyd Garrison and other radical abolitionists who sought to use moral arguments to overthrow slavery. But despite
the Garrisonians' persistence, and notwithstanding their refusal to countenance compromise with what they regarded as the unregenerate evil of slavery,
by the end of the 1830s only the most optimistic abolitionists believed the
overthrow of slavery was imminent. African American leaders, moreover, were
increasingly reluctant to abide by the dictums of the Garrisonians, whose noble intentions and lofty rhetoric regarding the virtues of racial justice did not
always translate into equitable treatment of those black Americans with whom
they came into contact. For many African Americans, white Garrisonians seemed

more concerned with theoretical debates concerning the meaning of slavery and freedom than they were with the day-to-day manifestations of racism as it was experienced by many blacks.[3]

Equally revealing of white attitudes were the sentiments of Harriet Beecher Stowe, whose 1852 novel, *Uncle Tom's Cabin*, did so much to bring the evils of slavery into white America's popular consciousness. Yet, while Stowe's anti-slavery credentials were solid, her racial views troubled many African Americans. Indeed, by advocating African colonization, she appeared to endorse the views of the American Colonization Society (ACS). Admittedly, in declaring that the "desire and yearning of my soul is for an African *nationality*," George, the character in *Uncle Tom's Cabin* who favored colonization, did express black nationalist sentiments. Yet Stowe's apparent admiration for Liberia pleased few blacks, and she was certainly unimpressed by the Haitians' black nationality: When George contemplated where a Christian, civilized black na-tionality was most feasible, he answered his own question by stating "Not in Hayti; for in Hayti they had nothing to start with." Asserting that a "stream cannot rise above its fountain," he claimed that the "race that formed the char-acter of the Haytiens was a worn-out, effeminate one." Inevitably, he contin-ued, "the subject race will be centuries in rising to anything."[4] Stowe's qualms about the Haitian character—expressed in terms that implied masculine cre-dentials were essential for the establishment of an effective nationality—along with her support for Liberian colonization, typified the views of many white Americans. For growing numbers of African Americans, the significant point was that from the late 1840s, independent action, separate from whites, seemed increasingly necessary.

This trend among blacks toward separate action had been evident at the 1843 National Convention of Colored Citizens. Although the delegates at that gathering narrowly rejected Garnet's militant resolution, they did en-dorse the political abolitionism of the Liberty Party. In so doing, they effec-tively renounced the principles of Garrisonian moral suasionism. Four years later, at the next national convention of African Americans, sentiment had shifted to the point where the delegates voted in favor of publishing Garnet's address. Jane H. Pease and William H. Pease have described the antebellum black leadership as "leaders without followers," but the events of 1847 suggest that the delegates to the National Colored Convention were responding to their constituents' frustrations with the political institutions and culture of an-tebellum America.[5] The democratic impulse that saw the expansion of the franchise in the Jacksonian era had not touched black Americans. Indeed, alongside whites' continuing repulsion toward the notion of racial amalgama-tion, the 1830s and 1840s witnessed a diminution of blacks' already minimal democratic rights: by 1847, all but five states had disenfranchised African Americans. Further disillusionment for blacks came with the electoral failure of the antislavery Liberty Party. While the emergence of the Liberty Party dur-ing the early 1840s had offered some hopes to opponents of slavery, its electoral failures signified the limitations of political abolitionism, as well as the depth of racism among white Americans. The successor to the Liberty Party, the Free Soil Party, did embrace an antislavery stance of sorts, but its very questionable abolitionist credentials were paralleled by an enduring reluctance to support the notion of equal rights for African Americans. These frustrations, coupled with the violence to which African Americans were subjected in both free and slave states, suggested that a change in tactics was required.

It was in this context that black leaders pondered the emigration question. Although most free blacks focused their energies on seeking their elevation within the United States, a few had emigrated to Liberia during the 1830s and 1840s.[6] But some blacks expressed interest in emigration to alternative destinations. One such movement occurred at the end of the 1830s, when sugar planters in the British West Indies recruited a number of African Americans to the island of Trinidad, to replace the labor that had formerly been provided by black slaves. In the United States, there was some curiosity from within the black community about the possibilities of emigration to Trinidad. During 1839–1840 two delegations, one from Baltimore and the other from Annapolis, were sent to the island to investigate conditions and assess its suitability as a destination for African Americans contemplating emigration. But interest in emigration was also evident well to the north of the slave state of Maryland. Members of Boston's black community, including activists aligned to the fervently anti-colonizationist Garrisonian wing of the anti-slavery movement, were endorsing emigration to the Caribbean during 1840. Between 1839 and 1842 "several hundred" American blacks took advantage of the Trinidad Legislative Council's offer of guaranteed employment. Once in Trinidad, however, many emigrants were soon disillusioned. Coming from a predominantly urban background, and unaccustomed to laboring in the cane fields, a number of the emigrants sought urban employment in Trinidad. Others returned to the United States, with vivid reports of broken promises and mistreatment at the hands of the planters. These emigrants, and opponents of the scheme, charged that the planters in Trinidad had been motivated not by an altruistic desire to assist black people, but by a determination to replace the labor they had lost following the end of slavery in the British Empire. This was not an entirely unfounded charge.[7] Nonetheless, although African American emigration to Trinidad ended in failure, it did suggest that emigration schemes to Caribbean destinations continued to have a certain appeal among black Americans.

Complementing that interest, from the mid-1840s, there was an increasing recognition among African American leaders that the struggle against racism transcended national boundaries. Again, the British West Indies proved to be the basis of an embryonic trans-national racial consciousness that became a significant influence on the African American leadership during the 1850s. One portent of this awareness was the willingness of the delegates to the 1847 National Convention of Colored Citizens to consider a proposal from a committee of Jamaican blacks for a commercial enterprise involving blacks in the

United States, Jamaica, and Africa. Arguing that "the relation existing between" black Jamaicans and their "brethren in North America" was one of "mutual sympathy and co-operation in all that pertains to the general welfare of the race," the authors of the proposal emphasized the value of "commercial enterprise." Agreeing that the fate of blacks in one region was related to the position of blacks elsewhere, the delegates accepted the Jamaicans' call for the establishment of a Jamaica Hamic Association. This organization, designed "to effect a correspondence with" the Jamaicans' "brethren in America, and friends throughout the world," was an early expression of economic pan-Africanism. Without abandoning the stay-and-fight doctrine, the delegates at Troy gave the Jamaicans' proposal a sympathetic hearing. Referring to the "advancement of our common cause," the participants at the 1847 meeting agreed that "a more intimate acquaintance with" their "brethren in those islands will be of mutual benefit and advantage."[8]

Another sign of shifting sentiment within black America concerned their attitude toward Africa. To be sure, most African Americans' opinion of the ACS did not undergo significant revision during the pre–Civil War period, and notwithstanding some blacks' depiction of Africa as their "rightful inheritance," Liberia's status improved only marginally. Liberia's July 1847 proclamation of independence, stemming partly from the desire of the ACS to divest itself of the burden of managing the colony, and reflecting the exigencies of international trade, rather than a heartfelt desire for independence on the part of the Liberians, drew only minor interest from black America.[9] Nonetheless, distinguishing what they considered the racist and proslavery motives of white colonizationists in the United States from the laudable achievement of political independence for the former ACS colony, the measured changes in the ways African Americans regarded Liberia were contemporaneous with other, more assertive statements in favor of emigration: Some black Americans were even willing to contemplate the virtues of settlement in Liberia. In January 1849, Henry Highland Garnet publicly recognized emigration as a legitimate "source of wealth and power" for African Americans. Writing to Frederick Douglass' *North Star*, he argued: "Emigration is often the source of wealth, prosperity, and independence. . . . I hesitate not to say, that my mind of late, has greatly changed in regard to the American Colonization scheme. So far as it benefits the land of my fathers, I bid it Godspeed, but so far as it denies the possibilities of our elevation, I oppose it. I would rather see a man free in Liberia than a slave in the United States." At the heart of Garnet's cautious advocacy of emigration was a conviction that Liberia "will be highly beneficial to Africa in a commercial and political point."[10] Garnet's late 1840s views on African emigration were iconoclastic, but in linking economics and politics he presaged the imperatives underpinning much of the black emigrationism of the following decade. By March 1849, Garnet was arguing that emigration was a feasible alternative for those African Americans who considered advancement in the United States to be an impossible objective.[11]

Significant though these late 1840s trends were, the unsuccessful resolution of the issues arising out of America's westward expansion held even more troubling portents for black Americans. The Mexican War of 1846–1848, widely regarded by African Americans and abolitionists as evidence of the growing power and influence of the slavepower, exposed large tracts of land in the west to white expansion. With the forces of slavery and freedom vying for ascendancy in the west, the nation's political leaders sought a political solution to the conflict that had its origins deep in the nation's culture and economic system. To the chagrin of black Americans, the centerpiece of the ultimately unsuccessful Compromise of 1850 was a new Fugitive Slave Act, designed to replace a 1793 bill of the same name. Intended to enable slaveowners to more easily reclaim their property in human flesh, this new legislation provoked outrage among African Americans, who condemned it as "the most cruel, unconstitutional and scandalous outrage of modern times."[12]

The Fugitive Slave Act added new urgency to the emigration question. This interest extended beyond the black elite. As Granville B. Blanks, a free black resident of Michigan stated, the new law "aroused my mind and excited in me a purpose to examine for myself what would be the probable future history of my people." Writing in 1852, Blanks had concluded that "our present Constitution," and the "prejudices" that were so deeply entrenched in the nation's culture, made "it is impracticable, if not impossible, for the whites and blacks to live together, and upon terms of social and civil equality."[13] Although Blanks's doubts regarding the possibilities of black and white Americans co-existing together sounded very much like the views of many white colonizationists, the growing pessimism among African Americans, in conjunction with the very real fear that ex-slaves who had long found sanctuary in the North would be hunted down and returned to their former owners, prompted many blacks to examine emigrationism afresh.

Following the passage of the Fugitive Slave legislation in September 1850, thousands of black Americans fled across the border into Canada. For many blacks, Canada was nothing more than a refuge from the slaveocracy; for others, however, Canada became a potential site for a large-scale and permanent migration of African Americans. Prominent advocates of Canadian emigration during the 1850s included Henry Bibb, Mary Ann Shadd, and James Theodore Holly. Canada, of course, was a long way from Haiti, and of the major proponents of Canadian emigrationism during the early 1850s, only Holly became a prominent advocate of African American emigration to the Caribbean. Nonetheless, in articulating an ideology of Canadian emigrationism, Holly and others not only foreshadowed some of the racial, economic, and political themes that would be expressed most forcefully when Haitian emigrationism reached its zenith on the eve of the Civil War; they also encountered many of the difficulties that would plague emigrationists of all persuasions for the duration of the 1850s. Perhaps most significant, during the early 1850s Holly, Bibb, and others, explicitly acknowledged the connections between the African American struggle for freedom and equality in continental North America, and the status of blacks in the Caribbean and Latin America.

Henry Bibb was the best known proponent of Canadian emigrationism during the early 1850s. Born into slavery in Kentucky in 1815, Bibb eventually escaped to the North in 1842, where he soon became active in the antislavery cause. After dabbling with the Liberty Party during the 1840s, Bibb's advocacy of emigrationism during the 1850s was based on earlier expressions of support for separate black institutions. As one of the composers of the 1848 Address to the Colored People of the United States, Bibb had endorsed the ideal of integration. Significantly, however, he had also accepted the "institutions of a complexional character" might be necessary for a number of years, in order to attain the "very idea of human brotherhood."[14] Bibb's subsequent turn to emigrationism, like that of other prominent African Americans, was in part an extension of this earlier endorsement of racially distinct organizations.

In 1850, along with a number of other African Americans alarmed by the Fugitive Slave Act, Bibb fled to Canada West, where he and his wife settled in the town of Chatham.[15] Assuming an important role among blacks in the region, Bibb not only worked to assist those African Americans who had settled there, but also encouraged others to emigrate to the area. As founder and editor of the *Voice of the Fugitive*, Bibb was able to articulate his emigrationist vision. In the process, he reiterated themes that had long interested black leaders, and presaged elements of the emigrationist ideology that would reach its apogee with the Haitian movement of the 1850s and early 1860s. Stressing the value of self sufficiency, Bibb insisted that blacks had to become "owners and tillers of the soil on which they live." The key to racial advancement, he emphasized, was for blacks to "produce what they consume."[16] Seeking to convince black Americans of the value of the principles he espoused, and praising the virtues of Canada as a destination for African American emigrants, Bibb called a North American Convention of Colored People. When the convention began in Toronto in September 1851, a number of prominent black leaders were present, including Martin Delany, about whom more is said later in this chapter. One notable absentee from the meeting—unable to attend because he lacked the necessary funds to make the journey to Toronto—was James Theodore Holly, an increasingly well-known figure within the black community in Canada.[17]

Born in 1829, James T. Holly became an important figure in the free black community during the decade preceding the Civil War. Praised by William Wells Brown as having "brought himself up to a point of culture not often attained by men even in the higher walks of life," Holly's willingness to translate his emigrationist ideology into personal action set him apart from Martin Delany, and other advocates of African American migration.[18] Descended from three generations of free blacks, Holly spent the first fifteen years of his life in Washington, D.C., where he and his elder brother Joseph followed the trade of their father in becoming shoemakers.[19] In Washington, James was fortunate to attend school, under the guidance of John M. Fleet, an African American doctor. In 1844, Holly's family moved to Brooklyn, New York, in part to avoid the problems caused by prejudice in the South. In New York, James' education continued under the guidance of the Reverend Felix Varella, a Spanish Catholic priest, who gave Holly his first Bible. Like his elder brother, who by 1848 was an active participant in the abolitionist movement, and a contributor to the *North Star,* James became interested in ameliorating the condition of the black race. New York City, with its impressive array of black social and cultural institutions, was conducive to both Hollys' interest in their race. For James Holly, good fortune came in the guise of Lewis Tappan, a wealthy white abolitionist. Impressed with Holly's scholarly instincts, Tappan offered him a clerkship with the American Missionary Association. From that position, Holly gained useful experience and valuable contacts among abolitionists and missionaries.[20]

After the death of Holly's father in 1850, the family moved to Burlington, Vermont. At this point Joseph and James Holly's reformist ideologies diverged. In early 1850, Joseph Holly wrote an open letter to Henry Clay, president of the ACS. This letter, published by Frederick Douglass in the *North Star*, was a bitter denunciation of white colonizationists. "We are here, and here we remain," he asserted, "we can't be coaxed, cheated, hissed, or kicked out of our country."[21] While Joseph Holly was prepared to work within the traditional stay-and-fight philosophy, James was not; by mid-1850 he was corresponding with William McLain, secretary of the ACS. Enthusiastic about Liberia's future, Holly expressed interest in emigrating to the African colony. But his proposal for his own emigration was formulated under a carefully conceived plan for his own personal advancement. Possibly influenced by his former schoolmaster, Dr. Fleet (whose education had been financially supported by the ACS), Holly sought the assistance of the ACS in pursuing medical studies. Specifically, he aspired to become a hydropathic practitioner in Liberia. Confident that attitudes toward Liberia would change, Holly emphasized to McLain that he was motivated by a sense of duty to his race.[22] Underlying Holly's public altruism and optimism, however, there was almost certainly private frustration and pessimism. He knew all too well the precarious and marginal nature of the freedom enjoyed by "free" blacks in the United States. Considering, too, the declining value attached to his own trade of a shoemaker in the industrializing economy of antebellum America, it is perhaps not surprising that an intelligent, educated person such as Holly would contemplate emigration.

The ACS, however, would not support Holly's proposal. Instead, informing Holly that Liberia's most pressing need was for teachers, McLain inquired whether the young man would emigrate in that capacity. Holly replied that he was interested in teaching in Liberia, and would continue his studies with that end in mind. But, noting that he would be happy to work as a shoemaker in Liberia "if the hereditary predisposition of my constitution to consumption and general debility did not admonish me that I must soon quit the seat, as a necessary precaution to preserve my health," he also signified the limits of his commitment to the Liberian venture.[23] As a later chapter reveals, Holly's quite understandable concern for his own physical well-being contrasted with his subsequent assertions concerning the need for a spirit of self-sacrifice—and a willingness to endure the most extreme physical hardship—among the African American populace.

In September 1850, Holly again wrote to McLain, expressing the wish that he could devote his time fully to his studies, but stating that his circumstances precluded him from so doing.[24] Although Holly did not hear from the ACS secretary again, his interest in emigration did not abate. His attention now turned northward. In May 1851, Holly wrote to Henry Bibb, urging blacks in Canada to establish a refuge for fugitive slaves. But Holly viewed Canada as potentially much more than a refuge for individual blacks fleeing the terrors of the Fugitive Slave Act. African American emigration to Canada could play a part in a grander scheme on behalf of the black race. Let "the moral, pecuniary, and if needs be the physical means of an extended and powerful influence," he wrote, "be concentrated to crush the infernal institution of American slavery."[25] In this way, emigration was conceived as one part of the antislavery struggle. At the heart of this philosophy was a conviction that a foreign power could play a part in the fight for emancipation. These proved to be recurrent themes among black emigrationists and nationalists during the 1850s and early 1860s.

Holly continued to press for the settlement of refugees in Canada, always careful to distinguish between emigration to that region, and to the other locations where it was suggested African Americans might relocate. He confronted a number of arguments against emigration to Canada. One criticism was that blacks could not thrive in a temperate climate. Rejecting that theory—which could easily be construed by defenders of slavery to argue that blacks were suited to slave labor in tropical climates—he stated that any race could adapt to a particular climate.[26] Alongside these essentially environmental arguments, Holly confronted the claim that emigrants to Canada would be abandoning the struggle for freedom in the United States. Endorsing Bibb's calls, Holly declared African Americans "should vigorously support this project [for emigration], and swarm in a ceaseless tide to Canada West," where they could "hang like an ominous black cloud over this guilty nation."[27] Holly thus believed that Canada's proximity to the United States was of no small significance. Abolitionists, black and white, had long spoken of free blacks being in a state of psychological bondage that precluded them from achieving meaningful freedom as long as millions of African Americans were enslaved. These abolitionists believed that to be of assistance in the fight against slavery, it was important for free blacks to remain as physically close to the slaves as safety permitted. Here, the legacy of the ACS continued to influence black thought and actions. For many black Americans, the notion that colonization in Africa was tantamount to an abandonment of the anti-slavery struggle remained a com-

pelling argument against the ACS. Accordingly, although a majority of abolitionists continued to advocate the stay-and-fight philosophy during the
1850s, the widely shared belief in the importance of proximity played a part in
shaping the emigrationists' outlook. African Americans who advocated emigration to Canada, or to the Caribbean, distinguished between their schemes,
where, they believed, emigrants would still be close enough to the United
States to play a role in the anti-slavery struggle, and plans for African emigration or colonization, where participants would be physically—and psychologically—far removed from the abolitionist battleground.

From the early 1850s, James Holly conceived these issues in unambiguously political terms. Many of the problems confronting African Americans, he
insisted, resulted from the fact that they were in "individual isolation" that
caused them to remain in a "state of anarchy." Although black emigrationists
were imbued with the ethos of individualism that was so dominant in antebellum America, Holly's statement implied that the individualism they espoused
was paralleled by a sense of collectivity—both as a means of mutual racial support, and as a means of promoting their goals. To surmount the long-
lamented absence of a collective political consciousness among African Americans, Holly proposed the establishment of a "center of unity," around which
the efforts of all blacks on, or near the American continent should revolve. In
1851, Holly favored Canada as the location for this political center. His rationale for favoring Canada attested to one of the major difficulties confronting African Americans. Explaining that if the proposed organization was situated in
the United States, it would be rendered ineffectual due to the rivalry between
various leadership factions, Holly hoped that a body centered in Canada would
be able to transcend such differences.[28]

Despite Holly's absence from the 1851 convention in Toronto, his influence was felt at the gathering because his call for the formation of a "North
American League"—comprising the black populations of Canada and the
United States—was presented by another delegate, John Fisher. Holly's proposal for the North American League was an important stage in the evolution
of antebellum black nationalist ideology. Holly envisaged several objectives for
the North American League. Besides establishing a comfortable asylum for
refugees from slavery, and encouraging the emigration of free blacks from the
United States to Canada, he hoped the League would assist emigrants to establish themselves as cultivators of the soil. The convention approved Holly's
proposal, and—perhaps reflecting the presence of William W. Anderson, sent
to North America by the Jamaican House of Assembly to assess whether African Americans could be enticed to settle on the island—resolved that the proposed union should also include the British West Indies. Adding detail to
Holly's calls to encourage emigrants to become landowning cultivators of the
soil, the delegates proposed that one component of the League should be a
North American and West Indian Federal Agricultural Union, which could
play a part in the destruction of slavery. It was anticipated that this cooperative

venture would encourage free blacks to become landowners, who could produce crops such as cotton, sugar, and corn—all staples of the southern economy—at more competitive prices than those produced in the southern regions of the United States.[29]

Although discussion about the proposed North American League continued for several months, nothing tangible materialized from the plans. This proved to be a typical pattern of emigrationism during the ensuing decade. Nevertheless, the ideas and aspirations behind plans such as the North American League were of enduring significance. They point to increasing doubts, at least on the part of the African American leadership, concerning the efficacy of the stay-and-fight philosophy. Implicit in the discussion about the North American League was an understanding that the fate of blacks in one region was related to the fate of blacks in other areas—a theme that would arise again during the 1850s, and beyond. Meanwhile, the continued exodus of several thousand African Americans to Canada in the wake of the Fugitive Slave Act testified to a general feeling of dissatisfaction and fear on the part of the black populace in the United States.

Following the 1851 convention in Toronto, Henry Bibb continued to advocate emigration to Canada. But from the early 1850s, Bibb's vision of black commercial nationalism extended beyond continental North America; he also recognized the potential of regions to the south of the United States. Like Holly, Bibb linked the fortunes of blacks in the United States and Canada to the fate and status of black people in the Caribbean. Declaring that blacks in the British West Indies could participate in an economic war against slavery, he argued that Jamaica's role would be crucial: not only was it geographically close to the United States, but—apparently unlike Canada—its principal crops could be brought into direct competition with the mainstays of the southern slave economy.[30] As later chapters explain, these matters of proximity and commercial potential were subsequently applied to arguments in favor of Haitian emigrationism. In the wake of America's market revolution, the notion of using commerce to undermine slavery rested on a quintessentially American faith in the power of the market.[31]

The influence of the market ethos on black emigrationists was also evident in another, more collective way. In October 1851, the committee appointed by the Toronto convention issued a report that included specific recommendations concerning the precise form that an agricultural union should take, and the means by which it should operate. The committee suggested that capital should be raised by "selling shares" in the union for fifty dollars, to be paid for in "ten annual installments." The money thus raised would be used to acquire tracts of land in Canada and Jamaica, and to buy the agricultural tools required to work those lands—which would then be sold to African American emigrants.[32] This proposal resembled schemes organized to facilitate the movement of white Americans to the western regions of the United States.

Plans for continental unity among blacks amounted to little in practice. Appointed in April 1852 as a "travelling agent" and "corresponding editor" for the *Voice of the Fugitive*, Holly embarked on a tour of five northeastern states to promote black emigration to Canada, and enlist subscribers to the newspaper.[33] With Bibb continuing to bring Holly more closely into the organization that was emerging in Canada, Holly and his wife arrived in Windsor, a small town just over the Canadian border, in June 1852. At this point, Holly assumed the positions of assistant editor and proprietor of the *Voice of the Fugitive*. Soon after, when Bibb left on a lecture tour, the twenty-two-year-old Holly took full charge of the newspaper. Although this was a significant opportunity for the young man, he found himself increasingly embroiled in a controversy surrounding the Refugee Home Society, an organization seeking to promote land ownership among blacks in Canada.[34]

The dispute over the Refugee Home Society was one expression of a much wider debate among African Americans—emigrationists and nonemigrationists alike—concerning blacks' acceptance of assistance from whites. On one level, the differences surrounding the Refugee Home Society overshadowed an underlying consensus regarding the importance of blacks taking matters into their own hands to advance their cause. Each of the protagonists in the dispute over the Refugee Home Society, moreover, shared a conviction that Canada offered the best prospects for black freedom. Nevertheless, the controversy over the Refugee Home Society highlighted substantial differences regarding black leaders' competing visions for the elevation of their race. A major participant in this debate was Mary Ann Shadd, an energetic advocate of Canadian emigrationism, and one of the best known black women activists of the antebellum period.[35] Shadd vigorously asserted the importance of black self-reliance, independent of any assistance—or interference—from whites. Insisting that black people should help themselves, she objected to the Refugee Home Society because it was dependent on white philanthropy. Paradoxically, it was necessary for individuals such as Holly and Bibb, who most loudly proclaimed the necessity of blacks becoming independent landowners, to accept white philanthropy to achieve that goal. Indeed, Holly's brand of separatism, with its embryonic thread of black nationalism, seemingly left room to accept aid from whites to accomplish those objectives. This was not the last time Holly would demonstrate a willingness to accept help from white people, an apparent contradiction in his thinking that his opponents were always willing to exploit. But the arguments of Holly's opponents were equally contradictory. Shadd, who—ostensibly at least—was more immediately concerned with the integration of blacks into white society, was opposed to the acceptance of aid from whites. Shadd, and those of her ilk, charged that organizations such as the Refugee Home Society fostered segregation of whites and blacks. It would be better, Shadd believed, if blacks sought to live as equals among whites, thereby demonstrating that fears and prejudices surrounding the results of racial integration were unfounded.[36] Each of these issues would be played out again, with much greater passion and urgency, when Haitian emigrationism became a reality at the end of the 1850s.

Meanwhile, the debate over emigration raged in Canada. Early in 1853, Samuel Ringgold Ward, who shared Shadd's skepticism of the Refugee Home Society, called a conference of blacks in Canada. After that meeting was held in April 1853, Holly and Bibb responded by calling a convention of their own. This gathering took place in Amherstburg, Canada West, in June 1853. Condemning Ward's conference for not being sufficiently "nationalistic," Holly and Bibb sought to rejuvenate interest in the principles that had been enunciated at the 1851 meeting. Starting from the premise that African Americans would benefit from a successful emigration program, they stressed the importance of cooperation between blacks in North America and the British West Indies. By lauding the potential impact of black commercial enterprises, the ideology of the marketplace was again evident.[37]

Holly assumed a central role at the Amherstburg convention, acting as secretary and chair of the Committee on Emigration. From that position he articulated his activist vision. Pointing to the inequalities confronting African Americans, the Report on Emigration submitted to the convention by Holly's committee suggested two possible courses of action. One option was a black revolution. Although this was described as "the boldest and probably the most glorious alternative," it was recognized that an African American revolution stood little chance of success; not only would the weight of numbers work to the favor of white Americans, but blacks were denied the means of communication essential for the orchestration of a successful revolt. Black leaders, ever mindful of the failure of Nat Turner's notorious 1831 uprising in Virginia, and of whites' vengeful reaction to that crisis, were perhaps also reticent to support revolutionary calls lest they be seen to be advocating a social conflagration such as that which had so devastated Haiti during the late eighteenth and early nineteenth centuries. According to the authors of the Report on Emigration, moreover, African Americans lacked the advantages of the curiously phrased "civilized warfare." Nevertheless, the report did state, in terms strikingly similar to those used by Henry Highland Garnet in 1843, that if those conditions were available to blacks, it would be valuable to strike against slavery, and leave the consequences to God. It would be better, they asserted, to be "dead freemen than living slaves."[38]

Concluding that an African American revolution was not viable, Holly and his fellow members of the Committee on Emigration urged blacks to direct their attentions to the more feasible alternative of emigration. As they emphasized, emigration was "emphatically one of the most important subjects that can engage the attention of an oppressed and denationalized people." Furthermore, they asserted that it was only through emigration that free blacks could improve their own condition, while at the same time work toward the abolition of slavery. Included in the Report on Emigration was an analysis of the advantages of the different regions in which emigrants could settle. Although Canada was favored as the most suitable site for a large-scale African American emigration, and although the committee noted there were some possibilities for emigration to Central America, the authors of the Report on Emigration gave favorable consideration to Haitian emigrationism. Here we find the first manifestations of James Holly's interest in the island republic. Not only was Haiti "wholly in the hands" of blacks, but it formed "the grandest centre of attractions for" the black "race wheresoever scattered around the globe." Arguing in favor of a large-scale migration to the island republic, Holly and the other members of the committee claimed that such a movement would protect the government there against the intervention of "any or all powers whatsoever"—including the slavepower—and would also "forward in an incalculable degree" the cause of black elevation in the United States. For the delegates at Amherstburg, black Americans had an obligation to Haiti: "Every coloured man," they declared, "should feel binding upon himself the duty to sustain the national existence of Hayti, intact against the intervention of any or all powers whatsoever, and should pursue a policy to that end."³⁹ African Americans were thus expressing a nascent sense of racial solidarity based around the survival of the first example of black nationhood. Black American emigration to Haiti, moreover, was being presented as a barrier to the expansionist aspirations of the southern slavepower. Both of these themes were central to Haitian emigrationism during the next decade.

The authors of the Report on Emigration confined their analysis to a discussion of sites on, or near the American continent. There were two reasons for that policy; one of which was spelled out publicly, while the other was implicit. Accepting that it was only by remaining physically close to the United States that emigrants could be of any assistance to the slaves and free blacks, the committee's report noted "we regard all measures calculated for our elevation, in order to be immediately practicable, must be strictly confined to a continental policy." Second, the specter of white colonization affected this desire to remain geographically close to the United States: Lurking behind support for continental emigration was a well-founded concern that an acceptance of emigration to Africa could be construed as an endorsement of the ACS, to which the delegates registered their opposition. The delegates at Amherstburg did acknowledge that the elevation of Africa was a worthy objective, but stressed that slavery in the United States was a much more urgent concern.⁴⁰

James Holly's emergent interest in Haiti stemmed in part from growing doubts concerning black emigration to Canada. Although he continued to regard the Refugee Home Society as a "highly useful and philanthropic organization," Holly wearied of the factional discord within the black leadership in Canada. Increasingly, too, he was aware of the prejudice that existed against blacks in Canada.⁴¹ In any case, Holly's position with the *Voice of Fugitive* terminated in late 1853, when Bibb was forced to close his paper. Early the following year, Holly returned to the United States, where he became principal of the black school in Buffalo, New York. Although Holly's interest in emigrationism did not recede, during the mid-1850s the chief advocate of black emigrationism from the United States was another man—Martin Robison Delany.

Delany's life and career are relatively well known, and the story of emigrationism to Africa has been analyzed in considerable detail elsewhere.[42] Nonetheless, some explanation of those subjects is required here, because the subsequent interest in Haitian emigrationism evolved partly from the failure of Delany's African alternative. Delany's background can be traced briefly. Born in Charleston, Virginia, in 1812, the son of a free mother and a slave father, in 1822 Delany fled north with his family to Pennsylvania. Interested from a young age in efforts to achieve black elevation, and influenced by the Reverend Lewis Woodson—described by historian Floyd Miller as a "father of black nationalism"—Delany's early efforts on behalf of his race were very much in the mainstream of abolitionist activity. During the 1830s, he supported efforts at black self-elevation, and served as an officer in the American Moral Reform Society. From 1843 through 1847, as editor and publisher of the *Mystery*, Delany continued to encourage African American self-reliance. In late 1847, he joined Frederick Douglass as corresponding editor of the *North Star.* By 1849, however, substantial divisions had emerged between Delany and Douglass. Notwithstanding these "increasingly marked" differences "between the positions of the two leaders on matters pertaining to the Afro-American community," and despite disputes over tactics and goals, Delany's split with Douglass also reflected personal rivalries.[43] After resigning from the *North Star* in June 1849, Delany returned to Pittsburgh, where he hoped to complete the medical studies he had commenced in the 1830s. Although he eventually succeeded in gaining admission to Harvard Medical School, Delany was allowed to complete just one term of the course before being expelled—for many students and staff at Harvard, the admission of Delany was an affront to the prevailing racial hierarchy.[44] Occurring at the same time as the nation was dividing over the Fugitive Slave Act, Delany's expulsion from Harvard reinforced his disillusionment with white America. For the next decade, that disillusionment led Delany to give serious, if inconsistent, consideration to African American emigrationism.

Of the antebellum African American leaders who have achieved significant acknowledgment beyond academic circles, Delany was the only one who could be regarded as an emigrationist. He has been acclaimed as "the first major Negro nationalist," and his 1852 work, *The Condition, Elevation, Emigration, and Destiny of the Colored People of the United States,* has been celebrated as the first major statement of black nationalist philosophy in the United States.[45] Yet Delany's brand of emigrationism was as pragmatic as that of his contemporaries, and the black nationalism he espoused demonstrated that he too was imbued with many of the values of the dominant culture of the country whose racism he so despised. Nothing more clearly demonstrates the fluidity of his attitudes than *The Condition, Elevation, Emigration, and Destiny of the Colored People of the United States.* Like other black leaders, Delany accepted principles that were well established in American culture. Predicating his proposals on the notion that African Americans' elevation "must be the result of *self-efforts*," and the work of their "*own hands*," Delany proposed that black advancement was contingent upon self-help, rather than the largesse of white Americans.[46]

Although these principles were well established within the black community and culture, Delany's work betrayed confusion and inconsistencies. This confusion attests to the ambiguities and contradictions within the black nationalism of mid-nineteenth-century America, ambiguities and contradictions that in turn reflected the hardships facing African Americans. Delany used *The Condition, Elevation, Emigration, and Destiny of the Colored People* to register his opposition to the ACS, condemning the organization on the grounds that it originated from the slaveholders' desire to "exterminate" the free blacks of the American continent. Not content to merely condemn the motives of the white colonizationists, Delany also criticized the ACS colony of Liberia: as well as its "unsuitable" location, its state of "pitiful" dependency on the ACS meant it fell far short of the model of an independent nation that was required to demonstrate blacks' capabilities. Delany saw some advantages in emigration to Canada, particularly as a refuge for fugitive slaves, but he believed that at some time it would be annexed by the United States. The regions favored by Delany in the text of *The Condition, Elevation, Emigration, and Destiny* were Central and South America, and the West Indies. Extolling Central and South America as "the ultimate destination and future home" of the black race on the American continent, he referred to the suitable climate, and the rich natural resources in those regions. Pointing out that whites constituted just one seventh of the population in those areas, he stressed that blacks did not suffer discrimination on account of their color.[47]

All of this amounted to a reasoned, thorough rejection of Liberia and advocacy of emigration within the Americas. Yet in an appendix to the same book, and contradicting his argument that stressed the need for blacks to remain close to the United States, Delany called for an expedition to eastern Africa, for the purpose of locating a suitable site for African American emigrants to settle.[48] Eastern Africa was a distant destination for African American emigrants, but it had the advantage of being a long way from Liberia, which was situated on the western side of the continent. No doubt Delany hoped to dissociate his proposal from the ACS scheme. In any case, the significant point is that in 1852 Delany's advocacy of emigration was both tentative and confused. This is not to censure Delany: The circumstances in which the African American leadership operated during the 1850s made consistency difficult. Black leaders could easily enunciate the broad goal of meaningful freedom for their race, but agreement on how that objective could be achieved, and indeed what that phrase should mean in practice, were understandably elusive. In essence, this was a manifestation of the persistent tension between means and ends that had long characterized abolitionism, and other antebellum movements for social reform.

The divisions among African American and abolitionist leaders were evident in their ambivalent responses to *The Condition, Elevation, Emigration, and Destiny*. Abolitionist Oliver Johnson, reviewing Delany's tract in the *Pennsylvania Freeman*, repudiated emigrationism, and criticized Delany for his suspicious attitude toward whites.[49] Although the *Liberator* gave a "friendly report," William Lloyd Garrison did express opposition to the separatist strain in Delany's thinking. For Garrison, like many other abolitionists, black proposals for emigration were in practice indistinguishable from white-sponsored schemes for black colonization.[50] While Henry Bibb was happy to quote Delany's preference for emigration to Canada West as a North American destination for American blacks contemplating emigration, he did use the columns of the *Voice of the Fugitive* to criticize what he regarded as Delany's overstated praise for free blacks vis-à-vis slaves.[51] Perhaps the most notable criticism came from Delany's erstwhile colleague, Frederick Douglass, who refused even to comment on the work. By the early 1850s, although Douglass had moved significantly beyond the moral suasionism of Garrisonian abolitionists, he remained committed to the stay-and-fight ideology. In part, the differences between Douglass and Delany were personal, as Delany's criticism of the "unjustifiable . . . cold and deathly silence" that Douglass "heaped" on the work implied. Delany was convinced that other critics were similarly motivated by personal rivalries. The real objective of the editors of the *Pennsylvania Freeman*, he argued, was "to disparage me, and endeavor to injure the sale of my book."[52]

Notwithstanding the personal aspect of the feuds within the black leadership, and despite the fact that individual black leaders moved back and forth between the emigrationist and stay-and-fight doctrines, there were significant differences between emigrationists and those who favored the stay-and-fight philosophy. Increasingly, these differences reflected tensions over the black nationalist response to the racism of white America. It was of course true that the turn to emigrationism, and the black nationalism with which emigrationism was often associated, reflected white America's refusal to grant equality to blacks. Responding to William L. Garrison's review of *The Condition, Elevation, Emigration, and Destiny*, Delany referred to this reluctant emigrationism, as well as his refusal to be bound to the traditional stay-and-fight ideology:

I am not in favor of caste, nor a separation of the brotherhood of mankind, and would as willingly live among white men as black, if I had an equal possession and enjoyment of privileges; but shall never be reconciled to live among them, subservient to their will—existing by mere sufferance as we, the colored people do, in this country.[53]

Delany, like other emigrationists, was convinced that the freedom enjoyed by blacks in the North was only marginally better than slavery—like slaves, free blacks were subservient to the whim of white Americans.

During mid-1852, Delany questioned Douglass on the lack of comment on his book in *Frederick Douglass' Paper.* Reiterating that African Americans needed to act separately of whites, Delany argued that blacks had to have a "position independently of anything pertaining to white men as nations."[54] Clearly, Delany was moving toward a more assertive emigrationist stance. But he did so only after efforts at self elevation in the United States had failed. Although Theodore Draper's argument that Delany's nationalism "was based more on unrequited love, on rejection by the whites, than on a self-sustaining independent need for separate national existence" is helpful, it does not completely explain the shift to emigrationism.[55] Considering the way in which personal rivalry permeated the African American leadership, it is fair to say that Delany's turn away from the stay-and-fight ideology also was based on unrequited love from blacks.

Delany was not the only African American leader invoking the notion of a black nationality during the early and mid-1850s. In fact, the notion of "nationality" was also evident among those who preferred to stay and fight for black rights within the United States. In May 1853, advocates of the stay-and-fight doctrine formally issued a "Call" in *Frederick Douglass' Paper* for a convention of African Americans. Howard Bell has described the 1853 convention as "without doubt, the most outstanding assemblage of the entire era."[56] Its real significance, however, lies not in the stature of those present, but in their interest in the theme of a black nationality. As the resolutions passed at the convention indicate, opposition to emigration did not preclude an individual from also embracing elements of black nationalism—a concept that embraced a variety of meanings. Indeed, the very amorphousness of the term "black nationalism" not only signified the breadth of the racism endured by the black communities in the United States, but was also a point of contention among black leaders. In turn, these contested meanings of "nationality" and "nationalism" were aspects of wider nineteenth-century debates concerning political and cultural constructions of the "nation."

For some African Americans, a concern for the collective well-being of their race within the United States translated readily into a form of incipient black nationalism. On this level, black nationalism could refer to the need for unity among blacks within the United States. Premised on the need for meaningful, rather than merely rhetorical cooperation among African Americans, this interpretation of nationality was reflected in the language used by the delegates to the 1853 Colored National Convention. The call for the formation of a national council, intended to coordinate and supervise African Americans' efforts to achieve meaningful freedom, betrayed an acceptance of the need for national efforts. Although calls for cooperation among African Americans were not tantamount to an advocacy of emigration, the stay-and-fight and emigrationist ideologies rested on the common assumption that the fate of blacks in different places was linked—and that formal collaboration was a prerequisite of racial advancement. This perception was expressed explicitly at the

1853 convention. With an elitism characteristic of the African American leadership, William J. Wilson, William Whipper, and Charles B. Ray's Report of the Committee on Social Relations and Polity called for cooperation among blacks, within as well as beyond the United States: "For the purpose of securing ourselves against encroachments, and making provisions for future emergencies, should they arise, our *relations* require the speedy linking together of the whole chain of enlightened mind among us, not only of the *States*, but of the whole *continent* into one *grand league*." Insistent that they should be accorded their rights as American citizens, the delegates to the 1853 meeting repudiated, once again, the scheme of the ACS.[57] For most black leaders, these calls for racial cooperation among black people in different nations were concomitant with demands for the extension of the rights of citizenship to African Americans. At the very least, however, even these black leaders who were a long way from suggesting African Americans should leave the United States, were accepting the necessity for racial cooperation, across international as well as regional boundaries. Internationalizing the struggle was thus a tactic, as well as an objective: The goal of meaningful freedom within the United States remained as important as ever.

There were other, more forceful expressions of "nationalistic" sentiments from Frederick Douglass, the most prominent advocate of the stay-and-fight ideology. Because he was not averse to advocating ideas most commonly associated with the emigrationist-nationalists, and because of his subsequent interest in Haiti, Douglass' views warrant some analysis. It would not be accurate to say he was appropriating the language and values of the emigrationist-nationalists, for even during the 1840s he had emphasized the importance of fostering links between African Americans. At the 1848 Colored National Convention, Douglass had helped draft an Address to the African American community that spoke of a unity among black peoples in terms very similar to those used by the emigrationists. "We are one people," he wrote, "one in general complexion, one in common degradation, one in popular estimation. As one rises all must rise, and as one falls, all must fall." The following year, Douglass called for the establishment of a National League of black people, designed to help them deal with the common problems they faced. Most significant, in a speech at the 1853 meeting of the American and Foreign Anti-Slavery Society, Douglass spoke of African Americans, slave and free, as "becoming a nation, in the midst of a nation which disowns them."[58] Given white Americans' response to certain Native American tribes' attempts to defend their sovereignty within the borders of the United States, many whites would have been far from reassured by Douglass' description of African Americans as an emergent nation-within-a-nation. In the same year, 1853, Douglass contemplated why some American blacks had elected to settle outside the United States. Although he regretted their example, and explained that "individuals emigrate—nations never," he understood why "men of superior ability and attainments" had emigrated. Rather than continuing "a contest against" overwhelming "odds," such as those which confronted blacks in the United States, they had "sought more congenial climes, where they can live more peaceable and quiet lives." Douglass thus acknowledged the right of individuals to emigrate, should the circumstances warrant such a course of action. Moreover, he went so far as to admit that "with an equal amount of education, and the hard lot which was theirs, I might follow their example."[59]

Advocates of the stay-and-fight theory were effectively turning to similar principles to those being advocated by the emigrationists. It is possible, as Howard Bell has argued, that the efforts to organize blacks on a national level on the "homefront" were in response to the "challenge of the emigrationists."[60] An equally plausible explanation, however, is that the form of black nationalism being advanced by advocates of the stay-and-fight school was also a response to the increasing oppression confronting free blacks in the North, and the apparent ascendancy of the southern slaveocracy. There was a vigorous debate between the emigrationists and advocates of the stay-and-fight philosophy. Nevertheless, without muting the extent and depth of those disputes, it is easy to overlook the common ground between the two groups. Indeed, it is somewhat misleading to describe them as two "groups": not only did individual black leaders change their minds frequently over the issue of emigration, but there were ongoing debates concerning a possible destination for African American emigrants. Above all, although it was the case that all emigrationists were nationalists, one did not have to be an emigrationist to be a nationalist.

Soon after the 1853 convention at Rochester, the faction led by Delany issued a call for a convention of emigrationists. This sparked a journalistic contest between advocates of the two philosophies, most of which was published initially in *Frederick Douglass' Paper*. Much of this debate was conducted not by Delany and Douglass, but by James Monroe Whitfield, representing the emigrationist perspective, and William J. Watkins, a close associate of Douglass. The son of the abolitionist William Watkins discussed in the preceding chapter, the younger Watkins was willing to change his mind when circumstances warranted; at the end of the 1850s he became an advocate of Haitian emigrationism.

James Whitfield was no less willing than other black leaders to contemplate a variety of strategies for African American elevation. Born in Boston, Whitfield moved at an early age to Cleveland, where he first expressed an interest in separate black settlements. During the late 1830s, he urged a concentration of blacks on the borders of the United States, especially in California. In 1841, he moved to Buffalo, New York, where he found employment as a barber. At that point, he also began writing poetry, quickly becoming one of the most highly respected black poets in the United States.[61] In July 1853, Whitfield attended the Colored National Convention held in Rochester, where he helped compose an Address to the African American community. Declaring "we address you as American citizens asserting their rights on their own native soil," the Address called for blacks to be granted equality in the United States.[62]

Within two months, however, Whitfield had forsaken the stay-and-fight philosophy, announcing in the columns of *Frederick Douglass' Paper* that he was in favor of emigrationism.[63] Whitfield's conversion to emigrationism was premised on an increasing sense of disillusionment with the United States. This disillusionment was evident in his best known work, *America and Other Poems*. Published in 1853, and dedicated to Delany, this volume was infused with an unambiguous political message that exposed the contradiction between American rhetoric on the one hand, and American racism on the other. His most famous poem, "America," began: "*America, it is to thee / Thou boasted land of liberty / It is to thee I raise my song / Thou land of blood, of crime, and wrong.*"[64] Considering Whitfield's skepticism regarding American freedoms, and given his literary reputation among the black community, he was well-placed to assume an important role as spokesperson for the emigrationists. His 1853–1854 exchanges with William J. Watkins over the emigration issue were subsequently published in pamphlet form, along with details on possible destinations to which African Americans might emigrate.[65]

Reviewing Delany's call for a convention, Douglass articulated his opposition to the concept of emigrationism. Describing the call as "unwise, unfortunate, and premature," he feared that enemies of the African Americans would "see in this movement a cause for rejoicing." It was of vital importance, he averred, that the enemies of the black race did not perceive divisions among African Americans: Unity—presumably under his leadership—was essential.[66] In reply, Whitfield conceded that the delegates to the Rochester convention had passed worthwhile resolutions. But suggesting that no tangible measures were being taken to reach the desired ends, he insisted that blacks take positive action to improve their position. As he put it, blacks had to create a powerful nation capable of earning the respect of others: "colored men can never be fully and fairly respected as the equals of the whites, in this country or any other, until they are able to show in some part of the world, men of their own race occupying a primary and independent position, instead of a secondary and inferior one, as is now the case everywhere." Describing a "reflex influence" that would result from the emergence of such a nation, Whitfield maintained this would be a powerful weapon against prejudice in the United States. It was blacks' destiny, he stated, "to develop a higher order of civilization and Christianity than the world has yet seen." By referring to concepts that held such wide currency in nineteenth-century America, Whitfield thus indicated the extent of the "Americanization" of blacks in the United States. But he went further. Speaking of blacks' "manifest destiny" through which they were to possess all the tropical regions of the American continent, as well as the adjacent islands, he echoed the strident rhetoric of recent American nationalism and expansionism. With regard to the details of the emigration, Whitfield raised the question of a selective or en-masse movement of African Americans. This was an important and contentious issue, because advocates of a large-scale movement of blacks from the United States appeared to accept white colonizationists' premise that blacks could never achieve meaningful freedom in the United States. Repudiating suggestions that emigrationists favored a large-scale exodus of African Americans, Whitfield implied that those who remained in the United States would benefit from the efforts of those who emigrated. By arguing against an en-masse emigration of African Americans, Whitfield further insinuated that he saw no contradiction between participating in the Emigration Convention, and urging equality for blacks in the United States.[67]

At that point of the debate William J. Watkins assumed the role of defending the stay-and-fight philosophy. Reiterating most of the anti-colonization arguments that had been widely accepted by the African American leadership since the establishment of the ACS, he proceeded to argue that enemies of the black race would not distinguish between "colonization" and "emigration." By denying that African Americans' position was as hopeless as the emigrationists assumed, Watkins expressed faith in God's justice, and stated that "we intend to stay *here* where God has placed us, and vindicate our dignity as men."[68] In explicitly masculinist terms, Watkins thus connected the tactics of black elevation to their Christian endeavors. Whitfield, too, appealed to these values. Invoking the self-help principle that antebellum Americans took so seriously, Whitfield stressed that blacks could not "call upon the Lord to do that for us which we should perform ourselves." Adamant that all the institutions of white America were implicated in a conspiracy to crush African Americans, he argued that blacks could elevate themselves more readily in other countries, where they had an "equal chance with other men."[69]

The Emigration Convention began in Cleveland, Ohio, in August 1854. That gathering represents one of the high points of the nineteenth-century emigration movement. For Delany it was the moment of his greatest influence over the movement. Yet, as this chapter has shown, many of the ideas that Delany, and others, would continue to advocate until the Civil War had already been broached during the early 1850s by Henry Highland Garnet, Henry Bibb, Mary Ann Shadd, and—most significantly—James Holly. Indeed, although Delany is more widely known than the other emigrationists of the 1850s, many of his ideas had been anticipated by people such as Bibb and Holly, who turned to emigration sooner, and more decisively, than did Delany. Moreover, while much of the focus during the late 1840s and early 1850s was on Canadian emigration, there were already important expressions of interest in the Caribbean region, including Haiti. As is seen later, it was in that direction that Holly's interest developed, most particularly toward Haiti. Over the next six years he would emerge as the major proponent of Haitian emigration. His ever more emphatic interest in the island republic, and his developing contribution to the black nationalist ideology that he believed connected African Americans to Haiti's past—and to its future—are major themes of the next chapter.

NOTES

1. Garnet's "Address to the Slaves," in *Negro Orators and Their Orations*, ed. Carter G. Woodson (1924; reprint, New York: Russell and Russell, 1969), 150–57; *Minutes of the National Convention of Colored Citizens: Held at Buffalo, on the 15th, 16th, 17th, 18th and 19th of August, 1843. For the Purpose of Considering their Moral and Political Conditions as American Citizens* (New York: Piercy and Reed, 1843), 13, 18–19.

2. *North Star*, 16 November 1849.

3. Jane H. Pease and William H. Pease, "Ends, Means, and Attitudes: Black-White Conflict in the Antislavery Movement," *Civil War History*, 18 (1972): 118–24.

4. Stowe, *Uncle Tom's Cabin; or, Life Among the Lowly* (1852; reprint, New York: Penguin, 1986), 608–9.

5. *Proceedings of the National Convention of Colored People, and Their Friends, Held in Troy, N.Y., on the 6th, 7th, 8th and 9th October, 1847* (Troy, N.Y.: J. C. Kneeland and Co., 1847), 31; Pease and Pease, *They Who Would Be Free: Blacks' Search for Freedom, 1830–1861* (New York: Atheneum, 1974), 288.

6. Between 1830 and 1839, the ACS despatched a total of 2,547 African Americans to Liberia. See Philip J. Staudenraus, *The African Colonization Movement, 1816–1865* (New York: Columbia University Press, 1961), 251.

7. Philip S. Foner, *History of Black Americans: From the Emergence of the Cotton Kingdom to the Eve of the Compromise of 1850* (Westport, Conn.: Greenwood Press, 1983), 304–5; Howard H. Bell, *A Survey of the Negro Convention Movement, 1830–1861* (New York: Arno Press, 1969), 127–28; Christopher Phillips, *Freedom's Port: The African American Community of Baltimore, 1790–1860* (Urbana: University of Illinois Press, 1997), 215–20.

8. *Proceedings of the National Convention of Colored People . . . 1847*, 21–25.

9. On Liberian independence, see Yekutiel Gershoni, *Black Colonialism: The Americo-Liberian Scramble for the Hinterland* (Boulder, Colo.: Westview Press, 1985), 13; Amos Beyan, *The American Colonization Society and the Creation of the Liberian State: A Historical Perspective, 1822–1900* (Lanham, Md.: University Press of America, 1991), 93.

10. *North Star*, 26 January 1849; Joel Schor, *Henry Highland Garnet: A Voice of Black Radicalism in the Nineteenth Century* (Westport, Conn.: Greenwood Press, 1977), 101–2.

11. *North Star*, 2 March 1849.

12. *Proceedings of the Colored National Convention, Held in Rochester, July 6th, 7th and 8th, 1853* (Rochester, N.Y.: Printed at the Office of *Frederick Douglass' Paper*, 1853), 4.

13. *Syracuse Daily Journal*, 14 August 1852, in *The Black Abolitionist Papers. Volume IV: The United States, 1847–1858*, ed. C. Peter Ripley (Chapel Hill: University of North Carolina Press, 1991), 131–32.

14. *Report of the Proceedings of the Colored National Convention, Held at Cleveland, Ohio, on Wednesday, September 6, 1848* (Rochester: John Dick, 1848), 17–21 (quote on 19). On Bibb, see Henry Bibb, *Narrative of the Life and Adventures of Henry Bibb, an American Slave* (New York; 1850); Fred Landon, "Henry Bibb: A Colonizer," *Journal of Negro History*, 5 (1920): 437–47; Roger W. Hite, "Voice of a

Fugitive: Henry Bibb and Ante-bellum Black Separatism," *Journal of Black Studies*, 4 (1974): 269–84.

15. One estimate suggested that perhaps twenty thousand African Americans fled to Canada as a consequence of the Fugitive Slave Act. See Fred Landon, "The Negro Migration to Canada after the Passing of the Fugitive Slave Act," *Journal of Negro History*, 5 (1920): 22, 27.

16. *Voice of the Fugitive*, 13 August 1851.

17. *Voice of the Fugitive*, 18 June 1851, 1 July 1851; Floyd J. Miller, *The Search for a Black Nationality: Black Emigration and Colonization, 1787–1863* (Urbana: University of Illinois Press, 1975), 111.

18. Brown, *The Black Man, His Antecedents, His Genius, and His Achievements*, 4th ed. (1865; reprint, Miami: Mnemosyne Publishing Co., 1969), 274.

19. The major study of Holly is David McEwen Dean, *Defender of the Race: James Theodore Holly, Black Nationalist Bishop* (Boston: Lambeth Press, 1979). See also Hollis R. Lynch, "James Theodore Holly: Ante-Bellum Black Nationalist and Emigrationist," (A Special Publication of the Center for Afro-American Studies, UCLA, 1977); J. Carleton Hayden, "James Theodore Holly (1829–1911), First Afro-American Episcopal Bishop: His Legacy to Us Today," in *Black Apostles: Afro-American Clergy Confront the Twentieth Century*, ed. Randall K. Burkett and Richard Newman (Boston: G. K. Hall & Co., 1978).

20. Holly, *Facts About the Church's Mission. A Concise Statement by Bishop Holly* (New York: Thomas Whittaker, 1897), 6; Lynch, "James Theodore Holly," 1–2.

21. *North Star*, 1 February 1850.

22. Holly to McLain, 25 June 1850, Domestic Letters, American Colonization Society Papers (microfilm), Australian National Library, Canberra (hereafter cited as ACSP).

23. Holly to McLain, 8 August 1850, ACSP.

24. Holly to McLain, 3 September 1850, ACSP.

25. *Voice of the Fugitive*, 7 May 1851.

26. *Voice of the Fugitive*, 16 July 1851.

27. *Voice of the Fugitive*, 4 June 1851.

28. *Voice of the Fugitive*, 30 July 1851; Miller, *Search for a Black Nationality*, 110.

29. *Voice of the Fugitive*, 24 September 1851; Lynch, "James Theodore Holly," 8; John W. Blassingame, ed., *The Frederick Douglass Papers. Series One: Speeches, Debates, and Interviews. Volume 2: 1847–54* (New Haven, Conn.: Yale University Press, 1982), 338n.

30. *Voice of the Fugitive*, 3 December 1851; Hite, "Voice of a Fugitive," 278–79.

31. On the market revolution, see Charles Sellers, *The Market Revolution: Jacksonian America, 1815–1846* (New York: Oxford University Press, 1991); Melvyn Stokes and Stephen Conway, eds., *The Market Revolution in America: Social, Political, and Religious Expressions, 1800–1880* (Charlottesville: University Press of Virginia, 1996).

32. *Voice of the Fugitive*, 22 October 1851; Miller, *Search for a Black Nationality*, 112.

33. *Voice of the Fugitive*, 8 April 1852; Lynch, "James Theodore Holly," 8.

34. Dean, *Defender of the Race*, 12; *Voice of the Fugitive*, 17 June 1852.

35. On Shadd Cary, see Harold B. Hancock, "Mary Ann Shadd: Negro Editor, Educator, and Lawyer," *Delaware History*, 15 (1973): 187–94; Jim Bearden and

Linda Jean Butler, *Shadd: The Life and Times of Mary Shadd Cary* (Toronto: NC Press, 1977); Jane Rhodes, *Mary Ann Shadd Cary: The Black Press and Protest in the Nineteenth Century* (Bloomington: Indiana University Press, 1998).

36. Miller, *Search for a Black Nationality*, 113.

37. Lynch, "James Theodore Holly," 9; Dean, *Defender of the Race*, 16; Miller, *Search for a Black Nationality*, 114.

38. *Minutes and Proceedings of the General Convention for the Improvement of the Colored Inhabitants of Canada, Held by Adjournments in Amherstburg C.W., June 16th and 17th, 1853* (Windsor, Canada West: Bibb & Holly, 1853), 3–5, 12–13.

39. *Minutes and Proceedings . . . 1853*, 1, 13–16.

40. *Minutes and Proceedings . . . 1853*, 8–10, 16.

41. *Liberator*, 4 March 1853; Lynch, "James Theodore Holly," 19.

42. See Cyril E. Griffith, *The African Dream: Martin R. Delany and the Emergence of Pan-African Thought* (University Park: Pennsylvania State University Press, 1975); Dorothy Sterling, *The Making of an Afro-American: Martin R. Delany, 1812–1885* (New York: Doubleday, 1971); Victor Ullman, *Martin R. Delany: The Beginnings of Black Nationalism* (Boston: Beacon Press, 1971).

43. Griffith, *African Dream*, 2–3, 12; Miller. "'The Father of Black Nationalism': Another Contender," *Civil War History*, 17 (1971): 310–19; Pease and Pease, *They Who Would Be Free*, 261.

44. Sterling, *The Making of an Afro-American*, 116–17; Griffith, *African Dream*, 12–13.

45. Lerone Bennett, Jr., *Before the Mayflower: A History of the Negro in America, 1619–1964*, Rev. Ed. (Harmondsworth: Penguin, 1966), 137.

46. Delany, *The Condition, Elevation, Emigration, and Destiny of the Colored People of the United States, Politically Considered* (1852; reprint, New York: Arno Press, 1968), 45.

47. Delany, *Condition, Elevation, Emigration, and Destiny*, 30–31, 169, 175–80.

48. Delany, *Condition, Elevation, Emigration, and Destiny*, 211.

49. *Pennsylvania Freeman*, 29 April 1852. See also Robert S. Levine, *Martin Delany, Frederick Douglass, and the Politics of Representative Identity* (Chapel Hill: University of North Carolina Press, 1997), 69.

50. Sterling, *The Making of an Afro-American*, 148; *Liberator*, 7 May 1852.

51. *Voice of the Fugitive*, 3 June 1852. Bibb's sensitivity to this freeborn/slave question might have been exacerbated in this instance because one of the free blacks Delany had noticed favorably in *The Condition, Elevation, Emigration, and Destiny of the Colored People* was Mary Ann Shadd, with whom Bibb had had more than a fair share of differences.

52. *Frederick Douglass' Paper*, 23 July 1852; *Pennsylvania Freeman*, 5 May 1852.

53. *Liberator*, 21 May 1852.

54. *Frederick Douglass' Paper*, 23 July 1852.

55. Draper, "The Fantasy of Black Nationalism," *Commentary*, 48 (1969): 30. My interpretation of Delany accords with that offered by Nell Irvin Painter, who has noted that "beyond his willingness to consider expatriation to Africa, which he came to see for only a select few, Delany's thinking about race, class, and 'elevation' was thoroughly American and right in step with that of his Afro-American peers." Bill McAdoo has offered a rather more harsh judgment on Delany, depicting him as one of the "chief spokesmen and prime movers of black zionism." See Painter, "Martin R.

Delany: Elitism and Black Nationalism," in *Black Leaders of the Nineteenth-Century,* ed. Leon Litwack and August Meier (Urbana: University of Illinois Press, 1988), 150; McAdoo, *Pre-Civil War Black Nationalism* (New York: David Walker Press, 1983), 23.

56. *Frederick Douglass' Paper,* 20 May 1853; Bell, *Survey of the Negro Convention Movement,* 166.

57. *Proceedings of the Colored National Convention . . . 1853,* 18–19, 24.

58. *Report of the Proceedings of the Colored National Convention . . . 1848,* 18; Pease and Pease, *They Who Would Be Free,* 251; Douglass, "The Present Condition and Future Prospects of the Negro People," May 1853, in *The Life and Writings of Frederick Douglass,* ed. Philip S. Foner, 4 vols. (New York: International Publishers, 1952), 2:246.

59. *Proceedings of the Colored National Convention . . . 1853,* 35–36.

60. Bell, "The Negro Emigration Movement, 1849–1854: A Phase of Negro Nationalism," *Phylon,* 20 (1959): 140.

61. *Frederick Douglass' Paper,* 25 November 1853; Richard Bardolph, "Social Origins of Distinguished Negroes, 1770–1865," *Journal of Negro History,* 40 (1955): 234; Miller, *Search for a Black Nationality,* 138.

62. *Frederick Douglass' Paper,* 15 July 1853; *Proceedings of the Colored National Convention . . . 1853,* 7–28.

63. M. T. Newsome, comp., *Arguments, Pro and Con, on the Call for a National Emigration Convention, to be Held in Cleveland, Ohio, August, 1854, by Frederick Douglass, W. J. Watkins, and James Whitfield. With a Short Appendix of the Statistics of Canada West, West Indies, Central and South America* (Detroit: George Pomeroy, 1854), 8–11; Miller, *Search for a Black Nationality,* 138.

64. Whitfield, "America," in *America and Other Poems* (Buffalo: James S. Leavitt, 1853), 9.

65. See Newsome, *Arguments, Pro and Con.*

66. Newsome, *Arguments, Pro and Con,* 7–8.

67. Newsome, *Arguments, Pro and Con,* 8–11.

68. Newsome, *Arguments, Pro and Con,* 11–13.

69. Newsome, *Arguments, Pro and Con,* 17, 27.

3

Contemplating Haiti: Black Emigrationism, 1854–1860

For African Americans in the northern states, the period from 1854 to 1860 was characterized by continuing debates regarding the virtues of emigration. Notwithstanding opposition from many black leaders, and despite the apparent indifference of many African Americans to questions of black nationalism, the continuing doubts about blacks' place in a society increasingly riven by the crisis over slavery meant the viability of the stay-and-fight ideology was under constant scrutiny. Writing in 1856, William Whipper—hitherto a staunch proponent of the stay-and-fight doctrine—told abolitionist Gerrit Smith that the "spirit of emigration has in all ages, promote[d] the progress and development of the oppressed." Although Whipper did not retreat from his denunciation of the American Colonization Society (ACS), he did assert that those black Americans who had relocated to Canada were engaged in a "practical antislavery work." In the face of continuing proscription within the United States, increasing numbers of black Americans were prepared to consider the virtues of emigrationism. For James T. Holly, and others, there was undeniable merit in Whipper's confident claim that emigration was an "agent of civilization."[1]

Yet although emigrationists agreed that African Americans should leave the United States, the question of where they should settle remained contentious. Martin Delany turned increasingly toward African emigration, although it was some time before he finally made up his mind in that direction. It is a premise of this chapter that the African option, although it embraced more than Delany's schemes, was essentially an aberration. Delany was slow to turn to Africa, and, in eventually doing so, he was forced to challenge black prejudices against that continent that had long focused on the activities of the ACS, and which reflected the influence of white America on mid-nineteenth-century African American culture. To the extent that African schemes did enjoy the attention of black American activists during the 1850s, they were mainly important in distracting the attention of contemporaries, and posterity, from the culturally and geographically more feasible alternative of Haiti. Accordingly, this brief discussion of Delany and African emigration complements a more substantial description and analysis of Holly's growing interest in Haitian emigration down to 1860, a phenomenon less emphasized by historians. More- over, although Delany focused his attentions on African emigrationism, he was conscious of Haiti's status as a tangible symbol of black revolution and independence.

The trends in the emigration movement of the late 1850s must be seen against the backdrop of the deepening North-South crisis. In the political sphere, the Compromise of 1850 had failed to resolve the sectional debate over the future of slavery. As white Americans continued to move westward, the slavery issue assumed ever greater significance. In early 1854, Senator Stephen A. Douglas of Illinois introduced a bill into Congress calling for the status of slavery in the western territories to be determined by the people who settled there. This concept of "popular sovereignty" raised the ire of many Northerners, who regarded it as an abject violation of the Missouri Compromise of 1820, which had defined the limits of slavery in the new territories. But it was African Americans who most clearly saw the implications of popular sovereignty. As Frederick Douglass concluded, "the only seeming concession to the idea of popular sovereignty in this bill is authority to enslave men." "To consider that right or authority," he asserted, "is a hell black denial of popular sovereignty itself."[2] Nevertheless, following a bitter Congressional debate, and with President Benjamin Pierce's support, Stephen Douglas' bill was passed. The Kansas-Nebraska Act added further fuel to the already smouldering sectional fire. In the western territories, the conflict between pro-slavery and anti-slavery settlers resulted in physical violence; during the mid-1850s the eyes of the nation were fixed on the events in "Bleeding Kansas." Clearly, the slavery issue was no longer confined to theoretical debate: Americans were killing each other over the issue.

If some black Americans still hoped for a political solution to the problems of slavery and racism, the 1850s proved a bitter disappointment. The emergence of the Republican Party in the mid-1850s brought little joy to African Americans. Like the Free Soilers before them, the Republican Party had scant interest in the plight of blacks. Placing the imperatives of political opportunism above moral considerations of immediatist abolitionism, most Republicans' primary concern was with the impact that the extension of slavery would have on *white* Americans. Although some leading members of the Republican Party, notably the Blair family of Missouri, did espouse anti-slavery principles, most Republicans emphasized the nonextension of slavery as the primary anti-slavery tactic, arguing that it was impossible to interfere with slavery in those states where it already existed. Many Republicans, moreover, accepted that any proposal to emancipate the slaves must be accompanied by a scheme to colonize African Americans outside the United States.³

No individual better demonstrated the Republicans' ambivalence on the questions of race and slavery than Abraham Lincoln. Debating the slavery issue in 1858, Lincoln assured his predominantly white audience that if the slaves were freed, his "first impulse" would be to send them to Liberia (although he did acknowledge that this was probably an infeasible objective).⁴ Although Lincoln might have had doubts about the practicability of a large-scale black exodus, his often quoted public endorsement for the idea of black colonization, and his subsequent support for two specific colonization schemes—including one that led to the settlement of five hundred African Americans on an island off the Haitian coast—compounded blacks' doubts regarding the Republicans' commitment to abolition and racial equality.

The political system's disappointing response to questions of race was paralleled by the judiciary's willingness to follow, rather than lead, white public opinion on the twin problems of slavery and racism. In 1856, the Supreme Court dealt a shattering blow to black aspirations, when it made its judgment in the case of Dred Scott, a slave who had sued for his freedom on the grounds that his master had taken him to an area where slavery had been prohibited under the terms of the Missouri Compromise. Rejecting Scott's claim, Chief Justice Roger Taney denied that African Americans were entitled to the benefits of citizenship.⁵ Even as abolitionists and blacks denounced Taney's statements, they understood he was articulating views that held wide currency among whites in the North as well as the South.

With their opportunities for social and civic equality diminishing, and with white racial attitudes hardening throughout the nation, a mood of pessimism was evident within black America during the late 1850s. The growing sense of disillusionment among African Americans was thrown into sharp relief by the South's response to John Brown's raid on Harper's Ferry, Virginia, in October 1859. Although Brown was widely derided as psychologically unstable, he did represent an abolitionist position, however extreme. Brown hoped that his assault on the federal arsenal at Harper's Ferry would foment a general uprising among the slaves. Instead, the attack was quickly suppressed and Brown and his co-conspirators at Harper's Ferry were killed or captured. Brown's dignity during his trial for conspiracy, his courage as he awaited execution, and his unwavering conviction in the righteousness of the anti-slavery cause, made him a valuable martyr for abolitionists. For many blacks, however, the speed with which the South closed ranks in condemning Brown, and the increasingly vitriolic defenses of the South's peculiar institution, served only to confirm their worst fears that an increasingly assertive slave power was determined to deny freedom and equality to all blacks, everywhere. It was in this context that African American leaders such as James Holly refined their ideology of black nationalism, grounded in a belief that the emigration of black Americans was an essential aspect of their quest for freedom and equality within the United States.

Meeting in Cleveland soon after the passage of the Kansas–Nebraska Act, the National Emigration Convention of Colored People began in late August 1854. This gathering represented a high point of antebellum emigrationism. Certainly for Martin Delany it was the point at which his influence among emigrationists was at its zenith. Approximately one hundred delegates from eleven states and Canada were in attendance when the convention commenced. A majority of those present were from western regions, with the largest contingent coming from the Pittsburgh area, where Delany was then residing. Evidently, he was able to convince a number of blacks living in and around the city of the benefits of emigration. The concentration of delegates from the west might also be an indication that the traditional, and perhaps more conservative, African American leadership was most influential in the east.[6] In any case, blacks living in western areas would have found it easier to attend the Emigration Convention, for the very practical reason that they did not have as far to travel as blacks resident in the east.[7]

The emigration convention was also distinctive in another way. Although black conventions of the period "generally seated women," one third of the delegates at Cleveland were women, including Delany's wife, and the widow of Bibb, who had died shortly before the convention began. We know little about the specific contributions made by the women present at the Cleveland convention, but there is evidence they were no mere ornaments at the meeting. Of the seven members of the Convention's Finance Committee, for example, four were women.[8] Involving women in public roles was inevitably controversial in antebellum America. Just as some white abolitionists had used the anti-slavery movement to challenge gender conventions, Delany had spoken on women's behalf on earlier occasions. At the 1848 National Convention he had provoked considerable debate when he had argued that women should be given greater responsibilities. In the end, Frederick Douglass—who the previous month had endorsed the first women's rights convention at Seneca Falls—offered a compromise proposal that did not refer specifically to women.[9] Delany's efforts to include women in the emigration movement might have reflected a commitment to gender equality. His own marital arrangements, whereby his wife Catherine provided the material support that often allowed him to engage in public life, amounted to a refutation of the prevailing domestic ideology.[10] But Delany's efforts on women's behalf—which he did not allow to interfere with his emigrationist or abolitionist activities—also constituted a pragmatic endeavor to broaden his base of support. In practice, moreover, most of the emigrationist leadership, with the notable exception of Mary Ann Shadd, were males.

As one of three secretaries to the 1854 convention, James Holly played an important part in the proceedings. However, it was Delany who was able to most effectively exploit the convention as a vehicle to enunciate his emigrationist vision. His Platform: or Declaration of Sentiments of the Cleveland Convention touched on two themes central to his philosophy. Besides asserting that no person could be independent unless they owned the land on which they lived, he introduced a principle on which he would subsequently expand: "we will never be satisfied nor contented until we occupy a position where we are acknowledged a necessary *constituent* in the ruling element of the country in which we live."[11]

Delany also presented to the convention a report to which all the members of the Business Committee—including Holly—signed their names, but which was clearly a reflection of his own increasingly emigrationist and nationalistic position. In "The Political Destiny of the Colored Race on the American Continent" Delany reiterated many of the principles he had expressed in his 1852 work. This essay, described by historian Sterling Stuckey as one of the "seminal political documents in American history," discussed the objectives of emigrationism, and the advantages of various sites for African Americans interested in making a new home for themselves outside the United States.[12] Insisting that blacks possessed the "highest traits of civilization," Delany contended that the black and colored races, who comprised two thirds of the world's population, were becoming increasingly unified. The time had come, he asserted, for them to "create an event." One means of so doing was by African Americans relocating to a region where they comprised "an essential part of the *ruling element*." It was for this reason that Delany gave only limited endorsement to Canadian emigration. Although he encouraged blacks in Canada to purchase as much land as possible, and agreed it was suitable as a "temporary asylum" for African Americans, he feared, as he had in 1852, that at "no very distant day" the British Provinces would be annexed by the United States. Delany continued to argue that the best way for blacks to solve their problems was by emigrating to the West Indies, and to Central and South America—regions where blacks' weight of numbers made them the "ruling element."[13]

Notwithstanding Delany's determination to assert blacks' strength of character, his document reflected the contradictory racial stereotypes that prevailed in mid–nineteenth-century America. On the one hand, in justifying African American emigration to those parts of the Americas where whites were in a minority, Delany appeared to endorse racial stereotypes that held wide currency among white people. For example, in describing the people of the "West Indies, Central and South America" as "generous, sociable, and tractable," he seemed to be representing blacks as essentially passive—just as apologists for slavery were prone to do. Furthermore, in asserting that the people in the West Indies, and Central and South America, were "susceptible of progress, improvement, and reform of every kind," Delany implied that those regions lagged behind the United States and other Western civilizations in such matters. All of this suggested that Delany considered African Americans as uniquely qualified to carry the virtues of industry and civilization south of the border. At the same time, however, he emphasized that not all black people were the impotent creatures their detractors often imagined them to be. In particular, he singled out Haiti as one place where whites had felt the full brunt of black power. The island republic, he declared, was

peopled by as brave and noble descendants of Africa as those who laid the foundations of Thebias, or constructed the everlasting pyramids and catacombs of Egypt—a people who have freed themselves by the might of their own will, the force of their own power, the unfailing strength of their own right arms, and their unflinching determination to be free.[14]

There is no way of assessing whether this section of "The Political Destiny of the Colored Race on the American Continent" was included at Holly's behest. But considering that black leaders had long lauded the Haitians' valor, and given that Delany had named his first son Toussaint L'Ouverture, after the most famous leader of the Haitian Revolution (he would later name another son Faustin Soulouque, after another Haitian ruler), there is no reason to think Delany did not concur that Haiti exemplified the positive traits that many black leaders believed were lacking in the African American populace.[15] This was not the first occasion on which Delany had referred to Haiti. In an 1848 letter to the *North Star*, he had referred specifically to Haiti's significance as an exemplar of black independence and accomplishment. While he did not dwell on the possibility of Haitian emigration in his 1854 tract, Delany's underlying position seemed unequivocal: "Upon the American continent . . . we are determined to remain."[16]

Yet there was less certainty about the question of where emigrants should settle than was suggested by Delany's tract. As Delany subsequently explained, during "secret" sessions, the delegates at Cleveland gave favorable consideration to the notion of African emigration; although no public pronouncements were made, they made Africa their ultimate destination.[17] The private decision to endorse African emigration, while publicly advocating emigration to regions on or near the American continent, attested to more than just the confusion that was evident among the black leadership. It also hinted at the telling legacy of the ACS, and implied that black leaders viewed potential emigration schemes as rivals, rather than complementary parts of an overall strategy. Differences between black leaders were inevitable, but during the 1850s emigrationists did spend considerable time and energy quarreling among themselves over the best destination for African American emigrants.

The lack of unanimity among emigrationists was evidenced by the expressions of support at the Cleveland convention for Canadian emigration, and by Holly's efforts to promote the Haitian alternative.[18] With regard to African emigrationism, the delegates were no doubt wary of embracing a plan that the black populace was likely to associate with the ACS scheme. Although the ACS succeeded in luring more than 4,500 African Americans to Liberia during the 1850s, most were southerners, many of whom were ex-slaves, emancipated on the specific condition that they emigrate to Liberia.[19] Notwithstanding the Liberian declaration of independence, few northern blacks endorsed the ACS during the pre–Civil War decade. Martin Delany's opinion of the ACS had certainly not changed, although his views did shift in subsequent years. Writing in 1855, he derided the ACS's plan as "the most pernicious and impudent of all schemes for the perpetuity of the degradation of our race."[20] For black emigrationists, the ACS's expression of general approval of the Emigration Convention was unhelpful, serving only to confirm many African Americans' suspicions concerning the links between black schemes for emigration on the one hand, and the ACS on the other.[21]

It was relatively straightforward for the delegates at the Cleveland convention to pass resolutions endorsing emigration. But having experienced disappointments on earlier occasions, those present at the 1854 meeting knew all too well the difficulties involved in taking proposals beyond the discussion stage. Let "us suggest to the reader," they remarked in their published account of the meeting, "that this Convention proved what it was intended to be, not merely a talking and theoretical, but an *acting* and *doing* Convention."[22] To transform that activist spirit into tangible action, a National Board of Commissioners was established, with Delany chosen to act as president, to facilitate an emigration movement.[23] Regrettably for the emigrationists, however, serious obstacles continued to impede the implementation of their plans. There were many factors inhibiting emigration, particularly emigration to Africa. Perhaps the major flaw in the emigrationists' theory, logistical questions aside, was that those blacks whom they would have encouraged to leave the United States were those with the most incentive to stay. Although Frederick Douglass bemoaned the fact that "education and emigration go together with us," the skilled, literate, and commercially successful minority of the African American population had more reason to remain in the United States than did the besieged black masses.[24] Members of this minority had managed, in the face of considerable adversity, to build a future for themselves in the United States. Moreover, because this minority often depended on the business of other, poorer blacks, they had cause to discourage a large-scale emigration of African Americans. Like the abolitionists' endeavors to undermine slavery through the free produce movement, the emigrationists' plan to attack slavery by waging an economic war against the slaveocracy was unrealistic. As well as demanding agricultural and entrepreneurial expertise, the emigrationists' schemes required capital that was in short supply in the black community. The minuscule number of African Americans with appropriate skills or resources were unlikely to contemplate emigration. These factors were to adversely affect the Haitian movement of the late 1850s and early 1860s.

Criticism of the 1854 Emigration Convention came from several directions. Douglass had little to say about the Cleveland meeting, but he did allow George B. Vashon (the first black graduate of Ohio's Oberlin College) to use the columns of *Frederick Douglass' Paper* to criticize the emigrationists. Typically, much of his criticism was of a personal nature. Vashon claimed that the constitution of the emigrationists' National Board of Commissioners was a copy of that written by the delegates at the 1853 convention in Rochester, to which the idea of emigration had been appended.[25] Vashon's comments point also to another characteristic of the era, for although he criticized the 1854 convention, he himself dabbled with the idea of emigration. Having spent two-and-a-half years working as a teacher in Haiti during the late 1830s, in August 1861 he would endorse emigration to the island republic.[26] Other critics of the 1854 convention charged that by referring only to the denial of equality to African Americans in the North, emigrationists were dealing with just one aspect of the overall problem facing black Americans. Proponents of emigration were thus accused of abandoning the slaves to their fate. Although emigrationists claimed to have an anti-slavery strategy, the delegates at Cleveland did acknowledge that their program appeared to offer little to the slaves. They also conceded their distance from those in bondage. These admissions did little to assuage their opponents.[27]

Nevertheless, there was continuing evidence of an interest in the separatist philosophy—even among advocates of the stay-and-fight philosophy. The debates at the 1855 Colored National Convention were evidence of this tentative interest. In the first instance, these discussions revealed the depth of ongoing African American antipathy to the ACS. The delegates' response to a letter from Jacob Handy of Baltimore, "eulogizing the Republic of Liberia, and advocating the colonization movement" is revealing of black attitudes during the mid-1850s. Howard Bell, pointing out that in earlier conventions letters of support for the ACS would have been "buried" in the business committee, has used the response of the 1855 convention to argue that the black leadership was shifting ground on the issues of colonization and emigration. As Bell suggested, the fact that there was even debate on the ACS signifies a shift from earlier conventions. However, while African Americans were increasingly likely to consider emigration schemes that were not tainted by the involvement of white colonizationists, the depth of the delegates' continuing resistance to the ACS was clear from their response to Handy's letter. Bell suggested that Handy's letter was handled "less respectfully" than the issue of Canadian emigration. But Bell's depiction of these events understates the antagonism prevalent among many black leaders on the issue of African emigration: not content to merely "return the letter" to Handy, George T. Downing, a devout opponent of black emigration and colonization, proposed it "be burned." By a vote of 33 to 20, his resolution was accepted by the convention. Although the delegates subsequently revised their decision to burn Handy's letter, their debates revealed that white-sponsored schemes for black colonization to Africa continued to arouse great passion among the black leadership.[28]

Evidently, feelings still ran deep about white-sponsored colonization schemes. Yet there were indications from the proceedings of the 1855 convention that African American leaders were distinguishing black-led schemes for emigration from white-sponsored programs for black deportation. Indeed, the outcome of a "spirited discussion" regarding the "question on the admission" of Mary Ann Shadd hinted at a greater willingness on the part of the black leadership to contemplate emigrationism. While some delegates at that meeting argued against admitting Shadd, Douglass defended her right to participate, even though he was well aware of her emigrationist ideas. The issue of nationality was also raised at the 1855 convention. Although the delegates accepted they were "part of this great nation," and while they asserted that their "interests cannot be entirely separated" from the United States, they did consider a proposal for Canadian emigrationism. The issue of black nationality was also addressed in a letter to the convention from J.W.C. Pennington, a senior and well-respected member of the black leadership. Alarmed by the territorial aggression of the United States, and referring specifically to Tennesseean William Walker's filibustering expeditions in Central America, Pennington urged the "liberal parties of all the parties and races of this Continent" to "combine in order to withstand the slave power of *this* republic." In calling for "a grand fusion Western Continent Anti-slavery Extension Convention," Pennington hoped that "gentlemen of talent from the British, French, Spanish and Danish Dominions, and also from Mexico and Central America" would be able to attend. Pennington did not suggest this convention should be limited to blacks, but it was significant that in arguing that it should "be held at some point where civilized law and order prevail," he nominated Haiti as an appropriate location.[29]

By 1855, although the delegates at the Colored National Convention continued to oppose the ACS, even the most ardent advocates of the stay-and-fight philosophy could not avoid the issues of emigration and black nationality. It was telling, too, that in contemplating emigration, the areas to the north and south of the United States, rather than Africa, appealed as regions where African Americans could find security and racial fraternity.

It was also during 1855 that James Holly traveled to Haiti, to investigate first-hand the prospects for African Americans emigrants. Holly had returned to the United States from Canada in early 1854, but his interest in emigrationism had not diminished. Besides writing the Introduction to *Arguments, Pro and Con*, the volume comprised of the exchanges between the emigrationists and their opponents in the period preceding the 1854 Emigration Convention, he had moved toward endorsing Haiti as the preferred destination for African Americans contemplating emigration. At the 1854 meeting, as was seen previously, he had endorsed Haitian emigration. And by proposing a resolution that January 1, the anniversary of Haitian independence, should be celebrated by blacks living outside the island republic, he had sought to promote the links between African Americans and Haiti's successful quest for independence.[30]

Intertwined with Holly's shift to Haitian emigrationism was a significant change in his religious orientation. Originally baptized as a Roman Catholic, he began to have misgivings about the Roman Catholic Church during the late 1840s when he lived in New York City. His teacher there, the Reverend Felix

Varella, considered sending Holly to Rome to study for the priesthood. For his part, Holly recalled many years later that he had "felt an inclination to labor in the ministry."[31] Details are elusive, but while Holly was in New York he might have attended St. Phillip's Protestant Episcopal Church. When his family moved to Vermont in 1850, Holly attended St. Paul's Episcopal Church. Attending confirmation on Good Friday, 1851, he was impressed with the ceremony performed by Bishop John Henry Hopkins. Holly found Hopkins' *The Primitive Church* doctrinally appealing. Paradoxically, Hopkins held strong anti-black, pro-slavery views, although Holly might not have been aware of those opinions. Nor was he deterred by the fact that most Episcopalians believed their faith should be reserved for whites. Instead, he was encouraged by more enlightened Episcopalians, such as Bishop Alonzo Potter, who sought to foster black participation in the Church. Holly was also influenced by his friend the Reverend William Monroe, pastor of the black Episcopal Church in Detroit. Holly formally renounced Catholicism in early 1852. As he noted more than four decades later, he had been gradually "weaned away from the unscriptural ways of" the Roman Catholic Church.[32] One historian, writing from an unambiguously pro-Episcopalian perspective, has emphasized that Holly explained in a letter to Bishop Hopkins that his eventual conversion to the Episcopal Church grew out of a "protest against the mind-enslaving system of unscrupulous domination" of the Roman Catholic Church, and his "awakening to the catholicity of the Protestant Episcopal Church."[33] In any case, after converting to the Protestant Episcopal Church, he was formally confirmed in his new faith in June 1852. The following year he was "admitted as a candidate for Holy Orders," and when he moved to Buffalo, New York, in 1856, his theological education continued under the Reverend William Shelton, rector of that city's most prominent Episcopal Church. Returning to the Detroit area in 1855, Holly received his Deacon's order from Bishop Samuel A. McCroskey.[34]

Holly's particular interest in Haiti, and his wider turn toward emigrationism, reflected personal, as well as ideological imperatives. In January 1855, Holly's elder brother, Joseph—who had not budged from his advocacy of the stay-and-fight philosophy—succumbed to tuberculosis, after a long illness. As David McEwen Dean has noted, this removed a "potential obstacle" to James' emigration plans.[35] Freed of opposition from within his family to the principles of emigrationism, Holly's interest in a movement from the United States became ever more explicit. Reflecting the cultural and hierarchical assumptions characteristic of the antebellum black leadership, Holly's emigrationism betrayed his deep commitment to the spiritual elevation of Haiti. In this way, his religious commitment merged with his wider plans for emigration. Appointed by the National Board of Commissioners at the 1854 Emigration Convention as "official commissioner" to visit Haiti, his designated task was to travel to the black republic to assess its suitability as a destination for African American emigrants. Holly sought to combine that endorsement with tangible support from

Episcopalian authorities. When he sought ordination, Holly made it clear that his specific goal was to become a missionary in Haiti. Hoping to examine the island republic as a possible field for Episcopal missions, during mid-1855 he sought the support of the Episcopal Church's Foreign Committee.[36]

Holly was not the only African American alert to Haiti's potential as a site for missionary activity. The Reverend Monroe, who had served as a missionary in Haiti during the late 1830s, also expressed interest in returning to the island. Yet, although Monroe was interested in Haiti, it was Holly who was the most vigorous advocate of emigration to the black republic. Armed with a letter of recommendation from Bishop McCroskey, Holly traveled to New York City, where his proposal was brought before the Episcopal Church's Foreign Committee. Although the Church approved in principle of the idea of establishing a mission in Haiti, no funds were forthcoming, at least officially. Holly did receive some private donations from sympathetic Episcopal clergy and laymen, and other emigrationists provided some scant assistance. Also relying on his own funds, and what he was able to borrow, Holly eventually secured enough money to finance his trip to Haiti. He sailed from New York in July 1855.[37]

Haiti had changed little since the 1820s. The rule of Jean Pierre Boyer, who had been president when African Americans emigrated during the 1820s, continued until 1843. Economic and agricultural conditions improved little during his long rule, and the racial divisions in Haiti were as marked in the 1850s as they had been in earlier decades. After Boyer's government fell, Haiti experienced renewed turmoil. Revolutions came in rapid succession, and the nation had four presidents in as many years. When General Jean-Baptiste Riché died in February 1847, the Haitian Senate elected Faustin Soulouque to the position of president. Initially reluctant to assume the presidency, Soulouque soon became comfortable with the idea of wielding power; by August 1849 he had consolidated his position to the point where he was proclaimed emperor. Like his predecessors, Soulouque had ambitions of securing and promoting Haiti's place in the world. To that end, he not only sought—unsuccessfully—to conquer neighboring Santo Domingo, but also to address France's continuing economic punishment of Haiti. In 1853, with Haiti beset by financial difficulties, Soulouque terminated the payment of the indemnity to France. But France was not prepared to allow its former colony to dictate the terms of their relationship, and when the French threatened to bombard Port-au-Prince, Soulouque was compelled to back down, promising to resume the payments.[38] This international disregard, or, more often, contempt, for Haiti, contributed significantly to its economic and social woes. When Holly arrived in the island republic it remained an underdeveloped agricultural country, with deep social divisions along racial lines.

For black Americans such as Holly, Haiti continued to present a paradox. On one hand, during the 1850s there were continuing expressions of pride in Haiti's status as an independent black republic. Significantly, this pride was not confined to proponents of Haitian emigrationism. In March 1858, the well-known black lawyer, physician, and abolitionist John S. Rock referred to the Haitians' valor. Disputing assumptions that black men were cowards, Rock told his audience that the "history of the bloody struggles for freedom in Haiti," when "the blacks whipped the French and English and gained their independence," stood as "a lasting refutation of the malicious aspersions of our enemies."[39] This sense of pride was a foundation on which Haitian emigrationism rested. But there was another set of imperatives, that reflected the cultural and political values of the African American community. By the 1820s, black Americans had formed contradictory views of the island republic and its contentious past; for African Americans during the 1850s, Haitians remained a remote "other," who were desperately in need of spiritual as well as material regeneration. Ironically, black Americans thus shared many of the values of their white oppressors, whose disdain for Haiti was expressed frequently during the antebellum period. Indeed, because Haiti continued to provoke strong passions among white Americans, it is worth considering in some detail the ways in which the black republic was depicted in historical and travelers' accounts in the period following the failed 1820s emigration movement. In some instances, representations of Haiti conformed to the crude and self-serving racial stereotypes that had long characterized outsiders' views of the island and its people. Jonathan Brown, a white northerner who had visited Haiti during the mid-1830s, was representative of this position. "The mass of the [Haitian] people," he wrote, "are not only uninstructed, but so profoundly stupid as to give rise to doubts if they are furnished with any intellect whatsoever. They know nothing of their age or of the events in their life."[40]

American observers such as Brown were not the only ones to make disparaging judgments about Haiti. James Franklin, an Englishman, had published his impressions of the island republic in 1828. Franklin sought to discredit those who were claiming Haiti was "a country in which wealth abounds, virtue flourishes, and freedom reigns triumphant." Following "several visits" to Haiti, he represented the island republic as devoid of moral, spiritual, political, and agricultural virtue. The "admirers of Hayti," he asserted, "have been very industrious in circulating the most deceptive accounts of the state of its commerce, by garbled and exaggerated specifications." Although Franklin acknowledged there were "some cases . . . in which instances of intelligence have been discovered in the Haytian citizen," he contended that such examples of intelligence only occurred "where individuals have had the advantages of a European education, or who, being the descendants of persons who previously to the revolution were possessed of wealth, had the means of travelling, for the purpose of acquiring the manners and customs of more enlightened nations." But such cases, in Franklin's view, were rare: "taking the people in the aggregate, they are far from having made any advances in knowledge." One of the ways by which Franklin highlighted Haiti's woes was by referring to the experiences of those African Americans who had emigrated to the island during the 1820s. Those emigrants who had settled on the Samaná Peninsula, he argued, had not had an easy time of it. Not surprisingly, the number of African Americans who remained there had "greatly diminished," with "numbers clandestinely leaving." The Haitian government's "assurances" to black Americans, he asserted, "were only made for the purpose of deluding them to form a settlement." In Franklin's view, the Haitian government's treatment of African American settlers was characteristic of a deeper malaise: "That the government of Hayti is the most inefficient and enervated of any of the modern republics cannot be denied."[41]

Franklin's assessment of Haiti sat easily alongside white Americans' long-standing views of the island republic. The Reverend John Beard, writing in the early 1850s, offered his impressions of Haiti, and of the capacities and characteristics of "the negro race." Writing in a period in which increasing attention was paid to the alleged "scientific" bases of racial difference, Beard offered a more sympathetic understanding of Haiti than that expressed by Franklin. But he did accept the prevailing view of black inferiority, tempered by a belief that such inferiority reflected environmental conditions, rather than biological predetermination. Although he concluded that "the negro is a man," Beard was equally certain that "the negro race is inferior to the highest style of man." He conceded that while "individuals belonging to that race have risen very high on the scales of civilized life," the "race at large cannot be accounted equal to some others." In Beard's view, this failure was a consequence of the fact that blacks had "no history." "It is no disparagement to the African," he wrote, "to say that they have realized but a small amount of social good in the island of Hayti, since the outbreak of its insurrectionary movements." The "legacy of slavery," along with the "prejudices, conflicting interests, and sanguinary wars," meant Haiti "has had a most rugged and perilous path to tread." Beard further qualified his criticism of Haiti's progress by stating that "the most cultivated of European nations," if they had been forced to endure circumstances similar to those confronting the black republic, "would have experienced great difficulty to hold itself erect." Moreover, in Beard's view, Haiti's leadership was evidence of the capacities of the African race. In "the patriotism of Toussaint, in the firmness of Christophe, in the moderation of Boyer, and in the wisdom of Riché," he declared, there was "enough to assure the impartial that in dark-coloured blood there is no incapacity for either government or social and civilized life."[42]

These writers did not exactly speak with one voice on Haiti. But the racialism that consistently underpinned their assessments of Haiti accorded with—and in turn shaped—the views of many Americans, including elements of the abolitionist movement. Indeed, prevailing American attitudes to Haiti were well summed up by a contributor to the *Liberator*. Writing in 1851, this observer pointed out that despite being blessed with rich natural resources, the Haitians were "an indolent people." Their "fathers," he continued, "made a vast quantity of sugar for [the] benefit of their owners; the present generation choose to make but little, and pervert a good share of that little into a very bad rum, which they are fools enough to like as well as white folks." Predicating his assessment upon the self-help ethos that was so dominant in antebellum America, the writer was convinced that intemperance was responsible for many of the Haitians' woes. Nevertheless, although his statement concerning the Haitians' alleged indolence echoed racial stereotypes that were common in the United States—among northerners and southerners alike—regarding black people's work habits, he was not willing to accept an equally common view regarding Haiti. The island republic, he insisted, was "by no means so wretched and unimportant as her studied depreciation by her oppressors and defamers of the African race would present her."[43]

Emigrationists such as Holly reflected, as well as confronted, these ambivalent attitudes toward Haiti. It was no coincidence that a similar ambivalence was evident in the cultural and political contest over savagery and civilization that raged in antebellum America. It was equally logical, given that the issues of race and slavery were at the center of that contest, that Haiti figured prominently in the slaveholders' defences of their peculiar institution. Frequently identifying Haiti as the worst example of barbarism and savagery, the slaveholders' condemnation of the island republic was central to their broader argument that the emancipation of the slaves throughout the New World had precipitated economic downturn.

For defenders of slavery in the United States, economic issues were inseparable from the wider struggle between savagery and civilization. Writing in 1855, David Christy asserted that the "free colored people of the West Indies" could "no longer be relied on to furnish tropical products," because they were "fast sinking into savage indolence."[44] Americans were not the only ones to exploit Haiti's economic grief to denigrate the value of free black labor. Writing in the late 1820s, James Franklin had declared that agriculture "has long been on the wane, and has sunk to the lowest possible ebb in every district of the republic." Yet although he asserted that he was "activated by no unfair nor unjust motives," Franklin's harsh judgments were no doubt shaped by contemporary events and debates. Writing at the same time as debates raged in Britain concerning the abolition of slavery throughout the Empire, Franklin disparaged the efficacy of free labor. The "system of labor so pursued in Hayti," he wrote, "instead of affording us a proof of what may be accomplished by" free labor "is illustrative of the fact, that it is by coercion, and coercion alone, that any return can be expected from the employment of capital in the cultivation of soil in our West India islands."[45]

In 1856, William J. Grayson utilized a poetic approach to defend the South's peculiar institution and disparage Caribbean blacks who had secured their freedom. His poetry was less than memorable, but his message was unambiguous:

> The bright Antilles, with each closing year
> See harvests fail, and fortunes disappear
> The cane no more its golden treasure yields
> Unsightly weeds deform the fertile fields

The negro freeman, thrifty while a slave
Loosed from restraint, becomes a drone or knave
Each effort to improve his nature foils
Begs, steals, or sleeps and starves, but never toils
For savage cloth mistakes the freedom won
And ends the mere barbarian he begun.[46]

Grayson's verse captured succinctly the southern rationale for the continuing enslavement of African Americans. For Grayson, an economic imperative merged seamlessly with claims that blacks in the post-emancipation Caribbean had discarded the benefits of civilization, and reverted to the barbarism—and inactivity—from where he believed they had originated.

J.D.B. De Bow, editor of *De Bow's Review*, and one of the South's best known defenders of slavery, used the example of emancipation in other slave societies to persuade non-slaveholding southern whites that the abolition of slavery would adversely affect their economic well-being. Arguing that the "world furnishes no instances" to show that the products of slave society could be "grown on a large scale by free labor," he asserted in 1860 that the "British West India Colonies" had been reduced from "opulence" to "beggary." For De Bow, however, Haiti provided the most salutary lesson of all: not only did "St. Domingo" share "the same" economic "fate" as other former slave societies, but the end of slavery there had led to dreadful bloodshed—which he emphasized had not been confined to the Haitian elites. This was a significant point, because issues of race frequently transcended class distinctions among southern whites. The survival of slavery in the United States rested, at least in part, on the fact that the slaveholding class enjoyed the allegiance of poor whites, who occupied a higher social station than any black. Indeed, although many whites often worked alongside blacks, the South's racial hierarchy reflected deep-seated fears among all of its white citizens. Here, too, Haiti offered lessons. As De Bow warned non-slaveholding Southern whites, "the poor whites" of St. Domingo were "massacred equally with the rich."[47]

Given these persistent attempts to denigrate Haiti, and present it as an example of barbarism, it was not surprising that the slavepower continued to refuse to countenance United States' recognition of the independent black republic of Haiti. Here, the politics of race, both domestic and international, rested firmly on cultural beliefs and social practices, as well as economic imperatives. Referring frequently to the bloodshed associated with Haiti's revolution, and emphasizing the island republic's economic woes, defenders of slavery in the United States successfully stifled attempts to recognize the island republic. For slaveholders, recognition of Haiti would not only be an apparent acknowledgment that violent revolution would ultimately be sanctioned by the United States, but would also be an admission that the black race was capable of self-government. This, in turn, would undermine one of the central planks of their defense of slavery; namely, that blacks required the paternalistic guidance of the white race.[48] As a subsequent chapter explains, when the Haitian government appointed James Redpath to oversee the American aspect of the black emigration to Haiti, they also commissioned him to secure U.S. recognition of the black republic.

The hostile depictions of Haiti, emanating from the North as well as the South of the United States, did not go unanswered. Free blacks continued to express pride in Haiti's history. This pride was expressed in a number of ways. During the mid-1850s, John Nelson Still, a Brooklyn businessman, and brother of abolitionist William Still, traveled the North with his diorama of *Uncle Tom's Cabin*. Besides highlighting scenes from Harriet Beecher Stowe's antislavery novel, and celebrating African Americans' military contributions to the American Revolution and the War of 1812, Still's diorama detailed the Haitian Revolution. Haiti's history was thus integrated into a broader narrative of black history and achievement.[49] African Americans were also conscious of the commercial relationship between the United States and Haiti. Speaking in Cortland, New York, in 1848, the black abolitionist Samuel Ringgold Ward suggested the U.S. "relations with the republic of Hayti should be placed upon such a basis as would relieve our commerce with that Republic from the inconveniences to which it is now subject, in consequence of the unjust treatment of our Government towards Hayti." "Why should Hayti," Ward asked, "who has maintained her independence half a century—two-thirds of the time that we have maintained our own—be treated in a manner so different?" Referring specifically to the interests of his particular audience, Ward argued that "New York, whose commerce with Hayti is greater than that of any other state of the Union," should be at the forefront of efforts to "induce our Government to treat our sister republic, Hayti, according to the claims of justice and propriety."[50] In this way, Ward hoped commercial considerations would prevail over the exigencies of racial politics, which for so long had precluded American recognition of Haiti. Of course, many white Americans regarded Haiti not as a sister in the family of nations, but as a poor cousin, who had not only failed to mature into adulthood, but who also sought to turn America's black children against their white parents.

Prominent white abolitionists repudiated such assumptions. In his 1861 lecture "Toussaint L'Ouverture," Wendell Phillips turned to "one of the most remarkable men of the last generation" to argue that the "negro race, instead of being that object of pity or contempt which we usually consider it, is entitled, judged by the facts of history, to a place close by the side of the negro."[51] Phillips was using Haiti's pre-eminent, albeit controversial revolutionary hero as a counter not just to the racism that was evident among those who defended slavery, but also to the racialism that permeated a good deal of white abolitionism.[52] Like others before him, Phillips praised Toussaint's military skill. But Phillips was not content to merely chronicle Toussaint's martial expertise. Determined to refute claims that post-colonial Haiti was nothing more than a model of barbarism, he also lauded Toussaint's "statesmanship," as being "as marvellous as his military genius." For Phillips, Toussaint's military prowess and statesmanship illustrated more than just the capabilities of an individual; he hoped also to demonstrate the "courage" and "endurance" of the black race. In the face of continuing political and economic proscription, Haiti had "become a civilized state," which carried on extensive commerce with the United States.[53]

There can be no doubt that James Holly, and other black Americans interested in emigration, were informed by these discourses about Haiti. It is more difficult, however, to ascertain with precision the extent to which the African American populace was aware of Haiti. Paradoxically, the southern slavepower's efforts to discredit the island republic perhaps served to increase Haiti's reputation among African Americans. But some black Americans, at least, also learned about the island republic from more direct sources. With the lively trade between the United States and Haiti, seamen continued to be important points of contact between the two nations. And along with the trickle of African Americans who relocated to the island republic, a handful of Haitians made their way to the United States. Although details of these individuals are inevitably sketchy, there is evidence of continuing encounters between black Americans and ˙Haiti. Even after the conclusion of the formal emigration movement of the 1820s there was some movement of people between the United States and Haiti. During the 1830s and 1840s a number of black Americans, some of whom were involved in missionary activities, visited Haiti. William Jennings, an agent for the *Colored American*, traveled to Haiti during the 1830s, sending back reports on agricultural and political conditions in the black republiċ.[54] There was also some movement in the opposite direction. In 1834, for example, one Evan Williams, identified only as a resident of Port-au-Prince, was admitted as an honorary member of the national convention of African Americans.[55] Williams' background is elusive, although his name suggests that he was an expatriate American, rather than a native Haitian. In any case, while there is no record that Williams took an active part in the proceedings of that convention, his presence does imply that certain American blacks did have some contact with Haiti.

James Holly sought to build on those contacts. On his arrival in Haiti in 1855, he was fortunate to obtain the support of John Hepburn, a black merchant from Virginia, and of Judge Emil de Ballette, an English-educated Haitian who had corresponded with the Reverend William Monroe concerning the "advisability of establishing an Episcopal mission in Haiti." Holly, handicapped by his inability to speak French, used their assistance to gain the attention of Haitian officialdom. As well as meeting with the ministers of the interior and the exterior, Holly was presented to Soulouque.[56] In these discussions, Holly pressed the emigration issue. Although he was unable to obtain the guarantees for black emigrants that he sought, Holly's efforts were of significance. Aware of the problems faced by black Americans who had emigrated to Haiti during the 1820s, he attempted to ensure that emigrants would be given every opportunity to succeed. He hoped the Haitian authorities would "offer encouragements" to African American emigrants, to help them establish themselves as cultivators. In addition to addressing Haiti's agricultural predicament, Holly sought to ensure that emigrants would be able to assist in the industrialization of Haiti. Besides wanting the Haitian government to "aid in the erection of manufacturing establishments, sugar refineries, grist and saw mills," he was hopeful that emigrants would not be required to pay import duties on tools and materials they took with them. Holly also raised the question of emigrants' rights in Haiti. Seeking an assurance that African Americans would be given equal civil and political rights as native-born Haitians, he asked that emigrants be granted "liberty of conscience in religious worship." Furthermore, although he did suggest emigrants be granted Haitian citizenship after one year's residence, he requested they be exempted from military service for seven years.[57]

To coordinate the emigration program, and supervise the embarkation of the emigrants, Holly urged the Haitian government to appoint a commissioner who would reside in the United States. Holly and other advocates of emigration envisioned they would have no trouble recruiting emigrants, provided the Haitians gave the assurances Holly outlined. The National Board of Commissioners, established at the 1854 Emigration Convention, would guarantee that at least two hundred families, or one thousand individuals, would emigrate annually for five years. If the guarantees were extended for a further two years, the commissioners were prepared to promise that another one thousand families, or "five thousand persons" would emigrate to Haiti. Holly envisaged that after seven years, the formal, organized scheme could be terminated, after which emigration would continue on a "voluntary and spontaneous" individual basis. He apparently made no estimate of the total number of blacks whom he thought would emigrate, but the figures cited above suggest a very selective emigration, the success of which would serve to alleviate the condition of the mass of blacks who remained in the United States. To enable the Haitian legislature to consider Holly's proposal, the secretary of the interior asked him to remain in the country for several months. A shortage of funds, however, compelled Holly to return to the United States. Although he subsequently claimed his proposals were "kindly entertained and considered," his attempt to extract specific guarantees regarding the rights of potential emigrants met with disappointment. Instead, he had to content himself with a general statement from the Haitian government announcing it would welcome African Americans emigrants at any time.[58]

Investigating the opportunities for emigration was one of Holly's motives for going to Haiti. He also spent considerable time assessing the feasibility of "establishing an Episcopal mission" in the black republic. After visiting the existing Protestant facilities in Haiti, he decided that the Episcopalians could establish a viable mission. In part, Holly's enthusiasm for this idea was based on what he judged to be a "hostile attitude from the Haitian government toward" the "Roman Catholic establishment." Holly's preoccupation with the shortcomings of the Roman Catholic Church, and his belief that the Episcopalians were better equipped to spread Christianity in Haiti, suggest the degree to which he had embraced many of the values of antebellum America. Leon Litwack has aptly described the black church on the eve of the Civil War as "the very bulwark and center of the black community," but—revealing again the extent to which Holly's vision of a black nationality entailed a significant modification of the existing Haitian nationality—his ideology of "Christian-emigrationism" represented a more assertive conjunction of religious faith with assumptions of African American superiority among black peoples. From his African American perspective, Holly was acting from the premise that the Haitian masses wanted to be imbued with Christianity—which he assumed was more advanced and representative of a civilized society than the Haitians' folk religion, with its strong African influences. Holly's inability to appreciate how deeply this so-called voodoo was embedded in Haiti's religious culture might have reflected the fact that he spent little time in the Haitian countryside. Remaining for the most part in Port-au-Prince, much of his attention was directed toward Haitian government officials and religious authorities.[59] In many respects, Holly saw what he wanted to see.

After returning to New York, Holly approached the Foreign Board of the Episcopal Church, hoping to gain its support for the establishment of a missionary station in Haiti. Describing the weaknesses of the Protestant churches in Haiti, he claimed the Roman Catholic Church was corrupt and out of favor with the emperor. Reflecting one of the most significant cultural tendencies of antebellum America, Holly interpreted and represented Haitian religious practices in gender-specific terms. This period witnessed what some scholars have labeled the "feminization" of American culture, including the religious culture. Although formal authority within the various denominations continued to be largely reserved for men, women were accorded increasing responsibility for religious matters, and were widely regarded as being blessed with a deeper religious sentiment than men. The common assumption that women were imbued with a deeper sense of spirituality was one of the premises of the prevailing domestic ideology, which in turn was one of the bases of antebellum Americans' conception of "civilization."[60] African Americans were not excluded from this ideological current. In Holly's view, while Haitian women were more religious than their menfolk, they were denied the opportunity to properly demonstrate the religious aspect of their nature. Echoing an earlier visitor to Haiti's remark that "none but females and a few stupid but upright negroes of the country are very frequent at mass," Holly asserted that only Haitian women attended the Catholic worship in their country. Arguing that Haitian men preferred the ceremony and symbolism of the Masonic Lodge, Holly—himself deeply interested in Masonry—sought to provide them with the opportunity to enhance their religious faith and demonstrate their commitment. Having been assured that Haitian Masons would flock to Episcopal services if they were offered, he envisaged there was a potential pool of recruits for Episcopalianism.[61] Although he was antagonistic to Catholicism, Holly's attempts to broaden the base of Christianity in Haiti was reflective of the domestic, as well as racial ideology of nineteenth-century America.

The Episcopal Church's Foreign Board did not offer immediate support to Holly, but it was prepared to help him articulate his views in public. When the board's members learned that he planned to deliver a series of lectures, describing what he had seen in Haiti, they arranged for him to speak in churches in New York City. During October and November 1855, Holly lectured on "The Religious Wants of Hayti" to audiences of black and white Episcopalians. Describing the opportunities Haiti offered for the diffusion of Christian civilization, Holly asserted that it would only be through the work of African American Episcopalian missionaries that such values could be imparted to the Haitians. Unfortunately for Holly, the Episcopal Church's financially precarious Board of Missions was not swayed by his arguments. In late November 1855, burdened by debt, and skeptical of the capabilities of black missionaries, the board notified Holly that it could not afford to commence missionary operations in any new fields. He was promised, however, that as soon as the necessary funds became available, he would be sent to Haiti as a missionary.[62]

Despite being rebuffed in his efforts to establish a mission in the island republic, Holly gratefully accepted the rectorship of a black Episcopal Church in New Haven, Connecticut. There, in 1856, he addressed that town's Literary Society of Colored Young Men. This lecture, published in 1857 as *A Vindication of the Capacity of the Negro Race*, was more passionate and revealing than his earlier speeches and tracts.[63] Here, too, we find Holly foreshadowing many of the themes on which he would subsequently expand in his 1860 series of "Thoughts on Hayti." All the while, he was moving toward an ever more explicit black nationalist ideology based around principles of Christian-emigrationism. Holly's lecture, the only publication of the Afric-American Printing Company (established at the 1854 Emigration Convention), and dedicated to the Reverend William Monroe, was largely comprised of a description of the Haitian Revolution, with a characteristically evocative assessment of the capacities of black people. *A Vindication of the Capacity of the Negro Race* betrayed two interrelated objectives. First, by detailing the history of the Haitian Revolution, and by connecting a religious imperative to black advancement, he sought to refute the "impious dogma of our natural and inherent inferiority." Second, he aimed to "inflame the latent embers of self-respect, that the cruelty and injustice of our oppressors, have nearly extinguished in our bosoms, during the midnight chill of centuries, that we have clanked the galling chains of slavery."[64]

Holly portrayed the Haitian Revolution as irrefutable evidence of the capabilities of the black race. Extolling the Haitians' "resuscitated manhood," he also detailed their patience in the face of adversity and brutality, representing these attributes as evidence of their civilized qualities. In an attempt to convince his audience of the legitimacy of the Haitian government, Holly compared it to that of the United States; indeed much of his tract was underpinned by a comparison of the United States and Haiti, suggesting perhaps that despite America's imperfections, for black emigrationists it remained a benchmark on which other political systems should be measured. Like others before him, Holly's emigrationist ideology rested upon frequently contradictory values and aspirations. Even while emigrationists such as Holly abhorred the racism that so defiled the political culture of the United States, they were seemingly convinced that the American system of government was the most advanced in the world—if not in practice, at least in potential. In short, although black emigrationists did not resile from criticism of the tainted political culture of the United States, they appeared to accept many of the premises of American exceptionalism.[65]

These assumptions and contradictions were evident in Holly's *Vindication of the Capacity of the Negro Race*. Depicting Haiti as a politically stable nation, he noted that Haiti had had "but eight rulers" since 1804; in the United States, by way of contrast, there had been "ten different chief magistrates" since 1809. "The fact is," Holly asserted, "there is not a nation in North America, but the United States, nor any in South America, except Brazil, that can pretend to compare with Hayti, in respect to general stability of government." This issue was significant in a number of ways. In the first instance, it was an obvious means of assuring African Americans that political conditions in Haiti were conducive to a successful emigration. Equally significant, Haiti's survival and stability were tangible signs that the United States should formally acknowledge the legitimacy of the government of the island republic. As Holly implied, Haiti had survived, despite the unrelenting hostility of the southern slavepower. He hoped African Americans would derive pride from these accomplishments. At the heart of his thesis was the matter of civilization, an issue of enduring concern to nineteenth-century Americans. For white Americans, the racial hierarchy associated with slavery seemed to confirm the ascendancy of white civilization over black savagery. Similarly, their westward sweep over the North American continent was evidence of the triumph of white civilization over Native American savagery. African Americans were more than just victims of these racial imperatives. Black leaders embraced the notion of civilization as vigorously as white Americans; for Holly, these concerns were couched in explicitly political terms. Refuting the assumptions inherent in many others' depictions of Haiti, Holly insisted the Haitians' "political stability," was indicative of "a vast remove from Barbarism." Besides proving that the Haitians' were "far ahead of the anarchy of some so-called civilized nations," their political stability was also evidence of "a high degree of civilization and progress."[66]

Holly did acknowledge the tension in Haiti between the "Republican and Monarchical" forms of government. He argued, however, that this tension was less significant than the fact that the "oscillation" between these two forms of government had "not unsettled the permanent stability of the national administration." Speaking just a few months before Congressman Preston Brooks from South Carolina would savagely assault anti-slavery Senator Charles Sumner of Massachusetts on the floor of the United States Senate, Holly contrasted the civilized elements of Haiti's political system to the United States. There, he pointed out, "a vagabond set of politicians, whose character for rowdyism disgraces the nation," were able "to enact such an odious law as the Fugitive Slave Bill." Turning Haiti's reputation as a despotic autocracy on its head, Holly argued that a "single necked despot is soon reached by the keen avenging axe of liberty." Such a system, he claimed, offered more protection to "personal liberty and the general welfare of the governed," than did American republicanism. Within the United States, Holly submitted, the same "axe of liberty" could "be hurled in vain and fall powerless among a nameless crowd of millions."[67] In Holly's view, the virtues of democracy were not self-evident to African Americans, whose numerical disadvantage was exacerbated by white Americans' refusal to include them as equals in the political system. For Holly, the Founding Fathers' determination to protect the rights of the minority from the tyranny of the majority had proved nothing more than a racially self-interested deception, effectively excluding African Americans from the polity.

Despite Haiti's status as the "black nationality of the New World," Holly conceded it had not fully realized its potential. In order to help it do so, he urged African Americans to emigrate to the island republic, taking with them "such of the arts, sciences, and genius of modern civilization, as we may gain from this hardy and enterprising Anglo-American race." Conceding, apparently, that blacks in the United States had benefited from their contacts with the white race, Holly thus implied that African Americans were more advanced than blacks in other parts of the world. Holly's work might have been, as August Meier has argued, a "clear cut statement of Negro nationalism," but it was a nationalism indubitably born of the American experience. Telling evidence of the influence of western values on Holly's philosophy can be found in the central place he accorded to Christianity in his nationalist ideology. Indeed, he was increasingly sure that Christianity and civilization were inseparable elements of an advanced nationality—just as they were supposed to be in the United States. Holly's thesis rested on the belief that if "one powerful negro sovereignty can be developed to the summit of national grandeur in the West Indies, where the keys to the eminence of both hemispheres can be held; this fact will solve all questions regarding the negro, whether they be those of slavery, prejudice or proscription." Asserting it would be better for African Americans to emigrate than "indolently remain" in the United States, "asking for political rights," which even if granted would be rendered worthless by "a social proscription stronger than conventional legislation," he understood black Americans were confronting a racist culture, as well as a tainted political system. To overcome these obstacles, Holly was very specific about where African Americans should emigrate. While Africa would be civilized and Christianized in the future, Holly was opposed to "utopian" schemes being "prematurely forced" upon the black race. Nor did he approve of efforts that sought "to rummage the graves of our ancestors, in fruitless, and ill-directed efforts at the wrong end of human progress."[68] Although he was determined to validate and celebrate the accomplishments of black people, in disparaging Africa and its peoples he was inadvertently endorsing the Anglo-Saxon view of a racial hierarchy. Holly, of course, was not the only emigrationist to reflect the Anglo-Saxon assumption of African inferiority, but in assuming black Americans were uniquely qualified to elevate Haiti to its rightful place on the world stage, he also implied the Haitians were lacking elements of modern civilization.[69]

All of these issues underpinned Holly's emergent ideology of Christian emigrationism, and shaped his ideology of black nationalism. But they did more. Underlying Holly's statements was a view of what constituted the nation. Like other black emigrationists, Holly was not always entirely consistent in his articulations of the ideal nation. But given the concept of black nationality entailed a cultural, as well as economic and political challenge to the prevailing racial order in the United States, it was perhaps not surprising that he sometimes shifted ground. It is well to remember, too, that because the task of the reformer almost always entails profound challenges to the social and political order, a certain flexibility, or pragmatism, is probably inevitable. Nevertheless, Holly and his coadjutors were consistent in their assumption that black Americans were destined to carry Christian civilization to Haiti, or other destinations. They were equally consistent, if somewhat less explicit, in their assumption that the nationhood they envisioned was one that did not seek to obliterate hierarchies. They did of course repudiate racial hierarchies, but they did not envisage a society where everyone was equal. Like white Americans, black emigrationists regarded hierarchies of merit and achievement as inevitable, and probably healthy.

Holly continued to lecture during 1856. Well aware that he had to appeal to different constituencies, he alternated between his passionate and nationalistic "Vindication" lecture, delivered primarily to black audiences, and a more tempered description of Haiti's religious needs, presented mainly before white audiences.[70] Typically, Holly sought to construct an organizational base to implement his objectives: His particular brand of emigrationism-nationalism was thus reflected in the "Protestant Episcopal Society for Promoting the Extension of the Church Among Colored People," that he and the Reverend William Monroe established in July 1856. Intended to propagate the Episcopal faith among African Americans, and build support "for the establishment of an Episcopal mission in Haiti," it was also hoped this new organization would promote emigration to the island republic.[71]

During 1856, Holly also made preparations for another emigration convention. Meeting in Cleveland in August 1856, the second gathering of emigrationists was preceded by none of the controversies and debates that had accompanied the 1854 emigration convention. The only newspaper to actively promote the 1856 Emigration Convention was the *Provincial Freeman*, under the guiding hand of Mary Ann Shadd Cary.[72] Evidently, for a time at least, opponents of emigrationism considered the best way to undermine the movement was to simply ignore it. Although most of the principal emigrationists were present at the 1856 meeting, Martin Delany was a notable absentee, unable to attend on account of illness. Despite his absence from the 1856 gathering, however, Delany was re-elected president of the National Board of Commissioners. While it is possible, as Cyril Griffith has claimed, that the emigrationists regarded Delany as the "guiding spirit for their movement," he was not in sole control.[73] Not only was there disagreement concerning the most suitable destination for African American emigrants, but it is ultimately misleading to depict the interest in emigration as representing a "movement," because that phrase connotes a cohesion that was clearly lacking from the emigrationist spirit of the mid-1850s. That lack of unanimity was evident in the responses from the delegates at the 1856 convention to one of Holly's proposals. Determined to use the convention to promote Haiti, Holly was chosen foreign corresponding secretary. Hoping to procure funding to return to Haiti, he reported to the convention on his trip to the island republic. Perhaps if he had completed a firm agreement with the Haitian authorities, he might have been able to convince the delegates that it would be best to concentrate exclusively on emigration to Haiti. The delegates at Cleveland, however, were not prepared to make such a commitment, although they did reaffirm their interest in the Caribbean as a whole.[74] Much of the problem for Holly stemmed from the fact that as president of the National Board of Commissioners, Delany's attentions were increasingly focused on Africa. The Board was not single-mindedly committed to African emigration. But nor was it going to be of any realistic assistance to Holly in his work on behalf of emigration to Haiti. Symptomatic of this problem was Holly's inability to obtain the funding that would have enabled him to return to the island republic—a situation he subsequently claimed "compromised" him with the Haitian authorities.[75]

Although Holly failed to convince the 1856 convention that emigrationist sentiment should be directed solely toward Haiti, his influence was reflected in the adoption of a plan to establish a North American and West Indian Trading Association. Designed as a "joint-stock venture," comprised of shareholders who would each pay fifty dollars, and intended to be under the control of a newly established Board of Trade, the Trading Association evidenced the free market bourgeois ethos that underpinned antebellum black emigrationism. The plan for a Trading Association closely resembled that proposed in 1851, and Holly was probably as much behind the 1856 scheme as he had been behind the earlier one. The Board of Trade, moreover, was made up of just six men, all from Connecticut, and four of them from Holly's St. Luke's Church in New Haven.[76] The delegates at Cleveland reaffirmed their intention to publish their own journal. A Board of Publication was organized to assist in the publication of the *Afric-American Quarterly Repository*, to be edited by James Whitfield. The emigrationists hoped their journal would not only present their side of the debate on the emigration issue, but would also "exhibit the intellectual capacities of the negro race."[77] Neither the Board of Trade nor the Board of Publication achieved any material results. Their significance, however, derives from the intention behind their establishment. The failure of both boards pointed to the difficulties faced by all African Americans: Lacking sufficient funds to implement their plans, schemes for black advancement stood little chance of success. Again, this is a point at which emigrationists and their opponents converged; although people such as Delany and Holly considered they were acting, whereas other leaders were merely talking, advocates of both philosophies were similarly constrained by financial difficulties.

The rivalry between African American leaders, including those who agreed on the virtues of emigrationism, hinted at another obstacle to black advancement in the United States. There was no single leader around whom emigrationists could coalesce. While Frederick Douglass was the best known black leader in nineteenth-century America, there was arguably no bona-fide leader of a mass movement among African Americans until the emergence of Marcus Garvey during the post–World War I period. In seeking to build a broad base of support, the leaders of the Haitian scheme of the Civil War era jostled with the proponents of African emigrationism for the mantle of leadership of the vaguely defined emigration movement. This process was evidenced by events at the 1856 Emigration Convention. Although that convention agreed to shift its central headquarters to Chatham, Canada West, where Delany was then residing, the composition of the Board of Trade was a reflection of Holly's status within emigrationist circles; Delany's role remained significant, but another center of emigrationist sentiment was growing around Holly's presence in New Haven.[78]

Not only did these two amorphous groups emphasize different locations for African American emigration, but they placed different emphases on the role of religion in the creation of the black nationality for which they were both striving. For his part, Delany continued to harbor serious doubts about the value of religion to black Americans. Claiming blacks were "highly susceptible" to religion, he had argued in 1852 that they placed too much faith in God. African Americans, he averred, "usually stand still," and "hope in God," waiting for "Him to do that for them which it is necessary they should do for themselves."[79] Conversely, as we have seen, Holly was increasingly convinced that the Christian religion, specifically the Episcopal Church, was destined to play a vital role in the elevation of the black race, both in the United States and elsewhere. By 1856, the main planks of Holly's Christian-emigrationist philosophy were firmly in place. But if Holly's emphasis on Christian regeneration accorded with the views of white Episcopalians, his focus on black nationality proved troubling to Church authorities. Unsurprisingly, Holly's requests for funds from the Episcopal Church authorities did not bear fruit. Eventually he realized that the future for black members of the Episcopal faith in the United States was undeniably bleak. Of course, not all white Episcopalians regarded blacks as their inferiors, and some had grave reservations about slavery, but under the influence of southern slaveholders, and northerners such as Bishop John Henry Hopkins, Episcopal Church policy reflected a belief in white superiority, as well as a conviction that blacks were unfit for the responsibilities of freedom.[80] Holly, of course, did not accept those assumptions, but—seeking to turn them to best advantage—continued to seek financial aid from the Church to enable black adherents to the Episcopal faith to emigrate to Haiti. Besides confronting the racialism that was evident among some leading white Episcopalians, Holly's chances of securing the Church's support were further hindered by the economic downturn that afflicted the United States during 1857 and 1858.[81]

In the wake of his disappointments with the Episcopalian authorities, Holly's cause suffered a further setback in 1858, when the Reverend Monroe shifted his attentions away from Haitian emigrationism. Discouraged by the failure of his Detroit congregation to grow (due in part to opponents of black emigration petitioning for his dismissal) Monroe moved to Brooklyn, New York. He again urged the Episcopal hierarchy to send him to Haiti as a missionary, but once more his request was denied. One factor behind the Church's Foreign Committee rejection of Monroe's application was a statement by two white Episcopalians from Detroit, who argued that although his integrity and motives were honorable, Monroe was not suited for missionary labors. Evident here was the racism among influential white Episcopalians that played a part in thwarting Holly's plans. Monroe, despairing of the possibility for Episcopalian assistance in the spiritual elevation of Haiti, turned his attention toward Africa; in May 1859 he emigrated to Liberia, to work as a missionary.[82] Monroe's change of heart typified the pragmatism of the African American leadership.

Holly demonstrated a similar pragmatism during 1858. Possibly discouraged by the failure of the Episcopal Church to provide him with funds to travel to Haiti as a missionary, and increasingly skeptical of blacks' ability to finance emigration to Haiti, independent of white assistance, he turned his attention in another direction in early 1858. In January of that year he was one of several black emigrationists who wrote to Francis P. Blair, Jr., a Republican congressman from Missouri, and advocate of African American colonization in Central America. Holly told Blair of the efforts he had made on behalf of Haitian emigrationism, but admitted that, for the time being at least, the scheme appeared to hold little promise of success. Stressing that African colonization was not a realistic option for black Americans, he argued "American intertropical emigration" was a more viable alternative. Holly's comments to Blair were premised on many of the assumptions that underpinned the ambiguous black nationalism of the 1850s. Characteristically, he emphasized the relationship between black and white Americans. Holly was hoping to impress, rather than antagonize Blair, but there is no reason to doubt he was sincere in his suggestion that one advantage of black emigration to Central America vis-à-vis African colonization was that emigrants to Central America would be able to "enjoy" a "constant intercourse" with "white Americans." Because they would not feel "as if they had lost their homes with us," African American emigrants would be "contented and happy in their lot." Praising Blair for his advocacy of black emigration, Holly assured him he could annually muster "two hundred emigrant families, or about one thousand free colored persons" for the next five years. After that initial period, Holly anticipated that emigration would regulate itself. He urged Blair to use his influence with the U.S. government, as well as with private citizens, to promote African American emigration to Central America. He also recommended that an "intelligent and able commissioner" be appointed to negotiate with the governments in the region. Presumably with himself in mind, he suggested that "this commissioner might be accompanied by some intelligent colored man, to be named by their Board or Central Committee, in whom they might repose the utmost confidence, when he brought back a report of the condition, prospects, and advantages, of that country."[83]

Holly's remarks to Blair are significant on several levels. In the first instance, his call for the appointment of a "commissioner" implied he was content to allow a white man to assume responsibility for negotiating an agreement on behalf of the prospective emigrants with the authorities in Central America. As later chapters reveal, this question of black emigrationists occupying positions subservient to whites became even more contentious when the Haitian Bureau of Emigration was established. Holly's overtures to Blair marked the first occasion since he had veered away from Canadian emigration that he had advocated African Americans going anywhere other than Haiti. His attention soon reverted to Haitian emigrationism, but there had been other expressions of interest in Central America during the 1850s.

Typically, the major black advocate of Central American emigration was no less flexible than Holly. This was James Whitfield, who was discussed earlier as the main advocate of the emigrationist position in the debate preceding the 1854 Emigration Convention. The National Board of Commissioners, organized at the 1854 Emigration Convention, commissioned Whitfield to travel to Central America, to investigate the possibilities for black emigration to that region. Like Holly, Whitfield discovered that the necessary funds were not easily available. Yet he maintained his interest in emigration; in January 1858, after Blair addressed the House of Representatives on the slavery question, Whitfield wrote to the *Missouri Republican*, endorsing his procolonization stance. Blair had several motives in advocating black colonization in Central America. Claiming "it is evident to every man of thought that the freed blacks, hold a place in this country which cannot be maintained," he described those African Americans who had fled to the North as "unwelcome visitors." In terms that reflected the racialism of nineteenth-century America, Blair spoke of the "badge" placed by nature on the African, which made "amalgamation revolting to our [white] race." Describing the rivalry between the United States and

Britain in Central America, Blair argued that sending black emigrants there would be the best means of insuring American influences predominated in the region.[84]

It is most revealing of the confused black nationalism of the antebellum period that there should be such interest on the part of black leaders in the ideas of a man like Blair. On the face of it, nothing could be more provocative than his assumption that blacks could not be assimilated in the United States, but, shipped overseas, could serve as an arm of American expansionism in regions where it was competing with Britain—a nation that had, since at least the early 1830s, proved more sympathetic to black rights and freedom than the United States. Yet Whitfield, at least, responded to Blair not only out of necessity born of blacks' vulnerability but with an apparent commitment to similar racialist assumptions. The "Saxon and the Negro," Whitfield asserted, "are the only positive races on this continent, and the two are destined to absorb into themselves all the others; and, like two positive poles, they repel each other; and if the one is destined to occupy all the temperate regions of this hemisphere, it is equally certain that the other will predominate within the tropics." Arguing that slaveholders were retarding "the march of civilization," Whitfield envisioned an organized emigration to Central America that would prove more efficient in despatching emigrants than the ACS. Praising Blair for his advocacy of black emigration, Whitfield hoped Congress would adopt the "same just and liberal policy."[85]

If Whitfield did genuinely believe in these racial imperatives, it presumably meant that by 1858 he had given up his earlier hope that blacks could be assimilated into American society. If that was the case, he might also have shifted ground on the question of selective or en-masse emigration, for if he believed the two races could not coexist as equals, then it is logical to assume he thought the only way all African Americans could secure real freedom would be through mass emigration. Although no details of his trip are available, it is thought Whitfield traveled to Central America in 1859.[86] But the African American interest in Central America was short-lived, and James Holly's flirtation with the idea did not last long. By the middle of 1858 he had again changed priorities; at a meeting in New York City in July he was again proclaiming the virtues of Haitian emigrationism.[87]

By that time, Holly was not the only African American expressing enthusiasm for Haiti. Indeed, interest in Haitian emigration was manifesting itself from several directions. In late 1858, the Convention of the Colored Men of Ohio considered the issues of colonization and emigration. As the proceedings of that convention reveal, the question of emigration to the Caribbean, and the associated issue of Haiti's status as an exemplar of the capabilities of the black race were occupying the minds of many African Americans. Although the delegates declared their opposition to a movement to Africa, emigration to regions closer to the United States proved more divisive. Characteristically, debates over emigration were contemporaneous with a discussion of the merits of Haiti as an agent of black advancement. E. P. Walker, who subsequently worked as an agent of the Haitian Bureau of Emigration, offered a resolution declaring that Haiti "sets the colored people" of the United States "an exam- ple of proper independence; and that, that government is doing more for the upbuilding of the black race, than all other instrumentalities proposed or con- troled [*sic*] by colored men." After discussion, Walker's resolution was "indefi- nitely postponed." But the debate did not end there. Reiterating the argument that emigration was a means of facilitating an economic assault on slavery, Walker and Joseph Dennis Harris (who would also later work on behalf of Hai- tian emigrationism) spoke in favor of emigration. Urging African Americans to "concentrate upon the West Indies, upon Central America, where by our supe- rior intelligence and energy, we would wield a wide influence, and many years would not pass away before we would have the world at our feet," Walker called on black Americans to use their particular skills and attributes to advance the cause of black progress. However, Walker and Harris were unable to per- suade a majority of the delegates of the virtues of emigration, and a resolution advising African Americans to devote their energies to advancing their rights within the United States, rather than abroad, was adopted.[88]

African American emigration to the Caribbean, particularly to Haiti, was also a topic of discussion in another western state. By early 1859, aware that the Haitian president had invited African Americans to emigrate to Haiti, blacks in Chicago were holding meetings to consider the idea.[89] H. Ford Doug- lass was reported as having delivered an "eloquent speech" in favor of the proj- ect, and the possibility that blacks might emigrate was sufficiently significant to prompt the editors of *Douglass' Monthly* to feel compelled to advise African Americans against leaving for Haiti. They claimed that by advocating emigra- tion, H. Ford Douglass was taking for granted the "old argument" of the ACS, that it was impossible for blacks to achieve equality in the United States.[90]

The repudiation of Haitian emigrationism in the columns of *Douglass' Monthly* suggests the divisions that existed between proponents of emigration- ism and the stay-and-fight ideology. But emigrationists also continued to have their fair share of disagreements among themselves. The continuing uncer- tainties over emigration had been evident at the third emigration convention, held at Chatham, Canada West, in August 1858. There, proponents of emigra- tion again discussed the merits of various schemes for black elevation. James Holly reported again on his 1855 trip to Haiti, but he was no more successful in gaining the support of the 1858 gathering than he had been two years ear- lier. As Holly stated later, "the whole policy of the movement changed" at the 1858 convention. This shift was reflected in a change of personnel.[91] William Howard Day, who had vacillated on the emigration issue for several years, re- placed Delany as president of the National Board of Commissioners. Although he had given favorable consideration to emigration at particular times during the 1850s, Day was not one of the more prominent emigrationists, and his support of the idea was, at best, circumspect. Day had moved to Chatham in early 1858, but despite his endorsement of Canadian emigration, his major concern was with the establishment of a black newspaper. Although Howard Bell has argued that Day's election to the "presidency of the Canadian wing of the African venture in 1858 represented his acceptance of the growing trend toward emigration and Negro nationalism," an examination of the resolutions and actions of the Chatham convention suggests the "movement" changed more than Day did.[92]

The delegates at Chatham refused to give specific approval to any particular destination, and they rejected the idea of mass emigration. Rather, they gave a half-hearted endorsement to emigration by declaring their support for efforts to gather information concerning suitable sites for individuals who chose to leave the United States. In order to attract African Americans with interests outside emigration, the convention agreed to change the name of their organization to the Association for the Promotion of the Interest of the Colored People of Canada and the United States.[93] The result of these changes was that the organization forfeited its active emigrationist spirit, in favor of a more general antislavery philosophy. Disappointed by that shift, and by the convention's refusal to actively support Haitian emigrationism, Holly removed himself from the organization. He understood that Day's declaration that he was "in favor of just such nationalities as that of Hayti" did not amount to active support for emigration. Holly's skepticism regarding Day's emigrationist credentials was not without foundation; at the 1858 convention of black Ohions, held just three months after the Chatham meeting, Day was to oppose emigration.[94]

Another emigrationist dissatisfied with the tenor of the 1858 Emigration Convention was Martin Delany, who attempted to gain support for the African alternative, particularly for a planned trip to assess the possibilities for African American emigration. Delany's advocacy of African emigration came after several years of deliberation over the question of a suitable destination for black emigration. Following the 1854 Emigration Convention, most of his efforts were directed toward the Americas. At the first annual meeting of the National Board of Commissioners, held in 1855, he reiterated his belief that the "only successful remedy for the evils we endure, is to place ourselves in a position of potency, independent of our oppressors." In a reversal of his earlier attitude he roundly endorsed emigration to Canada. And as well as informing his fellow commissioners that Holly was visiting Haiti, Delany again praised the island republic.[95]

Early in 1856, Delany moved from Pittsburgh to Chatham, Canada West, from where he continued to express interest in the Caribbean. Nothing eventuated, however, from his proposal that a "great Continental Convention" of black men be held in Kingston, Jamaica, and his attentions increasingly shifted toward Africa.[96] There are a number of explanations for this shift. Claiming that in "the winter of 1831–1832" he had "formed the design of going to Africa, the land of my ancestry," Delany subsequently explained that as early as 1850 he "had fully matured a plan for an adventure" to the region.[97] However, these suggestions that Africa was Delany's "first love" must be treated warily: As has been explained, not only was he a reluctant emigrationist, but during the 1850s he advocated emigration to a variety of locations. The publication in 1857 of works by Thomas J. Bowen and David Livingstone on Africa stimulated his interest in the continent, and his turn away from hemispheric emigration was reinforced by white Americans' growing interest in Central America—as exemplified by Francis Preston Blair's speech to the House of Representatives.[98] For some emigrationists, the chances of establishing an independent black nationality in the Americas would be jeopardized by U.S. territorial ambitions. Having expressed such fears about Canada, Delany must have worried that Central America was similarly threatened by white America's ebullient Manifest Destiny. At the 1858 Emigration Convention, Delany secured an "African Commission," authorizing him to undertake a "Topographical, Geological and Geographical Examination of the Niger River." But this was at best a vague endorsement, unsupported by any tangible assistance. Indeed the board noted it was "entirely opposed to any Emigration there [Africa] as such."[99] Delany was finding, like others before him, that although it was easy to enunciate grandiose plans, translating those proposals into action was an immeasurably more complex task.

Typically, the divisions among African Americans rendered Delany's quest even more difficult. During 1858 he was in direct competition with another group of African Americans who were looking toward Africa. In particular, Delany's efforts to raise funds to finance his proposed journey were hindered by the activities of the African Civilization Society, established in New York City in mid-1858. Endorsing the principles of emigrationism, the leaders of this organization anticipated an array of potential benefits deriving from a movement of black Americans to Africa. With Henry Highland Garnet as its president, the African Civilization Society aimed to Christianize and civilize Africa, destroy the international slave trade, promote the production of cotton and other products in Africa, and generally contribute to the elevation of black people around the world.[100]

These were characteristically ambitious goals, but the Civilization Society differed from Delany's group in two significant respects. In the first place, Garnet and others in the Civilization Society were willing to accept the assistance of whites. Although Delany later retreated from his refusal to countenance the assistance of whites, in 1858 he continued to proclaim that blacks had to act independently, and that accepting aid from whites would compromise that independence. This pointed to a constant dilemma confronting the emigrationist-nationalists of the 1850s: They could accomplish little without financial assistance from whites, which they were loath to accept because it would have exposed them to the same charges they made against opponents of emigration. Ironically, if emigrationists had been able to raise the necessary funds from within the African American community, it is doubtful that many blacks would have been prepared to leave the United States; as noted it would have been an indication that they were attaining wealth, and improving their position in American society. A second distinction between the two factions was the differing emphases they placed on religion. Although Delany did reflect the influence of western values, including Christianity, he had long expressed grave reservations concerning the influence of Christianity on the African American populace. Conversely, Garnet and his followers stressed the role that religion would play in the elevation of Africa. In this respect, members of the African Civilization Society were echoing the views expressed by James Holly.

Henry Highland Garnet's reputation as a black leader was based on more than the activist stance he had articulated at the 1843 National Convention. We have seen that he had expressed support for emigration in 1849, and following a stint in Britain during the early 1850s, he was commissioned by the United Presbyterian Church of Scotland to work in Jamaica as a missionary and teacher.[101] As Sterling Stuckey has remarked, Garnet's stay in Jamaica "contributed to his sense of the possibility for unity among people of African descent."[102] Perhaps with those possibilities in mind, Garnet wrote to the editor of the New York *Tribune* in June 1853, stating that a Jamaican planter was hoping to entice thirty African Americans to labor on his property. There was a labor shortage in Jamaica during the 1850s, and several emigrationists—including Delany—dabbled briefly with the idea of emigration to the British colony. Garnet's call, however, was opposed by Frederick Douglass, and nothing eventuated from his suggestion.[103]

After returning to the United States in 1856, by August 1858 Garnet was advocating black emigration. A key figure in the establishment of the African Civilization Society, he corresponded with cotton buyers, hoping to convince them of the viability of their scheme to use African-grown cotton to undercut Southern slaveowners on the world market. A principal advocate of that scheme was Benjamin Coates, a white man whose long-time membership of the ACS gave credence to those charging that the African Civilization Society was nothing more than a new version of the ACS—a suspicion reinforced by the fact that the African Civilization Society had access to more funds than did Delany's group.[104]

This question of funding proved an intractable problem for Delany. In an effort to raise the profile of his scheme, Delany established the African Civilization Society of Canada. He then wrote to William Lloyd Garrison, hoping to elicit his assistance in finding a publisher for his novel *Blake*.[105] That appeal yielded no results, but it did signify his willingness to seek help from a white man—a shift from his earlier insistence that blacks had to act independently if they were to gain equality and freedom. Moreover, given that the central character of *Blake* valorized a spirit of rebellion and independence, Delany's position was all the more contradictory.[106] Delany soon gave further evidence that he had retreated from his previous stance. In March 1859 he announced that he would cooperate with the New York-based African Civilization Society; after scraping together enough funds to finance his project, he departed for Africa in May.[107]

Conceivably, Delany might have believed his acceptance of aid from white colonizationists was merely a tactical concession, and that his long-term goals had not been compromised. However, other black leaders were skeptical of Delany's motives, and there was no shortage of opponents to the notion of black emigration to Africa. Indeed—despite Garnet's emphatic assertion that he was "*not* a colonizationist"—the African Civilization Society was widely construed as nothing more than the ACS in new garb.[108] As one black critic, James McCune Smith, stated, the "African Civilization Scheme is a feeble attempt to do what the American Colonization Society has failed to do; witness Liberia." "I do not see in your African Civilization scheme," Smith continued, "anything different in character or at all equal in force and power" to the ACS.[109] Garnet and Delany's opponents charged that the two men were succumbing to the notion that there was no place for blacks in American society.[110]

Nor did the emigrationists' assertions that they were advocating the emigration of a select minority appease their critics. Launching his new journal in January 1859, Frederick Douglass had noted that the editors expected to "insist upon it that we are Americans: *that America is our native land; that this is our home; that we are American citizens.*"[111] The following month, Douglass explained that although he had no objection to the civilization and Christianization of Africa, he was certain that the African Civilization Society, like the ACS, was premised on the "lying assumption, that white and black people can never live in the same land on terms of equality." Denying that the production of cotton in Africa would destroy slavery, he argued that slave labor could be "employed in raising anything which human labor and the earth can produce." Douglass had no objections to individuals who elected to leave the United States, but he did not sympathize with those who combined in societies to promote emigration.[112] He also responded to the environmental racialism which underpinned much of the white colonizationist sentiment—and which was often associated with the black emigrationists. In reply to a speech from Francis P. Blair, Jr., he denied that blacks were more suited to a tropical climate.[113]

Douglass and Smith were not the only opponents of African emigrationism; during 1859 and 1860 black leaders debated the issue at length. George T. Downing, who was identified earlier as a vocal critic of Liberia and the ACS, was equally critical of black schemes for emigration. On several occasions he linked the African Civilization Society to the ACS.[114] In countering such charges, Garnet rejected claims that blacks could never enjoy "equal privileges" with other classes in America. Nor did he accept suggestions that he was in favor of an en-masse exodus of African Americans. Rather, like other emigrationists, he believed the emigration of a minority would benefit the majority. Consequently, Garnet did not propose that African Americans should devote themselves solely to emigrationism: They should also continue to seek meaningful freedom within the United States.[115]

As the debate over emigrationism raged within the United States, Delany—accompanied by fellow emigrationist Robert Campbell—began his explorations in Africa. Despite his repeated condemnation of the ACS, and notwithstanding his attempts to distance his emigration plans from those of white colonizationists, Delany's first stop in Africa was Liberia. He sought to rationalize this apparent inconsistency by claiming he had never spoken directly "against Liberia," and although it is possible, as Cyril Griffith has suggested somewhat charitably, that Delany was hoping to steer Liberia away from its dependence on whites, his statements in favor of the erstwhile ACS colony effectively constituted a further retreat from the black nationalist principles he had espoused during the 1850s.[116] After failing to gain support from the Liberian authorities for his explorations in the Niger Valley, Delany embarked on his expedition. In Abeokuta, he and Campbell negotiated a treaty with the Alake (King), providing for the establishment of colonies of African Americans in Yorubaland. Delany and Campbell remained in Africa until April 1860, when they sailed for Britain. On reaching England, Delany set about generating interest in his scheme. Stressing that Britain would benefit from an alternate cotton supply, he made arrangements with cotton dealers who promised to handle the cotton he planned to produce when he returned to Africa.[117]

Returning to the United States in December 1860, Delany had some cause to be pleased with his accomplishments. Not only had he negotiated a treaty providing for the emigration of African Americans to Yoruba, but he had made contact with a number of wealthy and influential Englishmen.[118] However, aside from the organizational and logistical difficulties that continued to hinder emigration to Africa, Delany's black nationalism continued to betray profound—and perhaps ultimately irreconcilable—contradictions. An examination of his 1861 *Official Report of the Niger Valley Exploring Party* provides further proof of the influence of white America on his ideology of black nationalism. Delany's reservations regarding the influence of Christianity on the black population in the United States have been noted. Although he argued in the *Official Report* that religion had played its part in black culture, and that it was time for blacks to achieve temporal advancement, Delany made it clear that Protestant missionaries had done a fine job in the spiritual uplifting of native Africans. His underlying premise was that Protestant civilization was more advanced than African societies. He also quoted, with apparent approbation, an article from the *West African Herald* that called for British intervention in Africa.[119]

In addition to these contradictions, Delany faced other difficulties, not the least of which was the rivalry between various schemes working toward black American emigration to Africa. Delany's problems were typified by the arrival in the United States in June 1861 of two black colonizationists, Alexander Crummell and Edward W. Blyden, intent on generating support for Liberian colonization.[120] Compounding Delany's problems was the fact that the African Civilization Society had continued to function during his absence; because most of the interest in African emigration was centered in New York, it was to that organization—with its relatively well-established organizational base in New York City—that blacks interested in emigration turned. Although the Civilization Society's Reverend Elymas P. Rogers, sent to Africa on a mission of exploration, fell victim to malaria soon after his arrival in Liberia, and although Garnet's fund-raising mission to England failed to generate tangible support for African American emigration, the activities of the Civilization Society had further complicated Delany's mission.[121]

Despite Delany and Garnet's persistence, African emigrationism faced probably insurmountable obstacles. The only organization to send emigrants to Africa in the antebellum period was the ACS, but notwithstanding an increase in the number of black colonists sent to Africa during the 1850s, a majority of free blacks and their leaders continued to look askance at the society. The long-standing perception that the ACS was dedicated to the perpetuation of slavery compromised all other programs that looked toward Africa. That was certainly the case with the African Civilization Society, whose black leaders were implicated with the ACS by virtue of the fact that a number of white colonizationists endorsed the new organization. For his part, Delany was a reluctant emigrationist, who took several years to settle on the African alternative. No other individual so accurately represents the pragmatism—which in practice often amounted to positions that were plainly contradictory—of the antebellum black leadership. There were enormous financial and logistical difficulties standing in the way of African emigrationism, and the widespread belief, fueled by decades of propaganda against the ACS, and sustained by black as well as white Americans, that Africa was a backward, degenerate continent made African Americans understandably reluctant to try their fortunes in such a distant region.

Typically, however, one of the major factors militating against African emigration was the activities of other emigrationists, particularly those advocating a movement to Haiti. In practice, propagating the advantages of Haiti effectively highlighted the obstacles standing in the way of a successful movement to Africa. The most significant advocate of Haitian emigration was James Holly. For Holly, the establishment of a successful black nationality complemented an ideology of Christian-emigrationism that not only stood in opposition to the racial injustices of white America, but which also rested on the assumption that American blacks had unique qualities to offer black people elsewhere. For much of the 1850s, Holly labored to build support for black advancement via the emigration to Haiti of spiritually enlightened and vocationally appropriate African Americans. As succeeding chapters demonstrate, by mid-1860—when the Haitian Emigration Bureau was in operation—significant numbers of black Americans shared Holly's disillusionment with white America. For a time at least, they also shared his enthusiasm for the notion of African American emigration to the black republic.

NOTES

1. William Whipper to Gerrit Smith, 22 April 1856, in *The Black Abolitionist Papers. Volume IV: The United States, 1847–1858*, ed. C. Peter Ripley (Chapel Hill: University of North Carolina Press, 1991), 336.

2. *Frederick Douglass' Paper*, 24 November 1854.

3. On Republican Party attitudes to race and slavery, see Eric Foner, *Free Soil, Free Labor, Free Men: The Ideology of the Republican Party Before the Civil War* (New York: Oxford University Press, 1970).

4. Lincoln, in his "First Debate with Stephen A. Douglas," 21 August 1858, in *The Collected Works of Abraham Lincoln*, ed. Roy P. Basler, 9 vols. (New Brunswick, N.J.: Rutgers University Press, 1953), 3:15.

5. For examples of black frustration and anger at the Dred Scott decision, see Herbert Aptheker, ed., *A Documentary History of the Negro People in the United States*, 2 vols. (New York: Citadel Press, 1951), 1:392–94.

6. Jane H. Pease and William H. Pease, *They Who Would Be Free: Blacks' Search for Freedom, 1830–1861* (New York: Atheneum, 1974), 264.

7. *Frederick Douglass' Paper*, 11 August 1854.

8. Benjamin Quarles, *Black Abolitionists* (New York: Oxford University Press, 1969), 178; *Proceedings of the National Emigration Convention of Colored People; Held at Cleveland, Ohio, on Thursday, Friday and Saturday, the 24th, 25th and 26th of August, 1854* (Pittsburgh: A. A. Anderson, 1854), 9. See also Robert S. Levine, *Martin Delany, Frederick Douglass, and the Politics of Representative Identity* (Chapel Hill: University of North Carolina Press, 1997), 243 n.23; *Frederick Douglass' Paper*, 11 August 1854.

9. *Report of the Proceedings of the Colored National Convention, Held at Cleveland, Ohio, on Wednesday, September 6, 1848* (Rochester: John Dick, 1848), 11–12; Victor Ullman, *Martin R. Delany: The Beginnings of Black Nationalism* (Boston: Beacon Press, 1971), 163–64.

10. Nell Irvin Painter, "Martin R. Delany: Elitism and Black Nationalism," in *Black Leaders of the Nineteenth Century*, ed. Leon Litwack and August Meier (Urbana: University of Illinois Press, 1988), 151.

11. *Proceedings of the National Emigration Convention of Colored People . . . 1854*, 23–27.

12. Sterling Stuckey, ed., *The Ideological Origins of Black Nationalism* (Boston: Beacon Press, 1972), 22.

13. Delany, "Political Destiny of the Colored Race on the American Continent," reprinted in House of Representatives, *Report of the Select Committee on Emancipation and Colonization*, Report No. 148, 37th Congress, 2nd Session (Washington, D.C.: Government Printing Office, 1862), 40, 43, 45, 57.

14. Delany, "Political Destiny of the Colored Race," 42, 52.

15. Ullman, *Martin R. Delany*, 50.

16. Delany, "Political Destiny," 52; *North Star*, 6 October 1848.

17. Delany, *Official Report of the Niger Valley Exploring Party* (New York: T. Hamilton, 1861), 33.

18. *Proceedings of the National Emigration Convention . . . 1854*, 20–21; Lynch, "James Theodore Holly," 10.

19. Philip J. Staudenraus, *The African Colonization Movement, 1816–1865* (New York: Columbia University Press, 1961), 251.

20. Delany's "Introduction" to William Nesbitt, *Four Months in Liberia, or African Colonization Exposed* (Pittsburgh, 1855), 3–4.

21. *African Repository*, 31 (1855): 21–24.

22. *Proceedings of the Colored National Convention, held in Rochester, July 6th, 7th and 8th, 1853* (Rochester, N.Y.: Printed at the Office of *Frederick Douglass' Paper*, 1853), 6.

23. Floyd J. Miller, *The Search for a Black Nationality: Black Emigration and Colonization, 1787–1863* (Urbana: University of Illinois Press, 1975), 153; Ullman, *Martin R. Delany*, 65–66.

24. See Douglass' letter to Harriet Beecher Stowe, in *Proceedings of the Colored National Convention . . . 1853*, 35.

25. Miller, *Search for a Black Nationality*, 153–55.

26. Richard Bardolph, "Social Origins of Distinguished Negroes, 1770–1865," *Journal of Negro History*, 40 (1955): 234; *Pine and Palm*, 3 August 1861.

27. Pease and Pease, *They Who Would Be Free*, 266.

28. *Proceedings of the Colored National Convention, Held in Franklin Hall, Sixth Street, Below Arch, Philadelphia, October 16th, 17th and 18th, 1855* (Salem, N.J.: National Standard Office, 1856), 28, 33, 36–37; Bell, *A Survey of the Negro Convention Movement, 1830–1861* (New York: Arno Press, 1969), 179.

29. *Proceedings of the Colored National Convention . . . 1855*, 10, 17, 36–37; Bell, *Survey of the Negro Convention Movement*, 179

30. Newsome, comp., *Arguments, Pro and Con*, 1; Lynch, "James Theodore Holly," 10; Miller, *Search for a Black Nationality*, 160–61.

31. Holly, *Facts About the Church's Mission in Haiti. A Concise Statement by Bishop Holly* (New York: Thomas Whittaker, 1897), 6.

32. Holly, *Facts About the Church's Mission*, 6.

33. William F. Wipfler, *James Theodore Holly in Haiti* (New York: The National Council of the Episcopal Church, 1956), 3.

34. Miller, *Search for a Black Nationality*, 161. See also Dean, *Defender of the Race*, 22; Lynch, "James Theodore Holly," 2–4; George F. Bragg, *History of the Afro-American Group of the Episcopal Church* (1922; reprint, New York: Johnson Reprint Corporation, 1968), 192; James T. Addison, *The Episcopal Church in the United States, 1789–1931* (New York: Charles Scribner's Sons, 1951), 138.

35. Dean, *Defender of the Race*, 20.

36. Wipfler, *James Theodore Holly in Haiti*, 3; Lynch, "James Theodore Holly," 11; Miller, *Search for a Black Nationality*, 162.

37. Dean, *Defender of the Race*, 22; Lynch, "James Theodore Holly," 11.

38. Robert Debs Heinl and Nancy Gordon Heinl, *Written in Blood: The Story of the Haitian People, 1492–1971* (Boston: Houghton Mifflin, 1978), 201–8; James G. Leyburn, *The Haitian People* (1941; reprint, New Haven, Conn.: Yale University Press, 1966), 91; Robert I. Rotberg, *Haiti: The Politics of Squalor* (Boston: Houghton Mifflin, 1971), 78–81; Harold Palmer Davis, *Black Democracy: The Story of Haiti*, Rev. Ed. (1928; reprint, New York: Biblo & Tannen, 1967), 120.

39. *Liberator*, 12 March 1858.

40. Brown, *The History and Present Condition of St. Domingo* (1837; reprint, London: Frank Cass, 1972), 278.

41. James Franklin, *The Present State of Hayti (Saint Domingo) with Remarks on Its Agriculture, Commerce, Laws, Religion, Finances, and Population, Etc Etc* (1828; reprint, Westport, Conn.: Negro Universities Press, 1970), 2–3, 6, 11, 295.

42. Beard, *The Life of Toussaint L'Ouverture, the Negro Patriot of Hayti: Comprising an Account of the Struggle for Liberty in the Island, and a Sketch of Its History to the Present Period* (London: Ingram, Cooke, and Co., 1853), 316–17.

43. *Liberator*, 17 January 1851.

44. Christy, *Cotton is King . . .* (1855), in *Slavery Defended: The Views of the Old South*, ed. Eric L. McKitrick (Englewood Cliffs, N. J.: Prentice-Hall, 1963), 118.

45. Franklin, *Present State of Hayti*, 5–8.

46. Grayson, *The Hireling and the Slave . . .* (1856), in McKitrick, *Slavery Defended*, 61.

47. De Bow, "The Non-Slaveholders of the South," (1860), in McKitrick, *Slavery Defended*, 176.

48. David Nichols, *From Dessalines to Duvalier: Race, Colour, and National Independence in Haiti* (Cambridge: Cambridge University Press, 1979), 3.

49. Ripley, *Black Abolitionist Papers*, 4:111n.

50. *Cortland Democrat*, 16 September 1848, in Ripley, *Black Abolitionist Papers*, 4:28.

51. Phillips, "Toussaint L'Ouverture," in Phillips, *Speeches, Lectures, and Letters* (1884; reprint, New York: Negro Universities Press, 1968), 468.

52. For a recent analysis of this issue, see Paul Teed, "Racial Nationalism and Its Challengers: Theodore Parker, John Rock, and the Antislavery Movement," *Civil War History*, 41 (1995): 142–60.

53. Phillips, "Toussaint L'Ouverture," 479, 491–93.

54. Elizabeth Rauh Bethel, *The Roots of African-American Identity: Memory and History in Free Antebellum Communities* (New York: St. Martin's Press, 1997), 126.

55. *Minutes of the Fourth Annual Convention, for the Improvement of the Free People of Colour, in the United States, Held by Adjournments, in the Asbury Church, New-York, from the 2d to the 12th of June inclusive, 1834* (New-York: Published by order of the Convention, 1834), 13.

56. Miller, *Search for a Black Nationality*, 162–63; Lynch, "James Theodore Holly," 11.

57. Holly to Frank P. Blair, Jr., 30 January 1858, in Frank P. Blair, Jr., *The Destiny of the Races on this Continent, an Address before the Mercantile Library Association of Boston, Massachusetts, on the 26th of January, 1859* (Washington, D.C.: Buell and Blanchard, 1859), 36.

58. Holly to Blair, 30 January 1858, in Blair, *Destiny of the Races*, 36–37; Dean, *Defender of the Race*, 23

59. Miller, *Search for a Black Nationality*, 163; Litwack, *North of Slavery: The Negro in the Free States, 1790–1860* (Chicago: University of Chicago Press, 1961), 213.

60. See Ann Douglas, *The Feminization of American Culture* (New York: Knopf, 1978); Barbara Welter, "The Feminization of American Religion," in *Clio's Consciousness Raised: New Essays on the History of Women*, ed. Mary S. Hartman and Lois Banner (1974; reprint, New York: Octagon Books, 1976), 137–57.

61. Brown, *History and Present Condition of St. Domingo*, 274; Dean, *Defender of the Race*, 23; Miller, *Search for a Black Nationality*, 164, 168.

62. Wipfler, *Holly in Haiti*, 4; Miller, *Search for a Black Nationality*, 164.

63. See Holly, *A Vindication of the Capacity of the Negro Race for Self-Government, and Civilized Progress as Demonstrated by Historical Events of the Haytian Revolution; and the Subsequent Acts of that People Since Their National Independence* (New Haven, Conn.: William H. Stanley, 1857).

64. Holly, *Vindication*, 5–6.

65. Holly, *Vindication*, 8.

66. Holly, *Vindication*, 40, passim.

67. Holly, *Vindication*, 41–43.

68. Holly, *Vindication*, 45–46; Meier, "The Emergence of Negro Nationalism (A Study in Ideologies)," *Midwest Journal*, 4 (1951–52): 103.

69. See also R.J.M. Blackett, *Building an Antislavery Wall: Black Americans in the Atlantic Abolitionist Movement, 1830–1865* (Baton Rouge: Louisiana State University Press, 1983), 190.

70. Dean, *Defender of the Race*, 26.

71. Miller, *Search for a Black Nationality*, 167; Lynch, "James Theodore Holly," 12.

72. *Provincial Freeman*, 7 June 1856, 21 June 1856, 5 July 1856. Mary Ann Shadd had married Thomas Cary in January 1856. See Jim Bearden and Linda Jean Butler, *Shadd: The Life and Times of Mary Shadd Cary* (Toronto: NC Press, 1977), 185–86.

73. Cyril R.Griffith, *The African Dream: Martin R. Delany and the Emergence of Pan-African Thought* (University Park: Pennsylvania State University Press, 1975), 33; *Provincial Freeman*, 25 November 1856.

74. Dean, *Defender of the Race*, 27; Lynch, "James Theodore Holly," 12.

75. *Chatham Weekly Planet*, 21 February 1861. See also Dean, *Defender of the Race*, 27.

76. Miller, *Search for a Black Nationality*, 166–67; *Provincial Freeman*, 25 November 1856.

77. *Provincial Freeman*, 25 November 1856, 6 December 1856. Despite Joan R. Sherman's claim to the contrary, there is no evidence that any issues of the *Afric-American Quarterly Repository* were ever published. See Sherman, "James Monroe Whitfield, Poet and Emigrationist: A Voice of Protest and Despair," *Journal of Negro History*, 57 (1972): 174.

78. *Provincial Freeman*, 25 November 1856.

79. Delany, *The Condition, Elevation, Emigration, and Destiny of the Colored People of the United States, Politically Considered* (1852; reprint, New York: Arno Press, 1968), 37–38.

80. Dean, *Defender of the Race*, 29.

81. On the "Panic of 1857," see James M. McPherson, *Battle Cry of Freedom: The Era of the Civil War* (1988; reprint, Harmondsworth, Middlesex: Penguin, 1990), 189–91.

82. Miller, *Search for a Black Nationality*, 198–99; Dean, *Defender of the Races*, 29.

83. Holly to Blair, 30 January 1858, in Blair, *Destiny of the Races*, 35, 37.

84. *Speech of the Hon. Francis P. Blair, Jr., of Missouri, on the Acquisition of Central America; Delivered in the House of Representatives, January 14, 1858* (Washington, D.C.: Congressional Globe Office, 1858).

85. Whitfield to Blair, 1 February 1858, in Blair, *Destiny of the Races*, 38.

86. Sherman, "James Monroe Whitfield," 174–75.

87. Miller, *Search for a Black Nationality*, 186.

88. *Proceedings of a Convention of the Colored Men of Ohio. Held in the City of Cincinnati on the 23rd, 24th, 25th and 26th Days of November, 1858* (Cincinnati: Moore, Wilstach, Keys & Co., 1858), 7, 11–13.

89. *Chatham Tri-Weekly Planet*, 4 May 1859.

90. *Douglass' Monthly*, May 1859.

91. *Weekly Anglo-African*, 9 February 1861.

92. Bell, *Survey of the Negro Convention Movement*, 214–15; Miller, *Search for a Black Nationality*, 141–42.

93. *Chatham Tri-Weekly Planet*, 23 August 1858; Richard Blackett, "Martin R. Delany and Robert Campbell: Black Americans in Search of an African Colony," *Journal of Negro History*, 62 (1977): 5.

94. Miller, *Search for a Black Nationality*, 181; *Chatham Tri-Weekly Planet*, August 23, 1858; *Proceedings of a Convention of the Colored Men of Ohio . . . 1858*, 13.

95. Delany, "Political Aspect of the Colored People of the United States," *Provincial Freeman*, 13 October 1855. See also Delany, *Official Report of the Niger Valley Reporting Party* (New York: T. Hamilton, 1861), 36.

96. *Provincial Freeman*, 31 May 1856.

97. Delany, *Niger Valley Exploring Party*, 32–33.

98. Hollis R. Lynch, "Pan-Negro Nationalism in the New World Before 1862," *Boston University Papers on Africa*, 2 (1966): 167; Sterling, *Making of an Afro-American*, 163; Delany, *Niger Valley Exploring Party*, 36; Blackett, "In Search of an African Colony," 3.

99. Delany, *Niger Valley Exploring Party*, 39–40.

100. Garnet, et al., *The African Civilization Society* (New York: Office of the Civilization Society, 1859).

101. Benjamin Quarles, "Ministers Without Portfolio," *Journal of Negro History*, 39 (1954): 33–34; Earl Ofari, "*Let Your Motto Be Resistance*": *The Life and Thought of Henry Highland Garnet* (Boston: Beacon Press, 1972), 58–66.

102. Stuckey, "A Last Stern Struggle: Henry Highland Garnet and Liberation Theory," in *Black Leaders of the Nineteenth Century*, ed. Leon Litwack and August Meier (Urbana: University of Illinois Press, 1988), 145–46.

103. *Frederick Douglass' Paper*, 2 September 1854; Ronald V. Sires, "Sir Henry Barkly and the Labor Problem in Jamaica, 1853–1856," *Journal of Negro History*, 25 (1940): 216–35; Griffith, *African Dream*, 31–32.

104. Ofari, *Henry Highland Garnet*, 69; Richard K. MacMaster, "Henry Highland Garnet and the African Civilization Society," *Journal of Negro History*, 48 (1970): 101; Miller, *Search for a Black Nationality*, 191–92; Jane H. Pease and William H. Pease, *Bound with Them in Chains: A Biographical History of the Antislavery Movement* (Westport, Conn.: Greenwood Press, 1972), 185–86; Coates, *Suggestions on the Importance of the Cultivation of Cotton in Africa in Reference to the Abolition of Slavery in the United States through the Organization of an African Civilization Soci-*

ety (Philadelphia: C. Sherman and Son, 1858); Blackett, "In Search of an African Colony," 7–8.

105. Miller, *Search for a Black Nationality*, 194–95.

106. See Delany, *Blake, or the Huts of America* (1859–62; reprint, Boston: Beacon Press, 1970).

107. Delany, *Niger Valley Exploring Party*, 45; Miller, *Search for a Black Nationality*, 195–97.

108. *Weekly Anglo-African*, 19 September 1859.

109. *Weekly Anglo-African*, 12 January 1861.

110. *Liberator*, 4 May 1860.

111. *Douglass' Monthly*, January 1859.

112. *Douglass' Monthly*, February 1859.

113. *Douglass' Monthly*, March 1859.

114. *National Anti-Slavery Standard*, 17 September 1859; *Weekly Anglo-African*, 21 April 1860; Bell, *Survey of the Negro Convention Movement*, 229–34; Pease and Pease, *They Who Would Be Free*, 270–72.

115. *Weekly Anglo-African*, 17 March 1860. See also Pease and Pease, *They Who Would Be Free*, 269.

116. Delany, *Niger Valley Exploring Party*, 60; *Weekly Anglo-African*, 1 October 1859; Griffith, *African Dream*, 44.

117. Blackett, "In Search of an African Colony," 17; Miller, *Search for a Black Nationality*, 225–27.

118. Miller, *Search for a Black Nationality*, 250.

119. Delany, *Niger Valley Exploring Party*, 102–11, 121, 133–34.

120. Hollis R. Lynch, *Edward Wilmot Blyden: Pan-Negro Patriot, 1832–1912* (London: Oxford University Press, 1967), 27; Wilson Jeremiah Moses, *Alexander Crummell: A Study of Civilization and Discontent* (New York: Oxford University Press, 1989), 134–41.

121. Miller, *Search for a Black Nationality*, 228–31, 251, 258–60; *Weekly Anglo-African*, 9 February 1861, 11 January 1862; MacMaster, "Garnet and the African Civilization Society," 109–10.

4

James Redpath and the Haitian Bureau of Emigration

The year 1861 proved to be as tumultuous for black Americans as it was for their white compatriots. As the Union ruptured, and then plunged into Civil War, emigration to Haiti was an issue of wide debate within the black communities of the northern states and Canada. Under the aegis of a Haitian Bureau of Emigration, agents were spreading the emigrationist gospel, a weekly newspaper was promoting the virtues of the Haitian scheme, and emigrationist sentiment was directed primarily toward Haiti. Significantly, the promoters of Haiti enjoyed the concrete advantage over all other emigrationists of considerable financial resources; in providing substantial material support to the movement, the Haitian government advanced the emigrationist issue well beyond the theoretical dialogues that had long frustrated many black activists. However, after a flurry of emigration that saw two thousand African Americans—including several hundred from Louisiana —emigrate to Haiti between 1859 and 1862, the scheme ground to a halt amid much criticism within the United States of its weaknesses and, in particular, the difficulties faced by its settlers. Thereafter, black Americans increasingly looked to a northern victory in the Civil War as the best means of improving their position. With the stay-and-fight philosophy at last having tangible prospects of success, it was easy for blacks at the time, and for historians since, to regard emigration to Haiti as a minor phenomenon.

Nevertheless, the Haitian scheme represented a more significant climax to antebellum emigrationism than the African schemes of Martin Delany, Henry Highland Garnet, and others. Not only did black leaders who had previously opposed any form of colonization or emigration lend their support to the Haitian movement, but the scheme engaged the attention of at least some of the black populace. A central figure in this process was James Holly, whose ideology of Christian-emigrationism ever more explicitly connected the material and political well-being of black people everywhere to their spiritual condition. This chapter, examining the motives and objectives of those who worked for the Haitian Bureau of Emigration, and analyzing the shifts in black thought that underpinned the trend toward Haitian emigrationism, not only demonstrates the apprehensive mood that permeated the ranks of black activists in the Civil War period, but also attests to their flexibility and pragmatism. Equally, it is fruitful to search not just for disjunctions, but for consistencies among black leaders: Amid the ideological and tactical shifts associated with emigrationism, there were underlying continuities that have often been overlooked in the quest to establish nineteenth-century African American emigrationism as an antecedent of twentieth-century black radicalism. Besides revealing a good deal about the extent to which black Americans had become Americanized, an analysis of the pronouncements by the employees of the Haitian Bureau says much about their attitude toward blacks outside the United States.

It is one of the ironies of antebellum black emigrationism that despite the interest that had been expressed in Haitian emigration by Holly, and other African Americans during the 1850s, the central figure in the administration of the Haitian movement was a white man, James Redpath. To appreciate Redpath's interest in African American emigration to Haiti, it is necessary to consider not only the three visits he made to the black republic during 1859 and 1860, but also his reformist background over the longer period. Little has been written about Redpath, who in many ways was an emblematic figure of nineteenth-century America. Redpath's public life not only touched several aspects of antebellum reform, but also denoted the tenuous nature of reformism as a career. Born at Berwick-on-Tweed, Scotland, in 1833, Redpath elected not to enter the ministry, as his father desired, preferring instead to become a printer. At the age of sixteen, in collaboration with his father, Redpath wrote *Tales and Traditions of the Border.* However, his writing career was interrupted the following year by the family's migration to the United States. The Redpath family settled on a farm in Allegan County, Michigan, but it was not long before Redpath found employment in a printing office in the town of Kalamazoo. He remained there briefly, before moving to Detroit, from where his newspaper articles attracted the attention of Horace Greeley, editor of the New York *Tribune.* Greeley was sufficiently impressed to offer Redpath a position in New York, and the young journalist moved east.[1]

During the early 1850s, Redpath became interested in the plight of African Americans. By 1854, he was corresponding with William Lloyd Garrison; in a letter published in the *Liberator,* Redpath detailed the risks that an "ultra abolitionist" such as he took in traveling through the South. Explaining that he could "not endure procrastinating men," Redpath foreshadowed his increasingly activist approach to the slavery issue.[2] After resigning his position on the *Tribune* in 1855, he embarked on a tour of the South, to make a firsthand assessment of the conditions there.[3] When he ran low on funds, Redpath journeyed to St. Louis, where he found work with the Missouri *Democrat*. Despatched to Kansas, his reports on the conflict there attracted national attention.[4] Redpath spent much of the period between 1855 and 1859 in Kansas, although he did make a number of trips east, as well as another trip to the South. Following the formation of the Republican Party in 1856, Redpath initially placed high hopes in the new organization.[5] But he eventually concluded—as did many African Americans—that the Republicans were unwilling to act against slavery in ways that would lead to meaningful freedom for blacks.

This disappointment was one factor impelling Redpath toward an increasingly activist philosophy. While in Kansas, Redpath met John Brown, whose murderous deeds at Pottawatomie Creek in 1856 had abhorred many Americans. Redpath, however, admired Brown, sympathizing not only with his antislavery goals, but also with the methods he was prepared to use. Redpath's views of Brown, and his assessment of Brown's actions, warrant some analysis, for it is there further evidence is found of Redpath's disillusionment with the opportunities for genuine reform in the United States. It was from that sense of alienation that his interest in black emigrationism stemmed. Both Brown and Redpath were advocates, and one certainly a practitioner, of what might be labeled the "practical action" doctrine. In two eulogies of Brown, Redpath expanded upon sentiments he had already expressed in his 1859 work, *The Roving Editor; or, Talks with Slaves in the Southern States*. This book, documenting Redpath's peregrinations throughout the South, was also a vehicle by which he articulated his antislavery philosophy, and offered a critique of the nation's political institutions and values. Antagonistic to the notion of gradual emancipation, he argued the federal government should legislate immediately to end slavery. Efforts to merely restrict slavery to the states where it already existed, he insisted, were insufficient. Believing that violence might be required to end slavery, and defending the slaves' right to rebel, he served as an intermediary between Brown and his eastern supporters in the period preceding Brown's unsuccessful assault at Harper's Ferry. Not surprisingly, Redpath defended Brown's actions. Indeed, Redpath paid "homage" to Brown, for "first showing how, and how alone, the gigantic crime of our age and nation can be effectively blotted out from our soil forever." For Redpath, Brown was a model of Christian masculinity. Conjoining Brown's religious faith with his valor and commitment to the principles of abolition, Redpath expressed his admiration for Brown: "I admire you for your dauntless bravery in the field; but more for your religious integrity of character and resolute energy of anti-slavery zeal. Rifle in hand, you put the brave young men of Kansas to shame; truth in heart, you rendered insignificant the puerile programmes of anti-slavery politicians."[6]

Resonating through Redpath's writings was a deep sense of disenchantment with the political culture of antebellum America. Echoing the long-

standing principles of immediatist abolitionism, Redpath doubted "the ultimate efficacy of any political anti-slavery action which is founded on Expedi-
ency." The "morals of the counting room," he believed, were antithetical to
the values of true reformism. But where some radical abolitionists remained
true to the cause of nonviolence through the late 1850s, Redpath was prepared "to urge the friends of the slaves to incite insurrections, and encourage
in the North, a spirit" that would lead ultimately to "civil and servile wars." Invoking the memory and spirit of the American Revolution, Redpath declared
that if "the fathers were right in *their* rebellion, how much more right will be
the slaves in *their* rebellion?"[7] Redpath's anti-slavery philosophy thus led
him to countenance a violent end to the peculiar institution. In subsequent
years, that activist spirit was transformed into support for African American
emigrationism.

Unlike many abolitionists, Redpath's militant opposition to slavery was
premised on firsthand encounters with the South's peculiar institution. This
effort to lend credibility to abolitionism was not unusual among opponents of
slavery, but few abolitionists actually traveled through the South, as Redpath
did. "In this volume alone," he wrote in *The Roving Editor*, "of all American
anti-slavery or other books, the bondman has been enabled in his own language, (if I may employ the familiar phrase of political essayists and orators), to
'define his position on the all-engrossing question of the day.' " Redpath thus
sought to authenticate his opposition to slavery. Yet, although he was determined to give voice to the slaves, Redpath was nonetheless very much a product of his age, in that he betrayed a condescension toward blacks that was
characteristic of nineteenth-century America, and which had long permeated
the white abolitionist movement. "It is very easy," Redpath declared, "to ascertain the opinions of simple people, from the peculiar expression of their
eye." As is seen here, Redpath's confidence in his own ability to judge character was similarly evident during his tenure as general agent of the Haitian Bureau of Emigration. But, while many white Americans sought to persuade
themselves, and the slaves, that an insurrection against the slavepower was
doomed to fail, Redpath argued that the "slave quarter is the Achilles heel of
the South." On this point, Redpath referred again to the heroes of the American Revolution. In this instance, however, he also emphasized the limits of the
Revolution. Alluding to Nat Turner's rebellion, Redpath asserted that "one
insurrection in Virginia, in 1832, did more for the emancipation cause than all
the teachings of the Revolutionary Fathers." Looking beyond the War of Independence for an example of revolutionary deeds, Redpath stressed the need
to "strike a blow for the slaves—as Lafayette and his Frenchmen did for the
revolutionary sires." But Redpath also acknowledged that a rebellious spirit
was not entirely absent from the black race. Southern slaves, he suggested,
could "strike a blow for themselves, as the negroes of Jamaica and Hayti, to
their immortal honor, did." Redpath concluded *The Roving Editor* with a
warning. Having stated that slavery could "never be extended into Mexico,"

and certain that "westward, slavery cannot go," he cautioned those who contemplated slavery's expansion southward into the Caribbean. "The islands of American Archipelago," he noted, "are to-day almost exclusively in the hands of the liberated African race. *The first serious attempt at annexation will put them entirely in the hands of the blacks.*"[8]

In *The Public Life of Captain John Brown*, published in 1860, Redpath was equally unambiguous in his support for a direct strike at slavery. "I think that John Brown did right," Redpath wrote, "in invading Virginia and attempting to liberate her slaves."[9] Similar sentiments were evident through *Echoes of Harper's Ferry*, published later in 1860. Brown's "heroic Christianity," Redpath declared, was a model for other opponents of slavery. If slavery was to be destroyed, he averred, the North had to "act on the aggressive." Although he remained dubious about America's political culture Redpath envisaged that northern militance could be expressed politically. Rather than being intimidated by southern threats of secession, he suggested northerners should organize a national convention to revise the Constitution, with or without the approval of the slave states. Appealing to a range of values dear to nineteenth-century Americans, he argued that if the southern states did secede, "we of the North would gain in character, in influence, in strength, and in pocket."[10]

Through all of these texts, one point was clear: Speaking out against slavery would never destroy the peculiar institution—it was necessary to act. In essence, this was the same conclusion that most of the African American leadership had reached during the preceding twenty years—although, of course, there were probably insoluble differences over what constituted the most effective form of action. Seen in conjunction with his skepticism about American society and its political system and culture, Redpath's laudatory accounts of Brown's deeds accorded with sentiments expressed by many black activists. As seen here, agents of the Haitian Bureau also praised Brown. But there was another, more direct link between black emigrationism, Haiti, and the methods adopted by Brown: Brown was hailed widely in the black republic. Although he failed to liberate the slaves, there was considerable sympathy among Haitians for the way in which the martyred abolitionist was prepared to risk his life on the slaves' behalf. And unlike many Americans, Haitians obviously had fewer qualms about a violent assault on slavery. In early 1860, one American visitor described "a day of mourning" on behalf of Brown that had been observed in Haiti. Besides paying their respects to Brown, and building a monument to commemorate his deeds, the Haitian people donated money to the late abolitionist's family.[11] These links played a part in convincing Redpath that African American emigration to Haiti would significantly advance the cause of black freedom everywhere.

Redpath made his first trip to Haiti in January 1859, for "the purpose of describing the country and its people." He stayed for two months in Haiti, studying the black republic's history, politics, and geography. It was during Redpath's visit that the government of Emperor Faustin Soulouque fell.[12] Soulouque's reign had been far from distinguished, and after nearly twelve years in office, with the economy weakened by falling prices for cotton and coffee, and with his government bruised by the failed forays into Santo Domingo, Soulouque's grip on power had become increasingly tenuous during the 1850s. When he left Port-au-Prince in late 1858, discontent with his régime surfaced; in January 1859 he abdicated, following a coup d'état led by General Fabre Geffrard. The son of a mulatto mother and a black father, Geffrard attempted to use that background to gain influence with both the black and mulatto elements of Haitian society. Fifty years after the Revolution, there were still deep divisions and conflict between blacks and mulattoes in Haiti. Geffrard ruled for eight years, during which time he endeavored to improve Haitians' standard of living. Money was spent on public works, and resources were devoted to developing medical and educational facilities. And, like his predecessors, Geffrard sought to increase the production of agricultural goods, particularly cotton.[13]

Haiti's agricultural output had never reached the levels achieved prior to the Revolution. Arguing that the country had too many traders, and not enough producers, one foreign visitor noted during the 1850s that the existence of successive military governments had been a constant drain on the nation's resources. Those governments, it was noted, had made only token efforts to improve agricultural production, a situation exacerbated by the fact that agriculture was left almost wholly to "the poor and ignorant," who, at best, were "only moderately industrious."[14] As had been the case on earlier occasions, one favored method by which it was hoped to improve agricultural production was by encouraging the immigration of black American farmers, whose expertise would lead to a general improvement in the island's agricultural practices. Although Soulouque's government had refused to grant the guarantees sought by James Holly in 1855, it had expressed interest in enticing African American immigrants. In 1858, Soulouque had gone so far as to despatch agents to the United States to generate interest in emigration.[15] But it was not until Geffrard assumed the presidency that more active steps were taken to implement a movement of African Americans to Haiti.

Given that the instability and violence associated with Haitian politics had created a powerful imprint on the minds of Americans, it was not surprising that African American emigrationists were keenly interested in the power shifts in the island republic. Redpath placed great importance on the role of the leader in Haitian society. His depiction of Soulouque left no scope for misinterpretation: "Brutal, ignorant, a worshipper of snakes and a hater of intelligence, the enemy of commerce, education, progress, a man of burly figure and grotesquely autocratic carriage." But Redpath described Soulouque's successor differently. Perhaps hoping to ingratiate himself with the new president, Redpath praised Geffrard as a "gentleman of fine talent, culture and courtly address, the foremost Haytian of his age." Not satisfied with that public endorsement, Redpath dedicated *Echoes of Harper's Ferry* to Geffrard, thereby explicitly connecting the black struggle for freedom in the United States to the Haitians' quest to establish a powerful black nationality.[16] During the early months of 1859, Redpath became convinced that both of these objectives could be served by a successful emigration of African Americans to Haiti. Before he left Haiti, he put a series of questions to the new government, regarding the terms under which black Americans might emigrate. When he returned to the United States in April 1859 he set out to promote such a movement.[17]

On reaching the United States, Redpath discovered there was already an interest among African Americans on the question of Haitian emigration. During 1858 and 1859, blacks in Ohio and Illinois were expressing curiosity about Haitian emigration. But significant interest in Haitian emigration was also surfacing farther south, in Louisiana. During 1859 and 1860, approximately five hundred African Americans left New Orleans for the island republic, pushed from Louisiana by violence and repression, and pulled to the island republic by the prospect of political freedom and material gain. As with emigration from the northern states, the movement from Louisiana had the support of the Haitian government.

Louisiana was, in many respects, a likely source of emigrants for Haiti. The state's geographical proximity to the black republic facilitated the transportation of emigrants, and the fact that a relatively large proportion of Louisiana blacks could trace their ancestry to the émigrés from the Haitian Revolution rendered the island somewhat less alien than it was to African Americans elsewhere. Possibly, too, those personal connections meant that Haiti's language, as well as its Catholicism and its voodoo, would not be unfamiliar to Louisiana blacks. As John Blassingame has noted, although "many" New Orleans slaves "received conventional religious instruction from their masters or sat in the galleries of their churches," voodoo "held sway over a large part of the black population."[18] But the movement of African Americans from Louisiana to Haiti was also a consequence of the general racism directed toward black Americans, and of the specific circumstances under which Louisiana blacks lived and worked during the late 1850s. Between 1858 and 1860 free blacks in a number of Louisiana parishes found themselves under intense pressure from the white authorities. This pressure was in part born of a determination to "prevent" any involvement on the part of free blacks in "the presidential canvass of 1860."[19] Typically, too, in encouraging free blacks to leave their midst, whites assured African Americans they would be better off elsewhere. "The enjoyment of your natural rights and privileges," one editor wrote, "may be found in your native country—Africa or in Hayti, or in one of the West Indies Islands."[20]

Another imperative appeared to be at work in St. Landry Parish, from where a number of African Americans left for New Orleans, and then on to Haiti. In 1859, several "prominent" white slaveholders urged the Louisiana state legislature to prohibit the ownership of slaves by African Americans.[21] There were relatively few black slaveowners in St. Landry, or anywhere else in Louisiana for that matter. But amid the racial and political tensions of the late antebellum period, that black minority was an ever more direct affront to the racial hierarchy on which social relations in the South were based. As the white planters of St. Landry explained, the ownership of slaves by free blacks was "repugnant to the laws of good society, good government, Nature, and Nature's God."[22] The racism that underpinned such sentiments became more virulent in the late 1850s. Indeed, the period witnessed a well-organized intimidation of free blacks, including, on occasions, violent attacks that foreshadowed many southern whites' subsequent reaction to African American emancipation.[23]

Notwithstanding the endorsement of black emigration from a number of Louisiana's white citizens, and the intimidation of blacks in certain locales, some of the state's whites expressed ambivalence regarding the potential departure of large numbers of free blacks, particularly from New Orleans. This ambivalence reflected the somewhat atypical pattern of race relations in New Orleans. Although it would be easy to romanticize race relations in antebellum New Orleans, it was the case that to an extent unknown elsewhere in the United States, free blacks had been accepted into the local community. This relatively liberal attitude also influenced slavery in New Orleans. As John Blassingame remarked, not only were slaves in New Orleans "generally better fed, housed, and clothed than slaves in the countryside," but "many" were also "highly skilled."[24] Another sign of the relatively liberal racial attitude of New Orleans whites was their willingness in 1858 to allow the Haitian authorities to appoint a consul to serve in the city.[25] Given that the Federal Government continued to deny recognition to Haiti, the Louisiana authorities were a step ahead of their federal counterparts on this issue.

The atypical nature of race relations in antebellum New Orleans was further evidenced by the responses from the crescent city's white newspaper editors to the prospect of African American emigration. Although they expressed serious reservations about Haiti, and stressed the difficulties confronting blacks who sought to settle in the black republic, the city's white leaders did acknowledge that emigration might be of benefit both to Haiti, and to African Americans who relocated there. In discussing the possibility of an exodus of free blacks to Haiti, the editors of the New Orleans *Daily Picayune* revealed a familiar contempt for contemporary Haiti, condemning the republic's political history and leadership, and emphasizing that the island had never reached the economic heights of the pre-Revolutionary period. Lacking the public infrastructure of a modern state, the island's "moral condition" was allegedly deficient. Moreover, as their reference to Haiti as "this anomalous State" revealed, the editors of the *Picayune* shared the same concerns regarding Haiti that had long guided U.S. foreign policy toward the black republic. Of course, because of the "close proximity" of Haiti to Louisiana, these concerns were all the more urgent for residents of that state. Typically, too, the *Picayune*'s editors referred to the "crisis which the Haytian people are now undergoing." As the editors described it, the instability surrounding the overthrow of Soulouque, and the subsequent rise of Geffrard, were but the most recent episodes of Haiti's turbulent history. While they admitted that Geffrard seemed "to be acting in good faith," and was making "an earnest and powerful effort" to "rescue" Haiti "from barbarism," they were not about to let their black readers forget the island's woes. Consequently, although those African Americans "who emigrate from our shores to Hayti may expect to find a fine field for diligent persevering industry," the editors of the *Picayune* had "certain reservations" regarding the island republic. In short, black Americans should think very carefully before leaving the United States for the black republic.[26] During the same week, moreover, that the *Picayune* discussed the prospects for black Americans in Haiti, the paper used Haiti to rail unambiguously about the "incapacity of the negro for self-government." It was claimed that even "under the most favorable circumstances" blacks had proved themselves unable to establish and sustain a political system that could deliver social and economic stability.[27]

In cautioning New Orleans blacks about conditions in Haiti, the editors of the *Picayune* were not acting solely out of altruism. With a hint of pride, as well as the familiar conviction that African Americans had benefited from their contacts with white society and values, they commented that it was "principally" from the "free colored people of New Orleans" that the Haitians hoped to recruit immigrants. "It is evidently here," they continued, "that Hayti expects to find the class of people she needs to achieve the salutary reaction which is to save her from barbarism and put her once more on the road to civilization." Motivated no doubt by a concern that an exodus of the city's blacks would have a detrimental impact on the white population, and deprive the city of its skilled black workforce, the *Picayune*'s editors rhapsodized about race relations in New Orleans. "Our free colored population," they wrote, "form a distinct class from those elsewhere in the United States." Rather than "being antipathetic to the whites," it was argued that the city's free blacks "have followed in their footsteps, and progressed" alongside them, "with a commendable spirit of emulation, in the various branches of industry most adapted to their sphere." In general, "the free colored people of Louisiana, and especially of New Orleans," were described as "a sober industrious and moral class, far advanced in education and civilization." Some of the city's "best mechanics and artisans," along with "the great majority" of the "regular, settled masons, bricklayers, builders, carpenters, tailors, shoemakers, &c" were black; their "sudden departure," the *Picayune* asserted, "would certainly be attended with some degree of annoyance." If such self-interest was typical among white southerners, such candor was rather more unusual.[28]

Having cautioned African Americans about Haiti, the editors of the *Picayune* proceeded to outline the potential benefits of emigration that might accrue both to Haiti and to black American emigrants. In describing the island republic's need for "a nucleus of intelligent, enlightened, industrious people of their own color," who could "show" the Haitians "what industry, activity, and enterprise can achieve," the *Picayune* editors reiterated what James Holly and other proponents of Haitian emigration had been arguing since the mid-

1850s: A migration of black Americans to Haiti was analogous to "that of our own settlers," who confront "dangers and difficulties innumerable." The significant difference, however, was that whereas settlers in North America found only obstacles in their path, Haiti was at least ruled by a government "anxious to help." The black republic, moreover, not only had "intelligent men in the principal cities," but had "already" put in place "systematic measures" that would make migrants' mission more viable. Black Americans' job would "not be so much" one of building as one of "repair."[29]

Perhaps aware that many New Orleans whites conceded the virtues of the city's black population, and sensing an opportunity to import such skilled blacks, the Haitian governments of Soulouque and Geffrard formally endorsed the immigration of African Americans from Louisiana. To facilitate a movement to Haiti, in 1858 Soulouque commissioned Colonel Emile Desdunes, the Haitian-educated New Orleanian who was serving as Haitian consul to New Orleans, to act as an agent for emigration. The following year, after Geffrard's accession to power, Desdunes' appointment as agent of emigration was confirmed. Seeking initially to capitalize on the distressed situation of those free blacks outside New Orleans who were suffering the ostracism and violence of local whites, Desdunes offered free transportation to Haiti, along with "assurances of social equality and political rights." Evidently, Desdunes was persuasive enough, and conditions in a number of Louisiana parishes sufficiently troubling, to persuade 150 free blacks, many from St. Landry Parish, to sail for Haiti in May 1859. Subsequently, 195 more free blacks, including another group from St. Landry, along with a number from East Baton Rouge Parish, also accepted Desdunes' offer. Thereafter, emigration continued on a smaller scale until early 1860, when a group of 80 free blacks left the troubled Opelousas Parish for the black republic.[30]

The departure of several hundred blacks during January 1860 prompted the editors of the New Orleans *Times Picayune* to assess the movement. Given that the emigrants were, as the editors of the New Orleans *Bee* described them, "all wealthy and industrious persons—farmers and mechanics," their departure was a matter of some interest. As was the case six months earlier, the editors of the *Picayune* seemed uncertain whether to endorse African American emigration. Still worried that the "sudden departure" of well-qualified blacks would be "sensibly felt," they were concerned too that those who left the United States for Haiti had taken with them "a considerable amount of capital." Although they painted a sanguine picture of race relations in New Orleans, the *Picayune* editors did admit that conditions outside the city were less favorable. In particular, they took the opportunity to emphasize that conditions for blacks in the free states were far from advantageous for blacks. With all that in mind, they could not but "bid" the emigrants "God-speed" if they determined to better themselves by emigrating to Haiti.[31]

Although it is relatively easy to delineate the sentiments of the white residents of Louisiana regarding black emigration to Haiti, the reactions of the black emigrants themselves are harder to determine. Nonetheless, certain conclusions can be drawn. The first point to make is that the departure of approximately five hundred free blacks in a twelve-month period signifies that, like their northern brethren, free blacks in the South found little cause for optimism during the late 1850s and early 1860s. This was evidently true even among those blacks who lived in the relatively liberal city of New Orleans, and among the tiny minority of African Americans who owned other blacks. Of course, one option for disillusioned Louisiana blacks was Liberian colonization. As they had for decades, white colonizationists proclaimed the virtues of the ACS colony. But, while a handful of blacks did decide to make a future for themselves in Liberia, such people were generally slaves, or ex-slaves, as in the case of the "McDonogh Negroes," who were the former property of one of Louisiana's most famous sons.[32]

Haiti was, for some blacks at least, an immeasurably more appealing destination than Liberia. But despite their optimistic appraisals of Haiti, perhaps the most telling evidence of the Louisiana emigrants' experiences is that large numbers of them chose to return to the United States, some even before the end of 1859. Others, however, remained in Haiti, fearful that the vigilante activity that had initially driven them from their home parishes would be resumed anew if they returned. Such was the depth of those fears that some blacks, disillusioned with conditions in Haiti, elected to join a small colony of African Americans that had been established in Vera Cruz, Mexico. Of those who stayed in Haiti, there were some success stories. A number of emigrants involved themselves in trading and merchant activities; Charles Boisdoré, for example, an emigrant from St. Martin Parish, was by late 1861 reported to have achieved the position of "chief armorer for the Haitian government's Port-au-Prince arsenal."[33] But such successes were relatively rare, and the fate of the Louisiana emigrants to Haiti was a precursor to that of the much larger number of African Americans who were to leave the northern states and Canada under the auspices of the Haitian Bureau of Emigration.

Notwithstanding the eventual failure of the emigration from Louisiana to Haiti, the movement attracted the attention of blacks and whites in the North. The June 1859 departure to Haiti was reported in Horace Greeley's New York *Tribune*, and a report in *Douglass' Monthly* suggested that more than two thousand African Americans would emigrate to the island republic before the end of 1859.[34] Redpath watched these events with keen interest. While he favored a movement of African Americans to Haiti, Redpath was careful not to give his unequivocal approval to emigration until he was certain that settlers would be well treated in their new country. Commenting on reports that efforts were being made to induce blacks in Missouri to emigrate to the island republic, he counseled patience, advising African Americans to bide their time. Writing in mid-1859, he pointed out that Soulouque had also wanted black Americans to make their homes in Haiti; what the Haitian leader had really been hoping to acquire, however, was a supply of "good slaves." Although he stressed that Geffrard was a man of "very different character," Redpath reminded blacks that the government in Haiti was a "Military Monarchy," and that until certain guarantees were provided, African Americans were better off staying in the United States. He also warned that once in Haiti, emigrants could not leave until they received official permission from the government. Until more specific assurances were offered to prospective emigrants, Redpath believed African Americans should remain in the United States.[35]

The following month, June 1859, Redpath returned to Haiti, where he again toured the countryside, gathering information. Conferring once more with government officials on the emigration question, he asked Geffrard for guarantees that emigrants would be given every opportunity to succeed. Redpath's specific requests closely resembled those of James Holly four years earlier, although there is no evidence the two men were collaborating at this stage. In August, a report from A. Jean Simon, the Haitian secretary of state for foreign relations, outlined the conditions under which a movement of African Americans to Haiti could take place. It was emphasized that the primary purpose of encouraging the emigration of black Americans was to aid the development of agriculture in Haiti. Soon after, the Haitian government issued an official "Call for Emigration," setting forth the reasons why African Americans should settle in Haiti, and undertaking to provide the guarantees of assistance that Redpath had requested.[36]

No formal arrangements were finalized before Redpath left Haiti in September, but there was continuing interest in Haiti among African Americans. In late 1859, William P. Newman, a black resident of Canada West, visited Haiti on behalf of the American Baptist Free Mission Society.[37] Newman's emigrationist ideology, like that of Holly, rested on a missionary impulse. Sending back favorable reports to Canada and the United States, Newman asserted that Haiti needed "more men and women," and that although the country was not "*Paradise*," it could be made so. As well as stressing the political significance of Haiti's independence, Newman presented an idealized—albeit chauvinistic—image of Port-au-Prince: "We have beef, and plums for pudding, and I assure you, wine and women are not wanting." But Newman expressed particular enthusiasm for the Haitian countryside. Besides the "grand mountains, doubtless full of mineral wealth," the "fertile valleys," and "sublime forests," he asserted that there "is not a country in the world where farming will pay better than Hayti."[38] Like Holly and Redpath before him, Newman questioned the Haitian Government about the conditions under which an emigration might take place. Once again, the authorities gave an encouraging, if noncommittal response.[39] Newman concluded that although certain factors might work against an emigration to Haiti, it was the "only country" near the U.S. that made "men of African origin the white man's peer." In arguing that Haiti could sustain twenty times its existing population, he implied support for a large-scale emigration of African Americans. But he stressed it would be best for emigrants to have definite arrangements with proprietors of land in Haiti before they left the United States. Assuring African Americans that Haitians were "very anxious to have Christian colonies established among them," and seeking to allay prospective emigrants' concerns regarding their right to choose their own religious affiliations and practices, Newman argued that although "Hayti's national religion" is "called Catholic," it "tolerates the religions of the world and approves of christianity." And, seeking perhaps to ensure that emigrants would acculturate more easily into Haitian society, he suggested that African Americans emigrate in colonies "of not less than one hundred families each."[40]

Newman was not the only African American promoting Haitian emigration. Despite the failure of the 1858 Emigration Convention to endorse Holly's plans, his interest in Haiti was undiminished. As he had since the mid-1850s, Holly continued to conceive emigration in terms of blacks' religious well-being. In August 1859, he convened those blacks who shared his interest in establishing a mission in Haiti. Representatives from just three Episcopal churches were present at the fourth convention of the Protestant Episcopal Society for Promoting the Extension of the Church Among Colored People, but they did pass resolutions reflecting Holly's Christian-emigrationist philosophy.[41] Such resolutions, however, were largely meaningless unless funds could be procured to transform plans into action.

It was with the aim of establishing a mission in Haiti that Holly turned again to the Foreign Committee of the Episcopal Church. As they had on previous occasions, however, Church authorities turned down his application, pleading financial difficulties.[42] But Holly, determined to translate his philosophy of Christian-emigrationism into practical action, was also working in another direction in his efforts to encourage black emigration to Haiti. Beginning in June 1859, he published a series of "Thoughts on Hayti" in the *Anglo-African Magazine*, wherein he outlined his reasons for favoring black emigration, and detailed the benefits that blacks in both the United States and Haiti would derive from such a movement. In analyzing Holly's "Thoughts on Hayti," and in labeling him a "fanatical crusader," whose ideas were "much too sophisticated for many of his constituency to have appreciated or assimilated," historian James O. Jackson revealed as much about his own values as he did about Holly. Moreover, while there is merit in Jackson's statement that Holly's "Thoughts" were "among the earliest Afro-American nationalistic statement designed to initiate a movement for the liberation of Africans throughout the world," Holly was in fact no different from most others associated with the Haitian scheme, in that his attitudes were products of a distinctly American black experience.[43] It was an experience that produced black nationalists whose ambivalence about remaining in the United States was paralleled by their sense of difference from black people in other regions. Jackson's comment needs to be modified not only by analysis of what Holly wrote in his "Thoughts" but also of the attitudes of others who, through the same disillusioning black experience of the 1850s, were also to respond to the new opportunities presented in Haiti.

Predicating his thesis on the "Important position" the Haitian "Nationality holds in relation to the Future Destiny of the Negro Race," Holly's "Thoughts on Hayti" expanded on the themes he had earlier raised in his *Vindication of the Negro Race for Self-Government*. As he had for most of the 1850s, Holly linked Haitian independence and black nationality to "the cause of God."[44] In greater detail, Holly spelled out how an effective black nationality required cultural and religious elevation, as well as political independence. Although black people everywhere could be proud that Haiti had "preserved her national independence," Holly conceded that the island republic labored under considerable "disabilities." These difficulties were attributed to the fact that Haiti's black nationality "sprang into being from the lowest depths of degradation and slavery." Such a background, Holly argued, precluded the "dissemination of sound religious morality," which he considered the "basis of public virtue." Insisting that "Literature," and "the Arts and Sciences" were "inseparable concomitants of political sovereignty in making up true national greatness," he implied that African Americans could contribute these elements to Haiti's black nationality. Holly's biases were further evidenced by his statements regarding Haiti's religious practices—and by his continued inability to appreciate the role of voodoo in Haiti. Holly's turn away from Catholicism has been noted, but his prejudice against "Romanism" was exacerbated in the case of Haiti, because, as he put it in 1859, the island republic had been influenced by "the corruptest forms of that corrupt Church." Holly, however, was not prepared to excuse other denominations. Mindful of the Episcopalians' refusal to provide tangible support to his plans to engage in missionary work in Haiti, he noted that "Protestant Christianity, with her thousands of missionaries penetrating everywhere else, has dared to almost totally neglect these benighted people, who are perishing for want of the light of the Gospel." Confident of his own ability to shape events, Holly was evidently convinced that he could play a part in introducing the "pure religion of Jesus" to Haiti.[45]

Yet, Holly understood that he could not elevate Haiti single-handedly. In the third installment of his "Thoughts on Hayti," he outlined how an emigration of African Americans would remove "the National Disabilities of the Haytien People." Emigration to Haiti, Holly argued, would stir "up her stagnant waters of social life," ensure "her rich internal resources" would "be adequately developed," increase "her population," and guarantee that "new ideas of progress" were "infused into the national mind." Holly also noted, however, that emigration should be on the basis of "a select, judicious and discreet movement." In this regard, his comments accorded with his 1858 remarks to Congressman Francis Preston Blair, Jr., when Holly had envisaged the emigration of no more than 45,000 or 55,000 African Americans over two decades. Although that was a significant proportion of the free black community, it was far from a huge inroad into the entire African American population, which by the end of the 1850s numbered more than 4.5 million. The issue of selective versus en-masse emigration was a potentially problematic aspect of the Haitian scheme, raising as it did the whole question of whether emigrationists believed there was any hope for the elevation of black people in the United States. But in August 1859, Holly was as concerned with addressing Haiti's requirements, as he was with theorizing about the fate of African Americans. Underpinning his pronouncements was a conviction that Africa was in no position to help Haiti's immediate needs. Although he extolled the achievements of earlier African civilizations, he was certain the continent would not be an appropriate source of emigrants to Haiti. Indeed, he exhibited a condescension toward Africa that paralleled the most patronizing views expressed by white Americans. "The barbarism of the inhabitants of that savage continent," Holly noted, "could not do otherwise than retard, instead of promoting the national development of that people."[46]

The fourth chapter of Holly's "Thoughts" was also concerned with the objectives of an emigration to Haiti. Referring to the role of education as a means of elevation, Holly stressed that all members of society should have access to schooling. Besides lamenting that education "has borne its choicest fruits among the upper classes," he remarked that "the sisters" of young men were denied educational opportunities in Haiti. Holly did not specify what type of education he favored for Haitian women, but his acknowledgment that women should receive an education accorded with the views of radical abolitionists and other reformers in the United States. Similarly, in arguing that education was "essential to a proper culture of national patriotism," Holly envisioned what might be labeled a black republican motherhood—a racially refined version of the ideology of republican motherhood that was so widely valued in nineteenth-century America.[47] Here, the black nationalism of antebellum emigrationists was again reflective of blacks' experiences within the United States.

With these objectives in mind, Holly hoped that African American emigrants could help address Haiti's educational deficiencies. Again, this question was linked to the question of who should go to Haiti, and how the movement should be organized. Holly's comments on these issues reflected his aversion to Liberian colonization and his assumption that slaves lacked many of the civilized qualities of free blacks. As well as referring to the mortality rate among colonists in Liberia, he argued that even if recently freed American slaves were able to emigrate, they were unable to carry civilized qualities with them. Decrying the "*heathenish* system of Liberian colonization," he regretted that "slaves just emancipated on the plantations of Alabama, Mississippi and Louisiana" were "sent off by ship loads, steeped in all the ignorance and degradation of slavery, to add to the darkness and superstition of Africa, making her ancient confusion worse confounded." Rather than compare his plans for Haitian emigration to African colonization, he referred instead to the "pilgrim settlers of New England." Nothing could be closer to white America's self-image

and national mythology than the experience of the Pilgrims, and Holly's reference to this much acclaimed group signified the extent to which African
Americans were influenced by these American cultural and historical symbols.
Moreover, Holly's argument that "the emigration movement" to Haiti
"should assume the shape of well-organized religious communities," reflected
the seventeenth-century example of the Pilgrims and Puritans who had colonized New England. And although he insisted that young men "must be qualified for the Christian ministry," Holly no doubt anticipated that he would play
a key role among the "educated ministry" whom he anticipated would lead the
emigration movement. Holly's thesis rested on a conviction that proper organization—along the lines utilized by Eli Thayer during the 1850s emigration to Kansas—was an essential prerequisite for a successful emigration. A lack
of organization, Holly argued, had played a part in undermining African
American emigration to Haiti during the 1820s.[48]

In his fifth essay, Holly referred at length to the 1820s emigration to Haiti.
Partly because of their own false expectations, and partly because they were
not sufficiently removed from the experience of slavery, he posited that those
African Americans who left for Haiti during the 1820s were doomed to disappointment. Holly sought to convince potential emigrants that excessive servil-
ity, and unrealistic ambitions, would have an equally destructive effect on a
new movement to Haiti. Lacking the "principle of self-reliance," the emigrants who traveled to Haiti during the 1820s "wilted away before the obstacles that presented themselves in their pathway in Hayti." Although Holly was
certain that African Americans could carry the benefits of civilization to Haiti,
he cautioned potential emigrants not to anticipate becoming a political elite in
the island republic. Again, the emigration scheme of the 1820s was instructive.
Echoing the arguments of Henry Highland Garnet, who attributed the failure
of the earlier scheme to the emigrants' exaggerated ideas of what life would be
like in their new country, Holly asserted that during the 1820s men who had
occupied menial positions in the United States had "entertained the false conception that they were fitted to be the rulers" of the "heroic and independent
people" of Haiti. Holly—who soon after would express satisfaction that a
"much wanted self-reliance" was "now being successfully developed" among
African Americans—believed that by the 1850s black Americans were better
qualified to make a success of emigration to Haiti. Garnet, criticizing the
1820s emigrants for lacking patience and perseverance, noted that African
Americans who went to Haiti willing to work "would be amply rewarded." In
particular, he emphasized that experienced and hard-working farmers were required in Haiti. For Garnet, and other proponents of Haitian emigration, the
elevation of Haiti's agricultural system remained the vital component of the
plan to undermine American slavery—and provide the economic foundation
on which an influential black nationality could be based.[49]

This emphasis on black Americans' ability to regenerate Haiti's agricultural
system entailed potentially contradictory imperatives. On the one hand, Holly

argued that self-reliance and a willingness to act assertively were essential for the success of any emigration program. Like other emigrationists, he was convinced the "colored people of the United States" were the "only people in a proper position to contribute to the national regeneration" of the black republic. Anticipating that "American emigrants" could become the "industrial civilizers of Hayti," Holly suggested they would "occupy the same position in that country as the Bourgeoisie do in Europe." At the same time, however, Holly might well have been hoping to assure the Haitian authorities that African American immigrants would not constitute a threat to their leadership. He was adamant, therefore, that black Americans should not suppose they would wrest control of the island republic from the Haitians. "What could be more preposterous," he wrote, "than the deplorable phantasy that the American negro is fitted to be the political ruler of the self-emancipated freemen of Hayti?"[50]

Returning to imagery and language he had first used in 1853, the final installment of Holly's treatise was concerned with the plight of "denationalized people" such as blacks. It was essential, he argued in November 1859, that black people establish a nationality that accorded with the "civilization" and "demands" of the nineteenth century. Reiterating that Haiti, rather than "the savage kingdoms of Africa," was the most viable site for the attainment of that nationality, Holly asserted that a "successful emigration" of African Americans could play a telling part in ensuring the development of the black nationality already underway in Haiti. For Holly, racial justice—including an end to slavery—would occur only when the "corrupt public sentiment of the North" was transformed. If that statement was congruent with the views of Garrisonian abolitionists, so too was Holly's argument that when northern opinion was transformed, the South would be deprived of the "moral aid and comfort" it had long received from the "church and state (of the North)." In Holly's view, fugitive slaves must continue to play a telling part in publicizing the evils of slavery. But while he placed great emphasis on remaking the conscience of the North, Holly did not neglect the international support that was lent to American slavery. The United States, he reminded his readers, was not the only guilty party—the European powers were also complicit in the ongoing assault on African societies and cultures. To highlight the importance of a national base for black people, Holly drew a comparison between blacks and Jews, whom he argued were similarly denationalized. Although some Jews had achieved material comfort, and had done their best to find security in a number of nations, they were severely disadvantaged because they lacked a national identity.[51]

At the same time as Holly strove to interest black Americans in Haiti and a black nationality, James Redpath attended to the practical details of implementing a movement to the island republic. In July 1860, he returned to Haiti, where he completed the arrangements for the organization of a Haitian Bureau of Emigration.[52] The next month, Geffrard issued a formal decree, announcing that the bureau would be established, with its headquarters in Boston. Redpath was appointed general agent of emigration—a controversial appointment that was to be the subject of considerable criticism from within the black community. The Haitian government made an initial appropriation of twenty thousand dollars for the bureau, thereby setting it on a vastly more secure financial footing than any of the other emigration schemes that had been considered during the 1850s. In Haiti, the movement was to be under the joint supervision of Victorien Plésance, the secretary of state for foreign relations, and Auguste Élie, who was nominated director-general of emigration.[53]

The Haitian government was particularly keen to settle emigrants in the Artibonite Valley, in an area stretching sixty miles to the east of the township of St. Mark, which, it was anticipated, would be the primary receiving point for emigrants. The lands in the Artibonite Valley were described as being "fit for all sorts of cultivation," especially cotton and corn. The region had the added advantage of being the area of settlement chosen by the Louisiana blacks who had already emigrated. To assist the process of emigration, two Haitians were appointed inspectors, to survey lands and provisionally grant fifteen acres of land to each emigrant family, and ten acres to each single person. Redpath left Port-au-Prince in late September 1860; when he arrived in the United States the following month, he immediately set about organizing the Haitian Bureau of Emigration.[54]

To properly appreciate how the emigration of African Americans was expected to assist in the development of a black nationality, due attention must be given to the second part of Redpath's mission. In addition to promoting and directing African American emigration to Haiti, Redpath was expected to encourage the U.S. government to formally recognize Haiti's independence. As noted, the U.S. had never acknowledged the reality of the Haitian Revolution, primarily as a consequence of southern concerns that recognition would be tantamount to legitimizing the independent black republic, which they feared would encourage rebellion among the slaves. That fear also helps explain why the Haitian government appointed a white man to lobby for the recognition of their country: Although it would have been ideologically consistent to appoint a black person to carry out that task, the Haitian authorities realized that within the racist culture of the United States, a white man was more likely to be able to advocate successfully on Haiti's behalf.

The Haitian leadership perceived that American recognition of their black republic and African American immigration would both play a part in the elevation of the nation, and that the success of one would almost certainly enhance the other. To assist in securing recognition for Haiti, Redpath sought the support of the antislavery Congressman Charles Sumner, with whom he had been associated during the troubles in Kansas in the mid-1850s. Recognizing that many whites were in favor of black colonization, Redpath subsequently told Sumner that the "recognition of Haytien Independence would facilitate my work. It would give a greater impetus to emigration than anything that the Cabinet would do."[55] Redpath also tried to woo Abraham Lincoln, whose support for black colonization was well known. The issue of recognition occupied a good deal of Redpath's attention during the period when he worked for the Haitian government; in an effort to persuade Lincoln of the merits of recognition of Haiti, one of the bureau's agents, Richard J. Hinton, met with the president-elect in late 1860.[56] That meeting did not produce an immediate shift in U.S. policy toward the black republic, but reflecting commercial considerations, as well as a foreign policy freed from the constraints of the South's racial fears, U.S. policy did eventually change. In February 1862, Sumner introduced a bill that would grant recognition to Haiti, and to Liberia, which had also suffered diplomatic ostracism from the United States. After considerable debate, Congress eventually agreed to the proposal, and Lincoln signed the bill in June of the same year.[57]

It can only be speculated whether a more prompt U.S. recognition of Haitian independence would have given a significant fillip to the emigration movement. It is clear, nevertheless, that Redpath, and others, saw that the two matters were linked. Proponents of Haitian emigration were not the only ones to appreciate the significance of United States recognition of the island republic. Addressing the American Anti-Slavery Society (AASS) in May 1863, the black leader Robert Purvis identified a number of indications that the "good time" was "at hand." Among those signs, "the acknowledgment of the black republics of Haiti and Liberia" ranked with treaties suppressing the internal slave trade and the abolition of slavery in the District of Columbia.[58] For Purvis, and other black leaders, recognition of Haitian independence was a tangible and long-overdue acknowledgment of the capabilities of the black race.

Although Redpath's efforts to secure American recognition of Haitian independence ultimately bore fruit, a more immediate task confronting him when he formally established the Bureau of Emigration was to secure the services of a number of agents, who would be assigned to specific geographic areas. Their role involved disseminating information, particularly through the distribution of Redpath's 1860 publication, *A Guide to Hayti*, and the bureau's weekly newspaper. It was of great importance to recruit agents who had a high standing within the African American community. Even James Jackson, who was sharply critical of the appointment of Redpath, has conceded he was "shrewd enough" to employ prominent individuals to act as emigration agents.[59] Some, including Holly, were already known for their advocacy of emigration, while others, such as William Wells Brown and William J. Watkins, were better known as advocates of the stay-and-fight philosophy. Redpath hoped that the support of people such as Brown and Watkins would demonstrate that the Haitian scheme was very different from the colonization and emigration proposals that had preceded it. Most of the agents were black, but some—including John Brown, Jr.—were white. Realizing the importance of gaining the support, if not the services, of prominent abolitionists, Redpath also worked to gain Frederick Douglass's endorsement for the Haitian movement.

Although the uncertainties of the record make it impossible to determine conclusively the nature of each individual's motives, the significant point is that the commitment shown by the bureau's agents to Haiti was less surprising than might appear at first glance. Not only had they all expressed disenchant-ment with the traditional stay-and-fight philosophy, but a number of them had shown interest in emigration on earlier occasions. It was probably inevitable that this uniquely well-financed scheme would prove attractive to such men—through optimism about its greater viability, opportunism about its promise of employment or, most likely, a mixture of these motives even in the minds of single individuals. In the same way, in analyzing what these agents hoped would be achieved through the Haitian movement it is ultimately more important—as well as more feasible—to stress what it revealed in general about black attitudes than to pursue in detail the complexity of individuals' motives. Among a considerable range of opinions about the desirable scale of emigration there was unanimity that support for the Haitian scheme did not diminish African Americans' entitlement to freedom and equality within the United States. And the underlying conviction that they were indeed American was reflected in shared assumptions regarding their superiority vis-à-vis non-American blacks.

Holly was the first person to be officially appointed as an agent of the Hai-tian Bureau of Emigration. Appointed in November 1860, he spent two months working in New Jersey and Philadelphia before he was directed to be-gin lobbying in New England.[60] Holly eventually raised a colony of emigrants from his home town of New Haven. Leading this group to Haiti, Holly re-mained in the island republic until his death in 1911. In that respect, he was prepared to live by his injunctions concerning the value of emigration, al-though, as the next chapter explains, the way in which he represented the mis-fortunes suffered by his colony ultimately did little to promote the Haitian scheme. There was, moreover, a profound irony—or, more accurately, a con-tradiction—in Holly's appointment as an agent of the Haitian Bureau of Emi-gration. To be sure, Holly had evinced a willingness in the past to accept aid from whites—as a necessary means of achieving the goal of a black nationality. But having placed so much emphasis on the need for blacks to act independ-ently, and having labored so assiduously for Haitian emigration during the 1850s, it must have been galling for Holly to have found himself in the employ of a white man. He addressed this issue in 1861. Rationalizing the apparent in-consistency of working for a white man on the grounds that Redpath was merely the "white servant" of a black government, he argued that Redpath's appointment did not "detract one iota from the idea of negro sovereignty, na-tionality and independence."[61]

Redpath also secured the services of Henry Highland Garnet. In 1853 Gar-net had encouraged black Americans to make their homes in Jamaica, but his primary emigration interest was in Africa. Garnet's high profile within the black community, and his reputation as an uncompromising foe of racism, made him a potentially valuable asset to Redpath. Soon after the Haitian Bu-reau was established, the black preacher made it clear that he was interested in becoming directly involved in the venture. When Redpath visited New York City in October 1860, Garnet assisted in organizing lectures. Before the year's end he had been appointed agent for New York City and state.[62]

Although Holly and Garnet were already known for their advocacy of emigrationism, Redpath also secured the services of black activists who were associated with the stay-and-fight doctrine. William Wells Brown was one such prominent recruit. Born into slavery around 1813, Brown escaped from the South in 1834. Becoming one of the most prominent black writers in the antebellum period, Brown also involved himself in the reform issues—particularly abolitionism and temperance—that were so prominent in that period. During the 1840s, he lectured on behalf of the New York and Massachusetts anti-slavery societies, and was generally an adherent to the Garrisonian doctrine. When Garnet called the slaves to rebellion in 1843, Brown expressed opposition to the idea, but he would later give a more positive response to radical proposals for black freedom and equality. In 1849, he left the United States for Paris, where he represented the American Peace Society at the International Peace Conference. Remaining abroad for more than five years, Brown became well known in Britain for his anti-slavery endeavors.[63]

Another of the Haitian Bureau's prominent black agents was William J. Watkins. Unlike Brown, Watkins was born free, the son of a well-known Baltimore abolitionist and teacher. Watkins' father (who was encountered in chapter 1) was an early and devout opponent of the ACS. The elder Watkins maintained his opposition to all forms of colonization and emigration until his death in 1858, although he did migrate to Canada in 1852. The younger Watkins followed his father's interest in reform, and by the early 1850s he had secured a reputation as a dedicated and articulate member of the anti-slavery leadership. When he was appointed to the Haitian Bureau in 1861, Watkins was well known and well respected among the free black community in the North.[64]

Redpath also appointed H. Ford Douglass as an agent of the bureau. Born into slavery in Virginia, Douglass had lived in Cleveland, Columbus, and New Orleans during the 1850s. In each city he had been energetic among the African American community, and prominent in the fight for blacks' rights. Having served on the Committee on Emigration at the 1852 Ohio State Convention, Douglass regarded emigration as the best alternative for African Americans. Interested in the notion of black nationality, Douglass' emigrationism was also premised on a belief that it was the most feasible means of undermining slavery. Like other agents of the Haitian Bureau, Douglass' activism evinced considerable pragmatism. Although his advocacy of emigrationism was muted during the immediate pre–Civil War period, he continued to argue that African Americans should be prepared to work actively for their own freedom. Similarly, although he insisted he was "no advocate of revolution," by late 1860, Douglass was increasingly willing to consider the possibility of a violent overthrow of slavery. Above all, he wanted his "manhood recognized before the law."[65]

Little is known about the early activities of Joseph Dennis Harris, the other black agent of the Haitian Bureau whose attitudes are examined in some depth. Harris was a plasterer from Cleveland, who during the 1850s, played a prominent role in the Ohio State Anti-Slavery Society. Arguing unsuccessfully against William Howard Day's anti-emigration motion at the 1858 Ohio convention of African Americans, Harris asserted that blacks had sufficient numbers on the American continent, "if concentrated, to force freedom and respect" from their oppressors.[66] For Harris, emigrationism sat comfortably within a wide-ranging philosophy that emphasized the importance of African Americans fighting vigorously for their freedom.

At various times, all of these men underwent a similar process of disenchantment with the more traditional, moral suasionist method of antislavery agitation. Their pronouncements thus reveal much about the black experience and condition in mid-nineteenth-century America. Most of the bureau's agents had at some point supported the stay-and-fight ideology, but during the 1850s, two of the most prominent advocates of that doctrine were William J. Watkins and William Wells Brown. Watkins, in particular had been a vigorous opponent of emigrationism. In an 1854 article entitled "What Have the Abolitionists Done?," he stressed that African Americans were making progress in their fight for freedom. Contending that abolitionists had "given to the world a practical demonstration of the inherent power of Truth," he assured blacks—in specifically masculinist terms—that if they fought "manfully" they would achieve their victory.[67] The following year, arguing that blacks were entitled to equality in America, Watkins urged "every true friend" of his race to work for the improvement of blacks in the United States.[68]

But even as Watkins expressed optimism regarding blacks' chances of securing meaningful freedom in the United States, he revealed concerns about the immutability of American racism. On this issue, there was much to be learned from the white abolitionists. Disappointed that moral suasionism had failed to free the slaves, Watkins was also conscious of the racism that was evident even among the most radical wing of the abolitionist movement. Asking whether "the Abolitionists themselves act towards us as though they were devoid of prejudice against color, or condition?" Watkins answered emphatically: "No they do not."[69] It was in that context that both Watkins and Brown were increasingly willing to adopt activist techniques to fight slavery and oppression. One manifestation of that process was a support for political abolitionism—and, for Watkins, a break from the Garrisonians during the early 1850s. Hence Watkins' involvement in the Free Soil and Republican Parties, and his belief that slavery could be "better abolished under the constitution, than by trying to bring people up to the disunion standard." Indeed, as early as 1852, Watkins was reported as having "eloquently enforced the duty of every colored voter to sustain the Free Soil Party."[70] However, the ultimate failure of political abolitionism to secure emancipation for the slaves, coupled with the racism endemic to all white political parties, demonstrated the limits of the

American political system. In that context, emigrationism was potentially an appealing solution to the problems confronting African Americans.

Black emigrationism was premised on the notion of self-help, a doctrine that African American leaders of all persuasion continued to value during the 1850s. Convinced that African Americans had to "wake" from their "lethargic slumber," Watkins asserted that "our elevation depends very materially upon our own efforts." Little could be accomplished, he noted, while "tottering on the brink of despair." African Americans did not want sympathy or favors. Rather, they wanted "rights as men, as freemen, as citizens of the United States."[71] Complementing Watkins' conviction that blacks should not look to others for favors was his renunciation of religion as a panacea for African Americans' troubles. "The religion of the land," he stated in 1857, "is no better than its politics—not so good all things considered." Declaring that he had "no faith in the religion of the country," he told the delegates to the Cleveland Disunion Convention that he had seen "too much" of the "churches to have any confidence in them."[72]

Not only was Watkins prepared to prescribe activist methods to gain freedom for members of their race; during the 1850s he was not averse to advocating more overtly militant measures. In this respect, he was belatedly following the pronouncements of Henry Highland Garnet. In 1854, writing amid a debate regarding Boston abolitionists' failed attempts to prevent slave catchers from returning Anthony Burns to slavery in Virginia, an underlying principle for Watkins was that violence over the slavery issue had not been precipitated by African Americans, nor by abolitionists. Rather, slavery was "murder in the highest degree." It followed, then, that every "slaveholder" was "a murderer, a wholesale murderer."[73]

Watkins discussed these issues in a variety of contexts during the pre–Civil War decade. In an 1853 pamphlet entitled *Our Rights as Men*, he supported calls for the establishment of a black militia in Massachusetts. Although he maintained his long-standing policy of opposition to the ACS, the crisis engulfing the United States, coupled with the ongoing denial of freedom and equality to black Americans, rendered a change in tactics imperative. Watkins was adamant that he was "not a man of war," but he was sure that the "Juggernaut of American Prejudice"—which threatened to "crush the manhood out of us"—necessitated action. Referring to blacks' contributions in the American Revolution, he pointed to the inconsistency between the rhetoric of American liberty and independence, and the reality of American racism, as it was experienced by black Americans. Allowing African Americans to form their own military companies, Watkins asserted, was one means of acknowledging that they were worthy of the rights of citizenship.[74] For Watkins, the discrimination that blacks were forced to endure was all the more galling because groups of "foreigners" had obtained charters to form military companies. As "native-born American citizens," he declared in 1853, African Americans should have been entitled to the benefits of citizenship.[75] Many of the immigrants who settled in the United States in the 1840s and 1850s did compete with blacks for jobs and housing.[76] Yet, while Watkins's remarks echoed the rhetoric of those who worried about the influx of immigrants to the United States, his immediate concern—unlike the vociferous "Know Nothing" nativists of the 1850s—was to elevate blacks, rather than deny opportunities to recently arrived foreigners. During the 1850s, as conditions and prospects for blacks continued to deteriorate, Watkins was prepared to take his activist ideology even further. Having rejected unequivocally the notion of compensated emancipation (by which slaveholders were to receive financial compensation in return for freeing their slaves), and having announced that "Revolution was the order of the day," Watkins was one of those who argued at the 1858 Convention of Colored Men of Ohio that it was African Americans' "right and duty" to resist, "by force of arms when it was feasible."[77]

This question of violent means was thrown into sharp relief by John Brown's failed raid at Harper's Ferry. Many white abolitionists equivocated over Brown's violent methods. For their black coadjutors, however, the issue was rather less theoretical. Watkins' comment that Brown "died [so] that liberty may live and triumph" was a typical response. Similarly, although H. Ford Douglass pointed out that "he was no advocate of revolution," he did "believe in the right of self defence," and panegyrized Brown, asserting that if slavery could not be defeated by moral means, it would be a good thing if a "black John Brown" emerged in the South.[78]

In significant ways, the changes in William Wells Brown's attitudes paralleled those of Watkins. At the 1857 New England Anti-Slavery Convention, Brown defended the slaves' right to gain their freedom via revolutionary means. Three years later, he feared—as did other black abolitionists during that period of profound crisis—that the slave system was "going forward" as it "had never gone forward before." Explaining that there was no justice at all for free blacks in the slave states, he asserted that the situation was only marginally better in the North. Denied citizenship in the United States, he worried that the black race was "going backward." Invoking the familiar masculinist imagery, Brown argued that the United States was "determined" to "blot out," as far as it could, "everything that tends to show that the colored man is a man." Nonetheless, despite the deepening crisis, he told members of the AASS that African Americans "are not going to Africa—we are not going to leave this country at all—I say black people are not going to leave the United States."[79] At that point, Brown did not differentiate between white-sponsored schemes for black colonization, and the African Civilization Society, which purported to be a black-led organization.

Clearly, Brown and Watkins veered away from a passive form of the stay-and-fight doctrine during the 1850s. Although they did not lend their support to emigrationism, they were increasingly inclined to endorse activist, and ever more militant, measures to secure freedom and equality for African Americans. It is not surprising, then, that Redpath was prepared to employ Watkins and

Brown, for as we have seen, he too was convinced that positive, active steps had to be taken to destroy slavery. Referring to those who adhered to his philosophy as "Practical Abolitionists," Redpath was certain that those who continued to discuss theoretical questions about slavery failed to comprehend their "era." Unlike—or, perhaps because of—John Brown, Redpath was unwilling to organize an ill-conceived assault on slavery. It was in this context that Redpath, and others, embraced the notion of Haitian emigrationism.[80]

In the cases of Henry Highland Garnet, H. Ford Douglass, and J. D. Harris, there is ample evidence of their readiness during the pre–Civil War decade to embrace activist, and at times emigrationist philosophies to elevate their race. Garnet had called the slaves to rebellion, and had turned to emigrationism during the late 1840s and again during the 1850s. H. Ford Douglass and Harris had also given their support to emigrationism, although they had shown little consistency on the issue of a destination for African American emigrants. Both men, moreover, had also worked for more traditional anti-slavery societies before they joined the Haitian Bureau.

Having championed Canadian emigration during the early and mid-1850s, H. Ford Douglass had also pushed for blacks' civil and political rights in the United States. His advocacy of Haitian emigration during early 1859 has been noted; later that year, along with Harris, his attention turned toward Central America. Like other emigrationists, Harris had written to Francis Blair, Jr., assuring him that the "thinking portion" of the African American population appreciated the efforts he was making on behalf of emigration. Harris' comment not only signified the distance between the black leadership and populace, but also implied a lack of knowledge, if not outright opposition, on the part of the black masses toward emigration proposals. Harris offered to work as an agent for Blair, either disseminating information that would "awaken" African Americans, or as an emigrant, executing "some plan or expedition that might be devised."[81] Evidently, no response was forthcoming from Blair, and in February 1859 Harris accepted employment with the Ohio State Anti-Slavery Society. Then, in June 1859, Harris shifted ground again, establishing the Central American Land Company in Cleveland. Harris was the general agent of this organization, which also listed H. Ford Douglass as one of its agents. Although Harris and Douglass proposed sending an initial expedition to Central America before the end of 1859, they were unable to secure financial support for their plan.[82] In early 1860, Harris again wrote to Blair, discussing a plan for African American emigration to Honduras.[83] Blair needed no convincing of the virtues of black colonization, and besides lauding Haiti's accomplishments, he was a keen advocate of black colonization to Central America.[84] But Blair's endorsement did not translate into tangible assistance: ultimately, proposals for emigration to Central America came to nothing, and Harris and Douglass soon turned their attentions in other directions.

With the failure of the Central American Land Company, Harris dabbled briefly with the idea of African American emigration to Jamaica, while H. Ford

Douglass reverted to a more traditional antislavery point of view, working as a traveling agent for the Massachusetts Anti-Slavery Society. Although Douglass did have some ideas in common with the Garrisonians—like them, for example, he regarded the Constitution as a proslavery document—it was nonetheless indicative of the desperate mood of the pre–Civil War era that one who had worked for the emigrationist cause for most of the 1850s could fit into the New England abolitionist circle.[85] Not only do Douglass' shifts signify the pragmatic approach of the black leadership, but the Garrisonians' willingness to accept him into their fold attests also to their pragmatism. Although his advocacy of moral suasionism distinguished him from many of his African American coadjutors in 1860, Douglass' statements also indicated that he shared assumptions that held wide currency among that group. Not only was he increasingly convinced that the overthrow of slavery required violent means, but he refused to place his trust in either the Republican Party or Abraham Lincoln. Declaring in July 1860 that he did "not believe in the antislavery of Abraham Lincoln," Douglass charged that the Republican contender for the presidency was imbued with "proslavery character and principles." By May 1861—as the Civil War erupted—Douglass had concluded "the cause of the black man" in the United States was "hopeless."[86]

For Douglass and Harris, like other black leaders, a major factor behind the turn to Haitian emigrationism was disillusionment with the stay-and-fight ideology. Although the choice of Haitian emigrationism came after black leaders had toyed with other possible destinations, a further examination of the background of Redpath's agents reveals certain links with the island republic, that help explain why they accepted appointments with the bureau.

The most obvious of these links was that like Redpath and Holly, several of the bureau's employees had visited Haiti. In 1861, William Wells Brown spoke of his "long interest" in the island republic, and his background reveals several manifestations of his interest in the region. More than twenty years earlier, during the 1840s, Brown had visited Cuba, Haiti, and possibly other West Indian islands.[87] In 1855, following his European sojourn, one of the lectures Brown delivered in England was published under the title *St. Domingo: Its Revolutions and Its Patriots*. Stressing that blacks were human beings, who would fight to the death to win and maintain their freedom, he praised those who had participated in the Haitian struggle for liberation. Implicitly, Brown was suggesting that African Americans needed the verve and courage demonstrated by the Haitian revolutionaries. Brown also signaled an increasing willingness among certain elements of the African American leadership to countenance a violent assault on slavery. When discussing the brutality associated with the Haitian Revolution, Brown asserted "Let the slave-holders in our Southern States tremble when they shall call to mind these events." Perhaps most significant was Brown's conjoining of the American and Haitian Revolutions, through the agency of Toussaint L'Ouverture. As Brown stated,

Toussaint had played a part in transforming "the glorious sentiments of the Declaration of Independence" into a tangible reality.[88]

Back in the United States, Brown continued to refer to the example of the Haitians' valor in securing their independence. Addressing the Cleveland Disunion Convention in late 1857, he remarked that "St. Domingo is often referred to, to frighten the North out of the idea [of black freedom]." Pointing to the contradictory stereotypes presented of dark-skinned people, he noted that "we are told by others that God made the African for a slave, or he would not submit so quietly to be oppressed and dehumanized by his inhuman master." Brown hoped that "the people of the North only had the same determination to be free, that the colored people of St. Domingo had when Napoleon sent an army to reduce the Island again to slavery."[89]

Brown continued to express interest in Haiti, and he might have visited the island again in 1858. In any case, by 1861 he was actively promoting the Haitian scheme. This was not the first occasion on which he had expressed support for emigration to the Caribbean region. During 1851, he had proposed that the British government should "hold out inducements" to African Americans to encourage them to emigrate to Jamaica. For a brief period, he "felt that something could be expected." It was not long, however, before he concluded "that the mere offer of a free passage would be but slight inducement to a poor people." By late 1851, he was warning prospective emigrants to be "on their guard" about entering agreements to settle in the West Indies, lest they "find themselves again wearing the chains of slavery."[90]

J. D. Harris was another of the Haitian Bureau's employees who had visited the Caribbean. Following his flirtation with Jamaican emigration in late 1859, Harris embarked on a tour of Santo Domingo in 1860. Although he only visited the Spanish section of the island, he did comment on the Haitian Revolution in *A Summer on the Borders of the Caribbean Sea*, published soon after his return to the United States. On the one hand, like Holly, Harris was generous in his praise of the Haitians. Insisting there was nothing "low or cowardly" in Haiti's history, he regarded the island republic as "the field of unparalleled glory." Yet, although he valued the Haitian nationality, and respected the Haitians' achievement in ousting their French oppressors, there were passages in *A Summer on the Borders of the Caribbean Sea* in which Harris spoke in the same sensationalized language that was characteristic of antebellum discourses on the black republic. In "A Chapter of Horrors (which the delicate reader may, if he pleases, omit)," Harris declared solemnly that the "instances of barbarity" that accompanied the Revolution were "too horrible for description." Nevertheless, Harris did proceed to relate, in considerable detail, several examples of the violence and bloodshed that occurred during the turmoil in the French colony.[91] William J. Watkins, as far as can be determined, had not visited Haiti prior to his involvement with the bureau. Yet he did have a very tangible and personal link with the island republic, for his wife was Haitian; in mid-1861 he wrote that she had "her eye" firmly fixed on "the promised land."[92]

All these factors go part of the way toward explaining why certain black leaders turned to Haitian emigration. But as well as the flexibility they had demonstrated over previous years, and alongside the high-sounding principles that they enunciated, there was another, potentially significant consideration. An individual's conversion to Haitian emigrationism might well have been a response to material opportunities, as well as an ideological commitment to the principles of emigration and black nationalism. Having received the twenty thousand dollar appropriation from the Haitian government, Redpath was able to offer his agents steady employment and a reasonable wage. It is not inconceivable that black abolitionists would have modified their earlier opposition to emigrationism in order to gain a degree of financial security. Similar considerations could well have applied when Harris accepted an appointment as lecturer for the Ohio State Anti-Slavery Society in early 1859, and when H. Ford Douglass took the apparently inconsistent step of working for the Massachusetts Anti-Slavery Society in 1860. Not surprisingly, these abolitionists have left no record that pecuniary interest played any part in their decisions. But in a society where even elite blacks lived on the economic fringes of society, any offer of steady employment must have been a powerful inducement.

Although they concurred on many points, agents of the bureau expressed varying opinions regarding the proposed scale of emigration to Haiti. This question had dogged emigrationists since the early 1850s, but the establishment of the Haitian Bureau added new urgency to the issue. Redpath, insisting that emigration had to be under the auspices of a well-ordered scheme, denied charges that the program called for an en-masse movement of African Americans. Nevertheless, he called for relatively large numbers to emigrate to Haiti. Late in 1860, he suggested that "at least" fifty thousand American blacks could immediately be settled in Haiti; in March 1861, he stated that the island republic would receive, within twelve months, "a large and more valuable accession to her population than Liberia had received during all the many years it has existed." In numerical terms, this would have entailed an influx of more than ten thousand emigrants to Haiti.[93] Later, Redpath claimed he began operations with the intention of sending ten thousand emigrants in the first three years, and one hundred thousand after five years. The long-term objective might have been to despatch half a million African Americans to Haiti over a twenty five-year period. Nonetheless, while that would have been a significant movement, Redpath was right to point out that it would not have been a "universal exodus" of African Americans.[94]

There were occasions when some of Redpath's black agents also seemed attracted to the idea of a large-scale emigration—just as James Whitfield had been in his correspondence with Francis P. Blair, Jr. In his "Thoughts on Hayti" Holly had stressed the need to carry out emigration on a selective basis "for some time to come." But he did appear to leave the way open for an en-masse movement in the future.[95] Perhaps for tactical reasons, Harris, in seeking Blair's support, stressed that the white and black races could never exist in the United States on "terms of equality," a view that was implicitly consistent with a large-scale emigration. And, even though he argued that emigration should be on a selective basis, his statement that Haiti's "rich resources invite the capacity of 10,000,000 human beings to adequately use them" could easily be interpreted—or construed—as an implicit advocacy of an en-masse emigration of African Americans. Even more emphatic was Holly's 1857 declaration that "the social ostracism of the colored people in the United States" was "complete and irremediable." Pointing to the disparity between the values enshrined in the Declaration of Independence and the Constitution, and the reality of American racism, he concluded that African Americans had "nothing to look for" in the United States. Holly's statements betrayed his conviction that black people could never achieve equality in the United States. Theoretically at least, that left the way open for an en-masse emigration of African Americans.[96]

Despite Holly's comments, most black agents of the bureau could not openly or consistently consider a proposal for an en-masse emigration because of the continuing need to distance themselves from any association with the ACS. We have seen that William Wells Brown spoke out against the ACS in May 1860. Other agents also denounced the ACS. In 1860, just four months before H. Ford Douglass began working for the Haitian movement, he criticized the ACS scheme. "God never intended," he argued, "that this guilty nation should get rid of its sins and their consequences in that way." Opposition to the ACS was predictable from any black leader, but Douglass did not differentiate between that organization and black plans for emigration when he wrote the "colored man is here for weal or woe, and he must remain here for all time."[97] Evidently, in accepting Redpath's offer of employment, he acted on the premise that the Haitian scheme, because it called for only a selective emigration, and because it promised to strengthen an existing black nationality, was actually assisting African Americans in their quest for meaningful freedom in the United States.

Other agents of the bureau argued along similar lines. William J. Watkins had earlier described the ACS scheme as "the most formidable, the deadliest enemy of the peace, prosperity, and happiness of the colored population of the United States." Asserting that African Americans were entitled to equality in the United States, he urged "every true friend" of his race to work for the improvement of blacks in America.[98] Until he began advocating on behalf of the bureau in 1861, he did not distinguish between black proposals for emigration, and the ACS program. Indeed, it will be recalled that as an associate editor of *Frederick Douglass' Paper*, he had led the journalistic battle against James Whitfield and the other emigrationists in the period preceding the 1854 Emigration Convention. Again, however, Watkins' views shifted. In advocating Haitian emigrationism, he stressed that the ACS scheme, based as it was on the "assured invincibility" of white American prejudice, necessarily implied a rejection of the notion that African Americans could elevate themselves while they remained in the United States. By contrast, the Haitian movement "emanated from a branch of our people who cannot but have the welfare of the whole race at heart." Rather than relying on prejudice, Watkins suggested, the Haitian project sought to challenge it. Haitian emigrationists insisted that their movement could defeat oppression in the United States: by settling in the black republic, African American emigrants would be confronting, rather than running away from, American racism.[99]

Besides eschewing the ACS, Haitian emigrationists were careful to distinguish their scheme from black-organized proposals for African emigrationism. Redpath's trenchant criticism of African emigrationism, no doubt made with a black audience in mind, reflected stereotypes common to the nineteenth century. In Africa, he wrote, the "various tribes" were still "separate and hostile," whereas in Haiti they were all "represented and united." But that reference to the value of Haiti's nationality was insufficient. By describing Africa as "a Pagan and Barbarous country" Redpath appealed to values shared by black and white Americans alike. And by extolling African Americans as "Christians and civilized men," he perhaps sought to flatter his audience—and deter them from contemplating emigration to Africa.[100]

William Wells Brown's denunciation of the African Civilization Society as a "begging concern" was a typical rejection of the values Haitian emigrationists believed white colonizationists were seeking to instill among African Americans.[101] In April 1860, pointing out that Henry Highland Garnet was "almost the only colored officer in the Civilization Society," Brown disputed one of the major assumptions that he believed underpinned African colonization—that there was no hope for civic or social elevation of the free black population in the United States. As his critique of the African Civilization Society revealed, Brown was not prepared to distinguish between the ACS scheme and black proposals for emigration to Africa. Although he agreed that "every true friend of humanity would rejoice to see some plan put in motion to civilize and elevate the long-neglected people of Africa," he had no confidence in the Civilization Society, whose agents "represent that there is no hope for the moral, social, or political elevation of the free colored people in the United States."[102] Indeed, Brown regarded the African Civilization Society as a thinly disguised version of the ACS. This perception was common among free blacks, and Brown's comments were perhaps predictable. But he too was vulnerable to the charge of hypocrisy. Considering that he had worked alongside white Garrisonians, and given that he would soon be employed by Redpath, another white man, it was perhaps duplicitous for Brown to criticize Garnet on those grounds.

Garnet's concurrent advocacy of Haitian and African emigrationism was unique among the employees of the Haitian Bureau. Just as he saw no incongruity between advocating emigration to Africa while simultaneously continuing the fight for freedom in the United States, he saw no contradiction in recommending emigration to both Haiti and Africa. Rather, he regarded the two movements as complementing, rather than competing with, each other. It was "in the power of the colored men of America," Garnet claimed, "to supply the wants of both countries, and thus give the death blow to slavery, and bless our scattered race throughout the world." For Garnet, differentiating between Haitian and African emigration was inseparable from the issue of selective versus en-masse emigration. Believing that Haiti required a different type of emigration than Africa, he argued that movements to both regions could be conducted at the same time. Whereas Africa required a select minority—"*a few to direct the labor*"—he claimed the island republic needed a "population to develope [*sic*] her agricultural and mineral resources and defend her against the invasion of a slave power of the Western world." Although Garnet's allusion to white southerners' Caribbean ambitions represented a point of view shared by many African Americans, his implicit endorsement of an en-masse emigration, particularly his public assertion that Haiti was capable of holding "ten million inhabitants," rekindled fears that the Haitian movement was in some way allied to the Colonization Society.[103]

Underscoring Haitian emigrationists' efforts to distance their movement from schemes for African colonization and emigration was a conviction that a movement to the island republic offered the best opportunity for African Americans to contribute to a viable and vigorous black nationality. In part, this belief was premised on the notion of geographic proximity. Redpath argued that whereas the ACS scheme sought to take black Americans "far beyond the sphere on which they could operate against Slavery," the aim of the Haitian movement was to build up a black nationality that could "tell with great efficiency *against* slavery."[104] Redpath thus enjoined the nationalistic fervor of the nineteenth century to two other concepts close to the heart of antebellum Americans: the idea that individuals and groups inhabited distinct "spheres"; and the ethos of efficiency, which itself transcended spheres. Other converts to the Haitian scheme also addressed the question of black nationalism; it is appropriate, therefore, to analyze further the meanings they ascribed to the term, and the role they believed it could play in the elevation of the black race.

An essential tenet of the emigrationists' black nationalist philosophy was a belief that blacks had to act for themselves. This, of course, was not a new concept. But Haitian emigrationists differed from proponents of the stay-and-fight philosophy, and from advocates of emigration to Canada or Africa, over the question of where they should act to elevate themselves. Where Haitian emigrationists maintained it would be more valuable for skilled blacks to work on behalf of their race in Haiti, their opponents continued to regard such ideas as a dangerous distraction from the task at hand in the United States. Indeed, one of the most persistent charges leveled against Haitian emigrationism was that talk of leaving the United States served to unsettle the African American populace. William Wells Brown's response to that charge is illustrative of the emigrationist leadership's perception that the black populace had to take greater responsibility for its own elevation. For Brown, and other proponents of Haitian emigration, while the badge of race denoted a common oppression, self-improvement and elevation were largely contingent on individual effort and enterprise. Brown did not dispute the charge that talk of emigrationism had an unsettling effect. Instead, he asserted that emigration was an effective means of shaking black Americans out of their lethargic state. More would be gained by going to Haiti "to develop the resources of the Island," he argued, than would be achieved by remaining in the United States. Claiming that blacks' "greatest misfortune" was that they were not a migratory race, he reasoned that prejudice against the ACS—which he had helped maintain—had created a strong aversion to any suggestion that African Americans should leave their "native land." Noting that the objections to emigration centered on the feeling that blacks should not leave the land of their birth, thereby forsaking the slaves, he argued that on close examination, that line of thinking had little validity. He denied that blacks could exert any meaningful influence in the United States, where they occupied only menial positions. In Haiti—unlike Africa—black American emigrants would still be close enough to the United States to play a part in the anti-slavery struggle. And because most African Americans were too poor to become landowners, Brown suggested it would be in the best interest of all African Americans if some accepted the Haitian government's offer of a free grant of land, with "all the rights of natives."[105]

The importance black Americans attached to the issue of land ownership has been noted. Haitian emigrationists concurred with that concept, but by 1861 they had largely given up hope that the Jeffersonian ideal of all men becoming landowners was a realizable objective for most of the black populace in the United States. As Brown noted in 1861, "for the last twenty-five years," in "State and National Conventions," African American leaders had been "urging our people to leave the cities and towns and betake themselves to farming." But because "we are too poor to purchase farms," blacks "must emigrate" if they were to "become tillers of the soil." It was better, Haitian emigrationists argued, for blacks to become landowners in the island republic than it was for them to stay in the United States, where they would indefinitely remain in a position of servitude to white men.[106]

The question of a black nationality was inseparable from the issue of racial prejudice. Emigrationists asserted that a strong black nationality would compel white Americans to revise their attitudes toward the black race. There were two, closely connected aspects to this process. On one hand, African Americans had to develop self-esteem, without which it was futile to attempt to convince whites that blacks were their equals. Emigrationists concluded, however, with varying degrees of enthusiasm, that this sense of self-esteem could not develop amid the racist environment of white America. Redpath, too, addressed this issue. Accepting that the black race had produced "eminent men," he regretted that their genius had not been recognized by white men and women.

In Haiti, however, the black race could "develop itself in freedom." With no prejudice to contend against, Redpath asserted that African Americans could do "more for the Cause of the Slave" in the black republic than they could in the United States.[107]

As the next chapter reveals, the Civil War ultimately played a part in undermining the Haitian movement. Yet among some emigrationists there was a realization that even if the Civil War did lead to emancipation for the slaves, prejudice against African Americans would continue—and, given the prevalence of racism in the ostensibly "free" North, perhaps become even more acute. William J. Watkins did not begin lobbying on behalf of the Haitian scheme until August 1861. When the Civil War had broken out four months earlier he might have hoped that emancipation would soon result. But like his contemporaries, he realized quickly that emancipation was not imminent, and that racism was a problem to which no easy answer could be found. Following a visit to Oberlin, Ohio, in late 1861, Watkins described the prejudice against blacks that existed there. He wrote of the "deep-seated hostility of Northern dough-faces to colored people, even in the most favored Republican localities." As the Civil War progressed, he remarked, "prejudice against us appears to increase in virulence and power." To ensure that African Americans were not ignored, he argued, they had to be "seen and *felt* in this conflict."[108]

Watkins' argument that black emigration would ensure whites were aware of their presence was contradictory—a large proportion of the white population, regarding a black exodus as the best possible solution to the "black problem," would not have distinguished between proposals for a selective or en-masse emigration of African Americans. Partly as a consequence of that common white view, many black leaders continued to argue that the best way for African Americans to exert an influence was by remaining in the United States, and agitating for an end to slavery and oppression. Watkins, however, considered Haitian emigration as the most effective means of proving that black Americans were capable of looking after their own affairs, and that they would go to any lengths to obtain their freedom. Although he thought the Civil War might lead ultimately to the emancipation of the slaves, he also insisted that a black nationality was required to overcome the prejudice of white America. Like other abolitionists, he had long emphasized that blacks could not rely on the efforts of others if they were to secure meaningful freedom: African Americans' status would be determined by their own actions. The Civil War, Watkins asserted, had compelled black Americans to "study" themselves, and the "untoward circumstances" that surrounded and affected them. By late 1861, he was pleased to declare that blacks were "talking and resolving less," and "thinking and acting more."[109] Presumably, Watkins believed Haitian emigrationism had played a part in that process.

This issue of blacks assuming responsibility for their own well-being was connected to the question of religion. We have seen that emigrationists disagreed over the extent to which organized religion, and a faith in God, were helping or hindering African Americans in their quest for freedom and equality. But there was agreement that black Americans had to act for themselves, and that they should not expect God to do their duty for them. Even emigrationists such as Garnet and Holly, men closely connected with the Christian churches, stressed that African Americans should not wait for God to achieve their elevation. All emigrationists agreed that African Americans had to be active agents in their own elevation. Watkins, refining arguments he had been expressing since the early 1850s, insisted in September 1861 that "God will no more save lazy black men, than He will lazy white men."[110] The underlying attitude was clear: African Americans could rely on neither white Americans nor God for their elevation; rather, they had to help themselves, and the Haitian movement was encouraging them to do so.

According to the proponents of Haitian emigration, there was nothing haphazard about the means by which African American emigrants in Haiti would set about elevating their race. Redpath and the black agents of the bureau were optimistic that the creation of a vigorous black nationality would play a prominent part in challenging the oppression of blacks everywhere. An integral aspect of this thesis was the "reflex influence" that would derive from the successful emigration of a minority of African Americans. In his "Thoughts on Hayti" Holly had returned to this notion of a "reflex influence" that would "exert" a positive effect "on the condition of the colored people" of the United States, "and on the destiny of the negro race throughout the world." A "strong, powerful, enlightened and progressive negro nationality," Holly wrote, would be "capable of commanding the respect of all nations of the earth."[111] Watkins, too, was convinced that when blacks could demonstrate they were "strong and powerful" they would "command respect." Disillusioned with the idea that blacks' efforts to demonstrate their civility would automatically compel whites to grant them equality, and asserting in ever more vigorous language that it was time for blacks to demand equality, emigrationists were challenging the long-standing belief that African Americans could earn respect from white Americans. For the employees of the Haitian Bureau, emigrationism was the most viable means of accomplishing that process. As Watkins stated, a "righteous and powerful Negro Government" would "do more to elevate" the black race in the "estimation of the civilized world than the delivery of eloquent orations or the adoption of flaming resolutions."[112]

Although the advocates of the Haitian movement believed their work in favor of emigrationism was important in the elevation of the black race, they insisted that they remained dedicated to the fight for meaningful freedom within the United States. Like Henry Highland Garnet, William Wells Brown was determined to prove his ongoing commitment to the slaves. Arguing that African Americans were natives of the United States, and that "our right to remain here we will maintain," Brown declared in 1861 that if the Haitian movement rested on the premise that blacks could not rise in the United States, he would oppose it. Arguing that a "powerful and influential" government in Haiti, capable of demonstrating "the genius and capabilities of the Negro" was "as good an Anti-Slavery work" as could be "done in the Northern States of the Union," he fused emigrationism with the goals of the stay-and-fight ideology.[113] If Brown's statement preserved a role for the stay-and-fight philosophy, the white leader of the Haitian movement was less optimistic about the emancipatory potential of emigrationism. Although Redpath claimed emigration to Haiti was the most productive means by which blacks could work for their own freedom, he conceded privately that his plan alone would not "kill slavery."[114]

Haitian emigrationists utilized many of the concepts—and language—articulated by earlier proponents of emigration. William J. Watkins stressed the importance of African Americans emigrating to a location where whites "did not constitute the ruling power."[115] J. D. Harris was thinking along similar lines when he reiterated, almost verbatim, Martin Delany's statement that no people could be truly free until they constituted an "essential part of the ruling element" in the country in which they lived. And Harris utilized that concept, again as Delany had before him, when he pointed out that although blacks could be free in Canada, they would not become "a very great people there." It was essential, he insisted, that blacks become "identified with the ruling power of a nation."[116]

If proponents of the Haitian scheme shared some of the rhetoric and values of other emigrationists, they held distinctly grandiose visions regarding the black nationality they hoped to see develop in the island republic. Redpath spoke of Haiti developing to the point where it was the "England of the Western Continent," an image also used by Harris, as well as by an anonymous contributor to the *Weekly Anglo-African*. Like Holly and Whitfield before him, Redpath hoped to build a "splendid colored Nationality in the tropics."[117] In fact, the black nationality he envisioned would be based around two tropical confederacies—one in the West Indies, with Haiti as its center, and the other in Central America.[118] Harris also spoke of the creation of a black nationality that would "divide the continent with the whites." Envisaging the development of two empires, an Anglo-American, and the other Anglo-African, he hoped the latter empire would "challenge the admiration of the world, rivalling the glory of their historic ancestors." But Harris also imagined that a black nationality in the Caribbean would be an extension of an American empire—the "headquarters of a colored American nationality, and supreme mistress of the Caribbean Sea."[119]

These remarks were suggestive of a clearly spelled out program for the development of a black nationality. Yet they also reveal a great deal more. The utterances of the bureau's representatives indicate the influence of America on African Americans—indeed, aspects of Haitian emigrationism paralleled the racial and social values of many whites. It was predictable that Redpath would betray such attitudes, but the black agents of the bureau shared many of his assumptions regarding the black race. To be sure, black emigrationists had recognized the positive aspects of Haiti's history. They did not, however, believe all blacks were equal, either within the United States or between nations. Con-comitant with the notion that Haiti was incapable of reaching its full potential without outside help was a conviction that African Americans were uniquely qualified to fulfill such a role. Holly had raised this issue in his "Thoughts on Hayti." He was certain that to be successful, emigrants "should come from contact with a maturer and better developed civilization than exists in the country to which they migrate." Holly, of course, regarded Christianity as an essential element of that civilizing process, and African Americans' belief that they had benefited from their exposure to Christianity was matched by the feeling that they were more "energetic" than blacks elsewhere. Harris hinted at this attitude when he claimed an "infusion of Northern blood" was one means by which "the more sluggish tropics" could be "quickened and given energy."[120] Redpath was thinking along similar lines when he argued that blacks in the United States and Canada had profited from their contact with the Saxon race. Like black emigrationists, he claimed blacks who had lived in America possessed, "to a greater or lesser extent," the Saxon character that he believed was lacking in Haiti. And, again like other emigrationists, he was con-vinced that blacks in North America had improved through their contact with Christianity.[121] Implicit within this conviction was a sense among African Americans that there was no contradiction between good business and Christi-anity. For Redpath, along with the black agents of the Haitian Bureau, these expressions of what was an important aspect of many nineteenth-century con-structions of masculinity sat easily alongside the widespread ideal of the Chris-tian gentleman who was also engaged in the marketplace.

There were other areas of common ground between Redpath and black emigrationists. Stressing that African Americans had to act to help themselves, Redpath argued that in the short term the missions of the black and white races were different. For black Americans to accomplish their mission, they had to preserve their "identity," a task he believed was proving impossible in the United States. Not only was the weight of numbers stacked heavily against Af-rican Americans, but—expressing a view that was shared by a number of black emigrationists—they were also disadvantaged because the "Saxon race" was "a race of fighters." Yet blacks had not perished beneath the white man's lash. Rather, Redpath believed they would "disappear in the white man's arms."[122]

Redpath's reference to miscegenation raised a theme prominent in both abolitionist and proslavery thought; his appraisal of racial differences was also a gendered one. In this way he merged explicit ideas of race with more subtle references and assumptions concerning gender. The association of the white race with masculine characteristics was common during the nineteenth cen-tury. Equally common was the depiction of the black race in feminine terms. Such a depiction could be implicit, as in the case of Harriet Beecher Stowe's 1851 argument that slaves' "instinctive and domestic attachments" were stronger than those of whites. But it could also be explicit, as in the white abo-litionist L. Maria Child's 1843 assertion that the "comparison between women and the colored race as *classes* is striking." Women and blacks, she wrote, were "characterized by affection more than intellect; both have a strong development of the religious sentiment; both are exceedingly adhesive in their attachments; both, comparatively speaking, have a tendency to submission; and hence, both have been kept in subjection by physical force, and considered rather in the light of property, than as individuals." Another observer, the Reverend John Beard, who had traveled to Haiti, also referred to the domestic characteristics of dark-skinned people. The "negro blood," he argued, was peculiarly "favourable to the development of the domestic affections." It was not only whites who accepted these assumptions. Holly described blacks as "a very domestic race," who were "strong in their local attachments."[123] Although each of these writers interpreted the phrase "domestic" slightly differently, for Haitian emigrationists the black republic offered an opportunity to overcome these assumptions—and to challenge the practices and stereotypes with which they were widely associated.

These issues played a part in shaping Redpath's longer term view of race relations. Even though he argued that the white and black races were different, and that for the latter to fulfill its destiny blacks had to separate themselves from whites, he believed the ultimate result would be the amalgamation of the races. The new race, he claimed, would combine the intelligence and strong will of the caucasian with the fine health and vigor of the blacks. He envisioned a single world government, that would render obsolete all races and nationalities.[124] Redpath's vision was a Utopian one, but such visions had sustained abolitionists, and other reformers, for decades. Indeed, it could be argued that the Garrisonians' plan for the abolition of slavery and racism via a moral regeneration of humankind, was no less Utopian than Redpath's proposal. The underlying difference between them, of course, was that Redpath rejected the Garrisonians' moral suasionism in favor of concerted "action."

We have no record of how the black agents of the Haitian Bureau regarded Redpath's long-term view of the black race. It is significant, nonetheless, that they agreed that African Americans were the only ones qualified to elevate Haiti. This view reflected more than condescension to non-American blacks: It also rested on hierarchical assumptions concerning the black community within the United States. Haitian emigrationists' advocacy of selective emigration reflected a need to separate their scheme from that of the ACS as well as a belief that only certain African Americans could be of service to the island republic. In this regard, emigrationists differentiated between free blacks and slaves. Reflecting assumptions shared by many white Americans, and echoing Holly's earlier remarks regarding the ex-slaves who had failed as emigrants to Haiti during the 1820s, one essayist in the *Pine and Palm* described the slaves as "children," who were unable to make decisions for themselves. Not only would newly freed slaves be of no benefit to Haiti, but it would be unfair to them as individuals to send them to languish on the island republic.[125]

In depicting the slaves as children, emigrationists unwittingly concurred with the views of many white Americans. The influence of white America was also evident in Haitian emigrationists' emphasis on market forces. Here, proponents of the Haitian scheme were refining views enunciated by Henry Bibb, Martin Delany, and other emigrationists, from the early 1850s. Statements like those by H. Ford Douglass, that by "concentrating free labor in the tropics," blacks would "be able to attack slavery with the most efficient of all weapons—competition," betrayed a firm belief in the market ethos. Harris revealed a similar respect for that quintessential American ideology, when he suggested that half a dozen African American emigrants, equipped with cotton gins, would do more for the elevation of their race, by the successful cultivation of cotton, "than all the mere talkers in as many years."[126] Redpath, too, believed that by producing the staples of the southern economy, and undercutting the slaveocracy on the world market, emigrants to Haiti would strike directly at the peculiar institution. Recognizing the importance of cotton to England, and with the aim of alerting British cotton merchants to the potential benefits of buying Haitian cotton, he corresponded with G. R. Heywood, secretary of the Cotton Supply Association in England. Arguing that slave labor was more expensive than free labor, he pointed out that the South was no longer a reliable supplier of the raw materials they required. Emigrationists placed unrealistic faith in the antislavery powers of free labor cotton. Haitian cotton might have weakened slavery in the United States, but the maintenance of slavery in the South also was based on social and political factors that transcended the profitability of slavery. To be fair to the emigrationists, however, they generally conceived their economic attack on the peculiar institution as but one aspect of their wider assault on slavery.[127]

With that in mind, Haitian emigrationists recognized the importance of dissuading the southern slaveocracy from pursuing any territorial ambitions it might have had in the Caribbean. White southerners, convinced that slavery had to expand if it was to survive, and worried about the consequences of what they regarded as the ascendancy of the free soil ideology in Washington, as well as in the West, did contemplate expansion in the Caribbean. Cuba had long been a potential target of southern expansionism; William Wells Brown also claimed the slavepower had also "had its eyes upon" Haiti for many years. Black Americans, Brown asserted, had a duty to protect freedom in the island republic. William J. Watkins, too, believed that the presence of African American emigrants in Haiti would deter the "corrupt and despotic [slave] power" from moving in that direction.[128] The emigrationists' desire to plant colonies of free blacks in the Caribbean—and particularly in Haiti—was a central component of their plan to promote a black nationality, for accepting the thesis that in the rapidly expanding United States slavery had to expand if it was to survive, it could be argued that emigrationists were actively promoting abolition, by denying southerners the opportunity to acquire additional territory for slavery. At this point, the relationship between emigrationism and the Haitian government's appointment of Redpath as an advocate of American recognition of the black republic is clear, because that recognition was another means of deterring the slavepower from fulfilling its expansionist aspirations in Haiti's direction.

Aware that African American leaders were concerned with the white South's plans to expand southward, Redpath sought to use those concerns to lure the foremost black abolitionist into supporting Haitian emigrationism. Redpath realized that if Frederick Douglass could be enticed into endorsing Haitian emigration, it would lend weight to the movement, and significantly enhance its chances of success. Redpath would have been well aware of Douglass' consistent and trenchant criticism of colonization. Even after his rift with William Lloyd Garrison, Douglass had continued to endorse the anti-colonization and anti-emigrationist philosophy that was characteristic of Garrisonian abolitionism. Indeed, he gave little heart to emigrationists, continuing to argue, as he had in 1849, "that the black man in this land has as much right to stay in this land as the white man."[129] Douglass was particularly critical of African colonization, but he rarely differentiated between the ACS scheme, and the proposals of Delany and other black emigrationists. A notable exception was in May 1853, when he told the American and Foreign Anti-Slavery Society of an "alternative" to African colonization. That alternative, he reasoned, was "not quite so desperate as that we must be slaves here, or go to the pestilential shores of Africa." In an affirmation of the proximity theory, he said it was possible for blacks to plant "themselves" at the "very portals of slavery." In tropical America or Canada, he noted, black emigrants could "keep within hearing of the wails of our enslaved people" in the United States. Speaking in terms strikingly similar to those employed by the emigrationists, he discussed the possibility that blacks might "mould them[selves] into one body, and into a powerful nation." Nonetheless, he did stress he would prefer to stay where he was, and that emigration to regions close to the United States should only be considered as a final alternative.[130]

That statement was the closest Douglass came to endorsing any plan of emigration until early 1861. In May 1859, he had explicitly opposed emigration to Haiti. But like other black leaders, he was affected by the crises of the immediate pre–Civil War period. In June 1860, he wrote to Redpath, admitting that he had "little hope in the freedom of the slave by peaceful means."[131] That comment was a sign of disillusionment; within months Douglass was willing to contemplate the previously unthinkable—outright endorsement of emigrationism. Sensing that Douglass' anti-emigrationist resolve was wavering, Redpath took steps to encourage a change of heart. By November 1860, he was in contact with Douglass, and was so confident of securing his support that in a report to Victorien Plésance he stated that although Douglass "has always hitherto opposed Emigration, I am likely to obtain his aid."[132] Even allowing for the fact that Redpath was keen to impress the Haitian authorities with his work ethic and powers of persuasion, and prove to them that the emigration scheme was likely to succeed, there was considerable cause to believe Douglass would endorse the Haitian program.

The failure of the Republicans to provide any guarantees of freedom or security to blacks during the 1860 election campaign, coupled with their continued statements that their goal was the preservation of the Union, rather than emancipation for the slaves, contributed to Douglass' shifting attitude toward the Haitian scheme.[133] By late 1860, he was prepared to make favorable comments about the Haitian scheme. Writing the month after Lincoln's victory in the presidential election, he reiterated that he had never supported emigration. Taking into account, however, that "the means of obtaining a living" were "becoming more and more limited" for African Americans, he could "raise no objections to the present movement towards Hayti." Emigration "may prove highly advantageous to many families," and would be of "much service to the Haytian Republic." In a statement that could easily have come from Holly, Delany, or any of the other advocates of emigrationism, Douglass declared: "let us go to Hayti, where our oppressors do not want us to go, and where our influence and example can still be of service to those whose tears will find their way to us by the waters of the Gulf washing all our shores." Supporting the notion of a black nationality, he stated, "We believe the inevitable logic of events points to the ultimate growth in the equatorial regions of the American continent of an empire controlled by the mixed races of African blood." Douglass thus raised many themes of the black emigrationist-nationalist philosophy. Implying that African Americans' opponents were hostile to Haiti, he also concluded that the emigration of a select few would exert an influence and create an example that would benefit all black people. Importantly, he remarked that the long-held objections against the ACS could not be leveled truthfully at the Haitian scheme. Typically for Douglass, the question of slavery was central, and his sense of bonding with those still in thraldom was evident. Moreover, praising Redpath as a person who had "given many proofs of his deep abhorrence of slavery," Douglass endorsed the leadership of the Haitian movement. Evidently, he had come to view Haitian emigrationism as a viable alternative for at least some African Americans.[134]

Douglass' views had shifted significantly. And he had not finished. The continuing uncertainties of early 1861 led him to give a further endorsement of the Haitian scheme in the May edition of *Douglass' Monthly*. Therein he announced that, along with his daughter, he had accepted an invitation from Redpath to visit the island republic. All of this gave Redpath considerable cause for optimism. However, events intervened, and in a postscript to the May 1861 article, written after the fall of Fort Sumter, Douglass informed his readers that he would be staying in the United States, to "watch the current of events." The recent turn of affairs, he explained, had "made a tremendous revolution in all things pertaining to the possible future" of blacks in the United States.[135]

Douglass's equivocation over the Haitian movement was unfortunate for Redpath and the Haitian Bureau. Nonetheless, by mid-1861, the scheme was operational. Redpath had established his abolitionist credentials during the 1850s. But like the black agents he employed, Redpath was aware that traditional anti-slavery strategies, and other emigration proposals, had not only failed to free the slaves, but had proved ineffectual in challenging American racism. In the case of William Wells Brown and William J. Watkins, it was also disillusionment with the stay-and-fight ideology; for J. D. Harris and H. Ford Douglass it was an awareness of the impracticability of other emigration proposals. The bureau's agents did not regard their support for emigration as a retreat from their earlier insistence that African Americans were entitled to equality in the United States. Careful to promote only a select emigration of the "right" kind of blacks, they believed that the establishment of a black nationality was the most effective means of elevating their race. With the southern slaveocracy apparently ascendant, and with the plight of the free blacks in the North deteriorating, new measures were required to enable African Americans to achieve meaningful freedom. Emigrationists had high hopes on the potential value of a successful movement of African Americans to Haiti. Such an emigration would help eradicate prejudice, contribute to the fight against slavery, and deter the slavepower from moving south.

These themes were evident on an individual as well as collective basis. By their advocacy of emigration to the island republic, agents of the Haitian Bureau were responding in one way to the crisis that all blacks in the United States faced during the 1850s and early 1860s. Redpath's offer of employment was one inducement, but without exception, the reform careers of the Bureau's agents betrayed a flexibility and pragmatism that were only predictable given the circumstances under which they labored. Opponents of emigration were generally not averse to the principles underpinning a black nationality, but they did harbor serious reservations about the value of such a nationality on the fight for freedom within the United States. Worried, too, that talk of emigration distracted African Americans from the important tasks confronting them in the United States, they feared that discussion about emigration would be perceived by enemies of their race not only as a sign that they were going to run away, but also that they accepted that there was no place for blacks in American society. In principle, stay-and-fighters perceived little difference between black-organized schemes for emigration, and the colonization proposals formulated by whites. Nevertheless, by the end of 1860, the proponents of Haitian emigration had articulated an ambitious black nationalist ideology, with equally ambitious objectives; and—moving well beyond the theoretical discussions of other emigration proposals—a movement of African Americans to the island republic was underway.

NOTES

1. There is no adequate biography of Redpath. This brief biographical sketch is derived from two dated sources: Charles F. Horner, *The Life of James Redpath and the*

Development of the Modern Lyceum (New York: Barse & Hopkins, 1926), 7–18; and Alvin F. Harlow's entry on Redpath in the *Dictionary of American Biography*, ed. Allen Johnson et al., 20 vols. (New York: Oxford University Press, 1935), 15:443–44. See also John R. McKivigan's "Introduction" to Redpath's *The Roving Editor; or, Talks with Slaves in the Southern States* (1859; reprint, University Park: Pennsylvania State University Press, 1996), xiv–xxv.

2. Redpath to Garrison, 26 July 1854, Anti-Slavery Collection, Rare Books and Manuscripts Room, Boston Public Library (cited by courtesy of the Trustees of the Boston Public Library); *Liberator*, 4 August 1854.

3. Jim A. Hart, "James Redpath, Missouri Correspondent," *Missouri Historical Review*, 57 (1962): 70.

4. John R. McKivigan, "James Redpath, John Brown, and Abolitionist Advocacy of Slave Insurrection," *Civil War History*, 37 (1991): 295–96; Hart, "Missouri Correspondent," 70–71. Together with Richard J. Hinton, Redpath later wrote *Hand-Book to Kansas Territory and the Rocky Mountains Gold Region: Accompanied by Reliable Maps and a Preliminary Treatise on the Pre-Emption Laws of the United States* (New York: J. H. Colton, 1859).

5. Horner, *Life of James Redpath*, 66.

6. Horner, *Life of James Redpath*, 56; Redpath, *The Roving Editor* (New York: A. B. Burdick, 1859), ii.

7. Redpath, *The Roving Editor*, iv. See also Willis D. Boyd, "James Redpath and American Negro Colonization in Haiti, 1860–1862," *The Americas*, 12 (1955): 170; McKivigan, "Advocacy of Slave Rebellion," 300–301; Horner, *Life of James Redpath*, 56.

8. Redpath, *The Roving Editor*, 2, 28, 84, 256, 303, 305.

9. Redpath, *The Public Life of Capt. John Brown* (Boston: Thayer & Eldridge, 1860), 8.

10. Redpath, *Echoes of Harper's Ferry* (Boston: Thayer & Eldridge, 1860), 6, 8, 457.

11. *National Anti-Slavery Standard*, 24 March 1860.

12. Redpath, ed., *A Guide to Hayti* (1861; reprint, Westport, Conn.: Negro Universities Press, 1970), 9–10.

13. Robert Debs Heinl, Jr., and Nancy Gordon Heinl, *Written in Blood: The Story of the Haitian People, 1492–1971* (Boston: Houghton Mifflin, 1978), 209–16; Robert I. Rotberg, *Haiti: The Politics of Squalor* (Boston: Houghton Mifflin, 1971), 85; Seldon Rodman, *Haiti: The Black Republic* (New York: Devin-Adair, 1954), 21; Harold Palmer Davis, *Black Democracy: The Story of Haiti*, Rev. Ed. (1928; reprint, New York: Biblo & Tannen, 1967), 120–25.

14. Benjamin S. Hunt, *Remarks on Hayti as a Place of Settlement for African-Americans and on the Mulatto as a Race for the Tropics* (Philadelphia: T. B. Pugh, 1860), 8–10.

15. Howard H. Bell, *A Survey of the Negro Convention Movement, 1830–1861* (New York: Arno Press, 1969), 245.

16. *New York Tribune*, 25 June 1859; *Echoes of Harper's Ferry*, frontispiece. For varying assessments of Soulouque, see Harold Palmer Davis, *Black Democracy*, 120; David Nicholls, *From Dessalines to Duvalier: Race, Colour and National Independence in Haiti*, 3rd ed. (London: Macmillan, 1996), 83.

17. Redpath, *Guide to Hayti*, 10; *Douglass' Monthly*, May 1859.

18. Blassingame, *Black New Orleans, 1860–1880* (Chicago: University of Chicago Press, 1973), 6.

19. *Opelousas Courier*, 8 September 1860, cited in H. E. Sterx, *The Free Negro in Ante-Bellum Louisiana* (Rutherford, N.J.: Fairleigh Dickinson University Press, 1972), 301. See also Caryn Cossé Bell, *Revolution, Romanticism, and the Afro-Creole Protest Tradition in Louisiana, 1718–1868* (Baton Rouge: Louisiana State University Press, 1997), 84–85.

20. *Opelousas Patriot*, 6 September 1859, cited in Sterx, *Free Negro in Ante-Bellum Louisiana*, 298.

21. Carl A. Brasseaux, Keith A. Fontenot, and Claude F. Oubre, *Creoles of Color in the Bayou Country* (Jackson: University Press of Mississippi, 1994), 83.

22. Cited in Brasseaux, Fontenot, and Oubre, *Creoles of Color in the Bayou Country*, 83.

23. Sterx, *Free Negro in Ante-Bellum Louisiana*, 300–301. See also Richard C. Wade, *Slavery in the Cities: The South, 1820–1860* (London: Oxford University Press, 1964), 264–65; Joseph Logsdon and Caryn Cossé Bell, "The Americanization of Black New Orleans, 1850–1900," in *Creole New Orleans: Race and Americanization*, ed. Arnold R. Hirsch and Joseph Logsdon (Baton Rouge: Louisiana State University Press, 1992), 208.

24. Blassingame, *Black New Orleans*, 2. See also Roger A. Fisher, "Racial Segregation in Ante-Bellum New Orleans," in *Free Blacks in America, 1800–1860*, ed. John H. Bracey, Jr., August Meier, and Elliot Rudwick (Belmont, Calif.: Wadsworth, 1970), 37.

25. Rodolphe Lucien Desdunes, *Our People and Our History: A Tribute to the Creole People of Color in Memory of the Great Men They Have Given Us and of the Good Works They Have Accomplished*, trans. & ed. Sister Dorothea Olga McCants (1911; reprint, Baton Rouge: Louisiana State University Press, 1973), 112.

26. *Daily Picayune*, 15 July 1859.

27. *Daily Picayune*, 21 July 1859.

28. *Daily Picayune*, 15 July 1859.

29. *Daily Picayune*, 15 July 1859

30. Brasseaux, Fontenot, and Oubre, *Creoles of Color in the Bayou Country*, 83; Bell, *Revolution, Romanticism, and the Afro-Creole Protest Tradition*, 86–87.

31. *New Orleans Bee*, 16 January 1860; *Times Picayune*, 15 January 1860.

32. *Daily Picayune*, 28 April 1859.

33. Brasseaux, Fontenot, and Oubre, *Creoles of Color in the Bayou Country*, 84. See also Bell, *Revolution, Romanticism, and the Afro-Creole Protest Tradition*, 83–84.

34. *New York Tribune*, 29 June 1859; *Douglass' Monthly*, June 1859.

35. *Douglass' Monthly*, May 1859.

36. Redpath, *Guide to Hayti*, 93–99.

37. C. Peter Ripley, ed., *The Black Abolitionist Papers. Volume IV: The United States, 1847–1858* (Chapel Hill: University of North Carolina Press, 1991), 66n.

38. *Chatham Tri-Weekly Planet*, 20 December 1859; *Chatham Tri-Weekly Planet*, 22 March 1860.

39. Redpath, *Guide to Hayti*, 100–103.

40. *Weekly Anglo-African*, 23 June 1860; *Chatham Tri-Weekly Planet*, 21 June 1860.

41. Floyd J. Miller, *The Search for a Black Nationality: Black Emigration and Colonization, 1787–1863* (Urbana: University of Illinois Press, 1975), 233–34.

42. David McEwen Dean, *Defender of the Race: James Theodore Holly, Black Nationalist Bishop* (Boston: Lambeth Press, 1979), 32.

43. Jackson, "The Origins of Pan-African Nationalism: Afro-American and Haytian Relations, 1800–1863," (Ph.D. diss., Northwestern University, 1976), 160.

44. *Anglo-African Magazine*, June 1859.

45. *Anglo-African Magazine*, July 1859.

46. *Anglo-African Magazine*, August 1859; Holly to Blair, 10 December 1858, in Frank P. Blair, Jr., *The Destiny of the Races on this Continent, An Address before the Mercantile Library Association of Boston, Massachusetts, on the 26th of January, 1859* (Washington, D.C.: Buell & Blanchard, 1859), 35.

47. *Anglo-African Magazine*, September 1859. On Republican Motherhood, see, Linda Kerber, *Women of the Republic: Intellect and Ideology in Revolutionary America* (Chapel Hill: University of North Carolina Press, 1980), Chapter 9.

48. *Anglo-African Magazine*, September 1859.

49. *Anglo-African Magazine*, October 1859; *Weekly Anglo-African*, 22 December 1860, 25 February 1860, 26 January 1861.

50. *Anglo-African Magazine*, October, 1859, August 1859

51. *Anglo-African Magazine*, November 1859.

52. Redpath, *Guide to Hayti*, 10.

53. Boyd, "Colonization in Hayti," 172.

54. Redpath, *Guide to Hayti*, 110–11, 120–24; Boyd, "Colonization in Hayti," 172.

55. Redpath to Sumner, 17 March 1861, Haytian Bureau of Emigration, Reports and Correspondence, 1860–1861, Rare Books and Manuscript Section, Boston Public Library (HBE-BPL) (cited by courtesy of the Trustees of the Boston Public Library).

56. Redpath to Plésance, 12 December 1860, HBE-BPL.

57. Ludwell Lee Montague, *Haiti and the United States, 1714–1938* (1940; reprint, New York: Russell & Russell, 1966), 81–86.

58. *Liberator*, 22 May 1863.

59. Jackson, "Origins of Pan-African Nationalism," 198.

60. Redpath to Holly, 9 November 1860, HBE-BPL; Redpath to Plésance, 3 November 1860, 21 January 1861, HBE-BPL.

61. *Weekly Anglo-African*, 9 February 1861; *Chatham Weekly Planet*, 21 February 1861.

62. Redpath to Plésance, 3 November 1860, HBE-BPL; Redpath to Garnet, 17 December 1860, HBE-BPL.

63. See William Edward Farrison, *William Wells Brown: Author and Reformer* (Chicago: University of Chicago Press, 1969); Benjamin Quarles, *Black Abolitionists* (New York: Oxford University Press, 1969), 227.

64. Bettye J. Gardner, "William Watkins: Antebellum Black Teacher and Anti-Slavery Writer," *Negro History Bulletin*, 39 (1976): 625; C. Peter Ripley, ed., *The Black Abolitionist Papers. Volume II: Canada, 1830–1865* (Chapel Hill: University of North Carolina Press, 1986), 444n.

65. *Anti-Slavery Bugle*, 6 October 1860. See also Robert L. Harris, Jr., "H. Ford Douglas: Afro-American Antislavery Abolitionist," *Journal of Negro History*, 62 (1977): 219–20, 227.

66. *Proceedings of a Convention of the Colored Men of Ohio. Held in the City of Cincinnati on the 23rd, 24th, 25th and 26th Days of November, 1858* (Cincinnati: Moore, Wilstach, Keys & Co., 1858 in *Proceedings of the Black State Conventions, 1840–1865*, ed. Philip S. Foner and George E. Walker, 2 vols. (Philadelphia: Temple University Press, 1979–1980) 1:335; Ripley, *Black Abolitionist Papers*, 2:439–40.

67. *Frederick Douglass' Paper*, 8 December 1854.

68. *Frederick Douglass' Paper*, 18 May 1855.

69. *Frederick Douglass' Paper*, 10 February 1854.

70. *Anti-Slavery Bugle*, 28 November 1857; William C. Nell to William Lloyd Garrison, December 1852, in *Liberator*, 10 December 1852, repr. in *The Mind of the Negro as Reflected in Letters Written During the Crisis, 1800–1860*, ed. Carter G. Woodson (1926; reprint, New York: Negro Universities Press, 1969), 338.

71. *Liberator*, 12 December 1851, 28 November 1851; *Frederick Douglass' Paper*, 10 December 1852, 26 August 1853.

72. *Anti-Slavery Bugle*, 28 November 1857.

73. *Frederick Douglass' Paper*, 2 June 1854.

74. Watkins, *Our Rights as Men. An Address Delivered in Boston, Before the Legislative Committee on the Militia, February 24, 1853* (Boston: Benjamin F. Roberts, 1853), frontispiece, 4, passim; *Anti-Slavery Advocate*, August 1857.

75. *Boston Herald*, 23 April 1853 in Ripley, *Black Abolitionist Papers*, 4:154.

76. James O. Horton and Lois E. Horton, *In Hope of Liberty: Culture, Community, and Protest Among Northern Free Blacks, 1700–1860* (New York: Oxford University Press, 1997), 118–19.

77. *Proceedings of a Convention of Colored Men of Ohio . . . 1858*, in Foner and Walker, *Proceedings of the Black State Conventions* (quote on I:337).

78. *Weekly Anglo-African*, 17 December 1859; *Anti-Slavery Bugle*, 6 October 1860; Harris, "H. Ford Douglass," 227.

79. *National Anti-Slavery Standard*, 26 May 1860.

80. *Weekly Anglo-African*, 11 May 1861; *Pine and Palm*, 2 June 1861.

81. Harris to Blair, 10 December 1858, in Blair, *Destiny of the Races*, 34; Miller, *Search for a Black Nationality*, 150, 237.

82. Bell, *Survey of the Negro Convention Movement*, 212; Miller, *Search for a Black Nationality*, 237–38.

83. See Harris to Blair, 29 January 1860, in the Blair/Lee Papers, Princeton University, Princeton, New Jersey, reprinted in George E. Carter and Peter C. Ripley, eds., *Black Abolitionist Papers* (microfilm edition) (Sanford, N.C.: Microfilming Corporation of America, 1981), Reel 12, Frame 0463.

84. Blair, *Colonization and Commerce. An Address Before the Young Men's Mercantile Library Association of Cincinnati, Ohio, November 29, 1859* (Cincinnati; 1859), 6.

85. *Chatham Tri-Weekly Planet*, 8 October 1859; Harris, "H. Ford Douglass," 218, 224–27. See also the *Minutes of the State Convention of the Colored Citizens of Ohio, Convened at Columbus, January 15–18, 1851* (1851), as reprinted in Foner and Walker, *Proceedings of the Black State Conventions*, Vol. 1; *Provincial Freeman*, 11 April 1857.

86. *Liberator*, 13 July 1860, *Pine and Palm*, 18 May 1861. See also Eugene M. Berwanger, *The Frontier Against Slavery: Western Anti-Negro Prejudice and the Slavery Extension Controversy* (Urbana: University of Illinois Press, 1967), 135; James M.

McPherson, *The Struggle for Equality: Abolitionists and the Negro in the Civil War and Reconstruction* (Princeton, N.J.: Princeton University Press, 1964), 25.

87. *Pine and Palm*, 17 August 1861; "Supplement" to the *Pine and Palm*, 2 January 1862; Farrison, *William Wells Brown*, 74.

88. See Brown, *St. Domingo: Its Revolutions and Its Patriots. A Lecture Delivered Before the Metropolitan Atheneum, London, May 16, and at St. Thomas' Church, Philadelphia, December 20, 1854* (Boston: Bela Marsh, 1855), 25, 38. See also William Wells Brown, *The Black Man, His Antecedents, His Genius, and His Achievements*, 4th ed. (1865; reprint, Miami: Mnemosyne Publishing Co., 1969), 92–106.

89. *Anti-Slavery Bugle*, 28 November 1857.

90. *Pine and Palm*, 2 June 1861; *Liberator*, 24 October 1851.

91. Harris, *A Summer on the Borders of the Caribbean Sea* (New York: A. B. Burdick, 1860). 117.

92. *Pine and Palm*, 3 August 1861.

93. *Douglass' Monthly*, November 1860; Redpath to C. W. Jacobs, 25 March 1861, James Redpath Letterbook, Rare Book, Manuscript, and Special Collections Library, Duke University, Durham, North Carolina (JRL-DU); Philip J. Staudenraus, *The African Colonization Movement, 1816–1865* (New York: Columbia University Press, 1961), 251.

94. Redpath to Élie, 12 February 1862, Correspondence of James Redpath, Commercial Agent of Hayti for Philadelphia, Joint Commissioner Plenipotentiary of Hayti to the government of the U.S. & General Agent of Emigration to Hayti for the U.S. and Canada, 31 December 1861 to 12 May 1862, Schomburg Center for Research in Black Culture, New York Public Library, New York City (hereafter cited as CJR-NYPL); Redpath to Plésance, 22 November 1861, Letters and Reports of James Redpath, General Agent of Emigration to Hayti, to M. Plésance, Secretary of State of External Relations of the Republic of Hayti, Manuscript Division, Library of Congress, Washington, D.C. (LRJR-LC); *Pine and Palm*, 9 November 1861.

95. *Anglo-African Magazine*, August 1859, September 1859.

96. Harris to Francis P. Blair, Jr., 10 December 1858, in Blair, *Destiny of the Races*, 34; Holly, *A Vindication of the Capacity of the Negro Race for Self-Government and Civilized Progress, as Demonstrated by Historical Events of the Haytian Revolution; and the Subsequent Acts of that People Since Their Material Independence* (New Haven: William H. Stanley, 1857), 44–45.

97. *Anti-Slavery Bugle*, 6 October 1860.

98. Watkins, "The Evils of Colonization," 31 October 1854, in *Autographs for Freedom*, ed. Julia Griffiths, 2 vols. (1854; reprint, Miami: Mnemosyne Publishing Co., 1969), II:198–200; *Frederick Douglass' Paper*, 18 May 1855.

99. *Pine and Palm*, 28 September 1861.

100. Redpath, *Guide to Hayti*, 174; Redpath to G. R. Heywood, 10 April 1861, LRJR-LC.

101. *Liberator*, 26 August 1858; *Weekly Anglo-African*, 22 December 1859.

102. *Weekly Anglo-African*, 21 April 1860.

103. *Weekly Anglo-African*, 22 December 1860.

104. Redpath to George W. Wilson, 1 April 1861, JRL-DU.

105. *Pine and Palm*, 2 June 1861.

106. *Pine and Palm*, 17 August 1861.

107. Redpath, *Guide to Hayti*, 173–74; Redpath to W. S. Harris, 29 March 1861, JRL-DU.

108. *Pine and Palm*, 19 October 1861, 3 August 1861.

109. *Pine and Palm*, 20 November 1861.

110. *Pine and Palm*, 28 September 1861.

111. *Anglo-African Magazine*, November 1859.

112. *Pine and Palm*, 28 September 1861, 10 April 1862.

113. *Pine and Palm*, 3 August 1861, 17 August 1861, 2 June 1861.

114. Redpath to "My Dear Friends," 18 February 1861, JRL-DU.

115. *Pine and Palm*, 28 September 1861.

116. Harris, *Summer on the Borders*, 176; Harris to Francis P. Blair, Jr., 10 December 1858, in Blair, *Destiny of the Races*, 34.

117. Redpath to John Jones, 15 March 1861, JRL-DU; Harris, *Summer on the Borders*, 149; *Weekly Anglo-African*, 13 April 1861.

118. *Pine and Palm*, 18 May 1861.

119. Harris, *Summer on the Borders*, 181–82, 149.

120. *Anglo-African Magazine*, August 1859; Harris, *Summer on the Borders*, 158.

121. Redpath, *Guide to Hayti*, 174.

122. Redpath, *Guide to Hayti*, 171–73.

123. Stowe to Henry Ward Beecher, 1 February 1851, Harriet Beecher Stowe Letters, Beecher Family Papers, Manuscripts and Archives, Yale University, New Haven, Connecticut; Child, "The African Race," *National Anti-Slavery Standard*, 27 April 1843; Reverend John Beard, *The Life of Toussaint L'Ouverture, the Negro Patriot of Hayti: Comprising an Account of the Struggle for Liberty in the Island, and a Sketch of Its History to the Present Period* (London: Ingram, Cooke, & Co., 1853), 316; Holly to Frank P. Blair, Jr., 30 January 1858, in Blair, *The Destiny of the Races*, 35.

124. *Pine and Palm*, 18 May 1861.

125. *Pine and Palm*, 20 March 1862.

126. *Weekly Anglo-African*, 20 April 1860; Harris, *Summer on the Borders*, 90.

127. *Weekly Anglo-African*, 6 April 1861, 20 April 1861; Redpath to Heywood, 10 April 1861, LRJR-LC; Redpath to Plésance, 7 September 1861, LRJR-LC; Redpath to Heywood, 30 May 1861, JRL-DU.

128. *Pine and Palm*, 17 August 1861, 3 August 1861.

129. Douglass, "The American Colonization Society," Speech in Faneuil Hall, Boston, 8 June 1849, in *The Life and Writings of Frederick Douglass*, ed. Philip S. Foner, 4 vols. (New York: International Publishers, 1952), 1:394.

130. Douglass, "The Present Condition and Future Prospects of the Negro People," May 1853, in Foner, *Life and Writings of Frederick Douglass*, 2:252–53.

131. Douglass to Redpath, 29 June 1860, in Foner, *Life and Writings*, 2:487.

132. Redpath to Victorien Plésance, 3 November 1860, HBE-BPL.

133. Nathan I. Huggins, *Slave and Citizen: The Life of Frederick Douglass* (Boston: Little, Brown, and Co., 1980), 72.

134. *Douglass' Monthly*, January 1861.

135. *Douglass' Monthly*, May 1861.

5

Transplanting Black America: Emigrationism in Practice, 1861–1863

By transforming much of what had been confined to theoretical discourse during the 1850s into a tangible movement, the Haitian emigration scheme engaged the attention of free black communities throughout the northern states and Canada. In dispatching more African Americans abroad in the two years it was in operation than the American Colonization Society (ACS) ever managed to transport to Liberia in a similar period, the Haitian movement effectively challenged prevailing stereotypes concerning blacks' alleged apathy to their plight. Indeed, because Haitian emigrationism was directing black Americans to a very different destination than was the case with the ACS, its advocates' claims that emigration to the island republic was "essentially and diametrically opposed to the colonization project" was for a time sufficiently persuasive to suggest that the Haitian program was substantially more than a new incarnation of the ACS.[1] Ultimately, the Haitian scheme collapsed, in part because the political system in the North appeared to be countenancing challenges to slavery and racism, and partly because of the ongoing opposition to emigration from sections of the black leadership. As the Civil War ground on, most African American leaders reverted to the stay-and-fight ideology that had been so pervasive in the period preceding the passage of the 1850 Fugitive Slave Act. The failure of the scheme is best understood in the context of events in Haiti as well as within the United States; this chapter seeks to recapture—in so far as it is possible to do so—something of the emigration experience. This entails looking not only at the objections raised by dissatisfied emigrants (many of whom returned to the United States), but also considering their preconceptions and expectations.[2] In turn, this raises again the contested meanings that were attached to the concept of a black nationality.

The first group of African Americans to emigrate under the auspices of the Haitian Bureau sailed from New York in December 1860. Thereafter, emigrants continued to leave the United States until August 1862, when the bureau despatched its last group of colonists. Most of those who emigrated did so during 1861, particularly in the latter part of the year. Significantly, this was after the outbreak of the Civil War, suggesting that during the early part of that conflict many African Americans were not only skeptical that the war would lead to meaningful freedom, but were also concerned that the Confederacy might indeed triumph. By the time the final group of emigrants departed in August 1862, the bureau had despatched more than two thousand African Americans to the island republic.[3] If that was a relatively small number, it was adequate for the purposes of black leaders who continued to emphasize, not mass migration, but the raising of black consciousness by a successful selective emigration.

During the 1820s, dissatisfied emigrants had inflicted considerable damage on the Haitian emigration movement. This lesson was not lost on James Redpath, and other proponents of Haitian emigrationism, during the Civil War era. Even before the departure of the first group of colonists, Redpath sought to impress on the Haitian authorities the importance of ensuring that the reports emigrants sent back to the United States were favorable. The emigrants' statements, he told Victorien Plésance in late 1860, would "greatly influence" the movement's chances of success.[4] Although many of those who embarked for Haiti expressed great optimism about their prospects in their new homes, it is important to appreciate the magnitude of the emigrants' mission. Alongside the usual motive of self-interest, common to migrants in most circumstances, there was the added burden of being emissaries of a nascent black nationalism, that the movement's leaders hoped would fuse individual self-interest with the grander vision of a collective racial consciousness.

Although their early reports revealed an optimistic appraisal of conditions in Haiti, many emigrants were soon disillusioned. This disillusionment, as had been the case during the 1820s, was based in part on the profound cultural, linguistic, and religious differences between emigrants and native Haitians. Significantly, these differences resembled the differences that had emerged between African American settlers and native Africans in the ACS colony of Liberia. In each case, black Americans reflected the influence of their experiences within the United States. These experiences were both a raison d'être for the emigrationists' "civilizing" mission, and a reason behind the failure of the Haitian scheme. For the Haitian Bureau, preparing African Americans for life in Haiti was a difficult task, which suggested much about the contradictory impulses of emigrationism. In seeking to convince blacks of the virtues of migrating to Haiti, Redpath's role was that of a propagandist; at the same time, however, he also was required to caution prospective emigrants that life in Haiti could be demanding, even dangerous. From the moment of his appointment, there was a tension between these two functions. Although Redpath and other employees of the Haitian Bureau stressed that it was only through hard work and sacrifice that emigrants would succeed in Haiti, they also went to great lengths to depict the island republic as an attractive destination for emigrants.

One aspect of this task was to assure emigrants that they would be able to adapt to the social and cultural norms in Haiti. This, too, was a potentially contradictory objective: were the values and social systems with which black Americans were imbued to become the norm in Haiti; or were black American emigrants to become "Haitianized"? This question, at the heart of the emigrationists' black nationalist ideology, was of immediate concern to those blacks contemplating emigration. Redpath alluded to this matter in his 1861 *Guide to Hayti*. He pointed out that although the educated classes in Haiti spoke French, the "common people" spoke a "Haytian creole," which he claimed could be "easily acquired in three or six months" by living among the people. Redpath hoped to reassure African Americans that they would soon blend in with the Haitian populace. But implicit in his comment—and contradicting his assertion that black Americans would be "undisputed lords" on the island republic—was an assumption that emigrants to Haiti would not be mixing with the Haitian elite, and hence would be marginalized from the dominant positions in society. On one hand, Redpath, and other proponents of the Haitian scheme, were suggesting that black Americans' background and expertise meant they would occupy an indispensable, and presumably privileged, position in the black republic. Yet by implying that black Americans would be mixing with the common folk of Haiti, Redpath seemed to be suggesting that emigrants would be no better off than Haiti's lower classes, who were widely regarded by Americans as economically and socially disadvantaged and subject to the vagaries of political turmoil. Moreover, although black Americans had sharply felt the force of American racism, they were convinced they were more "civilized" than other dark-skinned peoples. Consequently, because many African Americans considered themselves superior to the majority of Haitians, and were actively encouraged in that belief by proponents of emigration, the implications of Redpath's comment were far from reassuring.[5] To the ultimate detriment of the movement, Redpath was never able to satisfactorily resolve this issue.

The question of religious differences between emigrants and native Haitians on which Redpath had touched, proved to be another matter of deep concern for prospective emigrants. Realizing that the black church was the most important institution in African America, Redpath, like James Holly before him, knew that potential emigrants to Haiti wanted assurances that they would be free to continue the religious practices that were so important to them. The church would be a source of strength and inspiration in their new country, and would serve as a link with the land they had left behind. After traveling to Haiti during the 1850s, Benjamin Hunt had raised doubts about the Haitian government's commitment to recognize all religions. But Redpath—conveniently leaving the vexed question of voodoo to one side—asserted that although Catholicism was the dominant religion in Haiti, the people there had for many years "professed no spiritual allegiance to the Pope." Claiming that Haitians tolerated different religions, he assured potential emigrants that Haitian Catholics had "never prosecuted Protestants."[6] To one potential emigrant, Redpath asserted that "no country is more tolerant" than Haiti. Henry Highland Garnet, too, sought to persuade African Americans that their religious values and practices would be tolerated in Haiti. Citing the "Haytien statute" book's "enlightened and liberal clause in relation to religious toleration," and pointing out that the Protestant churches in the United States tolerated "the devilism of chattel slavery," Garnet couched his argument in terms of black Americans' obligation to help Haitians in their journey toward civilization.[7]Redpath and other agents of the bureau were only partly successful in persuading potential emigrants that their religious freedom would be respected in Haiti; as is seen here, diplomatic developments rendered his task more difficult. And despite his assurances that the language problem was not an insurmountable one, and that emigrants would enjoy religious freedom, Redpath stressed that those who went to Haiti should be permitted, indeed actively encouraged, to settle in "neighborhoods." It was hoped that settling emigrants in colonies would render the transition from the United States to Haiti an easier one.[8]

Exacerbating the emigrants' sense of spiritual alienation were equally pressing material concerns. In fact, from the time of their arrival in Haiti, conditions were considerably more difficult than many emigrants, or Redpath, had envisioned. In large measure, these difficulties can be traced to the fact that most emigrants were ill-prepared for life in Haiti. This point is evidenced by an examination of their background. Here, we turn first to the series of "Statistics" published by the Haitian Bureau. Unfortunately, besides a series of arithmetic errors, these statistics provide frustratingly sparse information on the emigrants' background.[9] Notwithstanding these gaps in the historical record, however, it is clear that few emigrants were adequately equipped for the life of an emigrant in Haiti. This lack of preparation was manifested in a number of ways. Some of these difficulties arose from the aforementioned cultural and social differences, but Haiti's physical environment, which had been depicted in such arcadian terms by Redpath and other proponents of Haitian emigration, failed to meet many emigrants' expectations. A majority of emigrants, for example, were adversely affected by the Haitian climate. The change from the climate of the United States to the tropical conditions of Haiti struck many emigrants, particularly the very young and the elderly.

Redpath and other agents of the bureau had warned of the dangers involved in the transition from a temperate to a tropical climate, but as with their descriptions of the linguistic and religious problems, these difficulties were understated. Redpath's *Guide to Hayti* included a five-page section, "Diseases of

Hayti and their Remedies." Therein, Dr. W. P. Smith claimed—misleadingly, as it turned out—that "the catalogue of diseases in Hayti does not present anything nearly so complex in character, nor so many in varieties of types, as are known to exist in the colder latitudes." People of "sober, regular habits," he asserted, "who are cleanly in their persons, and whose constitutions are not injured by the use of spirituous liquors and other excesses, may live in Hayti to an advanced age without being subjected to many serious attacks of fever." The onus for good health was thus placed on the individual. In this way, because black leaders had long espoused the virtues of individual responsibility and self-help, Haitian emigrationists were again tapping into values long emphasized by the African American leadership. But for those who took the time to inquire, the experience of that community portended trouble for emigrants in Haiti. Although it had been clearly demonstrated in Philadelphia in 1793 that blacks who had been born and raised in temperate climates were as susceptible to yellow fever as whites, Smith asserted that while blacks from the United States "may certainly fall under the influence of the fevers" of Haiti, the attacks—"with certain rare exceptions"—would be "comparatively less virulent" than with the whites.[10]

Emigrants soon discovered that living in Haiti was considerably more hazardous to their health than they had been led to believe. This point is well illustrated by the experiences of those emigrants who settled in the St. Mark region. Of the African Americans who migrated to Haiti between 1860 and 1862, approximately one thousand settled in the area around the port of St. Mark.[11] The Haitian authorities were hoping to develop the lands in the valley of the Artibonite River (St. Mark is at the mouth of this river). Redpath had painted a glowing picture of St. Mark, a town with a population of between two and three thousand people. The town, he asserted, was "beautifully situated—very healthy, and with a mild climate." Another observer, writing in a much later period, was rather less sanguine about St. Mark, describing it as a "wretched town."[12] The experiences of the African American emigrants validated the latter assessment, with dozens of fatalities among the colonists who settled in and around St. Mark. Indeed, one of Redpath's own agents conceded in mid-1862 that there had been 125 fatalities among the approximately 1,200 emigrants who had settled in the St. Mark region.[13]

Redpath acted to ensure that reports of a high mortality rate did not undermine the movement. Emigrants were discouraged from leaving the United States during June, July, or August, when climatic conditions in Haiti were at their most debilitating. The bureau's agents warned emigrants of the risk of yellow fever, and described the precautions they should take to protect their health. Redpath persuaded Dr. J. M. Hawks to write a series of "Health Hints to Emigrants in Haiti," that were published in the *Pine and Palm*.[14] By late 1861, Redpath was urging the Haitian authorities to settle emigrants in the highland regions of the island, where it was believed conditions were more healthy. Redpath also sought to convince potential emigrants that because the rainfall in Haiti was far heavier in 1861 than was normally the case, emigrants had fallen ill in unusually large numbers. Even native Haitians, he insisted, had suffered more than usual from sickness during 1861. The final means by which Redpath sought to obviate the risk to the movement from reports of illness and mortality was to blame the emigrants themselves; as the Haitian scheme faltered, this was a pattern that was to become common among the movement's leaders. Those who became sick, Redpath argued, did so because of their own imprudence—by ignoring warnings concerning diet, exposure to the sun, abstinence from alcohol, and various other factors.[15]

Illness was not the only problem confronting emigrants. Redpath had made arrangements with the Haitian authorities to expedite the movement of emigrants onto their own land, but the process proved to be frustratingly cumbersome, particularly in the St. Mark region. The Haitian government undertook to provide emigrants with food and shelter for eight days. Emigrants were then expected to move onto the land granted to them by the government.[16] Although emigrants conceded the Haitians did all they could to provide food and shelter (often for much longer than eight days) they complained that the agents appointed by the Haitian authorities to survey the lands were inefficient. Emigrants repeatedly protested that they were kept waiting for months before receiving the lands that had been promised to them. One emigrant noted that the Haitian agents "move too slowly" in granting lands to the settlers. Expressing surprise at the "great number of emigrants" around the St. Mark region who had not moved onto their farms, another settler asserted that there seemed to be "a lack of energy on the part of the agents" there, who were not "pushing things forward" as they should have been.[17]

Another emigrant, Isaiah Jones, was even more critical of the Haitian authorities. Following his return to North America, Jones noted that "with the exception of Mr. Élie," the Haitian agents at St. Mark were not "qualified for the job." Even more alarmingly, he reported that the "overbearing" and "neglectful" agents frequently treated "the emigrants with brutality." Such depictions raised questions about the Haitians' commitment to the emigration project. For Jones, and other disgruntled emigrants to Haiti, the problems caused by the Haitian agents merged with other difficulties. In criticizing the Haitian authorities' mishandling of the emigration movement, Jones referred to the corruption and despotism associated with Haiti's political culture and institutions. Besides claiming that the majority of Haitians were "opposed to immigration," he and other immigrants discovered that Haiti's much vaunted political and social freedoms were all too often illusory. It might have been the case, as one long-term resident in Haiti asserted, that "many influential men in the Republic of Hayti had this [emigration] thing really at heart." But for Jones, and other emigrants, the reality they encountered in Haiti was less than encouraging. As Jones noted, as well as neglecting the emigrants' needs, the Haitian government tolerated—indeed, was responsible for—the severe infringements on civil liberties that were commonplace in the island republic.

Arguing that emigrants were denied the right of association, Jones reported that emigrants had been told that "no assemblage of more than fifty persons would be allowed." Those who disregarded that warning, Jones declared, "were liable to imprisonment." Of equal concern was Jones' comment that "freedom of speech does not exist in Hayti." Holly, and other leaders of the movement had defended the Haitian government, and praised the island republic's political system. For some emigrants, however, the denial of the rights of free speech and association could be attributed to the form of Haiti's government. "The Haytian government is a military despotism in the strictest sense of the word," Jones asserted on his return from St. Mark.[18]

Reports of the emigrants' difficulties soon filtered back to the United States, compelling Redpath to take steps to minimize the potential damage to the movement. Accusing the Haitian officials at St. Mark of "indolence and procrastination," he charged that their inaction contributed to the unnecessary loss of life among the emigrants. Later, he claimed that the actions of one of the agents, Mr. Orwell, had cost the movement "hundreds of emigrants."[19] To alleviate these problems at St. Mark, Redpath suggested in late 1861 that new agents be appointed there. He also proposed that black American representatives be despatched to St. Mark, to liaise between emigrants and the Haitian agents. Specifically, he suggested that J. D. Harris, author of *A Summer on the Borders of the Caribbean Sea*, and an ex-employee of the Haitian Bureau in the United States, be appointed to such an intermediary position.[20]

The Haitians were slow to respond to Redpath's proposal. One reason for their tardiness might have been—as Redpath suggested to Auguste Élie in February 1862—a lack of awareness concerning the situation at St. Mark. For their part, the Haitians' task was complicated by a lack of information concerning the arrival of emigrants. They often had little idea about when, and in what numbers, emigrants would arrive. The departure of more than four hundred emigrants from the United States in October 1861, for example, took the Haitian authorities by surprise. Despite indications from Redpath that there would be at least five hundred emigrants in that period, the Haitians were ill-prepared to cope with such an influx.[21] But Haitian officials also held the emigrants at least partly responsible for their own situation. Charging that the emigrants were "unreasonable," and overly fussy about the land that was granted to them, the Haitians' ability to fulfill their promises was complicated because emigrants often changed their minds about exactly where they wanted to settle. The Haitian government encouraged some settlers to work on the private property of Haitian landowners, "according to the wages of the share system." Emigrants were reluctant to do so, partly because they had migrated on the understanding that they would be given their own lands, and partly because they were reluctant to break up their settlement groups. Understandably, they did not wish to be the only English-speaking, Protestant workers among a group of native Haitians—to whom they probably considered themselves superior in any case.[22]

Although Redpath and the Haitian officialdom quarreled over who was responsible for the problems facing the St. Mark emigrants, the disjunction between the settlers' expectations and experiences can be attributed to a number of factors. The agents of the Haitian Bureau in the United States and Canada bore part of the responsibility, for not accurately depicting the conditions in Haiti. Of course, a number of the bureau's employees had not been to the island republic, and were reliant on the information that Redpath provided. The Haitian agents at St. Mark caused problems, and the Haitian government was slow to implement improvements. Nonetheless, many of the difficulties faced by the Haitian scheme were a consequence of the emigrants' background and lack of preparation for life in Haiti. Advocates of the scheme encouraged people with agricultural experience to emigrate. Moreover, the Haitian government's offer of a free passage to the island was, theoretically, available only to farmers and agricultural laborers. As the editors of the *Pine and Palm* remarked in September 1861, "we wish it to be clearly understood that there is no manner of use in any class of persons excepting farmers and laborers emigrating to Haiti."[23] Yet many emigrants, particularly in the early stages of the movement, did not have an agricultural background. This pattern reflected the geographic distribution of African Americans in the northern states, where a majority of blacks lived in urban areas. While black leaders had long sought to convince the African American populace that they should move to the countryside, where they would be better able to achieve self-sufficiency, most blacks found better economic opportunities in the cities. In addition, the extreme social isolation that black Americans encountered in rural areas would have been a factor pushing them toward the "relative social normality" that was available in urban communities of free blacks.[24]

Redpath endeavored to spread the emigrationist message in rural areas. One of the bureau's agents, the Reverend Josiah B. Smith, referred in June 1861 to the lack of knowledge about Haitian emigrationism in rural districts. In particular, Smith remarked that his visit to Pennsylvania, "particularly the interior part of it, is very opportune, for, as no agent has gone beyond the city of Philadelphia, and as our paper had not reached these small towns, but very little, or nothing at all, was known of our movement, or of Hayti." However, it was not always easy to promote emigration in agricultural districts. Alluding to the difficulties involved in spreading the emigrationist gospel beyond the towns and cities, William J. Watkins noted that it was effective to virtually go "from house to house."[25] Because such a process was necessarily time-consuming, and expensive, much of the agitation in favor of the Haitian scheme took place in towns and cities. African Americans living in rural areas found it more difficult to attend the meetings where emigration to Haiti was discussed; moreover, if they owned, or were buying their own farm, they had less incentive to emigrate. Another factor militating against the migration of rural blacks was the fact that of the relatively few African Americans who owned farms, many lived in the western districts of the United States, or in

Canada, which meant they had a longer (and consequently more expensive) journey to the east coast ports from where vessels left for Haiti. Efforts were made to defray the transport costs from inland regions to the coast, and Redpath sought to despatch a vessel to Toronto to collect emigrants from Canada. But he was not authorized to pay transport costs for those blacks who lived west of Pittsburgh or Detroit, and plans for a ship to leave Toronto with emigrants were eventually abandoned. A final factor discouraging black farmers from leaving North America was the fact that even if they did decide to emigrate, it was not possible to do so until they had sold their farm, which often took considerable time. Redpath's agents sometimes claimed there would be a large migration from a particular region—when the farmers there had disposed of their property. But the anticipated exodus never eventuated.[26]

Problems also arose in enticing agricultural laborers to emigrate to Haiti. Although not tied so directly to the land as the smaller number of blacks who owned the land upon which they worked, agricultural laborers were generally less well off, and hence unable to afford to make their way to the east coast points of embarkation. When arrangements were put in place to transport these prospective emigrants to the coast, confusion remained.[27] Given all of these difficulties, it was not surprising that blacks with an agricultural background were less likely to emigrate than those who lived in towns or cities. A report written in 1861 by a Haitian official stated that the "greater part" of the emigrants from the United States and Canada were from the "artisan class."[28] Although it is not possible to accurately quantify how many emigrants were accustomed to making their living on the land, it is clear many African American settlers arrived in Haiti with no agricultural expertise whatsoever.[29] Inevitably, these people found conditions in the island republic difficult.

Much of the responsibility for the emigrants' disenchantment rests with Redpath, and other employees of the Haitian Bureau. Although Redpath claimed to be only advising blacks with an agricultural background to leave the United States, he must have realized that many emigrants knew little or nothing about life on the land. In part, this problem arose because of the pressure placed upon Redpath to launch the scheme successfully, and generate interest in the movement. He was at pains to demonstrate to the Haitian authorities that he was encouraging only suitable applicants to emigrate. In February 1861, Redpath declared he could have sent "several shiploads" of emigrants to Haiti, but that he was "anxious to send only those who would cultivate the land." Later that year he stated that in "order to plant the movement firmly on an agricultural basis, I have announced that none save farmers and laborers will be accepted." A more accurate appraisal of the emigrants' background came from Henry Melrose, another employee of the bureau. He noted in March 1862 that although the early emigrants were people of good character, they were mainly townspeople, unaccustomed to agricultural labors.[30] As Melrose's statement implied, the issue of the emigrants' agricultural expertise was addressed belatedly during 1861. The bureau eventually received authorization to assist emigrants to make their way to the coast, thereby rendering it easier for blacks from inland regions to emigrate. By that stage, however, considerable damage had been inflicted on the movement, particularly because word of the early emigrants' difficulties had reached the United States.[31] Although William Wells Brown, and other agents of the Bureau, emphasized they were only accepting emigrants who were of the right character, and suitably qualified to succeed in Haiti, Redpath held them accountable for sending inappropriate emigrants. In February 1862, the general agent announced that henceforth agents would be held "personally responsible" for the type of blacks who emigrated.[32]

The Haitian Bureau's woes were compounded by a shortage of funds. Although Redpath had received an appropriation of twenty thousand dollars from the Haitian government, he was soon complaining that he was running short of money. After optimistically forecasting in October 1861 that the number of emigrants he sent would be "limited only by the funds" at his disposal, Redpath repeatedly asserted that the Haitians were slow to forward the money he required.[33] This shortage of funds did inhibit the Haitian movement, particularly in terms of arranging the transportation of emigrants. Indeed, the question of transporting the emigrants proved to be one of the bureau's most intractable problems. The aforementioned uncertainties concerning how many emigrants would be sailing on a particular date, coupled with deeper fears whether they would actually fulfill their commitment to sail, complicated the task of organizing transportation. Chartering vessels was often difficult, but after the outbreak of the Civil War, when vessels flying the Union flag became liable to attack from privateers, it was necessary to use British ships.[34] Redpath raised this matter with the Haitians; by October 1861 he was asserting it was "absolutely essential" for the Haitian government to purchase two ships for the specific task of transporting emigrants. Again, however, the wheels turned slowly, and by the time a contract for a steamer to sail regularly from New York to Port-au-Prince was signed in March 1862, it was too late to be of any consequence.[35]

Underpinning these logistical difficulties, the Haitian movement confronted a fundamental contradiction that rested at the very center of the question of black nationalism. The Haitian Bureau's propaganda spoke of the emigrants as the founders of a new black nationality. However, instead of realistically preparing emigrants for the privation that such a movement entailed, it painted a rosy picture of Haiti as a land of rich agricultural opportunities, where, with a minimum of effort, African Americans could make a comfortable living for themselves. This inconsistency was connected to another, deeper contradiction between the aims of the proponents of emigration, and the expectations of those who actually emigrated. Holly, Redpath, and other champions of the Haitian scheme regarded the emigrants as the vanguard of a new black nationality, that would contribute to the emancipation of the slaves, and help lead to equality for black people everywhere. In some cases, as with the frontier of the American West, and as with earlier expressions of the black nationalist-emigrationist ideology, these aspirations were gendered in such a way to explicitly connect the question of nationality to the masculine ideal. Certain emigrants noted that when they reached Haiti they felt as if they were men—for the first time in their lives. George Lawrence, an editor of the *Pine and Palm*, phrased the emigrationists' vision of "upbuilding black nationalities" in explicitly masculine terms. Emphasizing the importance of blacks demonstrating a "thorough capacity independently to compete with other peoples and our absolute equality to them," he enjoined African Americans to "not shirk the question, but meet it manfully." William J. Watkins, too, referred to the issue of black nationality in masculinist terms. "As I walked the streets of the capital," he noted after his arrival in Haiti in mid-1862, "I felt as no colored man anywhere in the United States can feel. I beheld her senators and representatives, her judges and her generals, with respect and admiration." It was only to be expected that leaders of the movement such as Lawrence and Watkins would express such enthusiasm for Haiti, but there is evidence that some other emigrants shared these sentiments. One such emigrant, James Nevitt, noted in 1861, "I am a man in Hayti, I feel as I have never felt before; that I was entirely free."[36]

Yet, only a minority of emigrants perceived their role in such a grandiose fashion. Most who chose to emigrate did so to escape the oppression they were forced to endure in America. The emigrationist leadership emphasized the importance of land ownership for blacks, and for many African Americans the opportunity to become a landowner was a powerful incentive. For most blacks, however, emigration and the prospect of becoming an independent landowner were conceived in terms of an opportunity for individual self-elevation, rather than as a step toward the creation of a black nationality. This was evidenced by the enquiries directed toward the bureau from potential emigrants, most of which were concerned not with the matter of a black nationality, but with such practical questions as wage levels, the cost of living, and soil conditions in Haiti.[37] Again, there was a gap between the antebellum black leadership and the African American populace, which suggests that although black nationalism was a dominant aspect of the rhetoric of antebellum emigrationists, it was a concept of rather less consequence to most emigrants. In a society that emphasized the virtues of individualism, it was perhaps only predictable that African Americans would perceive emigrationism as an act of individual self-advancement.

One consequence of the divergence of aims was that many emigrants, less concerned with the establishment of an independent black nationality than they were with individual security and self-advancement, were reluctant to undergo the hardships that were involved in emigrating to Haiti. Bearing in mind that Haiti had been represented as a land of opportunity, the bureau's propaganda had contributed to a feeling on the part of some emigrants that their skills would be in such great demand in the black republic that the native population would be keen to learn from them. It was perhaps not surprising that many emigrants were dissatisfied with conditions in Haiti. Again, Redpath responded to this dissatisfaction by criticizing the emigrants—just as he had done when emigrants' reports of ill health and mortality had reached the United States. Although he claimed that "five" emigrants had "been rejected for every one that has been accepted," he attributed many of their problems to a lack of ambition and self-reliance on the part of the emigrants. "Many will go to Hayti," he warned Victorien Plésance in January 1861, "because they are poor and persecuted and are in want of bread here: but the men who will leave America because their heart is interested in the prosperity of their race and the cause of freedom will prove to you by far—infinitely—the most desirable accessions to your population." A year later, seeking to explain the movement's problems, Redpath told the Haitians that American blacks lacked self-reliance. Referring to the damage being inflicted on the movement by one aggrieved emigrant, the editors of the *Pine and Palm* were even more trenchant in their criticism: "like many of the returned emigrants from Hayti, [he] was a lazy, good-for-nothing fellow."[38] By early 1862, however, even such emphatic critiques of the emigrants' character failed to rejuvenate what was a waning movement.

It was symptomatic of the whole Haitian movement that the very same blacks whom Redpath accused of lacking initiative were also those he sent to the island republic, despite his assurances that only the very best sections of the African American population would be selected to settle in Haiti. This put the Haitian scheme in a position analogous to the ACS, whose detractors had long focused on white colonizationists' belief that the same degraded blacks who could never be assimilated into American society were the chosen ones to redeem and elevate Africa. With regard to the Haitian movement, Redpath was not the only critic of the emigrants. Other agents, as well as some of the emigrants, agreed that a large proportion of settlers did not do enough to help themselves—and each other. Too many emigrants, it was claimed, were willing to wait around for the Haitian government to do their work for them. On his arrival in Haiti in late 1861, Joseph Dennis Harris expressed surprise at the number of emigrants "who had been there for months, still receiving a weekly supplement from the government." In June 1862, after Henry Melrose visited Haiti, he attributed the success of Harris' colony to the fact that its leader had instilled the proper ethic into the group.[39]

Although the emigrants were held responsible for their lack of initiative, the movement's leaders acknowledged that the settlers' apathy was not wholly their own fault. Although it would have been plausible to attribute some of their apathy to the problems arising from their ill health and difficulties of acculturation, leading emigrationists referred to other, what might be labeled "political" issues. Indeed, in explaining the alleged apathy among the emigrants, proponents of Haitian emigrationism referred again to the tenuous relationship between race and nationality that underscored antebellum emigrationism. As the editors of the *Pine and Palm* pointed out, there was "one unhappy result of our oppression; it makes any race inert and destroys their enterprise"; it was symptomatic of this perception that they also implied it would be easier to colonize whites than it was to colonize blacks. Perhaps most succinctly, Joseph E. Williams, another of the Haitian Bureau's agents, explicitly referred in March 1862 to "the enterprise" which moved "the Yankee nation."[40] This spirit of enterprise was often associated with the individualism of nineteenth-century America; but the Haitian authorities were also concerned with the emigrants' initiative. Nevertheless, although they also held the emigrants responsible for many of the difficulties they confronted, Haitian observers depicted their criticism in terms that emphasized the lack of cooperative spirit among the emigrants. One Haitian report asserted: "Strangers to each other for the most part, the truth of the matter is, the immigrants assist each other but very little."[41] Besides highlighting the contradictions of nineteenth-century black nationalism, these various explanations for the problems confronting the emigrants pointed to the divergence between the rhetoric of emigrationist ideologies, and the conditions facing a majority of African Americans.

Nothing better demonstrates these difficulties and differences than the experiences of the colony of emigrants led by James Holly. One of the most persistent criticisms leveled against the Bureau by its opponents was that although advocates of emigration were prepared to counsel African Americans to emigrate, the leaders of the movement were themselves unwilling to leave the United States.[42] Holly's departure from the United States was a potential rebuttal to this criticism. In the end, however, the fate of his colony served only to strengthen the hand of the anti-emigrationists. From Holly's perspective, the fusion of Christian and black nationalist imperatives underpinning emigration were unchanged. In 1860, he reiterated that it was vitally important for black ministers to emigrate to Haiti, where there was "an ample field" for them to demonstrate their usefulness.[43] But Holly's public appeals for support for emigration to Haiti met with little success during 1860 and early 1861, and following the appointment of Redpath as general agent of the Haitian Bureau of Emigrationism, it was unclear who really deserved the title of "leader" of the movement. Nonetheless, Holly was sufficiently well known in New Haven to attract the interest of some of the town's black population; in late April 1861 a colony comprising a contingent of New Haven blacks, along with a number of blacks from Canada West, left for Haiti, under his leadership.[44] Although the exigencies of emigrationism had compelled Holly to accept some individuals who were clearly not from the best and the brightest of the African American community, the departure of the New Haven colony was the culmination of many years' hard labor. Holly was not about to let the moment pass unacknowledged: In calling on the residents of New Haven—themselves "Descendants of the Pilgrims"—to support "this Mayflower expedition," he returned to the same rhetorical device he had employed in his "Thoughts on Hayti." Like the early New Englanders, his colonists were "sable pioneers in the cause of civil and religious liberty." En route to the island republic, and pushing the Mayflower analogy further, Holly's settlers pledged a "Madeira Compact," by which they vowed to labor on behalf of "the Kingdom of God in Hayti."[45]

At first glance, Holly's group enjoyed several advantages over other colonies. When the New Haven colony arrived in Haiti, they settled on President Geffrard's private estate ("Drouillard"). Given such a base, it might have been expected they would be able to avoid many of the problems confronting other emigrants. But Holly's colony soon ran into difficulties. Notwithstanding his long interest in Haitian emigrationism, and despite the fact that he had been to Haiti, and should therefore have been cognizant of the necessary health precautions for recent arrivals from the United States, the mortality rate among Holly's New Haven colony was the highest of the whole emigration program. Here, it is perhaps significant to recall that when Holly had visited Haiti in 1855, he had spent most of his time in towns. With little firsthand experience of rural conditions in the black republic, Holly was ill equipped to deal with many of the difficulties that arose. In early August 1861, he admitted publicly that from a "temporal point of view," members of his colony had "been sufferers from the very day" of their departure from New Haven. Holly, moreover, paid a high personal price in emigrating: By early 1862 four members of his own family (his mother, wife, a daughter, and an infant son) had died in Haiti. Discussing his "sad bereavement," he emphasized "that disease was precipitated upon every one who has sickened and died, by their own impudent disregard" of the warnings regarding "the habits we should observe in our new homes." Despite the deaths at Drouillard, however, Holly found cause for optimism. Writing to the editors of the *Pine and Palm*, he insisted that a high mortality rate was to be expected in any migratory movement. If that was not enough to alarm prospective emigrants, Holly went further. Besides describing the "sickness and death in our midst" as "one of the permissive dispensations of Almighty God," he declared that the deaths at Drouillard were a "triumphant witness on behalf of the noble cause of Haytian emigration."[46]

Redpath and other proponents of the Haitian movement realized that few African Americans shared Holly's willingness to die on Haitian soil. On returning to the United States, one member of Holly's colony refuted claims that most of those who had died at Drouillard had ignored warnings about "venturing through the burning sun and eating fruit." Many more had died, it was claimed, "from want of proper nourishments, care and attention." Although he conceded that some emigrants' woes were due to "imprudence and exposure," he argued that most of the illness and death was directly attributable to conditions in Haiti. With "all due respect for my reverend leader," he concluded, "I do not agree with his doctrine that we should be willing to sacrifice 400 out of every 1200 persons going to Hayti; neither do I wish them to die there that the soil may be enriched for the growth of cotton."[47] Opponents of the Haitian scheme quickly seized upon Holly's ill-judged remarks. As one contributor to the *Weekly Anglo-African* remarked, while decomposition took place more quickly in Haiti than it did in New England, using the corpses of emigrants to enrich "a soil already the richest in the world" seemed to be a "queer way to build colored nationalities."[48]

Redpath used the columns of the *Pine and Palm* to publicly disavow Holly's views of his colony. Rather than an example of the sacrifice necessary to advance the cause of emigration, the editors of the *Pine and Palm* described the deaths at Drouillard as "sad evidence of the fatal folly of refusing to obey the rules of living which experience has laid down for the tropics." Holly had conceded that many of the health problems faced by members of his colony were due to their imprudence; Redpath was more unequivocal in his criticism of the emigrants. This "excellent colony seems," it was argued, "by their own confession to have neglected all the rules which experience lays down for health in Hayti."[49] Notwithstanding Redpath's emphatic rebuttal of Holly's judgment of the value of the sacrifices made by the members of the New Haven Colony, the damage was already done—no matter the depth of the racism they encountered in the United States, by late 1861 few African Americans were willing to die in Haiti for the advancement of Holly's Christian-emigrationist dream. Given that Holly had explained in 1850 that one reason he could not emigrate to Liberia was because of the dangers that such a movement would have posed to his health, his assertions concerning the need for sacrifice among emigrants suggested a shift in his views that would have done little to encourage support among the black populace. Certainly, opponents of Haitian emigrationism used the divergence of opinion between Holly and Redpath to denounce the whole movement.[50]

With the problems facing the emigrants at St. Mark and Drouillard receiving wide publicity in the United States and Canada, the bureau was, by late 1861, encouraging departing emigrants to choose alternative locations. Consequently, subsequent groups of emigrants settled in a number of different regions, including Gonaives, Cape Haytien, and Archaie.[51] Although these people did not encounter such severe difficulties as those confronting the St. Mark emigrants, it was too late to have a decisive, rejuvenating effect on what was by early 1862 a waning movement. By that time, the African American community, which had earlier expressed interest in, if not support for Haitian emigrationism, was well aware that those who had chosen to emigrate had encountered hardship and privation.

Inevitably, the problems confronting emigrants in Haiti raised questions about the role of the leader of the Haitian Bureau in the United States. Rejecting the Haitian scheme in a January 1861 letter to the *Weekly Anglo-African*, "A Colored Presbyterian Minister" was particularly critical of Redpath, whom he described as "a third rate white man."[52] This type of criticism was common among those who remained committed to the stay-and-fight doctrine; but even among those who favored emigration, there were critics of Redpath. Considerable doubts existed regarding the appointment of a white man to lead a movement devoted to the establishment of a black nationality. Martin Delany, perhaps piqued that he had not been asked to head the bureau, questioned why Redpath had been appointed general agent, when there were black people eminently qualified to fill the position. Neither Redpath, "nor any other white man," Delany claimed, was "competent to judge and decide upon the destiny of the colored race or the fitness of any place for the bettering of their condition." Stressing that it was vitally important to develop a spirit of "*self-reliance*, on the principles of Black Nationality," he objected to the way in which whites such as Redpath were "granted all the positions of *honor and emoluments*," whereas blacks received "only the *subordinate*, with little or no pay!" As Delany noted, by appointing Redpath, the Haitian government was "acknowledging Negro inferiority." Redpath answered these criticisms by pointing out that there was "nothing humiliating in a black statesman employing a white man to do his business—whether it be political, financial, or commercial."[53]

It was symptomatic of the contradictions of nineteenth-century black nationalism that Delany criticized the appointment of Redpath, because Delany had not only accepted aid from whites to further his own emigrationist plans, but had also reached an accord with the African Civilization Society, a group that attracted the support of a number of white colonizationists. While he argued that these compromises did not demean or compromise his black nationalist philosophy, Delany's earlier statements concerning the necessity of black people acting independently of whites is suggestive of the pragmatism inherent in his reformism. Delany's criticism of Redpath's appointment, moreover, was an implicit critique of the nature of the Haitian black nationality. By early 1862, although Delany continued to claim that "abstractly considered, I have no objection to Haytien Emigration," his judgment regarding the black republic became more overt. Objecting "to the fearful manner in which" African Americans were "being misled into the belief that Hayti presents the natural advantages and facilities for a great and powerful nation," he argued that Haiti could not become "one of the national powers of the earth." Whereas Redpath had suggested that Haiti could occupy a place in world affairs analogous to that of England, Delany warned the island was too small to be of any great consequence in world affairs. He pointed to recent events to substantiate his claim that Haiti was not truly independent: the Spanish seizure of the Dominican Republic, which was located on the same island as Haiti; and the signing of a Concordat between the Haitians and the Roman Catholic authorities in Rome.[54] These two events did considerable damage to the Haitian emigration movement.

On the eve of the American Civil War, Spain announced the annexation of the Dominican Republic. Although the president of the Dominican Republic had asked Spain to annex his country, Fabre Geffrard declared that Haiti would never recognize the annexation, and supported an anti-Spanish insurgency that broke out across the border. When the Spanish responded by demanding the Haitians terminate their support for the Dominican rebels—a demand that was backed, in a classic display of gunboat diplomacy, by the stationing of a Spanish fleet off Port-au-Prince—Geffrard was forced to an ignominious back-down.[55] This affair had serious repercussions for the Haitian movement. Delany, and other critics of the Haitian movement, argued that Spain's seizure of the Dominican Republic was "the first step towards a total reduction of that island . . . to a miserable political dependence." Despite Redpath's assurances that there was "no danger to Hayti from the recent movement of Spain," the threat of a war between Spain and Haiti was a powerful deterrent against emigration. A two-month suspension of emigration to the island republic, and Redpath's assertion that he would not permit anyone to emigrate unless they had the "fullest knowledge" of the situation between Spain and Haiti, did little to reassure African Americans contemplating emigration. In April 1861, Redpath told Victorien Plésance that Haiti's diplomatic crises had "given a very serious check" to the emigration movement. Seeking to allay potential emigrants' concerns, and striving to convince African Americans that he was dedicated to their cause, Redpath announced that if "Hayti declares war against Spain, I will go as a volunteer." Redpath's declaration of personal bravado, however, did not assuage fears regarding Spain's Caribbean intentions. Moreover, agents of the Haitian Bureau were forced to deny rumors that France was also intending to annex Haiti. Emigrationist leaders spoke in terms of an African American Manifest Destiny in the Caribbean, but for Haitians, and for potential emigrants, talk of Spanish and French intervention renewed long-standing fears that Europeans were intent on the destruction of the Haitian nationality.[56]

These concerns were exacerbated by the signing of a Concordat between the Haitians and the Vatican. On taking power, Geffrard had been compelled to deal with the question of restoring relations between the Catholic Church and the Haitian government. In March 1860, a Concordat was signed, amid considerable discord in Haiti. African Americans, revealing a deep concern regarding the separation of Church and State, and probably influenced by the wave of nativist anti-Catholic sentiment that had swept the United States during the 1850s, feared the implications of this agreement for Haiti's independence. Skeptical about the Haitians' promises to respect the emigrants' religious freedoms, opponents of emigrationism seized on the Concordat to criticize the movement. This issue of religious freedom was linked to the question of black independence—and, by extension, the notion of a black nationality. In an editorial entitled "Forlorn Hope for Hayti," the *Weekly Anglo-African* asserted that under the terms of the Concordat, Geffrard was really conceding that "the *controlling* religious *influence must be white*." The next step in that process, they argued, was to "make the entire political process also *white*." In rhetoric echoing the sentiments of the emigrationists, the editors of the *Weekly Anglo-African* asserted that "the security of a people's rights consist in their *controlling* their own *political destiny*." Haitian emigrationists responded by arguing that the Concordat was a "wise act of political statesmanship," but real fears persisted regarding the rights of emigrants in Haiti, and of the Haitians' ability to maintain their independence.[57]

The strength of these perceptions cast doubt in many minds regarding Redpath's integrity and character. Redpath's abolitionist credentials were solid, and his declarations of support for black nationalism apparently authentic. Nonetheless, even such a devout friend of black Americans occasionally betrayed dubious intentions. Accordingly, although black leaders were not privy to Redpath's correspondence with the Haitian authorities, their skepticism regarding his motives was not entirely misplaced. This was clearly the case in July 1861, when Redpath wrote to August Élie, detailing the efforts he was making to organize the emigration of some of the increasingly large numbers of ex-slaves who were seeking refuge behind Union lines. In this instance, rather than focusing on the grand objective of a black nationality, Redpath referred instead to the requirements of the landowning class in Haiti. Speculating that ten to twenty thousand ex-slaves might be despatched to the black republic, and suggesting that the United States government might pay for the costs of transportation, Redpath noted that the "liberated" slaves would "be admirable laborers for your landed proprietors."[58] A charitable explanation for Redpath's statement would be that he foresaw the immense difficulties that would confront ex-slaves in the postbellum South, or that he envisaged ex-slaves who agreed to work for Haitian planters would eventually secure their own land in the island republic. But if he was thinking along those lines, he left no evidence to that effect.

Redpath's personal skills were no less questionable. Although John McKivigan has described Redpath as "an energetic administrator and skillful propagandist for his Bureau," the failure of the Haitian Bureau was in part due to Redpath's personal shortcomings.[59] As demonstrated by the volume of his correspondence, Redpath labored assiduously for Haitian emigrationism. But his frequent defensive protestations to the Haitian authorities about his industry—and his claim that he was "not one of those who are offended by kindly criticism"—must be judged alongside his readiness to attribute failures to the shortcomings of others.[60] His pedantic and dictatorial nature could alienate even his friends and colleagues. Evidence of Redpath's character is provided by his relationships with two other employees of the Haitian Bureau. Friction developed with Richard J. Hinton, a British-born reformer whose career bore parallels to that of Redpath. From the mid-1850s both men were actively interested in the welfare of African Americans, and both had known John Brown. The two men had cooperated to write *A Hand-Book to Kansas Territory and the Rocky-Mountains Gold Region*, so it would have come as no surprise when Redpath employed Hinton to work for the Haitian Bureau. Relations between the two men remained satisfactory for some time, but Hinton eventually antagonized Redpath by suggesting ways by which the bureau's journal could be improved. This prompted an angry tirade from Redpath: "God knows Hinton, I am your friend. . . . But I do *not* feel your friendship to be *priceless*. . . . I am the leader of the Haytian movement, and the editor consequently of the organ of it." Redpath claimed that the success of the movement depended, at that time, "on one person only"—himself. Arguing that his responsibility to the movement was greater than his responsibility to his friends, he decided that his "intimate" friendship with Hinton had to be suspended.[61]

Not only did Redpath fall out with friends such as Hinton, but his relationships with others could be similarly problematic. In November 1860, Redpath asked the Haitian authorities whether an "educated Haytian gentleman" could be sent to the United States to "speak with intending emigrants." The Haitians despatched Alexander Tate to serve in that capacity, but Redpath was soon charging that Tate was not a gentleman, but a "self-elected spy," who coveted the position of general agent. Redpath claimed that Tate was misrepresenting him, and doing a great disservice to the bureau. Soon after, threatening to resign unless the Haitian Government forced Tate to cease his slanders, Redpath suggested that Tate return to Haiti.[62] Such petulance did little to encourage confidence in the bureau.

Redpath's attitude toward his employees was no more reassuring. Writing in February 1862, he claimed that he had only been able to secure the services of "second class" men as agents. Such behavior lends credence to historian Willis Boyd's assertions that Redpath "was not an easy man to get along with," and that he was "deeply suspicious of his co-workers." Yet it is impossible to fully agree with James Jackson's essentially racial explanation for the white leader's weaknesses. Contrasting Redpath's shortcomings with James Holly's uncompromising commitment to Haitian emigration, Jackson has argued that Redpath's administrative and ideological deficiencies "invited distrust and suspicion." Ruing that Holly was "outmaneuvered" by Redpath for "the directorship of the project," Jackson rightly accused the general agent of a number of "blunders." Charging that Redpath "assumed leadership of the movement without establishing a base in black communities," Jackson implied that if a black person had been appointed general agent, this matter of credibility in the African American community would have been less problematic, and the movement more successful. But although Redpath was a "comparative stranger" to the black community, and although it is possible that an African American would have enjoyed wider support among black people, it is most doubtful if the appointment of a black person as general agent could have made a telling, decisive difference to the movement.[63] Such were the divisions within the black community, and so contentious was the question of emigrationism, that there was no single African American activist—not even Frederick Douglass—who was well known enough to command the unwavering respect and attention of the entire black populace. Indeed, the appointment of a black person as general agent would undoubtedly have inspired the same kind of jealousies and rivalries that had long been evident within the African American leadership.

Nonetheless, Redpath's behavior sometimes seemed to be at odds with the best interests of emigrationism. This was certainly the case in December 1861, when he announced a change in his reformist philosophy. Declaring that "many of the political doctrines" that he had previously advocated were "dangerous and abhorrent to the higher insight," Redpath stated that he intended to "retire from any political management" of the *Pine and Palm*, until such time as he had "attained a clearer and more human and Christian view of the duties of the freemen to the enslaved." No longer, for example, would he incite the slaves to rebel. This "change in political policy," he noted, was the result of a "change of heart—from an acceptance, full and unreserved, of the doctrines and plan of salvation of our Lord and Savior, Jesus Christ." Most curiously, at the same time as many blacks hoped the Civil War would lead to emancipation, he repudiated "war as an agency of freeing the oppressed."[64] This shift in Redpath's thinking—amounting to a return to the moral suasionist principles that had long dominated Garrisonian abolitionism—came at an inopportune moment in terms of his credibility within the African American community. In an article entitled "Redpath Repudiates Reason," one correspondent to the *Weekly Anglo-African* criticized the general agent's new philosophy, equating it with the views expressed by slaveholders who denied the slaves' right to resist. As the editors of the *Weekly Anglo-African* commented sardonically, "We felt sorry for friend 'Jeems' when he ran away from his fighting principles, although we knew he did not have to run far."[65]

These responses to Redpath's philosophical shifts were linked to the hopes and frustrations associated with the Civil War. The war tangibly affected the Haitian Bureau's ability to operate. Even before the outbreak of hostilities between the North and South, the impending conflict compelled Redpath to close the bureau's agency that had been established in New Orleans. It will be recalled that during 1859 and 1860 several hundred blacks had sailed from New Orleans for Haiti, and it was hoped that others could be convinced of the merits of emigrationism. To facilitate such a movement, Redpath had appointed an agent in New Orleans in November 1860. But in March 1861, as tensions between the North and South reached breaking point, Redpath was forced to close the New Orleans agency, thereby losing a potentially large number of emigrants.[66]

As the bureau lost New Orleans, there was a chance it might gain California. Just as white Americans flocked to California following the discovery of gold, blacks had also moved west; by 1860 California was home to more than four thousand African Americans.[67] During 1861, the Haitian Bureau received a number of enquiries from blacks in California. In October, Redpath told Victorien Plésance there were sixty or seventy African American families planning to leave California to settle in Haiti. To facilitate the movement of these people, Redpath advised the Haitian government to despatch James Holly to California. In promoting a movement of African Americans from California to Haiti, Redpath again touched on the question of blacks' nature—and their suitability as emigrants. Redpath argued that blacks from California would be successful emigrants, because "having once emigrated, they have none of the puerile prejudices and fears which chain down so many in the northern states to a menial position." Their spirit of self-reliance, he argued, as well as their previous experience with the pioneer life, would equip them well for life in Haiti.[68] But Holly never made it to California, and the bureau was unable to take advantage of the emigrationist sentiment that existed there among African Americans. Although more than 240 Californian blacks signed a petition in 1862 asking Congress to assist their plans for emigration, blacks in the West, like those in the North and the South, increasingly pinned their hopes on a Union victory in the Civil War.[69]

The Civil War affected Haitian emigrationism in other ways, too. Although proponents of the Haitian scheme pointed out that even if the "war should result in the abolition of slavery . . . it will not ameliorate the condition of the free black man, one iota," the conflict quickly robbed the Haitian Bureau of one very valuable potential ally. Having already postponed his planned trip to Haiti, Frederick Douglass began lobbying the U.S. government for the emancipation of the slaves. The "simple way," he declared in May 1861, to end the "savage and desolating war" being waged by the slaveholders was to "strike down slavery itself, the primal cause of the war."[70] By July, Douglass was expressing grave doubts about the Haitian Bureau. The Haitian movement, he wrote, had "become ethnological, philosophical, political and commercial." He contended that the Haitian movement was presenting itself as a "national" one, that was attempting to portray itself as the representative of a "national creed"—just as the detested ACS had done. Besides objecting to the refusal of the editors of the *Pine and Palm* to publish anti-emigrationist points of view, Douglass condemned the manner in which the leaders of the Haitian movement spread propaganda that appeared to subscribe to the theory that racial prejudice was inevitable. The Haitian Bureau, he alleged, had "propagated the favorite doctrine of all those who despise and hate the colored man, that the prejudice of the whites is invincible, and that the cause of human freedom and equality is hopeless for the black man in this country."[71] Redpath rejected Douglass' claim, but Douglass was a formidable adversary, whose influence and ability to thwart emigrationism were perhaps best measured by Redpath's earlier endeavors to recruit him to the Haitian cause.

Douglass was not the only prominent black opponent of Haitian emigrationism. From the time of his appointment, Redpath was compelled to devote considerable energy to defending the Haitian scheme against charges leveled by its black critics. Opponents of emigrationism undermined the movement in the press and at public assemblies. In the same way as the bureau's agents held meetings, opponents would speak at gatherings, denouncing the movement, and advising African Americans to remain in the United States. Venting his spleen against a "New York clique" that he blamed for many of the bureau's woes, Redpath sought to gain the upper hand in the propaganda battle over emigration. The main organ of the New York clique was the *Weekly Anglo-African*. According to Redpath, that newspaper—which initially had given the emigration issue a better hearing than the rest of the abolitionist press—

threatened the success of the scheme. During early 1861 Redpath began making arrangements to buy the *Weekly Anglo-African*. The purchase was completed in March 1861; in May the title of the paper was changed to the *Pine and Palm*. Redpath's actions, however, did not end the matter, for later in 1861 the anti-emigrationists began publishing a new *Weekly Anglo-African*, which regularly denounced the Haitian movement.[72]

Black leaders who opposed the Haitian scheme did not hesitate to use the emigrants' difficulties to dissuade other African Americans from setting off to the island republic. To that end, the revived *Weekly Anglo-African* published letters from dissatisfied emigrants. Along with their concerns regarding material and spiritual conditions in Haiti, returned emigrants broached the issue of Haiti's moral condition, a question of considerable significance for those who were representing the black republic as an exemplar of a civilized black nationality. One such correspondent was a former member of James Holly's ill-fated colony. Referring to the mortality rate among the members of Holly's colony, and suggesting that men "who have passed the age of 36 or 38 years" should not venture to Haiti, he also commented on conditions for women in the island republic. "I would not have women go there at all," he remarked in the euphemistic language typical of the period, "for reasons which I would prefer not giving in this communication." During a period in which the treatment of women was widely regarded as a measure of the state of "civilization," these were potentially serious allegations. Isaiah Jones, another emigrant to Haiti, also alluded to this issue. Although Jones and other disaffected emigrants focused on the day-to-day difficulties they encountered in Haiti, they also referred to the question of "civilization." Coupled with his aforementioned concerns regarding Haiti's political culture, Jones described the deep cultural and social divisions between Haitians and African American immigrants. As well as being perturbed by the various punishments inflicted by Haitian parents on their children, he noted that the "natives, male and female, generally go half clad, bordering on nudity." In so doing, he drew an implicit contrast between the civilized condition of African Americans, at least those in the North, and what was widely regarded as the primitive barbarism of the Haitians. Even Jones' use of the word "native" is significant, connoting as it did that Haitians had advanced little beyond the conditions in which blacks in Africa lived. Rather than becoming citizens in a black nationality that would challenge American slavery and racism, potential emigrants were being cautioned they would be reverting to a system of social and civic organization that verged on the "primitive." African Americans were denied many of the benefits of citizenship in the American republic, but they understood the values that were considered central to civilized societies. For black Americans such as Jones, the Haitians' way of life was at odds with the moral and spiritual values that the black leadership had long sought to instill in the African American populace.[73]

Compounding Jones' concerns was his judgment that a majority of Haitians were "opposed" to the immigration of African Americans.[74] Indeed, if the native Haitians were not actively opposed to the immigration of black Americans, there is evidence that some at least did not go out of their way to make the new arrivals welcome. Theft, for example, proved to be a problem, with several reports of immigrants' personal belongings being stolen by Haitians. Even Redpath was forced to concede the veracity of some of these reports.[75] All of this suggested that rather than contemplating emigration to the island republic, African Americans should follow the advice offered earlier by black abolitionist John Rock, and concern themselves with "civilizing the whites" within the United States.[76]

In responding to African American leaders who condemned emigration, Redpath again raised issues of race and nationality. Referring to the black community in the North, he expressed his dislike for the "petty cliques and hostile factions," who hated each other more than they detested "their common oppressors." Redpath also betrayed his perception of racial differences among the African American community. Claiming that much of the resistance to the movement was based not on a bona fide disapproval of the bureau's ends and means, but rather on factional allegiances, he argued that the "secret of the opposition" to the scheme was that the "*colored* cliques" of New York were opposed to the idea of a "*Black* Nationality." There were personal differences within the black leadership, but Redpath's claim that these divisions were based, at least in part, on differences of complexion, demands scrutiny. Although it is difficult to ascertain the extent of the division between African Americans of varying degrees of "blackness" during the antebellum period, there can be no doubt that such differences did exist. Redpath—perhaps transposing the very real differences that existed in Haiti between blacks and mulattoes—aimed to bridge the gap he perceived between the two groups within the United States. One way to do so was by employing both blacks and mulattoes as agents. Insisting that he "would not budge an inch" in favor of "either faction," he claimed that he took "good care to employ both equally." Redpath, who had noted after his travels though the South during the 1850s that "the mulattoes are invariably the most discontented of the colored population," explained that he had employed blacks such as Henry Highland Garnet and James Holly, and "colored" men such as H. Ford Douglass and Joseph Dennis Harris. Redpath's assertion that opposition to the Haitian scheme in the United States was based on caste differences is questionable, but opponents of the movement did not hesitate to exploit what the editors of the *Weekly Anglo-African* described as the "caste hatred" that existed in Haiti between blacks and mulattoes.[77]

Indeed, even before Redpath's appointment, Frederick Douglass had raised concerns about caste differences in Haiti. In mid-1859, Douglass, a mulatto, worried that Fabre Geffrard's rise to power in Haiti would lead to persecution of the island's mulatto population, who had long dominated the government. It "would be a sad thing to some of us, who have been hated and persecuted," Douglass noted, "for being too black, to go there and be hated and persecuted for being *too white.*" Redpath sought unsuccessfully to play down such fears, claiming that the "best feelings" existed between blacks and mulattoes in Haiti.[78] Rumors of conspiracy in the island republic, however, continued to be attributed to caste differences. In an August 1861 report to the Haitian authorities, Redpath referred to an article in the *Boston Traveller,* the headline of which spoke of a "Conspiracy to Overthrow the Government."[79]

Redpath's failure to convince the African American leadership that relations between blacks and mulattoes in Haiti were harmonious contributed to the continuing opposition to Haitian emigrationism, and to the general agent in particular, from several prominent African Americans. James McCune Smith, a well-regarded black resident of New York City who had studied medicine in Scotland after being denied admission to schools in the United States, was a devout critic of the Haitian scheme.[80] Smith assailed the movement from its inception, but he was no blind critic of all things Haitian. Nearly three decades earlier, in discussing the Haitian Revolution, he had lauded Toussaint L'Ouverture as an "extraordinary man," whose "vast and versatile genius" had played a telling part in establishing Haiti as an independent black republic.[81] Smith's youthful enthusiasm for Toussaint's heroism, however, did not translate into support for Haitian emigrationism during the 1860s. In an open letter to Henry Highland Garnet, Smith articulated his objections to Haitian emigrationism. Accusing Garnet of reneging on his earlier commitment to devote himself to the emancipation and elevation of African Americans, he urged him to "Shake yourself free from these migrating phantasms."[82] Because of Smith's high standing among the black population in New York City, Redpath was compelled to devote time to counteracting the influence of an individual whom he described as "an able" but "unprincipled" man.[83] Redpath was unable to silence Smith effectively; nor was he able to refute the claims of the other critics of the bureau, including George T. Downing (who had strenuously opposed the African Civilization Society), George W. Goines, and A. P. Smith.[84] Redpath attributed much of the opposition to the Haitian Bureau to the activities of black preachers. William J. Watkins, too, raised this issue. Arguing that "a bevy of selfish and ignorant preachers" were urging African Americans not to emigrate, he echoed Redpath's claim that black ministers were worried about losing their congregations.[85]

Characteristically, some of the most vociferous criticism of the Haitian scheme came from other emigrationists. Martin Delany's objections to the Haitian scheme have been mentioned, but other emigrationists also denounced the movement. From her base in Canada West, Mary Ann Shadd Cary was a vocal and persistent opponent of Redpath. Comparing the Haitian program to the ACS, she sought to convince blacks in Canada that they should not try their luck in the island republic. At one meeting where Watkins spoke on behalf of Haiti, she noted that although there were less than one hundred blacks in attendance, more than two hundred whites were present. As Shadd Cary presented it, because the Haitian scheme was being sponsored by whites, blacks should regard it with suspicion. She also criticized Redpath, questioning whether he was qualified to help blacks, and demeaning his contribution to the abolitionist cause. "Who," asked Shadd Cary, "is this James Redpath, in the hollow of whose hand lies trembling the destiny of our people?" Not content to censure the black employees of the bureau, she accused Redpath of "moral jugglery." A "few agents," she noted, "using the name [William Wells] Brown, and talking Redpath," were attempting to mislead blacks in Canada.[86] Claiming that the "thinking portion" of the black population was "not led astray" by the "new fangled movement of Mr. Redpath and his coadjutors," Shadd Cary declared after the departure of one group of emigrants that the "scene was in every sense humiliating." In a hierarchical tone, she thus suggested that only the lowly elements of the black population were departing for Haiti. As she had on earlier occasions, Shadd Cary counseled African Americans to settle permanently in Canada, where conditions were superior to those in the island republic.[87]

During late 1861, Redpath took steps to nullify Shadd Cary's influence.[88] But realizing perhaps that an African American would be more persuasive among the black community, the general agent left it to Watkins to counter Shadd Cary's criticisms. In a letter to the Toronto *Globe*, Watkins reassured potential emigrants that the Haitian government could fulfill its promises, and advised people not to be deceived by those who circulated stories about conditions in Haiti. Later, in a more direct attack on Shadd Cary, and urging opponents of the movement to be more consistent in their criticisms, Watkins pointed to the hypocrisy of those who opposed Haitian emigration at the same time as they advocated emigration to Canada.[89] Arguments between the two factions persisted, with Shadd Cary claiming in February 1862 that Redpath was seeking to "injure" her, and the school she ran. In April of the same year she renewed her attack on the Haitian Bureau, and reaffirmed that her school would survive.[90] It is difficult to measure the effect of Shadd Cary's criticisms of the Haitian movement, but the fact that Redpath and Watkins felt compelled to answer her charges demonstrates that they took her seriously.

Another emigrationist opposed to the Haitian movement was William P. Newman, who had initially endorsed the concept of emigration to the island republic. By mid-1861, asserting that the Haitians were "not capable of self-government," he argued that as well as "destroying themselves," they would "destroy everybody they govern." But the fact that the rulers of the island republic were despots was not the only problem. Referring to the example of widespread polygamy, Newman echoed other opponents of emigration in condemning the moral condition of the Haitian population. To further discourage emigration, he pointed to reports of cannibalism, and claimed that African Americans who had gone to Haiti were being forced to join the army—a claim that was particularly damaging when Redpath was busily denying reports that Haiti was on the verge of a war with Spain.[91]

There are a number of possible explanations for Newman's shifting views on Haitian emigrationism. Although one appraisal is that he was "undoubtedly" a "complainer," there are other explanations for his vehement denunciation of the Haitian Bureau.[92] Newman himself pointed to an incident that occurred when he was in Haiti, that led to him being temporarily gaoled there. This incident involved Newman's hat being knocked off by a Haitian policeman, for allegedly not tipping it in honor of a passing gentleman. Blaming Haitian officials for the affair, Newman noted that bizarre customs were the norm on the island. Redpath strenuously rejected those charges, insisting instead that Newman was responsible for the episode.[93] Besides Newman's anger over that incident, it is also possible that his animosity toward Haitian emigration stemmed from the fact that Redpath, not he, was offered the job of general agent of the bureau. For several months in mid-1861, rumors were circulating that various people had been offered positions with the Haitian Bureau; there must have been some conjecture that Newman had been offered a senior post with the bureau, because Redpath went to the trouble of explaining that Newman had not been offered the job of general agent.[94] As with the case of Shadd Cary, Newman's opposition to the Haitian scheme might also have stemmed from his advocacy of emigration to an alternative location, in his case Jamaica. During 1861 and 1862, he advised African Americans who felt they must emigrate to make their homes in Jamaica, where, he claimed, there was a great deal of interest in attracting blacks from North America.[95] Newman worked mainly among blacks in Canada, but one supporter of the Haitian scheme asserted that Newman's opposition would not jeopardize the success of the movement in the British Provinces, because his character was "too well known there." Redpath, however, took Newman seriously enough to plan a trip to Canada to expose him and "destroy his influence.[96]

It is evident, then, that the criticism from within the black leadership—from emigrationists and anti-emigrationists alike—played a telling part in undermining the Haitian movement. There is no reason to expect unanimity among African Americans on issues such as emigrationism. However, the tone of much of the debate over the Haitian scheme suggested again that as well as issues of substance, questions of personality also played a part in the debate. Although Redpath was prone to blame others for the bureau's failings, in denouncing the "petty intrigue" among the African American leadership, he did identify a real difficulty within the black community. Jane H. Pease and William H. Pease have described a pattern of "competition, rivalry, dispute, and distrust" among black leaders. These sentiments shaped arguments over the Haitian Bureau, as shown by an exchange, published in the *Weekly Anglo-African*, between Henry Highland Garnet and James McCune Smith. Highlighting what he regarded as Garnet's inconsistencies in his approaches to the difficulties confronting African Americans, Smith argued that Garnet was motivated less by a concern for the well-being of his race than he was by self-interest. "The sudden agility with which you wheeled about from African civilization to Haytien emigration," he asserted, "was not at all surprising to those familiar with your antecedents . . . [and] with such salary as in your judgment constituted 'a call.' "[97]

Nor was Garnet above personal criticism of his opponents. In a bitterly personal attack he accused the "warlike Doctor" Smith of doing nothing to help the "young people of New York," or, indeed, "those of the whole country." He argued that Smith was no better than his white brethren, who were not only prejudiced against blacks, but who also refused to employ them. Garnet's most bitter criticism of Smith came in late January 1861. To "my great astonishment," Garnet said, "you will persist in saying that this scheme, with all its extraordinary advantages, will certainly fail. Tell me, Doctor, what difference is there between your opinion of your own race and those of slaveholders and their apologists?" Garnet's appraisal of Smith was clear:

Both you and they [slaveholders and their apologists] deny the abilities of the black man. They say we cannot take care of ourselves: that we cannot thrive unless we are in a state of slavery or in the immediate presence of it; that we cannot live by our self-reliance; that we must have white masters; and that we are not capable of self-government.

In Garnet's view, Smith's arguments placed him "on the enemy's side. In the name of my race, whom you indirectly slander, I pronounce your charge as false as the Koran." Finally, Garnet depicted Smith's opposition in terms of individual freedom of choice. "I and thousands of others," Garnet told his adversary, "will think, speak, and act, just as we please." Implying that Smith was seeking to stifle free speech and debate, Garnet asserted that he would "exercise" his "freedom of opinion as far as" he could.[98]

Although African American leaders bickered over these issues, the black masses sensed that white America was belatedly—and reluctantly—beginning to understand what they had known all along: The Civil War was a struggle over the future of slavery. Although the war would not have occurred without slavery, few northerners initially viewed the struggle as a war against slavery. At the outbreak of hostilities, blacks had rushed to enlist in the Union armies, only to encounter the racism that had long plagued northern society. But as the war progressed, and as the casualty lists lengthened, the Union was ineluctably drawn toward acknowledging African Americans' aspirations. Abraham Lincoln, ever conscious of the constraints of the Constitution, and no less conscious of the racism among white Americans, did take tangible steps against slavery. In August 1861, he signed a bill sanctioning the seizure of all property, including slaves, that was being used to militarily aid the rebellion. That first Confiscation Act was followed by a more far-reaching bill in July 1862; two months later he issued the Preliminary Emancipation Proclamation.[99]

These steps—albeit frustratingly slow and ambivalent—were nonetheless significant, both in terms of James Redpath's ideological shift, and in terms of the fortunes of all emigrationist schemes. Redpath's shift away from direct action against slavery was out of step with developments in the Civil War. More broadly, although Lincoln was hardly a radical on the question of slavery, and was imbued with many of the racialist tenets that were evident in nineteenth-century America—including, for example, his advocacy of black colonization—the growing sentiment in favor of emancipation was a body blow for African American emigrationism. As the conflict progressed, there was renewed hope that white America would finally grant the freedoms that were so celebrated in its rhetoric. Consequently, with the Civil War lasting longer than anyone had anticipated, talk of emigrationism became more muted. Typically, however, even as black Americans saw their opportunities for advancement in the United States improve, they understood they would have to fight for their rights, and that white America would have to be compelled to accord better treatment to African Americans. Not surprisingly, the example of Haiti continued to loom large in the collective racial consciousness of black Americans. In the wake of the Emancipation Proclamation, as the black Reverend Jonathan C. Gibbs celebrated "freedom's joyful day," he referred specifically to the example of Haiti. As white Americans wondered whether blacks would have the courage to take the opportunity to participate in the Civil War, Gibbs not only recalled the contributions made by blacks in America's earlier wars, but also asked "what has made the name of Haiti a terror to tyrants and slaveholders throughout the world?" For Gibbs, the events in Haiti testified to the courage of black men, and served as a warning to southern slaveholders. As he asserted, "the terrible fourteen years' fight of black men against some of the best troops of Napoleon," that led to the French emperor's troops being "wiped out," had given the world unarguable evidence of the fighting spirit of black men. "There are some fights that the world will never forget," he noted, "and amongst them is the fight of black men for liberty on the Island of Haiti."[100]

The declining interest in emigration among the majority of black Americans must also be seen in the context of the reinvigoration of white-sponsored schemes to expatriate African Americans. Ultimately, these white schemes for black colonization proved spectacularly unsuccessful. But blacks continued to worry that support for emigration would be tantamount to an acceptance of white colonizationists' argument that blacks and whites could never co-exist as equals. This fear was compounded by the knowledge that white proponents of black colonization continued to espouse views that unashamedly reflected the assumption that racial difference precluded black advancement in the United States. James Mitchell, a white advocate of colonization, told Abraham Lincoln in 1862 that "our danger in the future arises from the fact that we have 4,500,000 persons, who, while among us, cannot be of us." For Mitchell, "persons of a different race" unavoidably formed "a distinct interest." Accordingly, although he argued he was making a "plea for the nationality of the negro," Mitchell's belief that Christian principles in the United States were damaged by the presence of blacks, and his assumptions regarding the immutability of racial difference, made his support for colonization reprehensible even to those blacks contemplating emigrationism.[101]

Black Americans' skepticism concerning the motives of white colonizationists was revealed in August 1862, when a delegation of African Americans met with Lincoln, who hoped to persuade them of the merits of emigrationism and colonization. Reiterating the well-worn argument that the underlying differences between the white and black races precluded African American advancement in the United States, and accepting apparently the immutability of white racism, the president asserted it would be "better for us both" if the races were "separated."[102] To encourage black colonization, Lincoln promised federal government support for the idea. But the response to Lincoln's proposals from the black leadership, and from the black community, suggested the depth of underlying antipathy to any scheme for colonization that appeared to rest on white attempts to expatriate African Americans, and deny their opportunities for advancement within the United States. As one black Philadelphian stated in May 1862:

To be asked, after so many years of oppression and wrong have been inflicted in a land and by a people who have been so largely enriched by the black man's toil, to pull up stakes in a civilized and Christian nation and to go to an uncivilized and barbarous nation, simply to gratify an unnatural wicked prejudice emanating from slavery, is unreasonable and anti-Christian in the extreme.[103]

African Americans' ongoing concerns regarding white attempts to promote black colonization were exacerbated when the United States Congress addressed the issue.[104] Redpath, not averse to seeking funds from sources other than the financially strapped Haitian government, knew that many in Washington favored black colonization. Consequently, in mid-1861 he sought unsuccessfully to utilize some of the one hundred thousand dollars allocated by Congress for black colonization under the provisions of the bill ending slavery in the District of Columbia.[105] For many black Americans, the notion of a white-sponsored scheme for black colonization was alarmingly reminiscent of the Colonization Society. Accordingly, African Americans' growing reticence to support Haitian emigration was one aspect of a deeper determination not to endorse any scheme that seemed to imply there was no future for blacks in the United States.

The Haitian movement ended not with a bang, but with a whimper. Although the bureau continued to advertise that emigrant vessels would leave monthly, and despite continued optimism in the bureau's public pronouncements, departures became increasingly irregular. The number of African Americans who emigrated declined sharply during 1862. Opponents succeeded in breaking up a number of emigrant groups, one such case being the colony that William J. Watkins labored long and hard to organize. With Redpath's encouragement, Watkins traveled to Haiti in June 1862, but stayed only until August. The demise of the Haitian Bureau, however, did not signify the end of Watkins' interest in emigration to the island republic. Here the black interest in Haitian emigrationism meshed, albeit temporarily, with Abraham Lincoln's support for colonization. One of Lincoln's favored schemes, that saw the emigration of several hundred African Americans to the Ile A'Vache—an island off the Haitian coast—was a dismal failure.[106] During 1863, Watkins worked on behalf of that scheme, helping to recruit blacks willing to be colonized on the Ile A'Vache. When that group sailed in April 1863, Watkins went with them. But the presence of Watkins—who soon returned to the United States, becoming by the end of the Civil War one of the earliest African American lawyers—was not enough to guarantee success for the Ile A'Vache venture.[107]

The Ile A'Vache project attracted considerable attention, but a combination of managerial ineptitude, dubious motives, and fraudulent dealings on the part of Bernard Kock, the American entrepreneur who had done much to persuade Lincoln of the merits of the scheme, as well as opportunism on the part of several of the Haitians involved in the project, doomed the scheme to failure. When 453 African Americans (a majority of them ex-slaves from Virginia) landed at the Ile A'Vache in June 1863, it soon became clear that matters were badly awry on the tiny island. Kock had been careful to emphasize the benefits that African Americans would derive from the project, and had agreed to help emigrants establish themselves on the island. His primary motive, however, was to secure a supply of laborers to exploit the island's timber resources. As the official lessee of the island, he stood to gain considerable financial benefit from the project. But Kock's corrupt record soon caught up with him, and with the emigrants expressing great discontent with conditions on the island, the Ile A'Vache project ground to an early halt. Following reports from James De Long, the American consul at Aux Cayes, and from Benjamin Whidden, the newly appointed senior U.S. representative in Haiti, Secretary of the Interior John P. Usher despatched D. C. Donohue to the Ile A'Vache to make a firsthand assessment of the situation on the island. Although conditions did improve somewhat during the two months during which Donohue was effectively in charge at the Ile A'Vache, it was too late to salvage the project. Lincoln sent a vessel to retrieve those African Americans who had survived their time on the island.[108]

Long before the demise of the Ile A'Vache scheme, the agents of the Haitian Emigration Bureau had turned their attentions in alternate directions. For some time, Henry Highland Garnet walked a fine line between support for Haitian and African emigrationism. As early as March 1861, however, he offered his resignation from the bureau. Redpath, initially reluctant to lose the services of such a well-known African American, eventually accepted the black preacher's resignation. Garnet's plans to visit Africa presented particular difficulties for the general agent. Differentiating between the black leadership and populace, Redpath declared "while Educated men see clearly enough that there is no possible inconsistency in advising masses to move in one direction while himself going in another, the great mass do *not* see it."[109] Besides betraying a hierarchical view of the black community, Redpath's comments revealed the underlying ambiguity over the question of select versus en-masse emigration that plagued the movement. By April 1862, Garnet was asserting that it was "the most ridiculous idea of the time to suppose that men who had watered their native soil with the sweat of their unpaid labor should not cling to its beauties and taste its benefits when freedom came." To aid in that process, Garnet—like a number of prominent African Americans—devoted himself to recruiting black soldiers for the Union Army.[110]

H. Ford Douglass also recanted on his emigrationist philosophy. After enlisting in the Union Army in 1862, he wrote in February 1863 that "national duties and responsibilities are not to be colonized, they must be heroically met and religiously performed."[111] William Wells Brown, demonstrating the same pragmatism that had characterized his earlier shifts on the emigration issue, also returned to the stay-and-fight camp. In May 1862, after severing his ties with the Haitian Bureau, he was reported as having supported anti-colonization resolutions at a Boston meeting of African Americans.[112] Another agent of the Haitian Bureau, Joseph E. Williams also repudiated emigrationism. After traveling to the island republic, Williams returned to the United States disenchanted with conditions in Haiti. In early 1862, to the delight of opponents of "the notorious Jim Redpath," Williams began lecturing "against the mischievous enterprise."[113]

In September 1862, Redpath's "official connection" with the Haitian Bureau ceased, and publication of the *Pine and Palm* was suspended. Accounting for the failure of the movement, Redpath absolved himself of responsibility. Typically, he insisted that he had been motivated by the highest principles, and rather than "mismanagement," the movement's failure was due to "misunderstandings" caused by differences of "language, prejudice, and characteristics." These were significant factors, but his argument that blacks in the United States—slave and free alike—were not self-reliant was rather more contentious, and self-serving.[114] Like a number of his former employees, Redpath was increasingly drawn toward an involvement in the Civil War. After leaving the Haitian Bureau, he put his journalistic talents to work as a correspondent for the Union Army. Presumably, involvement of that type did not compromise the philosophical position he had articulated several months earlier. Redpath's continuing interest in the black race was also expressed by his support for the candidacy of Salmon P. Chase for the presidency in 1864. When Chase's campaign ended in failure, Redpath directed his support to John C. Fremont, who was also highly regarded by abolitionist groups.[115] But Redpath remained interested in Haiti. After the demise of the Haitian Emigration Bureau, he turned his hand to publishing; one of the books he published in 1863 was a reprint edition of the Reverend John Beard's *The Life of Toussaint L'Ouverture*, that had been first published in 1853. Characteristically, in his

"Introduction" to Beard's work, Redpath took the opportunity to remark on the significance of "an independent negro nationality."[116]

There were enormous obstacles standing in the way of James Holly fulfilling the emigrationist aspect of his black nationalist philosophy. Nonetheless, he remained an optimist, ever ready to regard his personal efforts as a necessary sacrifice on behalf of a broader political–religious mission. In 1864, Holly explained his position: Declaring that he was "now a Haitian citizen, entitled to all the rights and immunities guaranteed to the same by the Constitution and laws of my adopted country," he anticipated that he would "live and die" in Haiti. Holly's family had paid a high price for his emigrationist vision, but he found strength from the fact that "the heritage" he expected "to leave" his "children" was "bound up with this first independent nation" of his "race." Often frustrated during the 1850s by white Episcopalians' indifference toward his Christian-emigrationism, Holly's devotion to the twin causes of black nationalism and Christianity had not wavered. Although he encountered personal difficulties in Haiti, Holly's black nationalist philosophy continued to entail potentially contradictory allegiances. His "political allegiance," he explained, was "to the government of this country," but his "ecclesiastical allegiance" was "to the church of another country." Holly's skills and commitment were eventually recognized by the American Episcopal Church in 1874, when he was appointed as the first black bishop. Holly remained in Haiti until his death in 1911, never wavering in his devotion to the Christian regeneration of Haiti—and, by extension, the black race.[117] As William Wells Brown's 1863 remark that "If there is any man living who is more devoted to the idea of a 'Negro Nationality' than Dr. Delany, that man is J. Theodore Holly" made clear, Holly's contemporaries were in no doubt about his black nationalist credentials.[118] Although Holly's role as an early advocate of black nationalism has not received the same attention from historians as Delany or Garnet, he was a significant figure, who served as a bridge between the African American activism of the antebellum period, and black leaders of the twentieth century, such as W.E.B. Du Bois and Marcus Garvey.

We can trace the post-emigrationist careers of the movement's leadership, but little is known of the majority of the emigrants. Many made their way back to the United States; others were absorbed into the Haitian population; and, most tragically, significant numbers undoubtedly died. Allston Wilson, an American with business interests in Haiti, spoke to several emigrants in 1863. Perhaps making use of their proficiency with the English language, a number of emigrants had initially secured work with foreign merchants in the Haitian capital. Subsequently, however, when threatened with conscription into the Haitian army, most of these people had fled to rural Haiti, to escape the draft.[119] In 1864 one visitor to Haiti reported that he could locate only two hundred of the original emigrants. In March of the same year, Edward L. Hartz, who was commissioned to help rescue the African Americans colonized on the Ile A'Vache, received a letter from James De Long asking whether "as an act of humanity" he could carry about forty blacks who had settled at Aux Cayes to the United States. De Long painted a grim, if by that time familiar, picture of the emigrants' fate in Haiti. Not only had the Haitian government failed to honor its promise to provide the emigrants with "lands and other accommodations," but without proper medical facilities, many emigrants had fallen victim to the "very sickly" environment. Separated from their friends and families back in the United States, African American settlers had "been in a destitute and suffering condition" since "their arrival." In response to De Long's request, Hartz took thirty-nine emigrants back to the United States.[120]

Despite the failure of the Haitian Emigration Bureau, and Haitian emigrationism in general, it is well to remember that the scheme not only provoked wide interest from a significant proportion of the black population, but also despatched more African Americans from the United States than the ACS was ever able to do in a similar period. Equally significant was the failure of black-sponsored schemes for emigration to Africa. The onset of the Civil War disrupted the emigrationists' plans but it would be misleading to blame that conflict for the failure of the Haitian movement. The same forces that served to bring on the Civil War were also largely responsible for the turn to emigrationism during the 1850s. The increasing North–South dichotomy, and the apparent strengthening of the slaveocracy; a realization that the means adopted by the abolitionists had failed; and, on the part of some African American leaders, an emerging sense that the fate of blacks in one region was related to the fate of blacks elsewhere all contributed to the emigrationism of the pre–Civil War decade. The Haitian movement emerged when black disenchantment with the United States was at its peak, and after plans for African emigration had proved impracticable. The outbreak of the Civil War, the subsequent Emancipation Proclamation, and the large-scale involvement of African Americans in the conflict overshadowed the Haitian scheme. Time would prove, however, that it was not only premature for African Americans to rest their hopes on a real shift in white sensibilities, but that many of the compelling reasons that had prompted talk of black nationalism and emigrationism remained valid long after the Civil War.

NOTES

1. *Pine and Palm,* 2 June 1861.

2. Here the historian is heavily dependent on the letters published in the black and abolitionist presses. Notwithstanding their claims that they were encouraging a full and frank exchange on the merits of the Haitian scheme, newspaper editors were free to include letters that supported their views on emigrationism, and equally free to exclude those letters that were at odds with their own views.

3. *Pine and Palm,* 12 October 1861, 14 August 1862.

4. Redpath to Plésance, 23 December 1860, Haytian Bureau of Emigration, Reports and Correspondence, 1860–1861, Rare Books and Manuscript Section, Boston Public Library (hereafter cited as HBE-BPL).

5. Redpath, ed., *A Guide to Hayti* (1861; reprint, Westport, Conn.: Negro University Press, 1970), 9, 131–35.

6. Benjamin Hunt, *Remarks on Hayti as a Place of Settlement for Afric-Americans and on the Mulatto as a Race for the Tropics* (Philadelphia: T. B. Pugh, 1860), 16; Redpath, *Guide*, 138–40.

7. Redpath to W. D. Harris, 29 March 1861, James Redpath Letterbook, Rare Book, Manuscript, and Special Collections Library, Duke University, Durham, North Carolina (hereafter cited as JRL-DU); *Weekly Anglo-African*, 26 January 1861.

8. Redpath, *Guide*, 93.

9. Regrettably, the two series of "Statistics of Haytian Emigration" published by the Haitian Bureau in the *Pine and Palm*, are inadequate for the purpose of analyzing with precision the background of those who emigrated to the island republic. Published in three installments (see the *Pine and Palm*, 12 October 1861, 19 October 1861, and 26 October 1861), the first set of statistics reveals that 558 emigrants had gone to Haiti in the period from December 1860 to September 1861. One major shortcoming of these early statistics is that they provide no indication of the ages of the emigrants, making it impossible to determine how many were of an age that would enable them to work on the land. Another important omission from the statistics of some of the early colonies, which renders it impossible to ascertain with precision how many emigrants had any agricultural expertise, is that no attempt was made to classify their occupations. That difficulty is only partially addressed in those cases where the emigrants' occupations are listed, for although a significant proportion were listed as "laborers," it was not specified what type of labor they were accustomed to performing. A surprisingly small number of emigrants were in the farmer or "cultivator" category, which helps explain many of the difficulties encountered by African American settlers in Haiti. In any case, we have to be wary of the number who claimed to have agricultural expertise, for bearing in mind that the Haitian government's offer of free passage was only open to farmers or farm laborers, it is likely that a number of African Americans who did not have an agricultural background claimed they did have such expertise, to avoid paying the passage to Haiti. A wide range of occupations were represented in the statistics, with a number of sempstresses, as well as teachers and shoemakers. In most cases, family units were not listed as such (exceptions being the first colony, which left New York City on 3 January 1861, and the seventh colony, which sailed from New Haven on 27 April 1861). The lists, however, do indicate that a significant proportion of the emigrants went to Haiti as families. Considering the pioneering nature of the scheme, it was perhaps surprising that so many dependents went to the black republic—although it should be remembered that the process of colonizing the American West also entailed the movement of thousands of family units.

Further evidence of the difficulties involved in ascertaining the emigrants' backgrounds comes from an examination of the "Recapitulation" of the first set of statistics. Therein, an attempt was made to classify the emigrants' geographical origins. Not only did the editors of the *Pine and Palm* admit that the first two colonies were despatched before they could be properly classified, but "birth place" and "last place of residence" were used in the same list, without differentiation. Moreover, although the bureau claimed that 585 emigrants had left for Haiti during the period covered by the first set of statistics, the list describing their last place of residence, or birth place, only accounts for 422 emigrants, including 62 whose origins were classified as "Unknown." Furthermore, the largest category in the sections dealing with "Education" and Religion" of the emigrants is "Unknown." Regarding the emigrants' education level the total "Unknown" was 300; concerning their religous orientation, 359 emigrants fell into the "Unknown" category. A further flaw in those statistics is that in neither case are the 585 emigrants accounted for: The total number in the "Education" list was 555, and for "Religion" it was 557. That problem is highlighted when the bureau's own figures for the total number of emigrants who had sailed to Haiti in the first 17 colonies (554), is contrasted with their figure of 585.

A second set of statistics was published in the *Pine and Palm* during April and May 1862 (see the editions for 17 April 1862, 1 May 1862, and 8 May 1862). In some respects, these statistics are more revealing that the earlier ones. Of a further 988 African Americans who had emigrated to Haiti under the auspices of the bureau, 393 were classified as adult males, and 242 as adult females. The remaining 353 emigrants were classified as "Minors" or "Infants"—a large proportion given the adverse conditions in Haiti. Of those emigrants listed in the section entitled "Trades and Callings," 197 claimed to be farmers, a figure that must be treated with some skepticism, for the reason just outlined. In addition, 64 emigrants classed themselves as laborers, but as in the earlier statistics, it is not specified what type of labor they were accustomed to performing. A chart indicating the emigrants' "Place of Nativity" indicates that the largest contingents came from Pennsylvania and Canada, but that reveals nothing about whether they came from rural or urban areas. Although there were no large communities of African Americans in Canada, as there were in Philadelphia and Pittsburgh, there were significant groups of blacks in Canadian towns such as Amherstburg, Windsor, and Chatham, suggesting that a number of the emigrants from the British Provinces might have come from urban areas.

In summary, the bureau's statistics provide frustratingly little help in assessing the emigrants' background. Although they reveal that more than fifteen hundred African Americans emigrated under the aegis of the bureau, they are too imprecise to be anything more than a very general guide: Much more can be deduced about African Americans' conditions and aspirations by addressing the problems they encountered in Haiti.

10. Redpath, *Guide*, 159–63. When an epidemic of yellow fever swept through Philadelphia in 1793, Dr. Benjamin Rush asserted that blacks would not contract the disease. After a number of blacks answered a call to volunteer for nursing and burial duties, it soon became clear they were far from immune from the disease. More than three hundred blacks perished before the crisis was over. See Winthrop Jordan, *White Over Black: American Attitudes Toward the Negro, 1550–1812* (Chapel Hill: University of North Carolina Press, 1968), 528–29; Julie Winch, *Philadelphia's Black Elite: Activism, Accommodation, and the Struggle for Autonomy, 1787–1848* (Philadelphia: Temple University Press, 1988), 15–17.

11. *Pine and Palm*, 12 June 1862, 10 July 1862.

12. Redpath, *Guide*, 165; Mabel Steedman, *Unknown to the World: Haiti* (London: Hurst and Blackett, 1939), 27.

13. *Pine and Palm*, 12 June 1862.

14. See *Pine and Palm*, 22 June 1861, 15 June 1861, 21 September 1861, 28 September 1861, 3 November 1861, 9 November 1861, 21 December 1861.

15. See Redpath to Plésance, 22 November 1861, Letters and Reports of James Redpath, General Agent of Emigration to Hayti, to M. Plésance, Secretary of State of External Relations of the Republic of Hayti, Manuscript Division, Library of Con-

gress, Washington, D.C., (hereafter cited as LRJR-LC); Redpath to Plésance, 9 March 1862, Correspondence of James Redpath, Commercial Agent of Hayti for Philadelphia, Joint Commissioner Plenipotentiary of Hayti to the government of the U.S. & General Agent of Emigration to Hayti for the U.S. and Canada, 31 December 1861 to 12 May 1862, Manuscripts, Archives and Rare Book Division, Schomburg Center for Research in Black Culture, New York Public Library, (hereafter cited as CJR-NYPL).

16. Redpath, *Guide*, 98.

17. *Pine and Palm*, 21 December 1861, 16 January 1862.

18. *Weekly Anglo-African*, 5 April 1862, 1 March 1862; M. B. Bird, *The Black Man; or, Haytian Independence. Deduced from Historical Notes, and Dedicated to the Government and People of Hayti* (1869; reprint, New York: Books for Libraries Press, 1971), 389.

19. Redpath to Élie, 12 February 1862, CJR-NYPL.

20. Redpath to Plésance, 20 October 1861, LRJR-LC; Redpath to Plésance, 22 November 1861, LRJR-LC.

21. *Pine and Palm*, 16 November 1861; Redpath to Plésance, 7 September 1861, LRJR-LC; Redpath to Élie, 23 September 1861, LRJR-LC.

22. *Pine and Palm*, 16 January 1862, 21 December 1861.

23. *Pine and Palm*, 21 September 1861.

24. Wilbur Zelinsky, "The Population Geography of the Free Negro in Ante-Bellum America," *Population Studies*, 3 (1950): 387–88.

25. *Pine and Palm*, 29 June 1861, 21 September 1861.

26. A. E. Newton to John Brown Jr., 4 March 1861, JRL-DU; Redpath to Plésance, 14 March 1861, HBE-BPL; *Pine and Palm*, 14 September 1861, 29 June 1861, 21 September 1861; *Weekly Anglo-African*, 20 April 1861.

27. *Weekly Anglo-African*, 20 April 1861.

28. *Pine and Palm*, 21 December 1861.

29. See above, n.9.

30. Redpath to "My Dear Friend," 19 February 1861, JRL-DU; Redpath to Plésance, 7 September 1861, LRJR-LC; *Pine and Palm*, 27 March 1862.

31. *Weekly Anglo-African*, 9 February 1861.

32. *Pine and Palm*, 2 January 1862; Redpath to Élie, 12 February 1862, CJR-NYPL.

33. Redpath to Élie, 5 October 1861, LRJR-LC; Redpath to Plésance, 11 August 1861, LRJR-LC

34. A. E. Newton to James Holly, 22 April 1861, JRL-DU.

35. Redpath to Élie, 5 October 1861, LRJR-LC; *Weekly Anglo-African*, 11 May 1861; Redpath to Plésance, 21 October 1861, LRJR-LC; *Pine and Palm*, 6 March 1862.

36. *Pine and Palm*, 22 June 1861, 4 September 1862, 9 November 1861.

37. See, for example, A. E. Newton to S. Langley, February 20, 1861, JRL-DU; and the descriptions of agricultural conditions in Haiti in the *Pine and Palm*, 15 June 1861, 26 October 1861, 13 November 1861.

38. *Pine and Palm*, 9 November 1861; Redpath to Plésance, 21 January 1861, HBE-BPL; Redpath to Élie, 13 February 1862, CJR-NYPL; *Pine and Palm*, 3 April 1862.

39. *Pine and Palm*, 2 January 1862, 12 June 1862.

40. *Pine and Palm*, 10 August 1861, 13 March 1862.

41. *Pine and Palm*, 21 December 1861.

42. *Weekly Anglo-African*, 7 December 1861; *Christian Recorder*, 26 October 1861. See also William Seraile, "Afro-American Emigration to Haiti During the American Civil War," *The Americas*, 35, (1978): 189–90.

43. Holly, *The Establishment of the Church in Hayti* (n.p.: n.p., 1860).

44. Holly's appeals for financial aid were published in two Episcopalian journals. See *The Calendar*, 17 November 1860, 21 November 1860, 1 December 1860, 8 December 1860, 9 February 1861, 16 February 1861, 9 March 1861, 30 March 1861, 6 April 1861, 4 May 1861, 11 May 1861; *The Church Journal*, 27 March 1861. See also Miller, *Search for a Black Nationality*, 241–42.

45. *Weekly Anglo-African*, 27 April 1861; Miller, *Search for a Black Nationality*, 242.

46. *The Calendar*, 31 August 1861; *Weekly Anglo-African*, 22 February 1862.

47. *Weekly Anglo-African*, 1 March 1862.

48. *Weekly Anglo-African*, 5 October 1861.

49. *Pine and Palm*, 28 September 1861; *Weekly Anglo-African*, 22 February 1862.

50. *Weekly Anglo-African*, 5 October 1861.

51. *Pine and Palm*, 10 July 1862.

52. *Weekly Anglo-African*, 19 January 1861.

53. *Chatham Tri-Weekly Planet*, 21 January 1861; Redpath to William J. Watkins, 4 March 1862, CJR-NYPL.

54. *Weekly Anglo-African*, 1 February 1862.

55. Robert D. Heinl and Nancy L. Heinl, *Written in Blood: The Story of the Haitian People, 1492-1971* (Boston: Houghton Mifflin, 1978), 221–22.

56. *Weekly Anglo-African*, 1 February 1862; Redpath to "Mr. Coffin," 2 April 1861, JRL-DU; *Liberator*, 12 July 1861; Redpath to Plésance, 6 April 1861, LRJR-LC; Redpath to William H. Johnson, 18 June 1861, cited in *William Henry Johnson Autobiography*, 50, included in George E. Carter and Peter C. Ripley, eds., *Black Abolitionist Papers* (microfilm edition) (Sanford, N.C.: Microfilming Corporation of America, 1981), Reel 3, Frame 0597; *Douglass' Monthly*, May 1861; *Pine and Palm*, 2 June 1861.

57. Heinl and Heinl, *Written in Blood*, 218–20; *Weekly Anglo-African*, 2 November 1861; *Pine and Palm*, 16 November 1861.

58. Redpath to Élie, 15 July 1861, LRJR-LC.

59. McKivigan, "James Redpath and Black Reaction to the Haitian Emigration Bureau," *Mid-America*, 69 (1987): 152. Similarly, William Seraile has referred to "the hard working Redpath." See Seraile, "Afro-American Emigration to Haiti," 194.

60. Redpath to George Lawrence, Jr., 18 May 1861, LRJR-LC.

61. Redpath to Hinton, 17 May 1861, 30 May 1861, JRL-DU.

62. Redpath to Plésance, 20 November 1860, 24 November 1860, HBE-BPL; Redpath to Plésance, 8 June 1861, LRJR-LC; Redpath to Élie, 6 June 1861, LRJR-LC; Redpath to Plésance, 19 June 1861, LRJR-LC; Redpath to Geffrard, 6 August 1861, LRJR-LC.

63. Redpath to Élie, 12 February 1862, CJR-NYPL; Willis D. Boyd, "James Redpath and American Negro Colonization in Haiti, 1860–1862," *The Americas*, 12 (1955): 174; James O'Dell Jackson III, "The Origins of Pan-African Nationalism:

Afro-American and Haytian Relations, 1800–1863," (Ph.D. diss., Northwestern University, 1976), 193, 221, 224–25.

64. *Weekly Anglo-African*, 19 January 1861; *Pine and Palm*, 14 December 1861, 21 December 1861.

65. *Pine and Palm*, 11 January 1862, 12 April 1862.

66. Redpath to Plésance, 2 March 1861, HBE-BPL; William P. Newman to George Lawrence, 31 May 1861, JRL-DU.

67. Rudolph M. Lapp, "The Negro in Gold Rush California," *Journal of Negro History*, 49 (1964): 81–82.

68. Redpath to Plésance, 13 October 1861, LRJR-LC; *Pine and Palm*, 8 June 1861, 29 June 1861, 17 August 1861, 16 November 1861.

69. See *Colonization of Free Blacks. Memorial of Leonard Dugged, George A. Bailey, and 240 other free colored persons of California, praying Congress to provide means for their colonization to some country in which their color will not be a badge of degradation* (Washington, D.C.: Printed for the House of Representatives, 1862).

70. *Pine and Palm*, 16 November 1861; *Douglass' Monthly*, May 1861.

71. *Douglass' Monthly*, July 1861. Redpath claimed he was fair in presenting both sides of the emigration debate. See Redpath to Plésance, 7 September 1861, LRJR-LC.

72. *Weekly Anglo-African*, 26 October 1861.

73. *Weekly Anglo-African*, 1 March 1862, 5 April 1862.

74. *Weekly Anglo-African*, 5 April 1862.

75. Redpath to Plésance, 13 October 1861, LRJR-LC.

76. *Liberator*, 3 February 1860.

77. Redpath to Plésance, 2 February, 1861, HBE-BPL; Redpath to Reverend G. Bishop, 25 May 1861, JRL-DU; Redpath, *The Roving Editor; or, Talks with Slaves in the Southern States* (New York: A. B. Burdick, 1859), 39; *Weekly Anglo-African*, 26 October 1861. On the relationship between blacks and mulattoes in the United States, see James Oliver Horton, *Free People of Color: Inside the African American Community* (Washington, D.C.: Smithsonian Institution Press, 1993), Chapter 6.

78. *Douglass' Monthly*, May 1859; Redpath to W. D. Harris, 29 March 1861, JRL-DU.

79. Redpath to Plésance, 24 August 1861, LRJR-LC.

80. David McEwen Dean, *Defender of the Race: James Theodore Holly, Black Nationalist Bishop* (Boston: Lambeth Press, 1979), 35.

81. Smith, "Toussaint L'Ouverture and the Haytian Revolutions," in *Masterpieces of Negro Eloquence: The Best Speeches Delivered by the Negro from the Days of Slavery to the Present Time*, ed. Alice Moore Dunbar (1914; reprint, New York: Johnson Reprint Co., 1970), 22.

82. *Weekly Anglo-African*, 5 January 1861, 12 January 1861.

83. Redpath to Plésance, 7 March 1861, HBE-BPL.

84. See, for example, *Liberator*, 17 May 1861; *Weekly Anglo-African*, 12 January 1862, *Christian Recorder*, 30 November 1861.

85. *Pine and Palm*, "Supplement," 2 January 1862; Redpath to Plésance, 2 February 1861, 23 February 1861, HBE-BPL.

86. *Weekly Anglo-African*, 19 October 1861, 14 December 1861, 28 September 1861.

87. *Weekly Anglo-African*, 28 September 1861, 19 October 1861, 26 October 1861.

88. *Pine and Palm*, 30 November 1861.

89. *Liberator*, 18 February 1862; *Pine and Palm*, 10 August 1861, 23 November 1861.

90. *Weekly Anglo-African*, 5 April 1862.

91. *Weekly Anglo-African*, 17 July 1861; *Christian Recorder*, 7 September 1861. See also Redpath to Plésance, 1 December 1860, HBE-BPL.

92. Jane H. Pease and William H. Pease, *Black Utopia: Negro Communal Experiments in America* (Madison: State Historical Society of Wisconsin, 1963), 72.

93. *Pine and Palm*, 7 September 1861; *Chatham Weekly Planet*, 21 March 1861; *Christian Recorder*, 7 September 1861; *Liberator*, 12 July 1861.

94. *Weekly Anglo-African*, 9 November 1861; 4 January 1862, 29 March 1862; *Pine and Palm*, 17 August 1861; Redpath to Plésance, 24 August 1861, LRJR-LC.

95. *Weekly Anglo-African*, 31 August 1861, 29 March 1862; *Pine and Palm*, 8 June 1861.

96. *Pine and Palm*, 14 September 1861; Redpath to Plésance, 7 September 1861, LRJR-LC.

97. Redpath to Plésance, 2 February 1861, HBE-BPL; Pease and Pease, "Negro Conventions and the Problem of Black Leadership," *Journal of Black Studies*, 2 (1971): 40; *Weekly Anglo-African*, 5 January 1861.

98. *Weekly Anglo-African*, 22 December 1860, 12 January 1861, 19 January 1861, 26 January 1861.

99. James M. McPherson, *Ordeal by Fire: The Civil War and Reconstruction* (New York: Knopf, 1982), 267–71.

100. *Christian Recorder*, 17 January 1863, in *The Voice of Black America: Major Speeches by Negroes in the United States, 1797–1973*, ed. Philip S. Foner, 2 vols. (New York: Capricorn Books, 1975), 1:287.

101. Mitchell, *Letter on the Relation of the White and African Races in the United States, Showing the Necessity of the Colonization of the Latter* (Washington, D.C.: U.S. Government Printing Office, 1862), 4–5, 27.

102. Abraham Lincoln, "Address on Colonization to a Deputation of Colored Men" (1862), in *Classical Black Nationalism: From the American Revolution to Marcus Garvey*, ed. Wilson Jeremiah Moses (New York: New York University Press, 1996), 211.

103. *Liberator*, 21 May 1862.

104. *Christian Recorder*, 23 August 1862, in Foner, *The Voice of Black America*, 1:282.

105. Redpath to Élie, 15 July 1861, LRJR-LC; Tinsley Lee Spraggins, "Economic Aspects of Negro Colonization During the Civil War" (Ph.D. diss., American University, 1957), 200.

106. On the Ile A'Vache episode, see Willis D. Boyd, "The Ile A'Vache Colonization Venture," *The Americas*, 16 (1959): 45–62; James D. Lockett, "Abraham Lincoln and Colonization: An Episode that Ends in Tragedy at Ile A'Vache, Haiti, 1863–64," *Western Journal of Black Studies*, 12 (1988): 178–84. A number of Whidden's reports on the Ile A'Vache situation are included in his reports to Secretary of State William H. Seward, reprinted in the Despatches from United States Ministers to Haiti, 1862-1906 (microfilm). National Archives, Washington, D.C. (National Ar-

chives and Records Service, Central Services Administration, Washington: 1955), Reel 1.

107. John W. Blassingame, ed., *The Frederick Douglass Papers. Series One: Speeches, Debates, and Interviews. Volume 2: 1847–54* (New Haven: Yale University Press, 1982), 442n.

108. Redpath to Watkins, 23 May 1862, CJR-NYPL; *Pine and Palm*, 12 June 1862, 4 September 1862; Benjamin Quarles, *Lincoln and the Negro* (New York: Oxford University Press, 1962), 191.

109. Redpath to Garnet, 25 March 1861, 29 March 1861, JRL-DU; *Weekly Anglo-African*, 6 April 1861.

110. *Weekly Anglo-African*, 26 April 1862.

111. *Douglass' Monthly*, February 1862; Robert L. Harris, Jr., "H. Ford Douglas: Afro-American Antislavery Abolitionist," *Journal of Negro History*, 62 (1977): 228–30.

112. *Liberator*, 2 May 1862.

113. *Weekly Anglo-African*, 12 April 1862.

114. *Pine and Palm*, 4 September 1862.

115. Alvin F. Harlow, "James Redpath" in the *Dictionary of American Biography*, ed. Allen Johnson et al., 20 vols. (New York: Oxford University Press, 1935), 15:444; James McPherson, *The Struggle for Equality: Abolitionists and the Negro in the Civil War and Reconstruction* (Princeton, N.J.: Princeton University Press, 1964), 266–67.

116. Redpath, editor's "Introduction" to *Toussaint L'Ouverture: Biography and Autobiography* (1863; reprint, New York: Books for Libraries Press, 1971), v.

117. Holly to the Reverend A. Cleveland, 22 September 1864, James Theodore Holly Papers, Archives of the Episcopal Church, Austin, Texas. (This material is reprinted courtesy of the Archives of the Episcopal Church.) See also Lynch, "James Theodore Holly," 15; Dean, *Defender of the Black Race*, 47–108.

118. Brown, *The Black Man, His Antecedents, His Genius, and His Achievements*, 4th ed. (1865; reprint, Miami: Mnemosyne Publishing Co., 1969), 274.

119. Boyd, "Colonization in Haiti," 181.

120. James De Long to Hartz, 1 March 1864, and "On board Mary C. Gray," Edward L. Hartz Papers, Rare Book, Manuscript, and Special Collections Library, Duke University, Durham, North Carolina.

Conclusion

Since the era of the American Revolution, emigrationism has been at the heart of the black experience in the United States. Although only a relative handful of African Americans emigrated during the antebellum period, the persistence and intensity of the debates surrounding the issue attest to the depth of feeling within black America regarding emigrationism. By exposing fundamental questions of racial and national identity, emigrationism casts light on the problems and dilemmas confronting African Americans.

Historians interested in black colonization and emigration have often focused on African emigrationism. As this study shows, however, that emphasis on African emigrationism has been at the historiographical expense of Haitian emigrationism. For many black Americans, Haiti was a more realistic and appealing destination than Africa. This contrast was well shown by the emigration movement of the 1820s. Repudiating white colonizationists' assumption that blacks were doomed to perpetual degradation as long as they remained in the United States, and rejecting claims by the white leaders of the American Colonization Society (ACS) that they favored the elevation of blacks, African Americans denounced the ACS as a racist organization, committed to the perpetuation of slavery. Indeed, for much of the antebellum period, black Americans—articulate leaders and obscure masses alike—vigorously asserted that the United States was their home. But the interest shown in Haitian emigrationism by African Americans during the 1820s reveals that some blacks were not averse to emigrationist schemes that could be clearly distinguished from that of the ACS. With white colonizationists working hard to recruit black Americans for their Liberian venture, the Haitian option proved a more tempting alternative for many northern blacks. Although the Haitian scheme of the 1820s can be described as a failure, the departure of six thousand African Americans to the island republic during the 1820s attested to the doubts held by many blacks regarding their future in the United States, and hinted at the links between Haiti and African America.

Although emigrationism was in abeyance for much of the 1830s and 1840s, the period from 1850 to 1862 was characterized by intense debate over emigrationism, with a number of black leaders articulating a black nationalist ideology that they hoped would play a part in overcoming American racism. Haitian emigrationism was an essential aspect of that black nationalism. While it would be misleading to ignore altogether Martin Delany and the interest in African emigrationism, and although emigrationists identified, and sometimes celebrated, black Americans' links with Africa, by 1860 it was widely accepted that Haiti, rather than Africa, was the most suitable and appealing destination for those blacks inclined to leave the United States. Not only was it easier to transport emigrants to Haiti than it would be to take them to Africa, but the island republic's geographical proximity to the United States meant it was possible to argue that those African Americans who emigrated to Haiti were not running away from the slaves. Whereas Africa had traditionally been presented in a negative fashion—a perception that Delany, and others, struggled unsuccessfully to overcome—black leaders in the United States had consistently spoken with pride of the Haitians' achievements, especially their success in ousting their colonial oppressors. And notwithstanding the wide knowledge of Haiti's turbulent political history, the existence of a government in the black republic that was modeled, at least in part, on principles that were recognizable to African Americans, gave that emigration movement a further advantage over its African counterpart, because the assistance provided by that government legitimized the scheme in a way that no African tribal chief could have done. In particular, the financial support provided to the Haitian movement by the authorities in Port-au-Prince allowed James Redpath to conduct the movement in a manner that Delany found impossible with his emigration proposals. By hiring agents, distributing his *Guide to Hayti*, and publishing the *Pine and Palm*, Redpath was able to generate a greater degree of interest in emigration than any other antebellum proponents of a black exodus from the United States. In the process Haitian emigrationism became much more than the hypothetical musings of the African American elite.

Haitian emigrationists held a further advantage over those who looked toward Africa. Delany's plans were impaired by the fact that the only African Americans to actually emigrate to Africa during the antebellum period did so under the auspices of the ACS. This made it difficult for Delany to dissociate his scheme from that of the ACS. It was easy, therefore, for his critics to charge that his plans were founded on the same racist premises as the ACS. Because Haitian emigrationism was directing black Americans to a very different destination, its advocates' claims that emigration to the island republic was "essentially and diametrically opposed to the colonization project" persuaded some African Americans that the Haitian movement was significantly more than a new incarnation of the ACS.[1] This issue was inseparably linked to the question of whether emigration should be limited to a select minority of the African American population. The alternative, an en-masse exodus of blacks, was fraught with difficulties: Besides the obvious logistical problems, the advocacy of a large-scale movement of blacks was tantamount to an admission that there was no place for free blacks in the United States—an apparent concession to the arguments of white colonizationists.

Unlike white colonizationists, however, African American emigrationists explicitly connected their schemes to the notion of black nationalism. Reflecting the dilemma of trying to reconcile their loyalty to their race with an attachment to the United States, the black nationalism of antebellum emigrationists was very much the product of a distinctly American black experience. Amid the deepening racial and political crisis of the mid-nineteenth century, Haitian emigrationists were often ambivalent about leaving America, and no less convinced of their differences from other Africans throughout the world. Analysis of Haitian emigrationism has revealed that the black nationalism of the 1850s was a more complex phenomenon than a stark depiction of the black leadership polarized into oppositional ideologies and factions would suggest. Although African American liberation has often been couched in terms of two, frequently contradictory principles—separatism, or integration—the issues have rarely been absolute, and the individuals concerned cannot be rigidly categorized, as some observers have assumed. Identifying and explicating the tensions within Haitian emigrationism during the Civil War era have demonstrated that antebellum black nationalism was an often tenuous fusion of cooperation and individualism, that is most fruitfully regarded as a continuum, to which assimilationists and emigrationists alike made telling contributions.

Through their discussions of a black nationality, emigrationists formulated a conception of "the nation." As this study shows, emigrationists did not speak with one voice on this issue. But some themes did recur, including the assumption that social, cultural, and economic hierarchies were part of the natural order. Accordingly, although antebellum emigrationists did repudiate hierarchies based on race, they did not offer an egalitarian vision of all blacks as equals. Rather, they envisioned hierarchies based on merit and achievement. In this way, their black nationalism was very much a reflection of—and no doubt a contribution to—broader American values.

It was perhaps not surprising that emigrationists articulated a nationalist vision that owed much to American culture, as well as to the experiences of black people in Africa and America. The frequency with which emigrationists invoked the notion of civilization was a telling barometer of the extent to which they were imbued with many of the values—and prejudices—of white America. Given, too, the central place of gender in the nineteenth-century cultural battle against "barbarism," it is equally significant that antebellum emigrationism was gendered in such a way to emphasize the masculine aspects of American ideology, especially its constructions of nationalism. As the westward march of white American "civilization" was couched in explicitly masculinist terms, black emigrationists' descriptions of their schemes as a means by which African Americans could assert their "manliness" were suggestive of the value attached to masculinity in antebellum America in general, and of the allegedly emasculating impact of slavery in particular.

These connections were potentially contradictory. Indeed, the story of Haitian emigrationism—and the associated issue of black nationalism—entails profound contradictions, for in promoting emigration to Haiti during the 1850s and early 1860s, James T. Holly and others were sure that African Americans were uniquely qualified to advance the cause of Haitian civilization. For African Americans contemplating the issue of black nationality, Haiti occupied an ambiguous, but essential place in their imagined community. Nevertheless, nineteenth-century Americans drew very different meanings from the contested story of Haitian independence. To white America, Haiti represented race war and rebellion; for black Americans, Haiti stood as a tangible symbol of black will and power. In particular, Haiti's status as the world's first independent black republic was a source of pride for black Americans, who lauded Toussaint L'Ouverture, and praised the Haitians' valor and persistence in the face of international hostility. Consequently, despite many disparaging depictions of Haiti, black Americans generally regarded Haiti in a more positive light than Africa—if nothing else, Haiti's status as the world's first independent black republic ensured it a place in African American consciousness.

White Americans' scorn for Haiti, however, did not mean the issue of emigration was a straightforward one for African Americans. The political, economic, and racial troubles that plagued Haiti, along with the ignominy of continuing European and American interference in its internal affairs, were antithetical to the images many black people preferred to project of an independent black nationality—even one that proved so troublesome to the United States' collective racial consciousness, and to its self-image as the benevolent protector of liberty in the Caribbean. Although there is compelling evidence that black Americans accepted that the Haitians had done much for the elevation of their race by establishing and maintaining their political independence, African Americans understood that social and economic progress remained elusive in the island republic. Paradoxically, too, in opposing emigration, some black Americans' depictions of the perceived lack of moral and social refinement in Haiti paralleled southern slaveholders' denunciations of the island republic.

For black Americans, then, Haitians were both subjects of admiration and objects of derision. Accordingly, while African Americans understood the significance of Haitian independence, Holly and others were also sure that Haiti had not reached its true potential. The black nationalism imagined by emigrationists regarded the black nationality that existed in the island republic as incomplete. Only when Haiti had achieved economic prosperity and social stability, it was argued, could the nation fulfill its potential as an effective beacon and agent of black liberation and elevation. Specifically, Haiti required an infusion of African American expertise and energy, and Christianity, if it was to reach its true potential as an exemplar of a black nation. Similarly, in assuming that African Americans were more advanced than other "Africans," black emigrationists were effectively, if unwittingly, endorsing many of the racial stereotypes that prevailed in nineteenth-century America. Haiti's ambiguous place in the African American consciousness was appropriate, given that nineteenth-century expressions of black nationalism were essentially born of adversity. This was—indeed, is—not unusual. But for Holly and other antebellum proponents of black nationalism, their pride in the accomplishments and virtues of the black race was in part a defensive reaction to the antipathy shown by white America to African America.

At the same time, then, as African Americans expressed pride in the Haitians' success in ousting the French and establishing an independent black nationality, the black nationalism espoused by Haitian emigrationists during the Civil War era was characterized by condescension, and a firm conviction that Haiti could only achieve its potential via the intervention of African Americans. Despite the racism and inequalities of American society, black emigrationists were evidently persuaded that their experiences in America rendered them more advanced than other descendants of Africa. In this way, African American emigrationists reflected, as well as confronted the racist culture of antebellum America, for in assuming the inferiority of Haitians and Africans, they echoed the views of many white Americans. Nineteenth-century American exceptionalism, it seems, transcended racial distinctions.

These imperatives were also evident in black Americans' attitude toward the broader ideological values underpinning nineteenth-century American expansionism. Although Manifest Destiny, as it was understood and articulated by many white Americans, frequently entailed an adherence to racialist principles, nineteenth-century black emigrationists expressed a Manifest Destiny of their own, that was both a reaction to, and a reflection of, those very same white racial attitudes. For Holly, and a number of other black emigrationists, their Manifest Destiny further reflected American culture in that it couched emigrationism in terms of a Christian mission. Here was America, in this case black America, seeking to re-make the world in its own image. This was not the only occasion that American reformers had sought to carry American values abroad; antebellum emigrationists were anticipating postbellum reformers who were active on the international stage, such as the members of the Women's Christian Temperance Union, whose reform efforts amounted to a form of cultural imperialism.[2] But given that black Americans suffered the racism of white America so severely, and given that the black nationalism of the antebellum era grew in part out of the injustices of American racism, it was profoundly ironical that black emigrationists were determined to transplant essentially American values overseas.

In reflecting the influence of American culture, some emigrationists emphasized the significance of Christianity. Antebellum black Christianity, however, was much more than a carbon copy of Anglo American Christianity. Rather, it was a complex amalgam, betraying the influence of Christianity, as well as the multiplicity of values and practices of African religions. Nevertheless, black Americans expressed disdain for the Haitians' voodoo, and their Catholicism. Nothing better encapsulates these paradoxes than Holly's commitment to an Episcopalian regeneration of Haiti. Although the Episcopalian authorities in the United States expressed only lukewarm support for Holly's missionary impulse, and although the denomination reflected the wider ambivalence of most churches to issues of race and slavery, Holly not only converted to the Episcopalian faith, but was also certain that it was through the agency of Episcopalianism that Haiti's spiritual regeneration could begin. For some emigrationists, particularly Holly, their perceptions of Haiti's religious predicament—and their assumption that African American Christianity could be an effective agent of the civilizing process—were a raison d'être for emigrationism. Here, again, the black nationalism of Haitian emigrationists reflected the Manifest Destiny in which American expansionism was typically represented and understood as an extension of God's will.[3]

The specific form—and implications—of the Haitian emigrationists' black Manifest Destiny served to distinguish Haitian emigrationism from schemes for African emigration. In his recent analysis of the black nationalism of Martin Delany, Alexander Crummell, and Henry McNeal Turner, Tunde Adeleke has argued that a "distinguishing feature of nineteenth-century black American nationalism" was "not so much its adaptations of Anglo-Saxon values as its relation to imperialist culture and ideology and the way that this connection helped to shape, legitimize, and strengthen the imperialist onslaught on Africa." Adeleke has contended that Delany, Crummell, and Turner "eventually concurred with much of the rationale for European imperialism."[4] Adeleke's argument has some merit with regard to the ideology of African emigrationism, but the ideology of the Haitian emigrationists did not serve the interests of those who sought to subdue the Haitian nationality. Rather, in seeking to render Haiti more secure from American or European expansionism, emigrationists such as Holly sought to augment the Haitian state by an infusion of "American" values. Such a situation was profoundly ironical, but it did not parallel the process that Adeleke claimed was at work among proponents of black American emigration to Africa.

Although Haitian emigrationism failed to achieve the very ambitious goals enunciated by its proponents, it did engage the interest of significant numbers of African Americans in the late antebellum period; this was perhaps the emigrationists' most significant achievement, for the interest shown in Haiti challenged the common view that the black populace was apathetic to its plight. At the same time, however, even as the interest in Haiti on the part of the African American populace suggested they were heeding their leaders' messages, the emigrants' experiences in Haiti point also to the divisions within black America, and to the ambiguities and contradictions of the black nationalism that was espoused by the movement's leaders. Emigrants, many of whom left the United States not because of a deep-seated commitment to the principles of black nationalism, however vaguely defined, but rather because they saw in the Haitian scheme an escape from oppression and an opportunity for individual self-advancement, encountered enormous difficulties in Haiti. Indeed, many African Americans who relocated to Haiti were soon disillusioned. Initially confident that their experiences and acumen would enable them to achieve material security in their new home, and hoping to find political and civic freedom in the black republic, emigrants soon realized that the Haitian authorities were unable—or unwilling—to fulfill the promises they had made. To the Haitian leadership the African American immigrants were a resource, a means of improving the island's productivity and prosperity; no doubt, too, many ordinary Haitians viewed the immigrants from the United States with deep suspicion. The emigrants' difficulties attested not only to the distinctions within African America, but were also suggestive of the profound differences between blacks in the United States and elsewhere. Paradoxically, as their black nationalist vision revealed, the African American leadership was itself aware of those distinctions.

The demise of Haitian emigrationism during the 1820s, and again during the 1860s, can be attributed in part to the settlers' difficulties and disappointments in the black republic. Important, too, were the vociferous denunciations of the scheme from a number of black leaders who refused to distinguish between the Haitian movement and that of the much-detested ACS. If nothing else, the strident opposition to the scheme from some black leaders hinted at the potential appeal of Haitian emigrationism. It is well to remember, too, that Haitian emigrationists were not the only ones who failed to achieve their goals. Although emancipation did occur as a consequence of the Civil War, advocates of the stay-and-fight doctrine failed to achieve equality for black Americans. Black recognition of the divergence between American rhetoric, and the reality of American racism, coupled with their understanding of the ongoing distinction between "freedom" and "equality," helps to account for the recurring interest in emigrationism through succeeding decades.

NOTES

1. *Pine and Palm*, 2 June 1861.

2. On the WCTU, see Ian Tyrrell, *Woman's World/Woman's Empire: The Woman's Christian Temperance Union in International Perspective* (Chapel Hill: University of North Carolina Press, 1991).

3. Richard Blackett has made a similar point with regard to the African emigrationists of the Civil War era. See Blackett, *Building an Antislavery Wall: Black Americans in the Atlantic Abolitionist Movement, 1830–1865* (Baton Rouge: Louisiana State University Press, 1983), 189.

4. Adeleke, *UnAfrican Americans: Nineteenth-Century Black Nationalists and the Civilizing Mission* (Lexington: University Press of Kentucky, 1998), 115.

Bibliography

PRIMARY SOURCES

Manuscript and Archival Material

American Colonization Society Papers (microfilm), Australian National Library, Canberra.

Anti-Slavery Collection, Rare Book and Manuscript Room, Boston Public Library.

Beecher Family Papers, Manuscripts and Archives, Yale University, New Haven, Connecticut.

Correspondence of James Redpath, Commercial Agent of Hayti for Philadelphia, Joint Commissioner Plenipotentiary of Hayti to the Government of the U.S. & General Agent of Emigration to Hayti for the U.S. and Canada, December 31, 1861 to May 12, 1862, Schomburg Center for Research in Black Culture, New York Public Library, New York City.

Despatches from United States Ministers to Haiti, 1862–1906 (microfilm). National Archives, Washington, D.C. National Archives and Records Service, Central Services Administration, Washington: 1955.

Edward L. Hartz Papers, Rare Book, Manuscript, and Special Collections Library, Duke University, Durham, North Carolina.

Haytian Bureau of Emigration, Reports and Correspondence, Boston, 1860–1861, Boston Public Library.

James Redpath Letterbook, Rare Book, Manuscript, and Special Collections Library, Duke University, Durham, North Carolina.

James Theodore Holly Papers, Archives of the Episcopal Church, Austin, Texas.

Letters and Reports of James Redpath, General Agent of Emigration to Hayti, to M. Plésance, Secretary of State of External Relations of the Republic of Hayti, Manuscript Division, Library of Congress, Washington, D.C.

Scrapbook of clippings of articles mostly relating to Haiti and John Brown by James
     Redpath, 1859–1861, Schomburg Center for Research in Black Culture,
     New York Public Library, New York City.

Newspapers and Periodicals

African Repository, 1825–1850
Anglo-African Magazine, 1859–1860
Calendar, 1860–1862
Douglass' Monthly, 1859–1862
Frederick Douglass' Paper, 1851–1859
Freedom's Journal, 1827–1829
Genius of Universal Emancipation, 1821–1825
Liberator, 1831–1865
New Orleans Bee, 1859–1860
New Orleans Daily Picayune, 1859
New Orleans Times Picayune, 1860
North Star, 1847–1851
Pine and Palm, 1861–1862
Provincial Freeman, 1853–1857
The Rights of All, 1829
Voice of the Fugitive, 1851–1853
Weekly Anglo-African, 1859–1863

Published Material

Aptheker, Herbert, ed. *"One Continual Cry": David Walker's Appeal to the Colored
     Citizens of the World (1829–1830)*. New York: Humanities Press, 1965.
Barskett, James. *History of the Island of St. Domingo: From Its First Discovery by Co-
     lumbus to the Present Period*. 1818; reprint, London: Frank Cass, 1971.
Basler, Roy P., ed. *The Collected Works of Abraham Lincoln*. 9 vols. New Brunswick,
     N.J.: Rutgers University Press, 1953.
Beard, Rev. John R. *The Life of Toussaint L'Ouverture, the Negro Patriot of Hayti:
     Comprising an Account of the Struggle for Liberty in the Island, and a Sketch
     of Its History to the Present Period*. London: Ingram, Cooke, and Co., 1853.
Bell, Howard H., ed. *Minutes of the Proceedings of the National Negro Conventions,
     1830–1864*. New York: Arno Press and the *New York Times*, 1969.
Bird, M. B. *The Black Man; or, Haytian Independence. Deduced from Historical Notes,
     and Dedicated to the Government and People of Hayti*. 1869; reprint, New
     York: Books for Libraries Press, 1971.
Blair, Francis Preston, Jr. *Colonization and Commerce. An Address Before the Young
     Men's Mercantile Library Association of Cincinnati, Ohio, November 29,
     1859*. Cincinnati: n.p., 1859.
———. *The Destiny of the Races on this Continent, An Address before the Mercantile
     Library Association of Boston, Massachusetts, on the 26th of January, 1859*.
     Washington, D.C.: Buell and Blanchard, 1859.

————. *Speech of the Hon. Francis P. Blair, Jr., of Missouri, on the Acquisition of Central America; Delivered in the House of Representatives, January 14, 1858.* Washington, D.C.: Congressional Globe Office, 1858.

Blassingame, John, ed. *The Frederick Douglass Papers. Series One: Speeches, Debates, and Interviews. Volume 1: 1841–46.* New Haven, Conn.: Yale University Press, 1979.

————. *The Frederick Douglass Papers. Series One: Speeches, Debates, and Interviews. Volume 3: 1855–63.* New Haven, Conn.: Yale University Press, 1985.

————. *The Frederick Douglass Papers. Series One: Speeches, Debates, and Interviews. Volume 5: 1881–95.* New Haven, Conn.: Yale University Press, 1992.

Brown, William Wells. *The Black Man, His Antecedents, His Genius, and His Achievements.* 4th ed. 1865; reprint, Miami: Mnemosyne Publishing Co., 1969.

————. *St. Domingo: Its Revolutions and Its Patriots. A Lecture Delivered Before the Metropolitan Atheneum, London, May 16, and at St. Thomas' Church, Philadelphia, December 20, 1854.* Boston: Bela Marsh, 1855.

Browne, Jonathan. *The History and Present Condition of St. Domingo.* 1837; reprint, London: Frank Cass, 1972.

Campbell, Robert. *A Few Facts Relating to Lagos, Abbeokuta, and Other Sections of Central Africa.* Philadelphia: King & Baird, 1860.

Carter, George E. and Peter C. Ripley, eds. *Black Abolitionist Papers.* Sanford, N.C.: Microfilming Corporation of America, 1981.

Clark, Benjamin C. *A Plea for Hayti, with a Glance at Her Relations with France, England and the United States, for the Last Sixty Years.* Boston: Eastburn's Press, 1853.

Coates, Benjamin. *Suggestions on the Importance of the Cultivation of Cotton in Africa in Reference to the Abolition of Slavery in the United States through the Organization of an African Civilization Society.* Philadelphia: C. Sherman and Son, 1858.

Colonization of Free Blacks. Memorial of Leonard Dugged, George A. Bailey, and 240 other free colored persons of California, praying Congress to provide means for their colonization to some country in which their color will not be a badge of degradation. Washington, D.C.: Printed for the House of Representatives, 1862.

Constitution of the American Society of Free Persons of Colour, for Improving Their Condition in the United States; for Purchasing Lands; and for the Establishment of a Settlement in Upper Canada, also the Proceedings of the Convention, with Their Address to the Free Persons of Colour in the United States. Philadelphia: J. W. Allen, 1831.

Delany, Martin. *Blake, or the Huts of America.* 1859–1862; reprint, Boston: Beacon Press, 1970.

————. *The Condition, Elevation, Emigration, and Destiny of the Colored People of the United States, Politically Considered.* 1852; reprint, New York: Arno Press, 1968.

————. *Official Report of the Niger Valley Exploring Party.* New York: T. Hamilton, 1861.

————. "Political Destiny of the Colored Race on the American Continent," reprinted in House of Representatives, *Report of the Select Committee on*

Emancipation and Colonization, Report No. 148, 37th Congress, 2nd Session. Washington, D.C.: Government Printing Office, 1862.

Dewey, Loring, ed. *Correspondence Relative to the Emigration to Haiti of the Free People of Colour in the United States, together with Instructions to the Agent Sent by President Boyer.* New York: Mahlon Day, 1824.

Dunbar, Alice Moore. *Masterpieces of Negro Eloquence: The Best Speeches Delivered by the Negro from the Days of Slavery to the Present Time.* 1914; reprint, New York: Johnson Reprint Co., 1970.

Foner, Philip S., ed. *The Life and Writings of Frederick Douglass.* 4 vols. New York: International Publishers, 1952.

———. *The Voice of Black America: Major Speeches by Negroes in the United States, 1797–1973.* 2 vols. New York: Capricorn Books, 1975.

Foner, Philip S., and George E. Walker, eds. *Proceedings of the Black State Conventions, 1840–1865.* 2 vols. Philadelphia: Temple University Press, 1979–1980.

Franklin, James. *The Present State of Hayti (Saint Domingo) with Remarks on Its Agriculture, Commerce, Laws, Religion, Finances, and Population, Etc Etc.* 1828; reprint, Westport, Conn.: Negro Universities Press, 1970.

Frazier, Thomas R. *Afro-American History: Primary Sources.* New York: Harcourt, Brace, and World, 1970.

Friemarck, Vincent, and Bernard Rosenthal, eds. *Race and the American Romantics.* New York: Schocken Books, 1971.

Garnet, Henry Highland et al. *The African Civilization Society.* New York: Office of the Civilization Society, 1859.

Griffiths, Julia, ed. *Autographs for Freedom.* 2 vols. 1854; reprint, Miami: Mnemosyne Publishing Co., 1969.

Griggs, Earl Leslie, and Clifford H. Prator, eds. *Henry Christophe and Henry Clarkson: A Correspondence.* 1952; reprint, New York: Greenwood, 1968.

Hamilton, William. *Address to the Fourth Annual Convention of the Free People of Color of the United States. Delivered at the Opening of Their Session in the City of New-York, June 2, 1834.* New York: S. W. Benedict, 1834.

Harris, Joseph Dennis. *A Summer on the Borders of the Caribbean Sea.* New York: A. B. Burdick, 1860.

Harvey, W. W. *Sketches of Haiti From the Expulsion of the French to the Death of Christophe.* 1827; reprint, London: Frank Cass, 1971.

Hassal, Mary. *Secret History, or The Horrors of St. Domingo in a Series of Letters: Written by a Lady at Cape Francois to Colonel Burr, Late Vice-President of the United States, Principally During the Command of General Rochambeau.* Philadelphia: Bradford & Innskeep, 1808.

Haytien Emigration Society. *Information for the Free People of Colour Who Are Inclined to Emigrate to Hayti.* Philadelphia: J. H. Cunningham, 1825.

Hill, Adelaide C. and Martin Kilson, eds. *Apropos of Africa: Sentiments of Negro American Leaders on Africa from the 1800s to the 1950s.* London: Frank Cass, 1969.

Holly, James Theodore. *The Establishment of the Church in Hayti.* n.p.: n.p., 1860.

———. *Facts About the Church's Mission in Haiti. A Concise Statement by Bishop Holly.* New York: Thomas Whittaker, 1897.

————. *A Vindication of the Capacity of the Negro Race for Self-Government, and Civilized Progress, as Demonstrated by Historical Events of the Haytian Revolution; and the Subsequent Acts of That People Since Their National Independence*. New Haven: William H. Stanley, 1857.

Hunt, Benjamin S. *Remarks on Hayti as a Place of Settlement for Afric-Americans and on the Mulatto as a Race for the Tropics*. Philadelphia: T. B. Pugh, 1860.

Katz, William Loren, ed. *Eyewitness: The Negro in American History*. New York: Pitman, 1967.

Lundy, Benjamin. *The Life, Travels, and Opinions of Benjamin Lundy, Including His Journeys to Texas and Mexico; With a Sketch of Contemporary Events, and a Notice of the Revolution in Hayti*. Compiled Under the Direction and on Behalf of His Children. 1847; reprint, New York: Negro Universities Press, 1969.

Mackenzie, Charles. *Notes on Haiti: Made During a Residence in that Republic*. 2 vols. 1830; reprint, London: Frank Cass, 1971.

McKitrick, Eric L., ed. *Slavery Defended: The Views of the Old South*. Englewood Cliffs, N.J.: Prentice-Hall, 1963.

McPherson, James M., ed. *The Negro's Civil War: How American Negroes Felt and Acted During the War for the Union*. New York: Pantheon Books, 1965.

Minutes of the National Convention of Colored Citizens: Held at Buffalo, on the 15th, 16th, 17th, 18th and 19th of August, 1843. For the Purpose of Considering their Moral and Political Conditions as American Citizens. New York: Piercy and Reed, 1843.

Minutes and Proceedings of the First Annual Convention of the Free People of Colour, Held by Adjournments in the City of Philadelphia, From the Sixth to the Eleventh of June, Inclusive, 1831. Philadelphia: Published by Order of the Committee of Arrangements, 1831.

Minutes of the Fourth Annual Convention, for the Improvement of the Free People of Colour, in the United States, Held by Adjournments, in the Asbury Church, New-York, from the 2d to the 12th of June inclusive, 1834. New York: Published by Order of the Convention, 1834.

Minutes and Proceedings of the General Convention for the Improvement of the Colored Inhabitants of Canada, Held by Adjournments in Amherstburg, C.W., June 16th and 17th, 1853. Windsor, Canada West: Bibb & Holly, 1853.

Minutes and Proceedings of the Second Annual Convention, for the Improvement of the Free People of Color, in these United States, Held by Adjournments in the City of Philadelphia, from the 4th to the 13th of June Inclusive, 1832. Philadelphia: Martin and Boden, Printers, 1832.

Minutes of the Proceedings of the Third Annual Convention, for the Improvement of the Free People of Colour in these United States, held by Adjournments in the City of Philadelphia, From the 3d to the 13th of June inclusive, 1833. New York: Published by Order of the Convention, 1833.

Minutes of the State Convention of the Colored Citizens of Ohio, Convened at Columbus, January 15–18, 1851. Columbus: n.p., 1951.

Mitchell, James. *Letter on the Relation of the White and African Races in the United States, Showing the Necessity of the Colonization of the Latter*. Washington, D.C.: United States Government Printing Office, 1862.

Moses, Wilson Jeremiah, ed. *Classical Black Nationalism: From the American Revolution to Marcus Garvey*. New York: New York University Press, 1996.

Mott, Abigail Field, comp. *Biographical Sketches and Interesting Anecdotes of Persons of Color. To Which is Added, a Selection of Pieces of Poetry*. 2nd ed. New York: Mahlon Day, 1837.

Nell, William C. *The Colored Patriots of the American Revolution*. 1855; reprint, New York: Arno Press, 1968.

Nesbitt, William. *Four Months in Liberia, or African Colonization Exposed*. Pittsburgh: n.p., 1855.

Newsome, M. T., comp. *Arguments Pro and Con, on the Call for a National Emigration Convention, to be Held in Cleveland, Ohio, August, 1854, by Frederick Douglass, W. J. Watkins, and James Whitfield. With a Short Appendix of the Statistics of Canada West, West Indies, Central and South America*. Detroit: George Pomeroy, 1854.

Phillips, Wendell. *Speeches, Lectures, and Letters*. 1884; reprint, New York: Negro Universities Press, 1968.

Porter, Dorothy, ed. *Early Negro Writing, 1760–1837*. Boston: Beacon Press, 1971.

Proceedings of a Convention of the Colored Men of Ohio. Held in the City of Cincinnati on the 23d, 24th, 25th and 26th Days of November, 1858. Cincinnati: Moore, Wilstach, Keys & Co., 1858.

Proceedings of the Colored National Convention, Held in Franklin Hall, Sixth Street, Below Arch, Philadelphia, October 16th, 17th and 18th, 1855. Salem, N.J.: National Standard Office, 1856.

Proceedings of the Colored National Convention, Held in Rochester, July 6th, 7th and 8th, 1853. Rochester: Printed at the Office of *Frederick Douglass' Paper*, 1853.

Proceedings of the National Convention of Colored People, and Their Friends, Held in Troy, N.Y., on the 6th, 7th, 8th and 9th October, 1847. Troy, N.Y.: J. C. Kneeland & Co., 1847.

Proceedings of the National Emigration Convention of Colored People; Held at Cleveland, Ohio, on Thursday, Friday, and Saturday, the 24th, 25th and 26th of August, 1854. Pittsburgh: A. A. Anderson, 1854.

Redpath, James. *Echoes of Harper's Ferry*. Boston: Thayer and Eldridge, 1860.

———, ed. *A Guide to Hayti*. 1861; reprint, Westport, Conn.: Negro University Press, 1970.

———. *The Public Life of Captain John Brown*. Boston: Thayer and Eldridge, 1860.

———. *The Roving Editor; or, Talks with Slaves in the Southern States*. New York: A. B. Burdick, 1859.

———, ed. *Toussaint L'Ouverture: Biography and Autobiography*. 1863; reprint, New York: Books for Libraries Press, 1971.

Redpath, James, and Richard Hinton. *Hand-Book to the Kansas Territory and the Rocky Mountain Gold Region: Accompanied by Reliable Maps and a Preliminary Treatise on the Pre-Emption Laws of the United States*. New York: J. H. Colton, 1859.

Report of the Proceedings of the Colored National Convention, Held at Cleveland, Ohio, on Wednesday, September 6, 1848. Rochester: John Dick, 1848.

Ripley, C. Peter, ed. *The Black Abolitionist Papers*. 5 vols. Chapel Hill, N.C.: University of North Carolina Press, 1985–92.

Rollin, Frank [Frances] A. *Life and Public Services of Martin R. Delany, Sub-Assistant Commissioner, Bureau of Refugees, Freedman, and of Abandoned Lands, and Late Major 104th U.S. Colored Troops.* Boston: Lee and Shepard, 1868.

Saunders, Prince. *Haytian Papers. A Collection of the Very Interesting Proclamations and Other Official Documents, Together with Some Account of the Rise, Progress, and Present State of the Kingdom of Hayti.* 1816; reprint, Boston: Caleb Bingham & Co., 1818.

———. *A Memorial Presented to the American Convention for the Abolition of Slavery, and Improving the Condition of the African Race, December 11th, 1818 .* Philadelphia: Printed by Joseph Richardson, 1818.

Smith, James McCune. *A Lecture on the Haytien Revolutions: with a Sketch of the Character of Toussaint L'Ouverture. Delivered at the Stuyvesant Institute, for the benefit of the Colored Orphan Asylum, February 26, 1841.* New York: Printed by D. Fanshaw, 1841.

St. John, Sir Spenser. *Hayti or the Black Republic.* 2nd ed. 1889; reprint, London: Frank Cass & Co., 1971.

Stowe, Harriet Beecher. *Uncle Tom's Cabin; or, Life Among the Lowly.* 1852; reprint, New York: Penguin, 1986.

Stuckey, Sterling, ed. *The Ideological Origins of Black Nationalism.* Boston: Beacon Press, 1972.

Sumner, Charles. *Independence of Hayti and Liberia. Speech of Hon. Charles Sumner, of Massachusetts, on the Bill to Authorize the Appointment of Diplomatic Representatives of the Republics of Hayti and Liberia, with the Debate Thereon; in the Senate of the United States, April 23 and 24, 1862.* Washington, D.C.: Congressional Globe Office, 1862.

Watkins, William J. *Our Rights as Men. An Address Delivered in Boston, Before the Legislative Committee on the Militia, February 24, 1853.* Boston: Benjamin F. Roberts, 1853.

Whitfield, James. *America and Other Poems.* Buffalo: James S. Leavitt, 1853.

Woodson, Carter G., ed. *The Mind of the Negro as Reflected in Letters Written During the Crisis, 1800–1860.* 1926; reprint, New York: Negro Universities Press, 1969.

———. *Negro Orators and Their Orations.* 1925; reprint, New York: Russell & Russell, 1969.

SECONDARY SOURCES

Addison, James T. *The Episcopal Church in the United States, 1789–1931.* New York: Charles Scribner's Sons, 1951.

Adeleke, Tunde. *UnAfrican Americans: Nineteenth-Century Black Nationalists and the Civilizing Mission.* Lexington: University Press of Kentucky, 1998.

Anderson, Benedict. *Imagined Communities: Reflections on the Origin and Spread of Nationalism.* London: Verso, 1983.

Bardolph, Richard. "Social Origins of Distinguished Negroes, 1770–1865," *Journal of Negro History,* 40 (1955): 211–49.

Baur, John Edward. "Mulatto Machiavelli: Jean Pierre Boyer and the Haiti of His Day," *Journal of Negro History,* 32 (1947): 307–53.

Bearden, Jim, and Linda Jean Butler. *Shadd: The Life and Times of Mary Shadd Cary.* Toronto: NC Press, 1977.

Bell, Caryn Cossé. *Revolution, Romanticism, and the Afro-Creole Protest Tradition in Louisiana, 1718–1868.* Baton Rouge: Louisiana State University Press, 1997.

Bell, Howard H. "The Negro Emigration Movement, 1849–1854: A Phase of Negro Nationalism," *Phylon,* 20 (1959): 132–42.

———. "Negro Nationalism: A Factor in Emigration Projects, 1858–1861," *Journal of Negro History,* 47 (1962): 42–53.

———. "Negro Nationalism in the 1850s," *Journal of Negro Education,* 35 (1966): 100–104.

———. *A Survey of the Negro Convention Movement, 1830–1861.* New York: Arno Press and the *New York Times,* 1969.

Bennett, Lerone, Jr. *Before the Mayflower: A History of the Negro in America, 1619–1964.* Rev. Ed. Harmondsworth: Penguin, 1966.

Berlin, Ira. *Many Thousands Gone: The First Two Centuries of Slavery in North America.* Cambridge, Mass.: Belknap Press of Harvard University Press, 1999.

———. *Slaves Without Masters: The Free Negro in the Antebellum South.* New York: Vintage Books, 1974.

Berlin, Ira, and Ronald Hoffman, eds. *Slavery and Freedom in the Age of the American Revolution.* 1983; reprint, Urbana: University of Illinois Press, 1986.

———. "Time, Space, and the Evolution of Afro-American Society," *American Historical Review,* 85 (1980): 44–78.

Berry, Mary Frances, and John Blassingame. *Long Memory: The Black Experience in America.* New York: Oxford University Press, 1982.

Berwanger, Eugene. *The Frontier Against Slavery: Western Anti-Negro Prejudice and the Slavery Extension Controversy.* Urbana: University of Illinois Press, 1967.

Bethel, Elizabeth Rauh. *The Roots of African-American Identity: Memory and History in Free Antebellum Communities.* New York: St. Martin's Press, 1997.

Beyan, Amos J. *The American Colonization Society and the Creation of the Liberian State: A Historical Perspective, 1822–1900.* Lanham, Md.: University Press of America, 1991.

Blackburn, Robin. *The Overthrow of Colonial Slavery, 1776–1848.* London: Verso, 1988.

Blackett, R.J.M. *Beating Against the Barriers: Biographical Essays in Nineteenth-Century Afro-American History.* Baton Rouge: Louisiana State University Press, 1986.

———. *Building an Antislavery Wall: Black Americans in the Atlantic Abolitionist Movement, 1830–1865.* Baton Rouge: Louisiana State University Press, 1983.

———. "Martin R. Delany and Robert Campbell: Black Americans in Search of an African Colony," *Journal of Negro History,* 62 (1977): 1–25.

Blassingame, John. *Black New Orleans, 1860–1880.* Chicago: University of Chicago Press, 1973.

Blight, David W. *Frederick Douglass' Civil War: Keeping Faith in Jubilee.* Baton Rouge: Louisiana State University Press, 1989.

Bolster, W. Jeffrey. *Black Jacks: African American Seamen in the Age of Sail.* Cambridge, Mass.: Harvard University Press, 1997.

Boyd, Willis D."The Ile A'Vache Colonization Venture," *The Americas,* 16 (1959): 45–62.

———. "James Redpath and American Negro Colonization in Haiti, 1860–1862," *The Americas,* 12 (1955): 169–82.

Bracey, John H., August Meier, and Elliot Rudwick. *American Slavery: The Question of Resistance.* Belmont, Calif., Wadsworth, 1971.

———, eds. *Black Nationalism in America.* Indianapolis: Bobbs-Merrill Co., 1970.

———. *Blacks in the Abolitionist Movement.* Belmont, Calif.: Wadsworth, 1971.

———. *Free Blacks in America, 1800–1860.* Belmont, Calif.: Wadsworth, 1970.

Bragg, George F. *History of the Afro-American Group of the Episcopal Church.* 1922; reprint, New York: Johnson Reprint Corporation, 1968.

Brasseaux, Carl A., Keith A. Fontenot, and Claude F. Oubre. *Creoles of Color in the Bayou Country.* Jackson: University Press of Mississippi, 1994.

Brewar, William M. "John B. Russwurm," *Journal of Negro History,* 13 (1928): 413–22.

Brooks, George E., Jr. "The Providence African Society's Sierra Leone Scheme, 1794–1795: Prologue to the African Colonization Movement," *International Journal of African Historical Studies,* 7 (1974): 183–202.

Burkett, Randall K., and Richard Newman. *Black Apostles: Afro-American Clergy Confront the Twentieth Century.* Boston: G. K. Hall & Co., 1978.

Cerutti, James. "The Dominican Republic: A Caribbean Comeback," *National Geographic,* 62 (1977): 538–65.

Cole, Hubert. *Christophe: King of Haiti.* London: Eyre & Spottiswoode, 1967.

Cruse, Harold. *The Crisis of the Negro Intellectual.* New York: William Morrow, 1967.

Curry, Leonard P. *The Free Black in Urban America, 1800–1850: The Shadow of the Dream.* Chicago: University of Chicago Press, 1981.

Dain, Bruce. "Haiti and Egypt in Early Black Racial Discourse in the United States," *Slavery and Abolition,* 14 (1993): 139–61.

Dash, J. Michael. *Haiti and the United States: National Stereotypes and the Literary Imagination.* Basingstoke, Hampshire: Macmillan, 1988.

Davis, David Brion. *The Problem of Slavery in the Age of Revolution, 1770–1823.* Ithaca, N.Y.: Cornell University Press, 1975.

Davis, Harold Palmer. *Black Democracy: The Story of Haiti.* Rev. Ed. 1928; reprint, New York: Biblo & Tannen, 1967.

Dean, David M. *Defender of the Race: James Theodore Holly, Black Nationalist Bishop.* Boston: Lambeth Press, 1979.

Desdunes, Rodolphe Lucien. *Our People and Our History: A Tribute to the Creole People of Color in memory of the Great Men They Have Given Us and of the Good Works They Have Accomplished.* Trans & ed. Sister Dorothea Olga McCants. 1911; reprint, Baton Rouge: Louisiana State University Press, 1973.

Dillon, Merton L. *Benjamin Lundy and the Struggle for Negro Freedom.* Urbana: University of Illinois Press, 1966.

Draper, Theodore. "The Fantasy of Black Nationalism," *Commentary,* 48 (1969): 27–54.

Du Bois, W.E.B."Haiti," in *Federal Theatre Plays.* New York: Random House, 1938.

———. *The Souls of Black Folk.* 1903; reprint, New York: Dover Publications, 1994.

Egerton, Douglas R. *Gabriel's Rebellion: The Virginia Slave Conspiracies of 1800 and 1802*. Chapel Hill: University of North Carolina Press, 1993.

————. " 'Its Origin is Not a Little Curious': A New Look at the American Colonization Society," *Journal of the Early Republic*, 5 (1985): 463–80.

Elkins, Stanley. *Slavery: A Problem in American Institutional and Political Life*. Chicago: University of Chicago Press, 1959.

Essien-Udom, E. U. *Black Nationalism: A Search for an Identity in America*. New York: Dell, 1964.

Farrison, William Edward. *William Wells Brown: Author and Reformer*. Chicago: University of Chicago Press, 1969.

Filler, Louis. *The Crusade Against Slavery, 1830–1860*. New York: Harper Torchbooks, 1960.

Foner, Eric. *Free Soil, Free Labor, Free Men: The Ideology of the Republican Party Before the Civil War*. New York: Oxford University Press, 1970.

Foner, Philip. *History of Black Americans*. 3 vols. Westport, Conn.: Greenwood Press, 1975–83.

Foster, Charles I. "The Colonization of Free Negroes in Liberia, 1816–1835," *Journal of Negro History*, 38 (1953): 41–66.

Fox, Early Lee. *The American Colonization Society, 1817–1840*. Baltimore: Johns Hopkins University Press, 1919.

Frazier, E. Franklin. *The Negro in the United States*. Rev. Ed. New York: Macmillan, 1957.

Freehling, William W. *The Reintegration of American History: Slavery and the Civil War*. New York: Oxford University Press, 1994.

Frey, Sylvia R. *Water from the Rock: Black Resistance in a Revolutionary Age*. Princeton, N.J.: Princeton University Press, 1991.

Fyfe, Christopher. *A History of Sierra Leone*. London: Oxford University Press, 1962.

Gardner, Bettye J. "William Watkins: Antebellum Black Teacher and Anti-Slavery Writer," *Negro History Bulletin*, 39 (1976): 623–25.

Gaspar, David Barry, and David Patrick Geggus, eds. *A Turbulent Time: The French Revolution and the Greater Caribbean*. Bloomington: Indiana University Press, 1997.

Geiss, Imanuel. *The Pan-African Movement*. Trans. Ann Keep. London: Methuen, 1974.

Genovese, Eugene. *From Rebellion to Revolution: Afro-American Slave Revolts in the Making of the Modern World*. New York: Vintage Books, 1979.

Gershoni, Yekutiel. *Black Colonialism: The Americo-Liberian Scramble for the Hinterland*. Boulder, Colo.: Westview Press, 1985.

Gold, Herbert. *Best Nightmare on Earth: A Life in Haiti*. New York: Touchstone, 1991.

Griffith, Cyril R. *The African Dream: Martin R. Delany and the Emergence of Pan-African Thought*. University Park: Pennsylvania State University Press, 1975.

Gross, Bella. "Freedom's Journal and the Rights of All," *Journal of Negro History*, 17 (1932): 241–86.

Hancock, Harold B. "Mary Ann Shadd: Negro Editor, Educator, and Lawyer," *Delaware History*, 15 (1973): 187–94.

Harlow, Alvin F. "James Redpath," in *Dictionary of American Biography*, 20 vols. ed. Allen Johnson et al. (New York: Oxford University Press, 1935), 15:443–44.

Harris, Robert L., Jr. "H. Ford Douglas: Afro-American Antislavery Abolitionist," *Journal of Negro History*, 62 (1977): 217–34.

Harris, Sheldon. *Paul Cuffe: Black America and the African Return*. New York: Simon and Schuster, 1972.

Hart, Jim A. "James Redpath, Missouri Correspondent," *Missouri Historical Review*, 57 (1962): 70–78.

Hartman, Mary S., and Lois Banner, eds. *Clio's Consciousness Raised: New Essays on the History of Women*. 1974; reprint, New York: Octagon Books, 1976.

Heinl, Robert Debs, and Nancy Gordon Heinl. *Written in Blood: The Story of the Haitian People, 1492–1971*. Boston: Houghton Mifflin, 1978.

Herskovits, Melville J. *Life in a Haitian Valley*. 1937; reprint, New York: Octagon Books, 1964.

———. *The Myth of the Negro Past*. 1958; reprint, Boston: Beacon Press, 1970.

Hickey, Donald R. "America's Response to the Slave Revolt in Haiti, 1791–1806," *Journal of the Early Republic*, 2 (1982): 361–79.

Hirsch, Arnold R., and Joseph Logsdon, eds. *Creole New Orleans: Race and Americanization*. Baton Rouge: Louisiana State University Press, 1992.

Hite, Roger W. "Voice of a Fugitive: Henry Bibb and Antebellum Black Separatism," *Journal of Black Studies*, 4 (1974): 269–84.

Hoetink, Harry. " 'Americans' in Samaná," *Caribbean Studies*, 2 (1962): 3–22.

Holly, Marc Aurèle. *Agriculture in Haiti*. New York: Vantage Press, 1955.

Horner, Charles F. *The Life of James Redpath and the Development of the Modern Lyceum*. New York: Barse & Hopkins, 1926.

Horsman, Reginald. *Race and Manifest Destiny: The Origins of American Racial Anglo-Saxonism*. Cambridge, Mass.: Harvard University Press, 1981.

Horton, James Oliver. *Free People of Color: Inside the African American Community*. Washington, D.C.: Smithsonian Institution Press, 1993.

Horton, James Oliver, and Lois E. Horton. *Black Bostonians: Family Life and Community Struggle in the Antebellum North*. New York: Holmes & Meier, 1979.

———. *In Hope of Liberty: Culture, Community, and Protest Among Northern Free Blacks, 1700–1860*. New York: Oxford University Press, 1997.

Huggins, Nathan I. *Slave and Citizen: The Life of Frederick Douglass*. Boston: Little, Brown, and Co., 1980.

Hunt, Alfred N. *Haiti's Influence on Antebellum America: Slumbering Volcano in the Caribbean*. Baton Rouge: Louisiana State University Press, 1988.

Jackson, James O'Dell III. "The Origins of Pan-African Nationalism: Afro-American and Haytian Relations, 1800–1863," Ph.D. diss., Northwestern University, 1976.

Johnson, Paul E., ed. *African-American Christianity: Essays in History*. Berkeley: University of California Press, 1994.

Jordan, Winthrop. *White Over Black: American Attitudes Toward the Negro, 1550–1812*. Chapel Hill: University of North Carolina Press, 1968.

Kerber, Linda. *Women of the Republic: Intellect and Ideology in Revolutionary America*. Chapel Hill: University of North Carolina Press, 1980.

Landon, Fred. "The Negro Migration to Canada after the Passing of the Fugitive Slave Act," *Journal of Negro History*, 5 (1920): 22–36.

Langley, Lester D. *The Americas in the Age of Revolution, 1750–1850*. New Haven, Conn.: Yale University Press, 1996.

Lapp, Rudolph M. "The Negro in Gold Rush California," *Journal of Negro History*, 49 (1964): 81–98.

Lawson, Bill E., and Frank M. Kirkland, eds. *Frederick Douglass: A Critical Reader*. Malden, Mass.: Blackwell, 1999.

Levine, Robert S. *Martin Delany, Frederick Douglass, and the Politics of Representative Identity*. Chapel Hill: University of North Carolina Press, 1997.

Leyburn, James G. *The Haitian People*. 1941; reprint, New Haven, Conn.: Yale University Press, 1966.

Litwack, Leon. *North of Slavery: The Negro in the Free States, 1790–1860*. Chicago: University of Chicago Press, 1961.

Litwack, Leon, and August Meier, eds. *Black Leaders of the Nineteenth Century*. Urbana: University of Illinois Press, 1988.

Lockett, James D. "Abraham Lincoln and Colonization: An Episode that Ends in Tragedy at Ile A'Vache, Haiti, 1863–64," *Western Journal of Black Studies*, 12 (1988): 178–84.

Lynch, Hollis R. *Edward Wilmot Blyden: Pan-Negro Patriot, 1832–1912*. London: Oxford University Press, 1967.

———. "James Theodore Holly: Ante-Bellum Black Nationalist and Emigrationist," *A Special Publication of the Center for Afro-American Studies*, UCLA, 1977.

———. "Pan-Negro Nationalism in the New World Before 1862," *Boston University Papers on Africa*, 2 (1966): 149–79.

MacCorkle, William A. *The Monroe Doctrine in Its Relation to the Republic of Haiti*. New York: Neale Publishing, 1915.

MacMaster, Richard K. "Henry Highland Garnet and the African Civilization Society," *Journal of Presbyterian History*, 48 (1970): 95–130.

McAdoo, Bill. *Pre-Civil War Black Nationalism*. New York: David Walker, 1983.

McKivigan, John. "James Redpath, John Brown, and Abolitionist Advocacy of Slave Insurrection," *Civil War History*, 37 (1991): 293–313.

———. "James Redpath and Black Reaction to the Haitian Emigration Bureau," *Mid-America*, 69 (1987): 139–53.

McPherson, James M. *Battle Cry of Freedom: The Era of the Civil War*. 1988; reprint, Harmondsworth, Middlesex: Penguin, 1990.

———. *Ordeal by Fire: The Civil War and Reconstruction*. New York: Knopf, 1982.

———. *The Struggle for Equality: Abolitionists and the Negro in the Civil War and Reconstruction*. Princeton: Princeton University Press, 1964.

Meier, August. "The Emergence of Negro Nationalism (A Study in Ideologies)," *Midwest Journal*, 4 (1951–52): 96–104; and 4 (1952): 95–111.

Miller, Floyd J. *The Search for a Black Nationality: Black Emigration and Colonization, 1787–1863*. Urbana: University of Illinois Press, 1975.

Miller, John Chester. *The Wolf by the Ears: Thomas Jefferson and Slavery*. New York: Free Press, 1977.

Montague, Ludwell Lee. *Haiti and the United States, 1714–1938*. 1940; reprint, New York: Russell & Russell, 1966.

Moses, Wilson Jeremiah. *Alexander Crummell: A Study in Civilization and Discontent*. New York: Oxford University Press, 1989.

———. *The Golden Age of Black Nationalism, 1850–1920*. Hamden, Conn.: Archon Books, 1978.

Murrin, John M. et al. *Liberty, Equality, Power: A History of the American People*. Fort Worth, Tex.: Harcourt Brace, 1996.

Nash, Gary B. *Forging Freedom: The Formation of Philadelphia's Black Community, 1720–1840*. Cambridge, Mass.: Harvard University Press, 1988.

Nichols, David. *From Dessalines to Duvalier: Race, Colour, and National Independence in Haiti*. Cambridge: Cambridge University Press, 1979.

Nye, Russel B. *William Lloyd Garrison and the Humanitarian Reformers*. Boston: Little, Brown, and Co., 1955.

Oates, Stephen B. *To Purge This Land with Blood: A Biography of John Brown*. 2nd ed. Amherst: University of Massachusetts Press, 1984.

Ofari, Earl. *"Let Your Motto Be Resistance": The Life and Thought of Henry Highland Garnet*. Boston: Beacon Press, 1972.

Pease, Jane H., and William H. Pease. *Black Utopia: Negro Communal Experiments in America*. Madison: State Historical Society of Wisconsin, 1963.

———. *Bound With Them in Chains: A Biographical History of the Antislavery Movement*. Westport, Conn.: Greenwood Press, 1972.

———. "Ends, Means, and Attitudes: Black-White Conflict in the Antislavery Movement," *Civil War History*, 18 (1972): 117–28.

———. "Negro Conventions and the Problem of Black Leadership," *Journal of Black Studies*, 2 (1971): 29–44.

———. *They Who Would Be Free: Blacks' Search for Freedom, 1830–1861*. New York: Atheneum, 1974.

Phillips, Christopher. *Freedom's Port: The African American Community of Baltimore, 1790–1860*. Urbana: University of Illinois Press, 1997.

Plummer, Brenda Gayle. *Haiti and the United States: The Psychological Moment*. Athens: University of Georgia Press, 1992.

Prichard, Hesketh. *Where Black Rules White: A Journey Across and About Hayti*. 1900; reprint, Freeport, N.Y.: Books for Libraries Press, 1971.

Quarles, Benjamin. *Black Abolitionists*. New York: Oxford University Press, 1969.

———. *Lincoln and the Negro*. New York: Oxford University Press, 1962.

———. "Ministers Without Portfolio," *Journal of Negro History*, 39 (1954): 27–42,

Reed, Harry. *Platform for Change: The Foundations of the Northern Free Black Community, 1775–1865*. East Lansing: Michigan State University Press, 1994.

Renehan, Edward J. *The Secret Six: The True Tale of the Men who Conspired with John Brown*. New York: Crown Publishers, 1995.

Rhodes, Jane. *Mary Ann Shadd Cary: The Black Press and Protest in the Nineteenth Century*. Bloomington: Indiana University Press, 1998.

Rodman, Seldon. *Haiti: The Black Republic*. New York: Devin-Adair, 1954.

Rotberg, Robert I. *Haiti: The Politics of Squalor*. Boston: Houghton Mifflin, 1971.

Schor, Joel. *Henry Highland Garnet: A Voice of Black Radicalism in the Nineteenth Century*. Westport, Conn.: Greenwood Press, 1977.

Segal, Ronald. *The Black Diaspora*. London: Faber and Faber, 1995.

Sellers, Charles. *The Market Revolution: Jacksonian America, 1815–1846*. New York: Oxford University Press, 1991.

Seraile, William. "Afro-American Emigration to Haiti During the American Civil War," *The Americas*, 35, (1978): 185–200.

Sherman, Joan R. "James Monroe Whitfield, Poet and Emigrationist: A Voice of Protest and Despair," *Journal of Negro History*, 57 (1972): 169–76.

Sherwood, Henry N. "The Formation of the American Colonization Society," *Journal of Negro History*, 2 (1917): 209–28.

————. "Paul Cuffee," *Journal of Negro History*, 8 (1923): 153–229.

Shick, Tom W. *Behold the Promised Land: A History of Afro-American Settler Society in Nineteenth-Century Liberia*. Baltimore: Johns Hopkins University Press, 1980.

————. "A Quantitative Analysis of Liberian Colonization from 1820 to 1843 with Special Reference to Mortality," *Journal of African History*, 12 (1971): 45–59.

Sigler, Phil Samuel. "The Attitudes of Free Blacks Towards Emigration to Liberia," Ph.D. diss., Boston University, 1969.

Sires, Ronald V. "Sir Henry Barkly and the Labor Problem in Jamaica, 1853–1856," *Journal of Negro History*, 25 (1940): 216–35.

Smith, E. Valerie. "Early Afro-American Presence on the Island of Hispaniola: A Case Study of the 'Immigrants' of Samaná," *Journal of Negro History*, 72 (1987): 33–41.

Smith, Elbert B. *Francis Preston Blair*. New York: Free Press, 1980.

Spraggins, Tinsley Lee. "Economic Aspects of Negro Colonization During the Civil War," Ph.D. diss., American University, 1957.

Staudenraus, Philip J. *The African Colonization Movement, 1816–1865*. New York: Columbia University Press, 1961.

Steedman, Mabel. *Unknown to the World: Haiti*. London: Hurst and Blackett, 1939.

Sterling, Dorothy. *The Making of an Afro-American: Martin R. Delany, 1812–1885*. New York: Doubleday, 1971.

Sterx, H. E. *The Free Negro in Ante-Bellum Louisiana*. Rutherford, N.J.: Fairleigh Dickinson University Press, 1972.

Stewart, James Brewer. *Holy Warriors: The Abolitionists and American Slavery*. New York: Hill & Wang, 1976.

Stokes, Melvyn, and Stephen Conway, eds. *The Market Revolution in America: Social, Political, and Religious Expressions, 1800–1880*. Charlottsville: University Press of Virginia, 1996.

Stuckey, Sterling. *Slave Culture: Nationalist Theory and the Foundations of Black America*. New York: Oxford University Press, 1987.

Teed, Paul. "Racial Nationalism and Its Challengers: Theodore Parker, John Rock, and the Antislavery Movement," *Civil War History*, 41 (1995): 142–60.

Thomas, Lamont D. *Rise to Be a People: A Biography of Paul Cuffe*. Chicago: University of Illinois Press, 1986.

Trouillot, Michel-Rolph. *Haiti: State Against Nation. The Origins and Legacy of Duvalierism*. New York: Monthly Review Press, 1990.

Ullman, Victor. *Martin R. Delany: The Beginnings of Black Nationalism*. Boston: Beacon Press, 1971.

Wade, Richard C. *Slavery in the Cities: The South, 1820–1860*. London: Oxford University Press, 1964.

———. "The Vesey Plot: A Reconsideration," *Journal of Southern History*, 30 (1964): 143–61.

Walker, Clarence. *Deromanticizing Black History: Critical Essays and Reappraisals.* Knoxville: University of Tennessee Press, 1991.

West, Richard. *Back to Africa: A History of Sierra Leone.* London: Jonathan Cape, 1970.

White, Arthur O. "Prince Saunders: An Instance of Social Mobility among Antebellum Blacks," *Journal of Negro History*, 60 (1975): 526–35.

White, Shane. *Somewhat More Independent: The End of Slavery in New York City, 1770–1810.* Athens: University of Georgia Press, 1991.

Winch, Julie. *Philadelphia's Black Elite: Activism, Accommodation, and the Struggle for Autonomy, 1787–1848.* Philadelphia: Temple University Press, 1988.

Winks, Robin. *The Blacks in Canada: A History.* London: Yale University Press, 1971.

Wipfler, William F. *James Theodore Holly in Haiti*. New York: The National Council of the Episcopal Church, 1956.

Wright, Donald R. *African Americans in the Early Republic, 1789–1831.* Arlington Heights, Ill.: Harlan Davidson, 1993.

Zelinsky, Wilbur. "The Population Geography of the Free Negro in Ante-Bellum America," *Population Studies*, 3 (1950): 386–401.

Index

About the Author

CHRIS DIXON teaches American History at the University of Newcastle, Australia. He has also held positions at the University of Sydney and Massey University, New Zealand. His other works include *Perfecting the Family: Antislavery Marriages in Nineteenth-Century America* (1997).

Recent Titles in
Contributions in American History

ISBN 0-313-31063-7

90000>

EAN

9 780313 310638

HARDCOVER BAR CODE